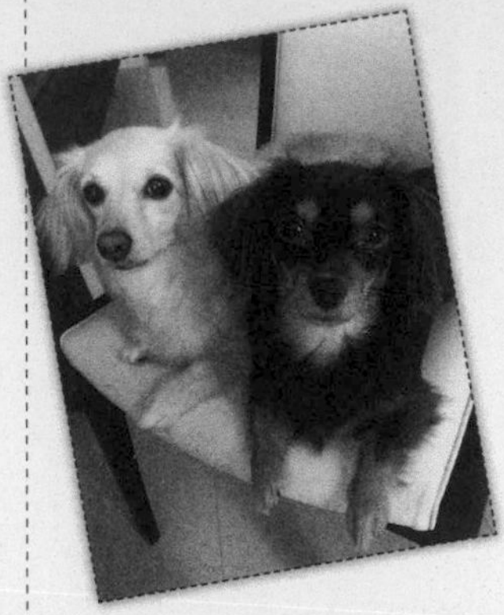

It's volume 15 already.
I can't believe it!
—Tsugumi Ohba

The second season of the anime is starting. We also revamped the cover design.
—Takeshi Obata

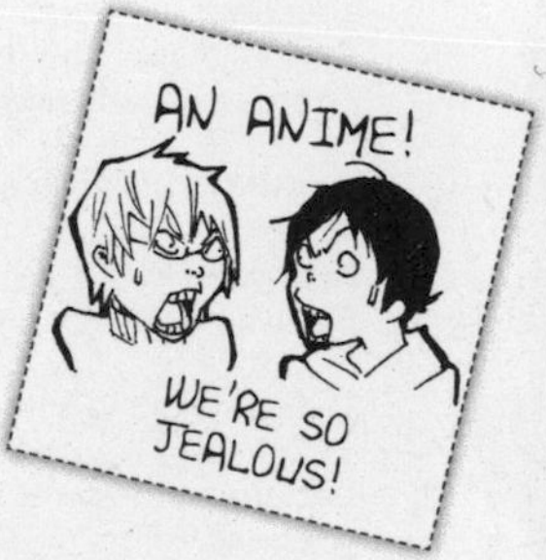
AN ANIME!
WE'RE SO JEALOUS!

Tsugumi Ohba

Born in Tokyo, Tsugumi Ohba is the author of the hit series *Death Note*. His current series *Bakuman。* is serialized in *Weekly Shonen Jump*.

Takeshi Obata

Takeshi Obata was born in 1969 in Niigata, Japan, and is the artist of the wildly popular SHONEN JUMP title *Hikaru no Go*, which won the 2003 Tezuka Osamu Cultural Prize: Shinsei "New Hope" award and the 2000 Shogakukan Manga award. Obata is also the artist of *Arabian Majin Bokentan Lamp Lamp*, *Ayatsuri Sakon*, *Cyborg Jichan G.*, and the smash hit manga *Death Note*. His current series *Bakuman。* is serialized in *Weekly Shonen Jump*.

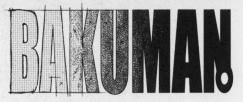

Volume 15

SHONEN JUMP Manga Edition

Story by **TSUGUMI OHBA**
Art by **TAKESHI OBATA**

Translation | **Tetsuichiro Miyaki**
Touch-up Art & Lettering | **James Gaubatz**
Design | **Fawn Lau**
Editor | **Alexis Kirsch**

Printed in the U.S.A.

Published by VIZ Media, LLC
P.O. Box 77010
San Francisco, CA 94107

10 9 8 7 6 5 4 3 2 1
First printing, October 2012

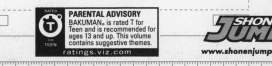

VIZ media
www.viz.com

www.shonenjump.com

BAKUMAN。

15

SUPPORT and FEELING

STORY BY TSUGUMI OHBA

ART BY TAKESHI OBATA

SHONENJUMP MANGA

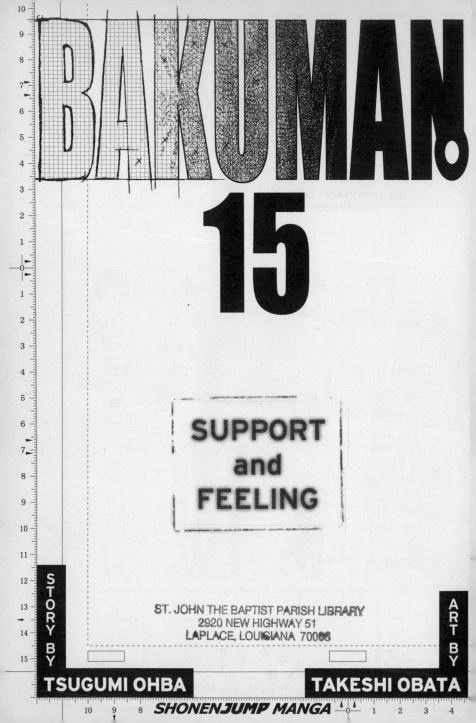

MAN。 バクマン。 vol. 15

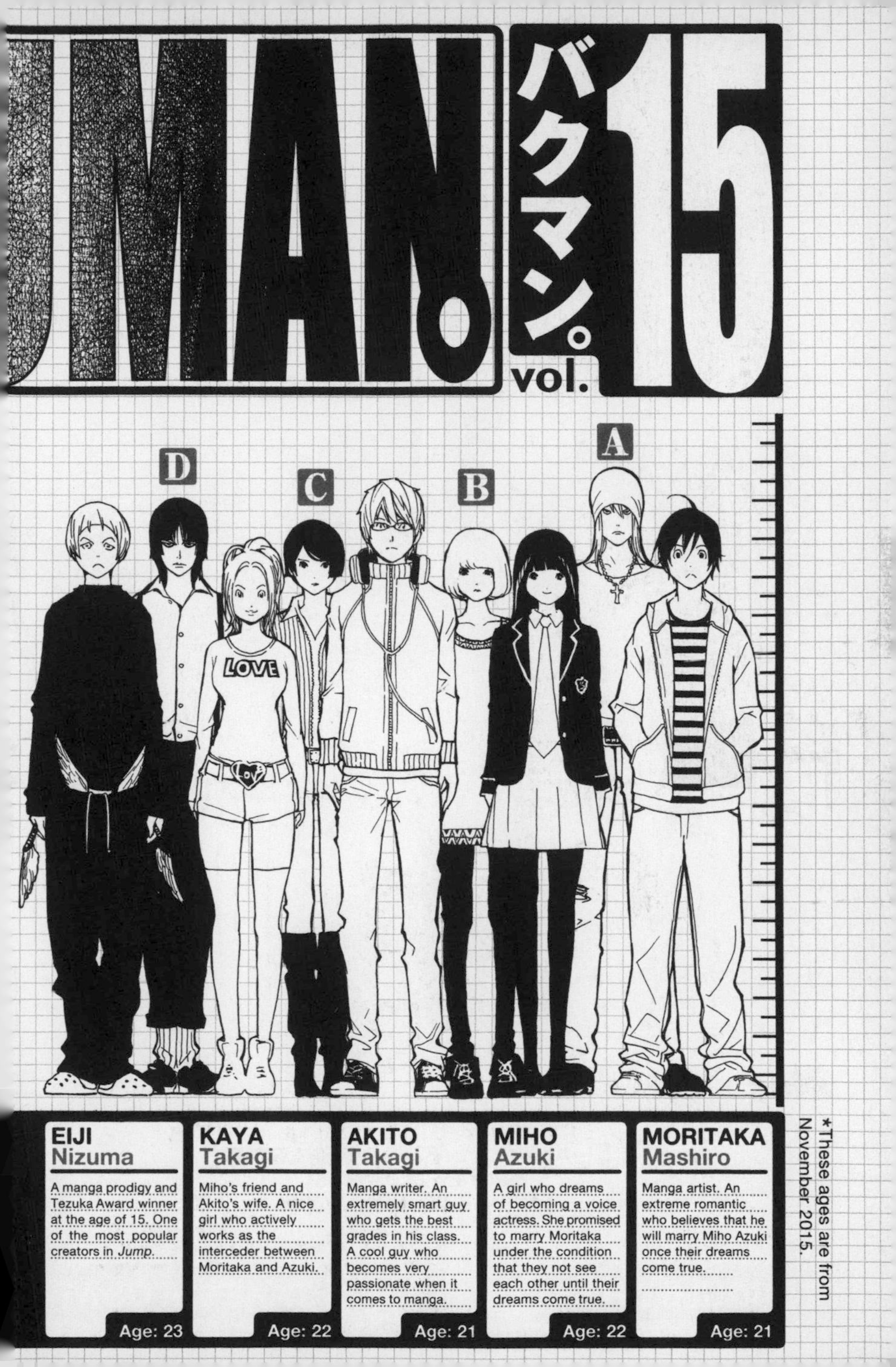

D
C
B
A
LOVE

EIJI
Nizuma

A manga prodigy and Tezuka Award winner at the age of 15. One of the most popular creators in *Jump*.

Age: 23

KAYA
Takagi

Miho's friend and Akito's wife. A nice girl who actively works as the interceder between Moritaka and Azuki.

Age: 22

AKITO
Takagi

Manga writer. An extremely smart guy who gets the best grades in his class. A cool guy who becomes very passionate when it comes to manga.

Age: 21

MIHO
Azuki

A girl who dreams of becoming a voice actress. She promised to marry Moritaka under the condition that they not see each other until their dreams come true.

Age: 22

MORITAKA
Mashiro

Manga artist. An extreme romantic who believes that he will marry Miho Azuki once their dreams come true.

Age: 21

*These ages are from November 2015.

STORY In order to attain the glory that only a handful of people can, two young men decide to walk the rough "path of manga" and become professional manga creators. This is the story of a great artist, Moritaka Mashiro, a talented writer, Akito Takagi, and their quest to become manga legends!

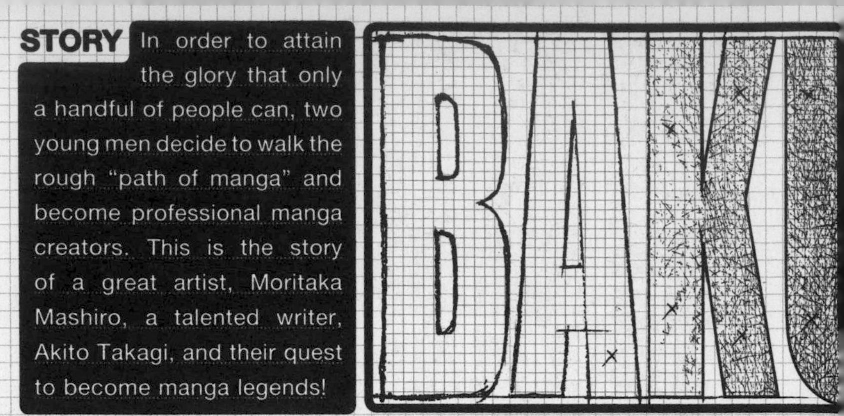
BAK

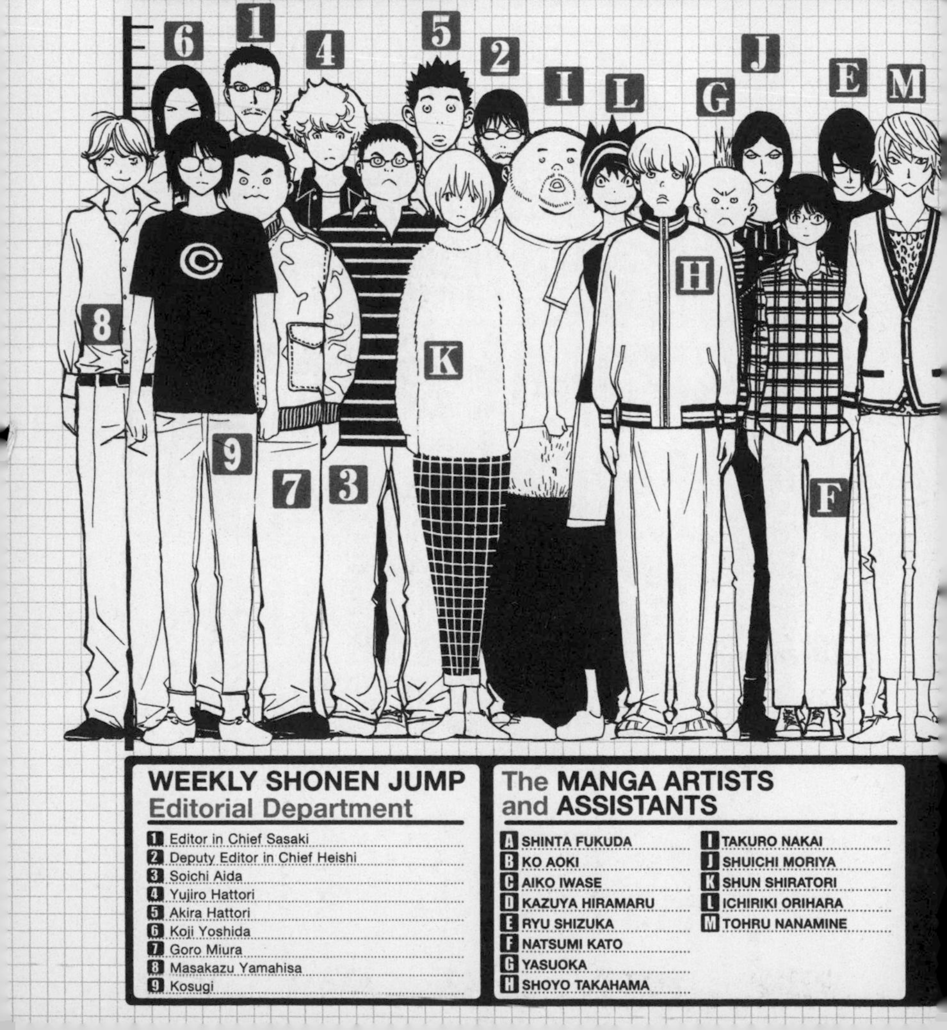
6
1
4
5
2
I
L
G
J
E
M
8
9
7
3
K
H
F

WEEKLY SHONEN JUMP Editorial Department

1. Editor in Chief Sasaki
2. Deputy Editor in Chief Heishi
3. Soichi Aida
4. Yujiro Hattori
5. Akira Hattori
6. Koji Yoshida
7. Goro Miura
8. Masakazu Yamahisa
9. Kosugi

The MANGA ARTISTS and ASSISTANTS

- A SHINTA FUKUDA
- B KO AOKI
- C AIKO IWASE
- D KAZUYA HIRAMARU
- E RYU SHIZUKA
- F NATSUMI KATO
- G YASUOKA
- H SHOYO TAKAHAMA
- I TAKURO NAKAI
- J SHUICHI MORIYA
- K SHUN SHIRATORI
- L ICHIRIKI ORIHARA
- M TOHRU NANAMINE

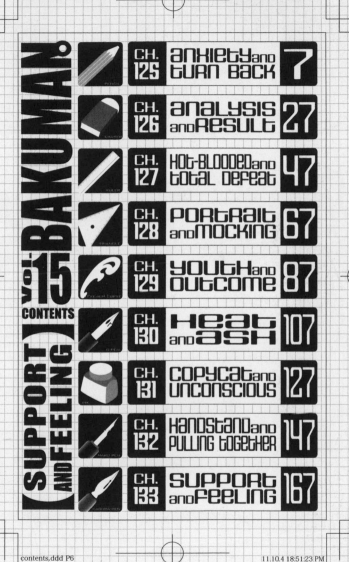

vol.BAKUMAN。

15

CONTENTS

[SUPPORT AND FEELING]

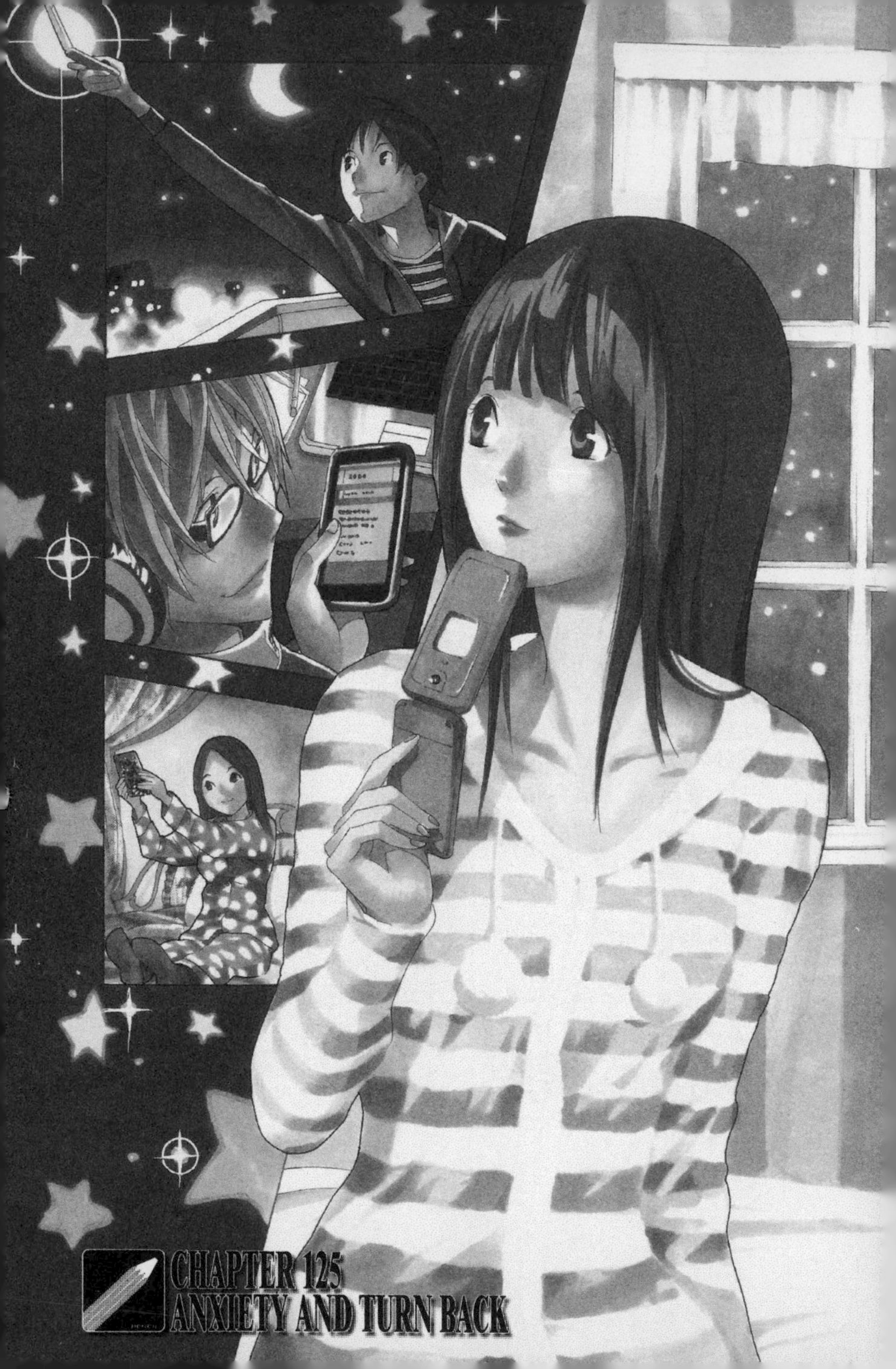
CHAPTER 125
ANXIETY AND TURN BACK

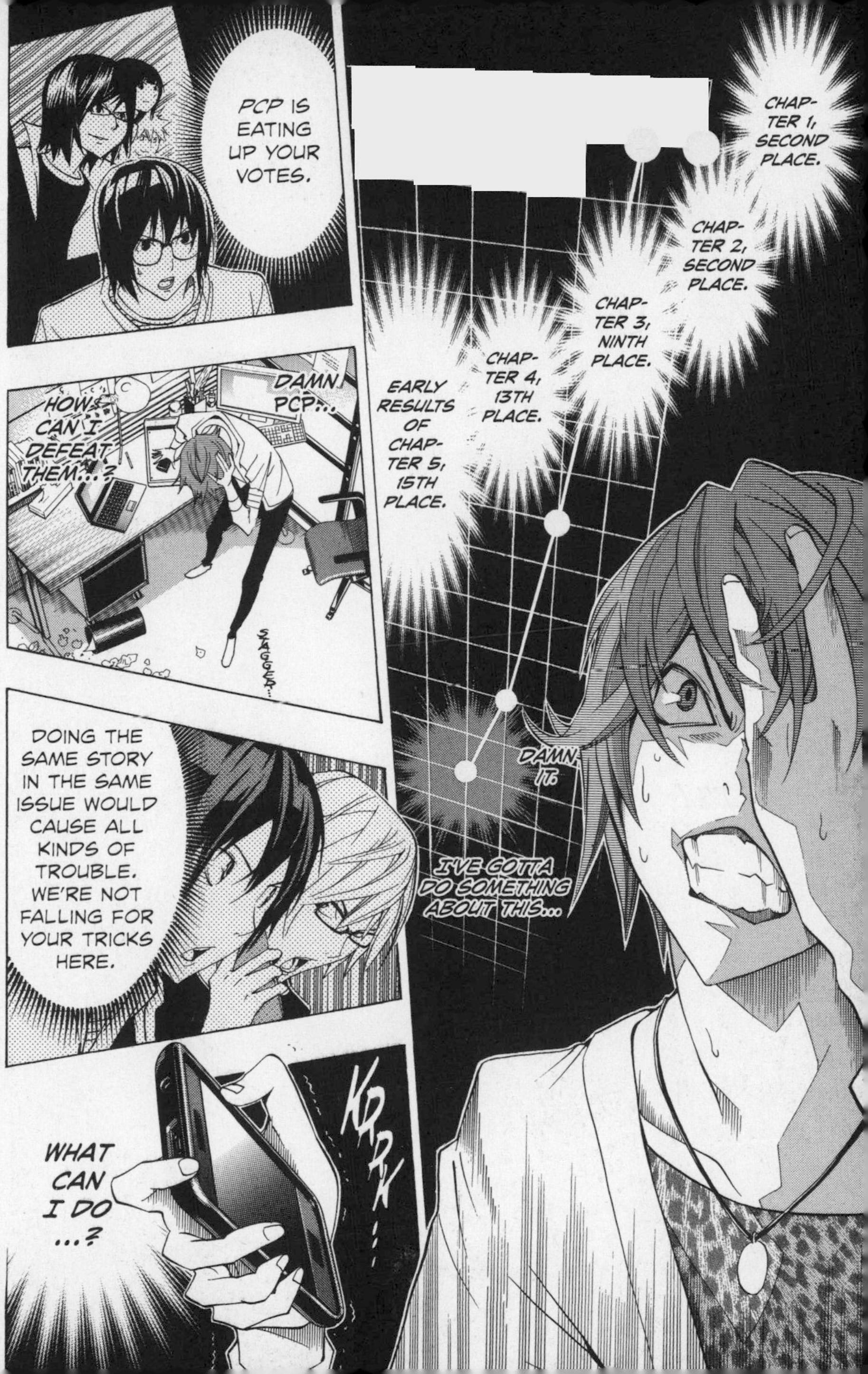

CHAPTER 1, SECOND PLACE.
CHAPTER 2, SECOND PLACE.
CHAPTER 3, NINTH PLACE.
CHAPTER 4, 13TH PLACE.
EARLY RESULTS OF CHAPTER 5, 15TH PLACE.
DAMN IT.
I'VE GOTTA DO SOMETHING ABOUT THIS...
PCP IS EATING UP YOUR VOTES.
DAMN PCP...
HOW CAN I DEFEAT THEM...?
STAGGER...
DOING THE SAME STORY IN THE SAME ISSUE WOULD CAUSE ALL KINDS OF TROUBLE. WE'RE NOT FALLING FOR YOUR TRICKS HERE.
KRRK...
WHAT CAN I DO ...?

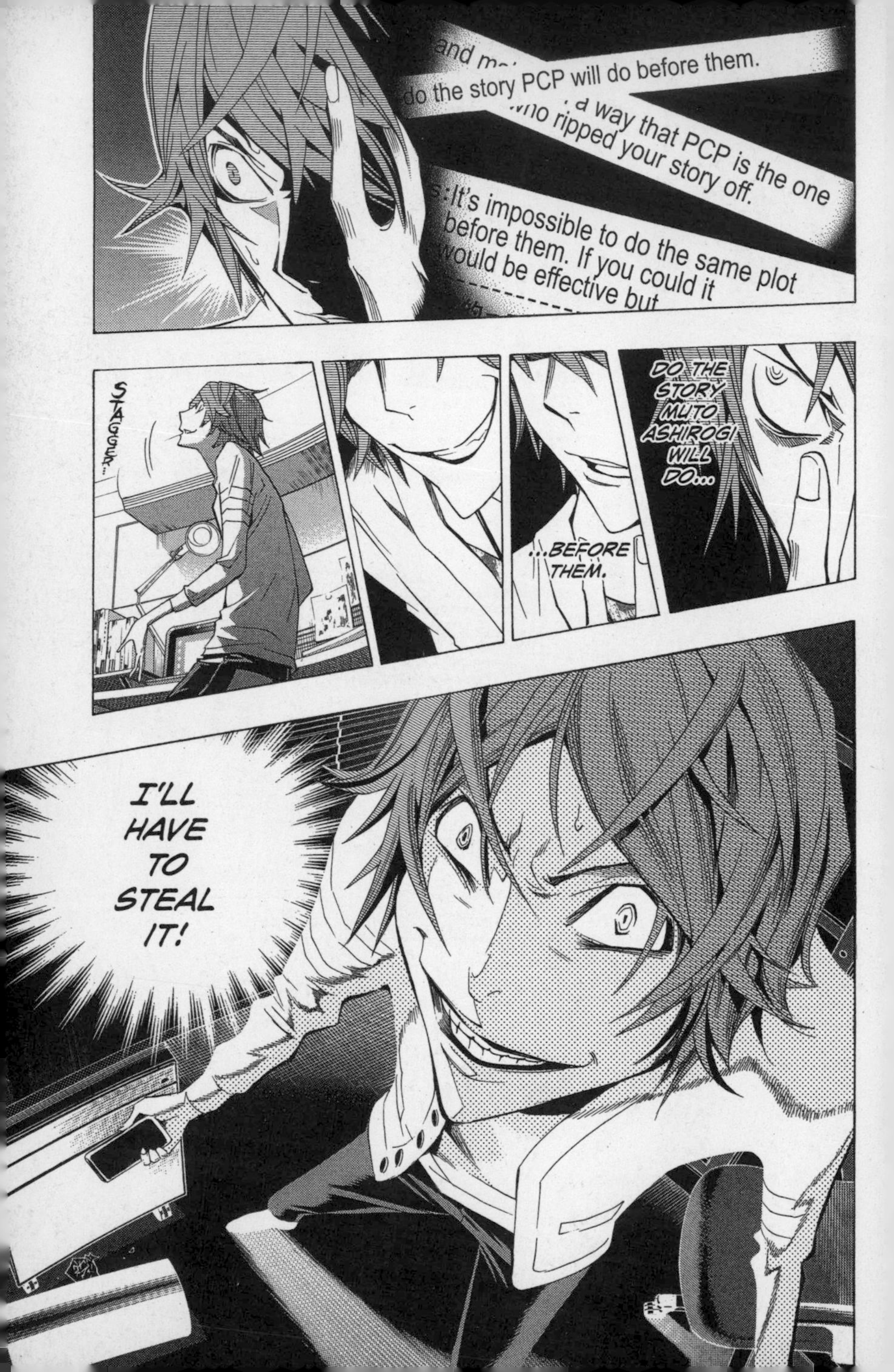

do the story PCP will do before them.
a way that PCP is the one
who ripped your story off.
It's impossible to do the same plot
before them. If you could it
would be effective but
DO THE STORY MUTO ASHIROGI WILL DO...
...BEFORE THEM.
STAGGER...
I'LL HAVE TO STEAL IT!

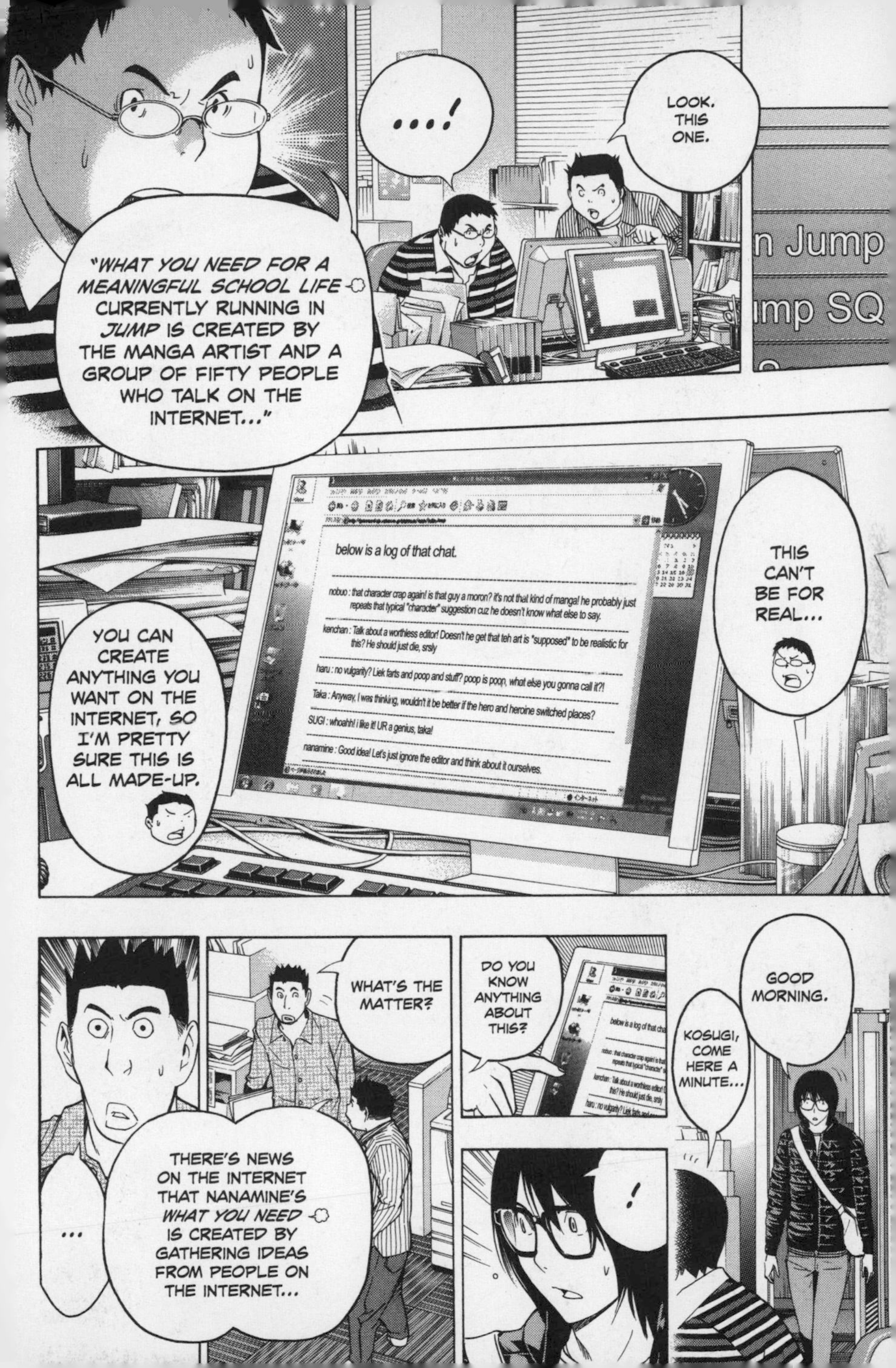

LOOK. THIS ONE.
...!
"WHAT YOU NEED FOR A MEANINGFUL SCHOOL LIFE CURRENTLY RUNNING IN JUMP IS CREATED BY THE MANGA ARTIST AND A GROUP OF FIFTY PEOPLE WHO TALK ON THE INTERNET..."
THIS CAN'T BE FOR REAL...
below is a log of that chat.
nobuo : that character crap again! is that guy a moron? it's not that kind of manga! he probably just repeats that typical "character" suggestion cuz he doesn't know what else to say.
kenchan : Talk about a worthless editor! Doesn't he get that teh art is "supposed" to be realistic for this? He should just die, srsly
haru : no vulgarity? Liek farts and poop and stuff? poop is poop, what else you gonna call it?!
Taka : Anyway, I was thinking, wouldn't it be better if the hero and heroine switched places?
SUGI : whoahh! i like it! UR a genius, taka!
nanamine : Good idea! Let's just ignore the editor and think about it ourselves.
YOU CAN CREATE ANYTHING YOU WANT ON THE INTERNET, SO I'M PRETTY SURE THIS IS ALL MADE-UP.
GOOD MORNING.
KOSUGI, COME HERE A MINUTE...
DO YOU KNOW ANYTHING ABOUT THIS?
!
WHAT'S THE MATTER?
THERE'S NEWS ON THE INTERNET THAT NANAMINE'S WHAT YOU NEED IS CREATED BY GATHERING IDEAS FROM PEOPLE ON THE INTERNET...
...

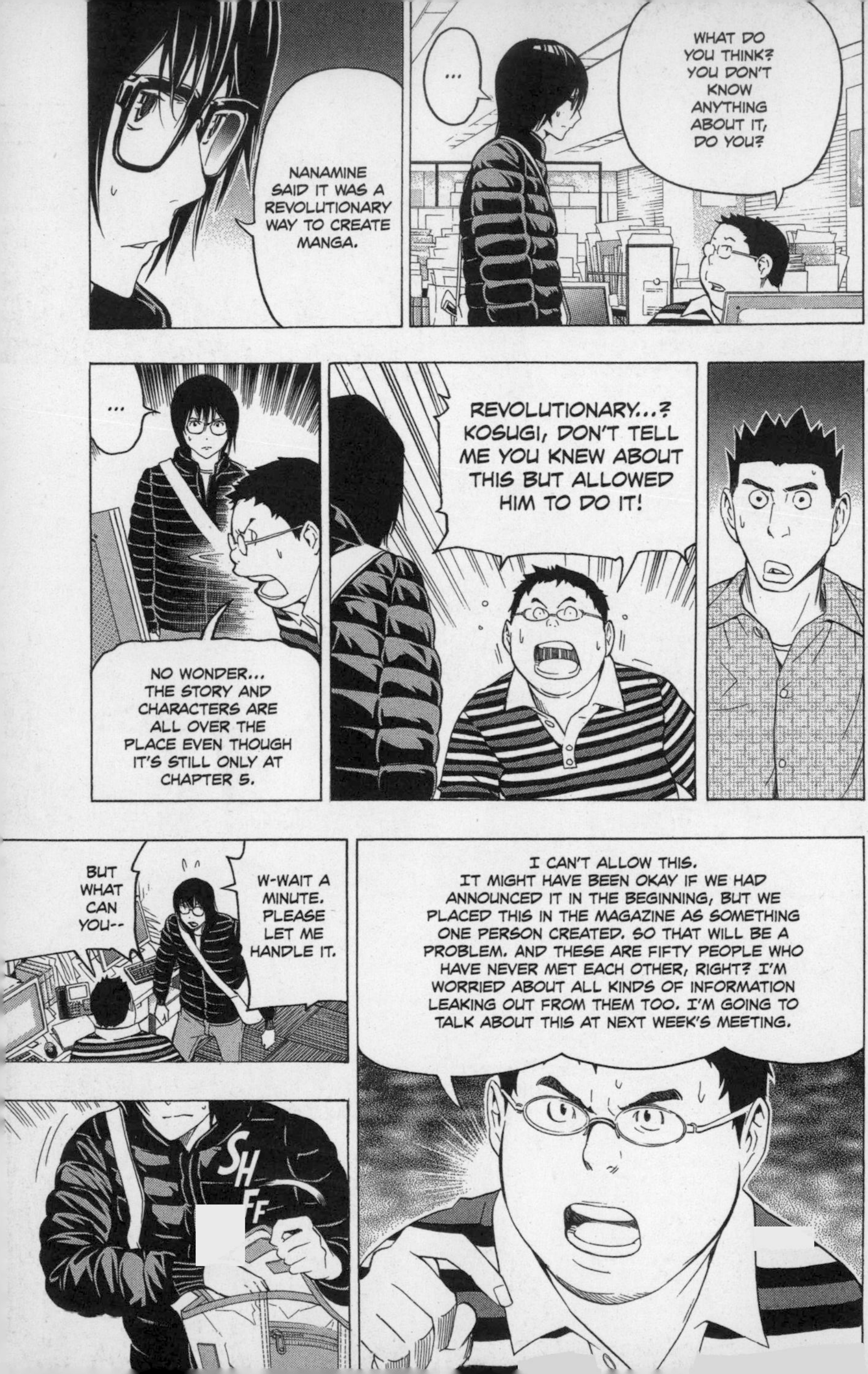
WHAT DO YOU THINK? YOU DON'T KNOW ANYTHING ABOUT IT, DO YOU?
...
NANAMINE SAID IT WAS A REVOLUTIONARY WAY TO CREATE MANGA.
REVOLUTIONARY...? KOSUGI, DON'T TELL ME YOU KNEW ABOUT THIS BUT ALLOWED HIM TO DO IT!
...
NO WONDER... THE STORY AND CHARACTERS ARE ALL OVER THE PLACE EVEN THOUGH IT'S STILL ONLY AT CHAPTER 5.
I CAN'T ALLOW THIS. IT MIGHT HAVE BEEN OKAY IF WE HAD ANNOUNCED IT IN THE BEGINNING, BUT WE PLACED THIS IN THE MAGAZINE AS SOMETHING ONE PERSON CREATED. SO THAT WILL BE A PROBLEM. AND THESE ARE FIFTY PEOPLE WHO HAVE NEVER MET EACH OTHER, RIGHT? I'M WORRIED ABOUT ALL KINDS OF INFORMATION LEAKING OUT FROM THEM TOO. I'M GOING TO TALK ABOUT THIS AT NEXT WEEK'S MEETING.
W-WAIT A MINUTE. PLEASE LET ME HANDLE IT.
BUT WHAT CAN YOU--
SHFF

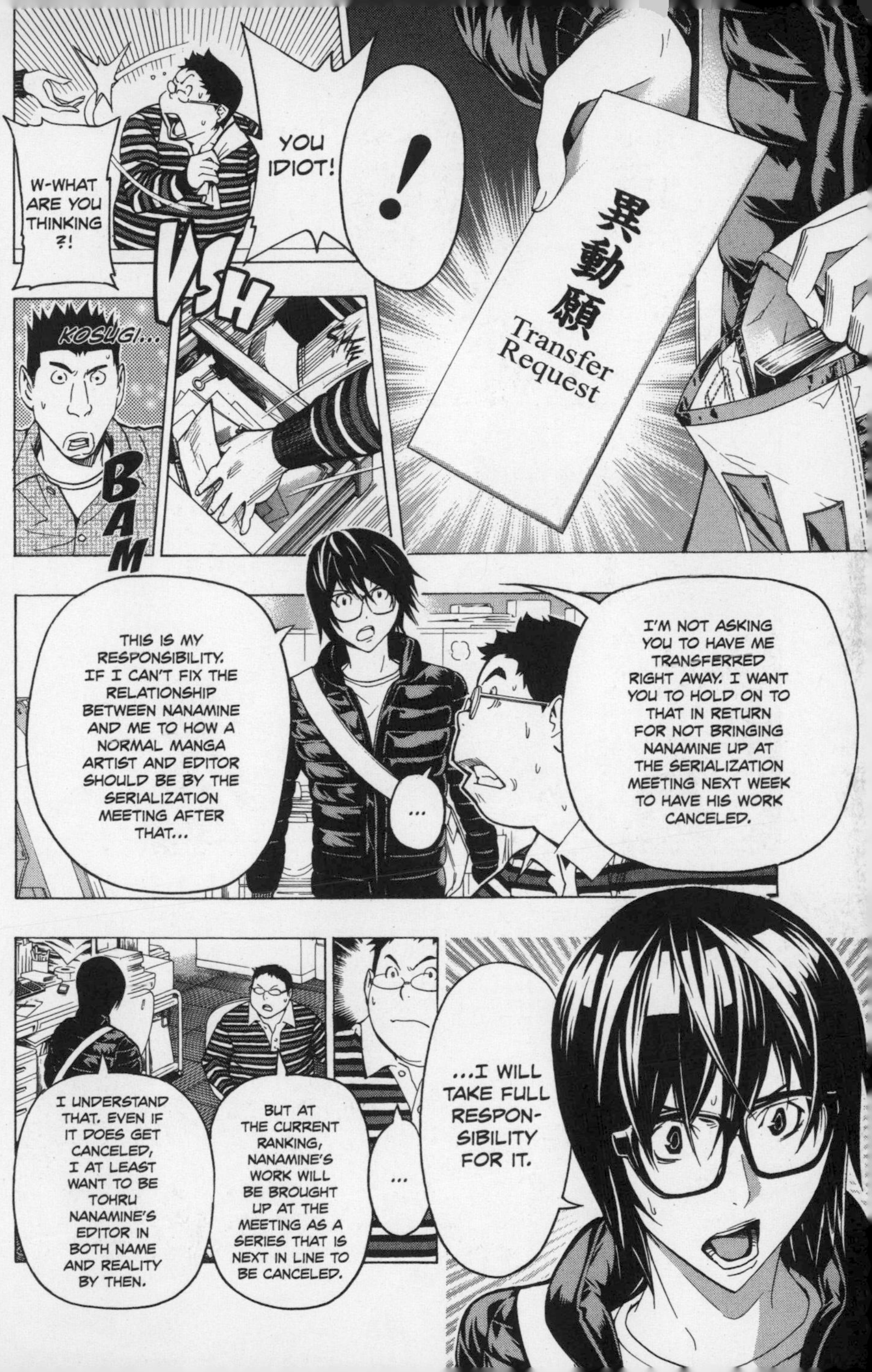

異動願
Transfer Request
!
YOU IDIOT!
W-WHAT ARE YOU THINKING?!
VSH
KOSUGI...
BAM
I'M NOT ASKING YOU TO HAVE ME TRANSFERRED RIGHT AWAY. I WANT YOU TO HOLD ON TO THAT IN RETURN FOR NOT BRINGING NANAMINE UP AT THE SERIALIZATION MEETING NEXT WEEK TO HAVE HIS WORK CANCELED.
...
THIS IS MY RESPONSIBILITY. IF I CAN'T FIX THE RELATIONSHIP BETWEEN NANAMINE AND ME TO HOW A NORMAL MANGA ARTIST AND EDITOR SHOULD BE BY THE SERIALIZATION MEETING AFTER THAT...
...I WILL TAKE FULL RESPON-SIBILITY FOR IT.
...
BUT AT THE CURRENT RANKING, NANAMINE'S WORK WILL BE BROUGHT UP AT THE MEETING AS A SERIES THAT IS NEXT IN LINE TO BE CANCELED.
I UNDERSTAND THAT. EVEN IF IT DOES GET CANCELED, I AT LEAST WANT TO BE TOHRU NANAMINE'S EDITOR IN BOTH NAME AND REALITY BY THEN.

READ THIS WAY

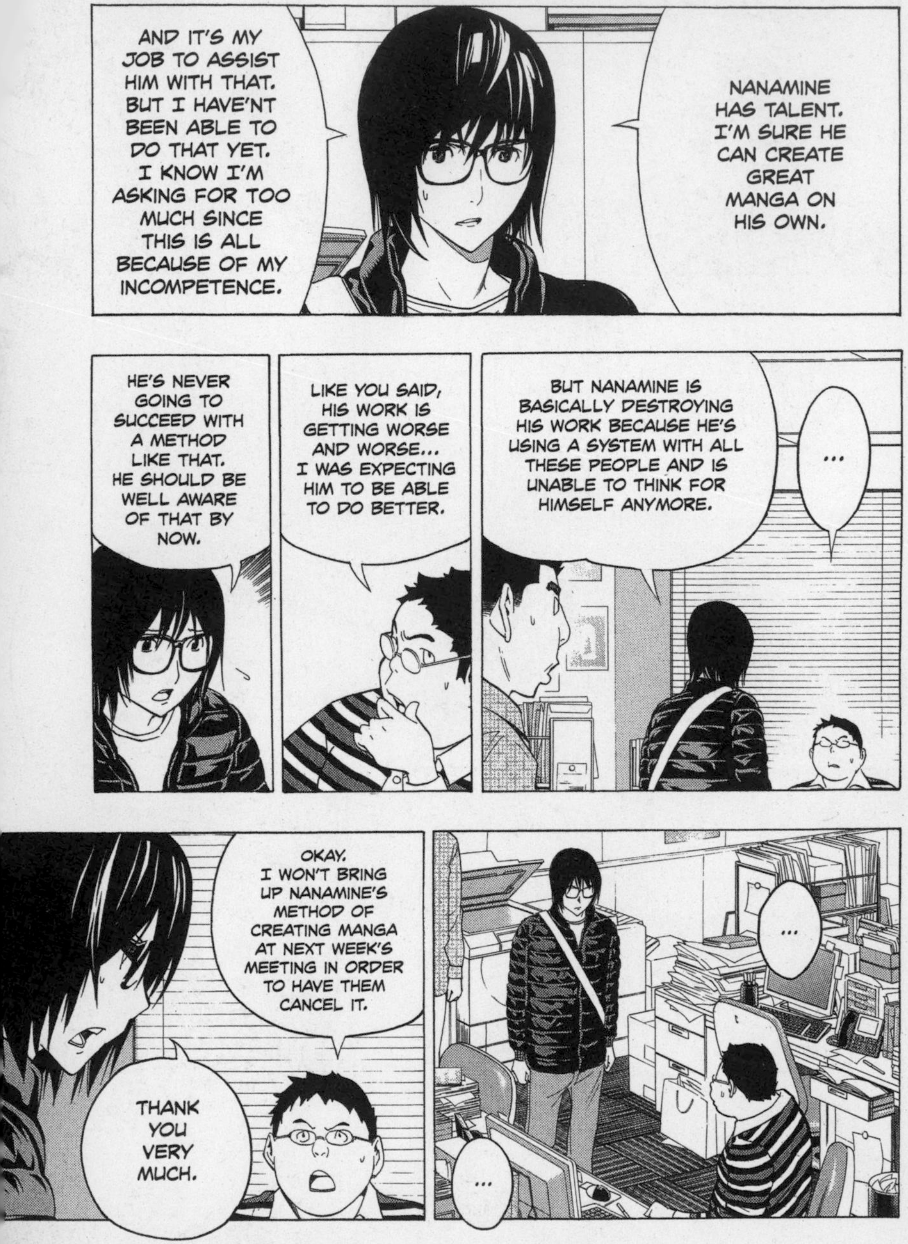
NANAMINE HAS TALENT. I'M SURE HE CAN CREATE GREAT MANGA ON HIS OWN.
AND IT'S MY JOB TO ASSIST HIM WITH THAT. BUT I HAVE'NT BEEN ABLE TO DO THAT YET. I KNOW I'M ASKING FOR TOO MUCH SINCE THIS IS ALL BECAUSE OF MY INCOMPETENCE.
BUT NANAMINE IS BASICALLY DESTROYING HIS WORK BECAUSE HE'S USING A SYSTEM WITH ALL THESE PEOPLE AND IS UNABLE TO THINK FOR HIMSELF ANYMORE.
...
LIKE YOU SAID, HIS WORK IS GETTING WORSE AND WORSE... I WAS EXPECTING HIM TO BE ABLE TO DO BETTER.
HE'S NEVER GOING TO SUCCEED WITH A METHOD LIKE THAT. HE SHOULD BE WELL AWARE OF THAT BY NOW.
...
...
OKAY. I WON'T BRING UP NANAMINE'S METHOD OF CREATING MANGA AT NEXT WEEK'S MEETING IN ORDER TO HAVE THEM CANCEL IT.
THANK YOU VERY MUCH.

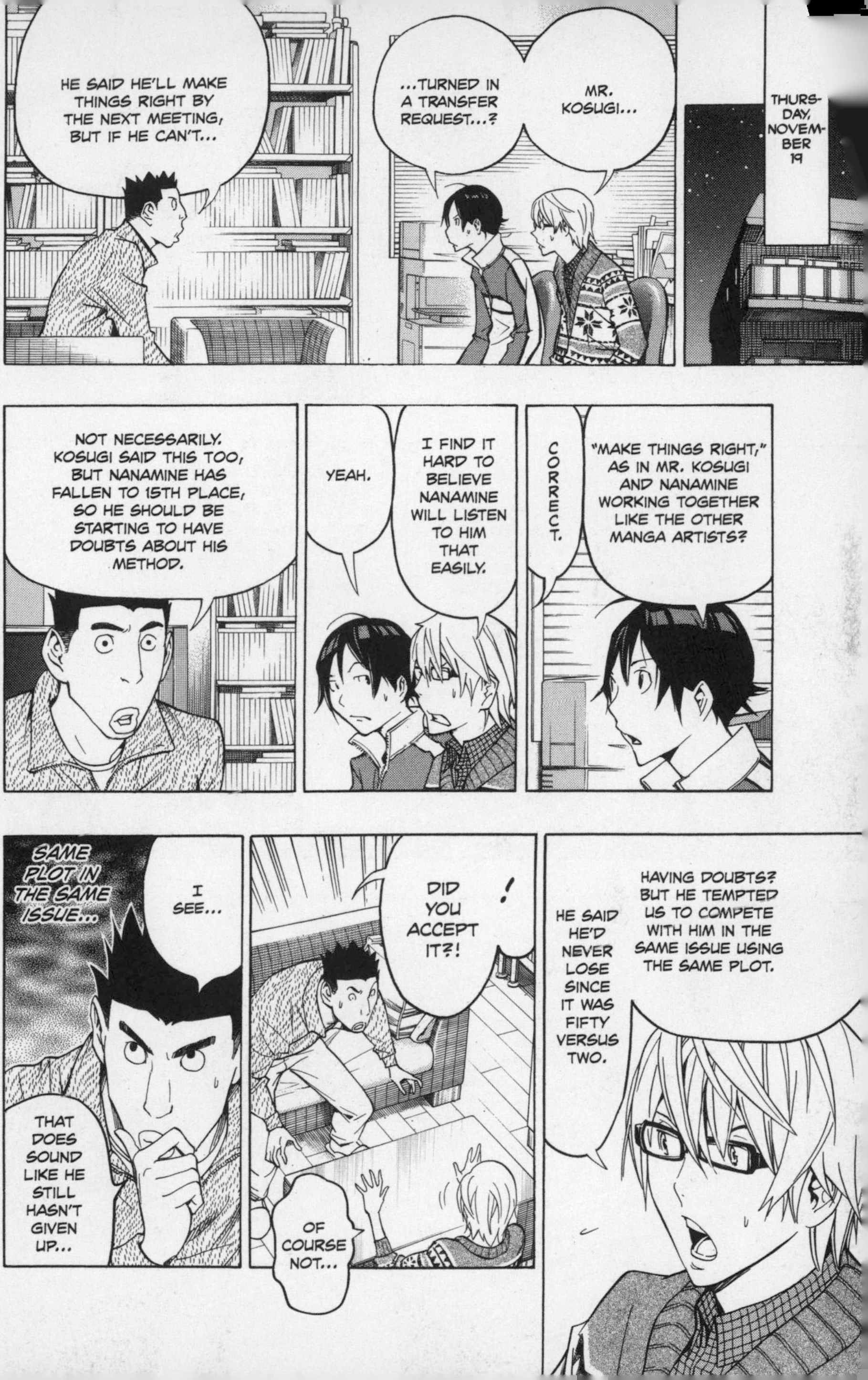
THURSDAY, NOVEMBER 19
MR. KOSUGI...
...TURNED IN A TRANSFER REQUEST...?
HE SAID HE'LL MAKE THINGS RIGHT BY THE NEXT MEETING, BUT IF HE CAN'T...
"MAKE THINGS RIGHT," AS IN MR. KOSUGI AND NANAMINE WORKING TOGETHER LIKE THE OTHER MANGA ARTISTS?
CORRECT.
I FIND IT HARD TO BELIEVE NANAMINE WILL LISTEN TO HIM THAT EASILY.
YEAH.
NOT NECESSARILY. KOSUGI SAID THIS TOO, BUT NANAMINE HAS FALLEN TO 15TH PLACE, SO HE SHOULD BE STARTING TO HAVE DOUBTS ABOUT HIS METHOD.
HAVING DOUBTS? BUT HE TEMPTED US TO COMPETE WITH HIM IN THE SAME ISSUE USING THE SAME PLOT.
HE SAID HE'D NEVER LOSE SINCE IT WAS FIFTY VERSUS TWO.
!
DID YOU ACCEPT IT?!
OF COURSE NOT...
I SEE...
SAME PLOT IN THE SAME ISSUE...
THAT DOES SOUND LIKE HE STILL HASN'T GIVEN UP...

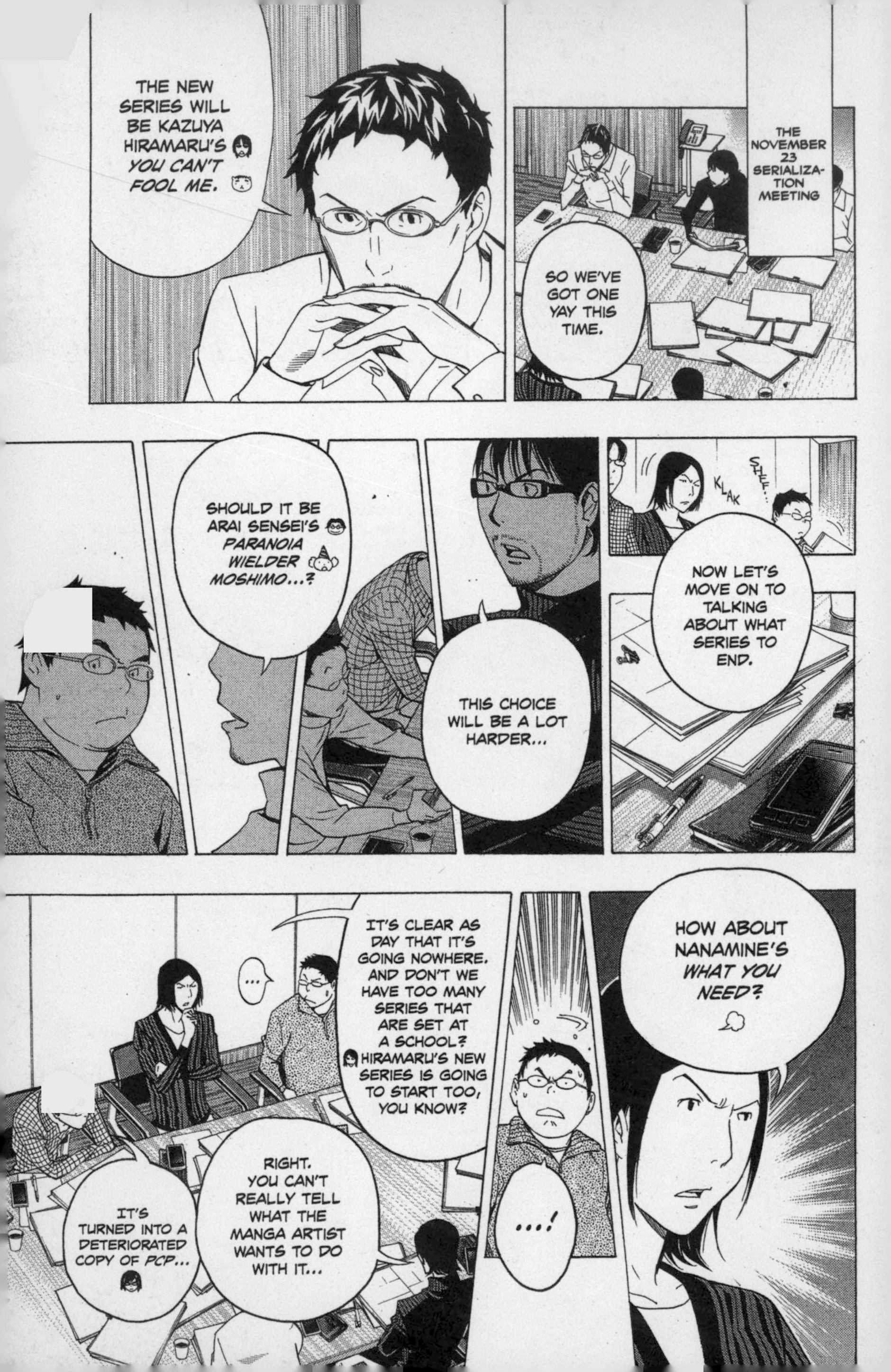
THE NOVEMBER 23 SERIALIZATION MEETING
SO WE'VE GOT ONE YAY THIS TIME.
THE NEW SERIES WILL BE KAZUYA HIRAMARU'S *YOU CAN'T FOOL ME.*
SHEFF...
KLAK
NOW LET'S MOVE ON TO TALKING ABOUT WHAT SERIES TO END.
THIS CHOICE WILL BE A LOT HARDER...
SHOULD IT BE ARAI SENSEI'S *PARANOIA WIELDER MOSHIMO...?*
HOW ABOUT NANAMINE'S *WHAT YOU NEED?*
...!
IT'S CLEAR AS DAY THAT IT'S GOING NOWHERE. AND DON'T WE HAVE TOO MANY SERIES THAT ARE SET AT A SCHOOL? HIRAMARU'S NEW SERIES IS GOING TO START TOO, YOU KNOW?
...
RIGHT. YOU CAN'T REALLY TELL WHAT THE MANGA ARTIST WANTS TO DO WITH IT...
IT'S TURNED INTO A DETERIORATED COPY OF *PCP*...

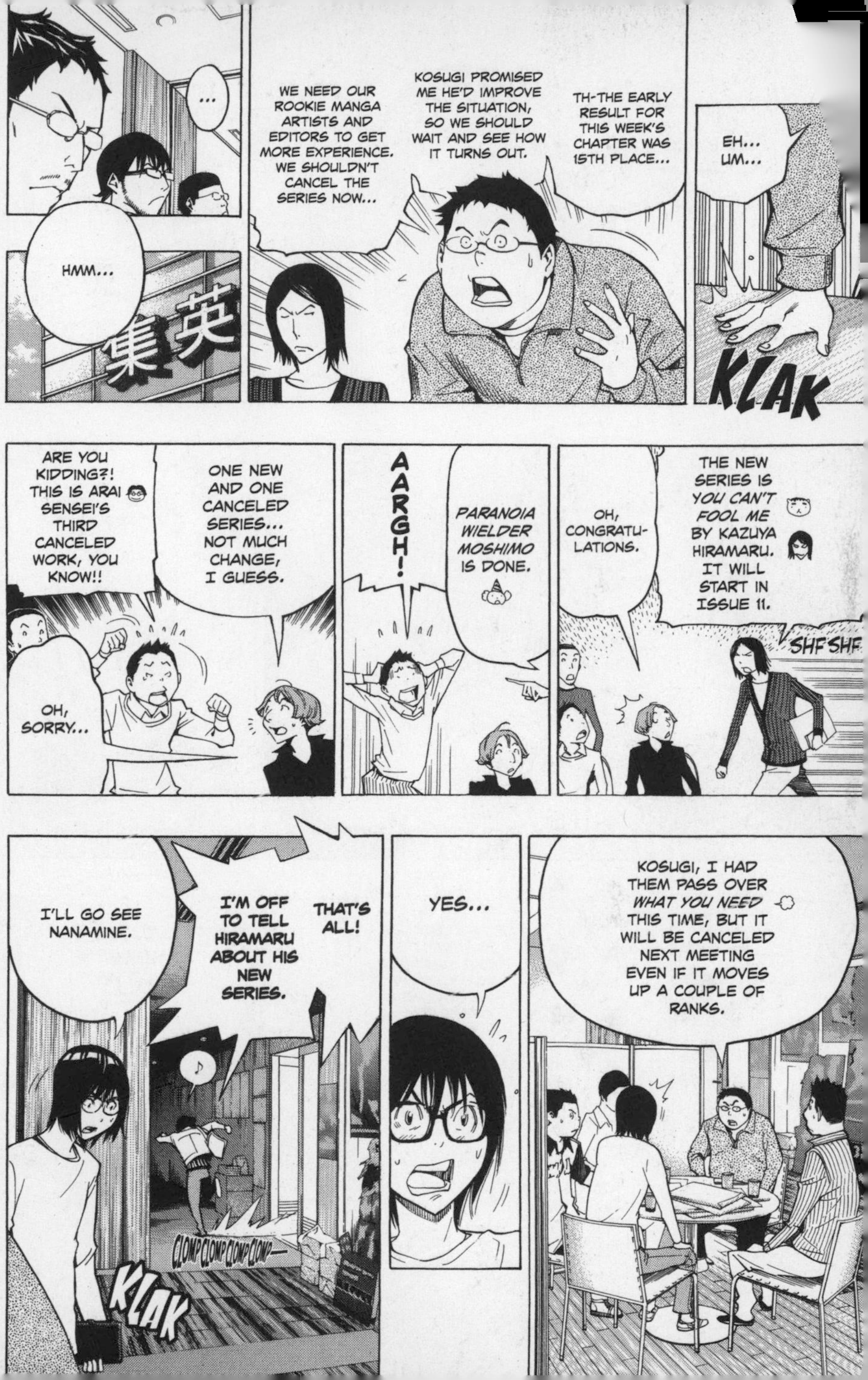
EH... UM...
KLAK
TH-THE EARLY RESULT FOR THIS WEEK'S CHAPTER WAS 15TH PLACE...
KOSUGI PROMISED ME HE'D IMPROVE THE SITUATION, SO WE SHOULD WAIT AND SEE HOW IT TURNS OUT.
WE NEED OUR ROOKIE MANGA ARTISTS AND EDITORS TO GET MORE EXPERIENCE. WE SHOULDN'T CANCEL THE SERIES NOW...
...
HMM...
集英
THE NEW SERIES IS *YOU CAN'T FOOL ME* BY KAZUYA HIRAMARU. IT WILL START IN ISSUE 11.
SHF SHF
OH, CONGRATULATIONS.
PARANOIA WIELDER MOSHIMO IS DONE.
AARGH!
ONE NEW AND ONE CANCELED SERIES... NOT MUCH CHANGE, I GUESS.
ARE YOU KIDDING?! THIS IS ARAI SENSEI'S THIRD CANCELED WORK, YOU KNOW!!
OH, SORRY...
KOSUGI, I HAD THEM PASS OVER *WHAT YOU NEED* THIS TIME, BUT IT WILL BE CANCELED NEXT MEETING EVEN IF IT MOVES UP A COUPLE OF RANKS.
YES...
THAT'S ALL!
I'M OFF TO TELL HIRAMARU ABOUT HIS NEW SERIES.
CLOMP CLOMP CLOMP CLOMP
I'LL GO SEE NANAMINE.
KLAK

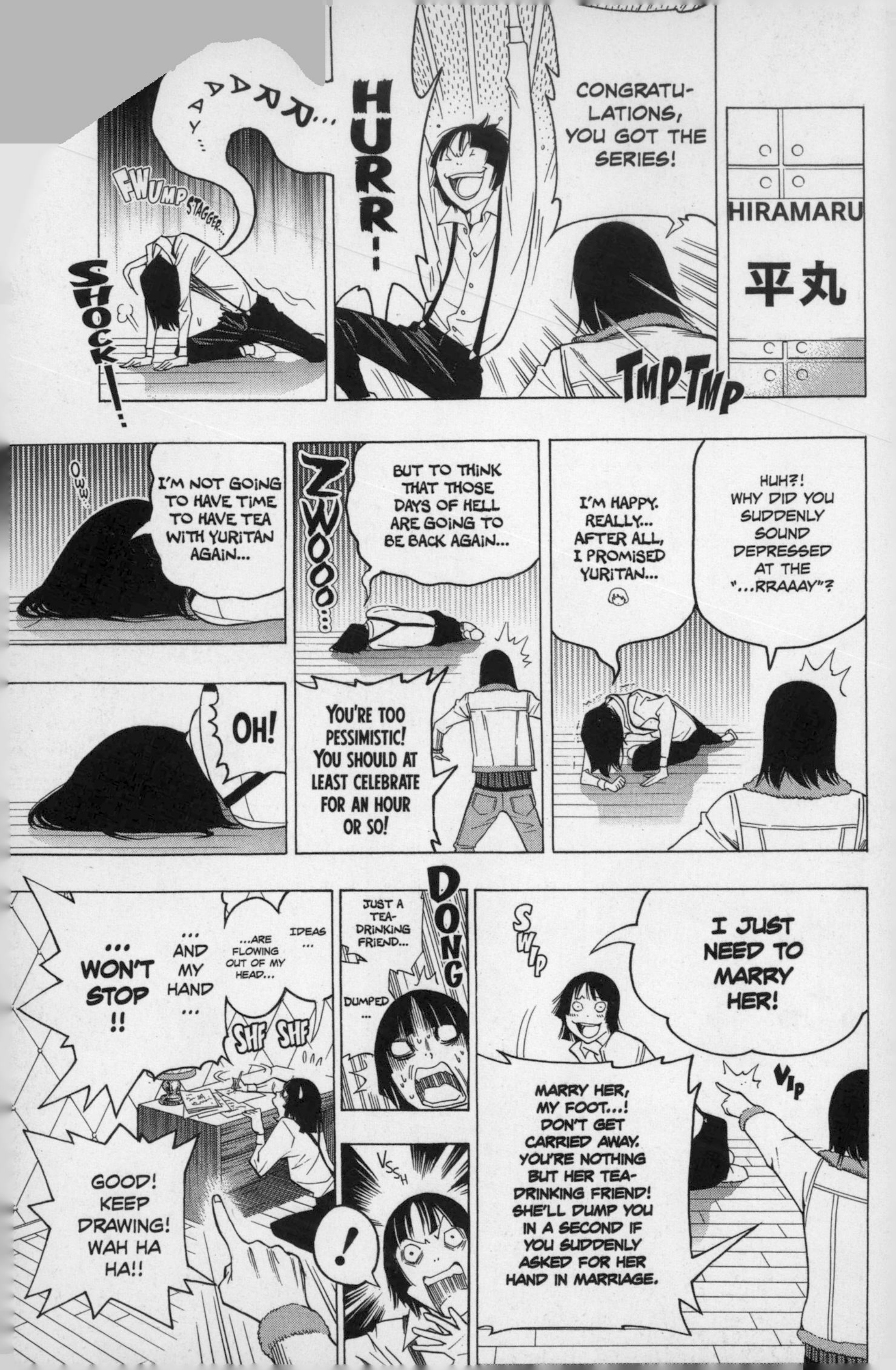
CONGRATULATIONS, YOU GOT THE SERIES!
HIRAMARU
平丸
TMP TMP
HURR!!
FWUMP
STAGGER...
SHOCK!!
HUH?! WHY DID YOU SUDDENLY SOUND DEPRESSED AT THE "...RRAAAY"?
I'M HAPPY. REALLY... AFTER ALL, I PROMISED YURITAN...
ZWOOO...
BUT TO THINK THAT THOSE DAYS OF HELL ARE GOING TO BE BACK AGAIN...
YOU'RE TOO PESSIMISTIC! YOU SHOULD AT LEAST CELEBRATE FOR AN HOUR OR SO!
OWW...
I'M NOT GOING TO HAVE TIME TO HAVE TEA WITH YURITAN AGAIN...
OH!
SWIP
I JUST NEED TO MARRY HER!
VIP
MARRY HER, MY FOOT...! DON'T GET CARRIED AWAY. YOU'RE NOTHING BUT HER TEA-DRINKING FRIEND! SHE'LL DUMP YOU IN A SECOND IF YOU SUDDENLY ASKED FOR HER HAND IN MARRIAGE.
DONG
JUST A TEA-DRINKING FRIEND...
DUMPED...
VSSH
!
IDEAS...
...ARE FLOWING OUT OF MY HEAD...
... AND MY HAND ...
... WON'T STOP !!
SHF SHF
GOOD! KEEP DRAWING! WAH HA HA!!

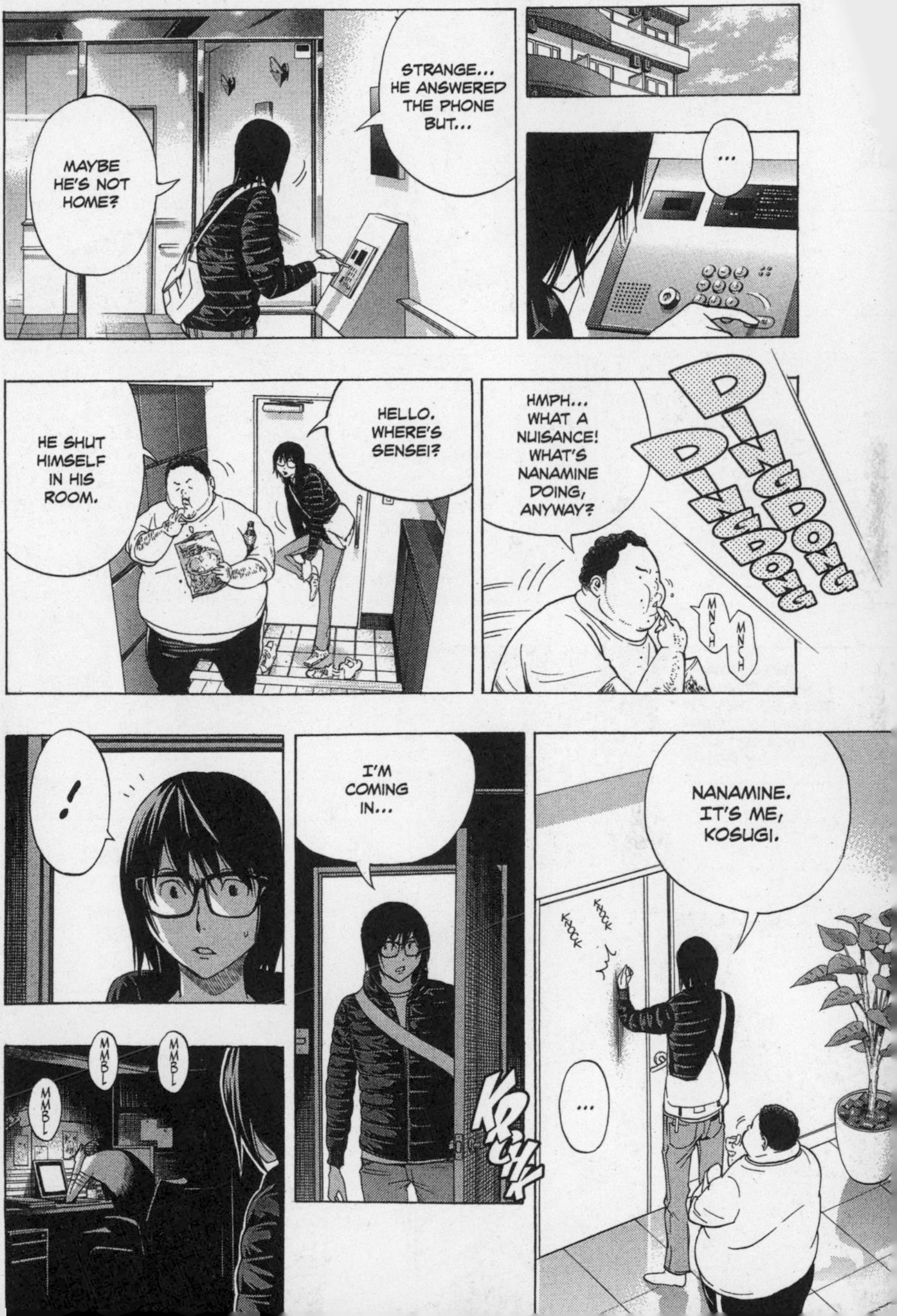
...
STRANGE... HE ANSWERED THE PHONE BUT...
MAYBE HE'S NOT HOME?
DINGDONG DINGDONG
HMPH... WHAT A NUISANCE! WHAT'S NANAMINE DOING, ANYWAY?
MNCH MNCH
HELLO. WHERE'S SENSEI?
HE SHUT HIMSELF IN HIS ROOM.
NANAMINE. IT'S ME, KOSUGI.
KNOCK KNOCK
...
I'M COMING IN...
K-CHAK
!
MMBL MMBL MMBL

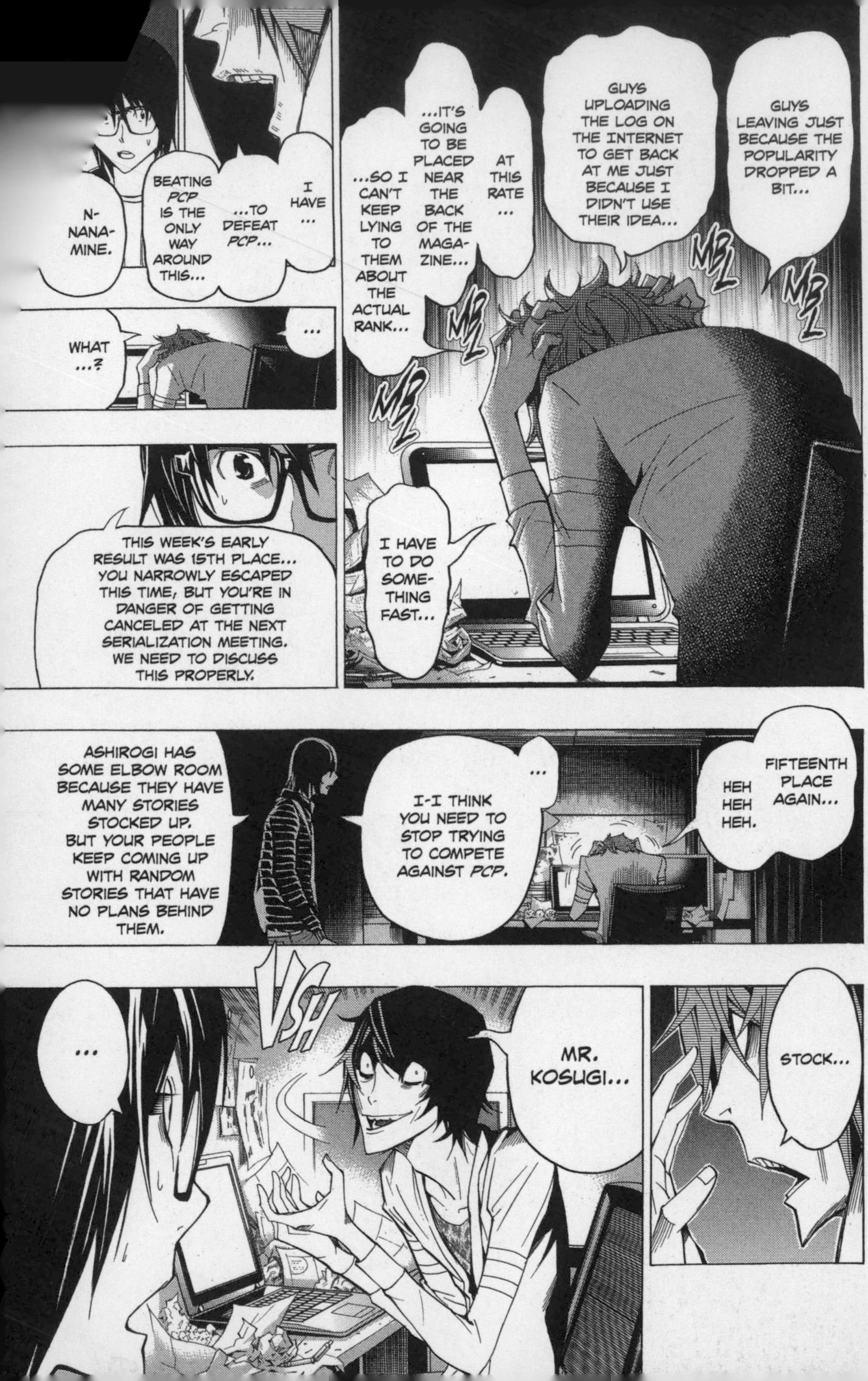
GUYS LEAVING JUST BECAUSE THE POPULARITY DROPPED A BIT...
MBL
GUYS UPLOADING THE LOG ON THE INTERNET TO GET BACK AT ME JUST BECAUSE I DIDN'T USE THEIR IDEA...
MBL
AT THIS RATE ...
...IT'S GOING TO BE PLACED NEAR THE BACK OF THE MAGAZINE...
...SO I CAN'T KEEP LYING TO THEM ABOUT THE ACTUAL RANK...
MBL
MBL
I HAVE TO DO SOMETHING FAST...
I HAVE ...
...TO DEFEAT PCP...
BEATING PCP IS THE ONLY WAY AROUND THIS...
N-NANAMINE.
...
WHAT ...?
THIS WEEK'S EARLY RESULT WAS 15TH PLACE... YOU NARROWLY ESCAPED THIS TIME, BUT YOU'RE IN DANGER OF GETTING CANCELED AT THE NEXT SERIALIZATION MEETING. WE NEED TO DISCUSS THIS PROPERLY.
FIFTEENTH PLACE AGAIN...
HEH HEH HEH.
...
I-I THINK YOU NEED TO STOP TRYING TO COMPETE AGAINST PCP.
ASHIROGI HAS SOME ELBOW ROOM BECAUSE THEY HAVE MANY STORIES STOCKED UP. BUT YOUR PEOPLE KEEP COMING UP WITH RANDOM STORIES THAT HAVE NO PLANS BEHIND THEM.
STOCK...
MR. KOSUGI...
VSH
...

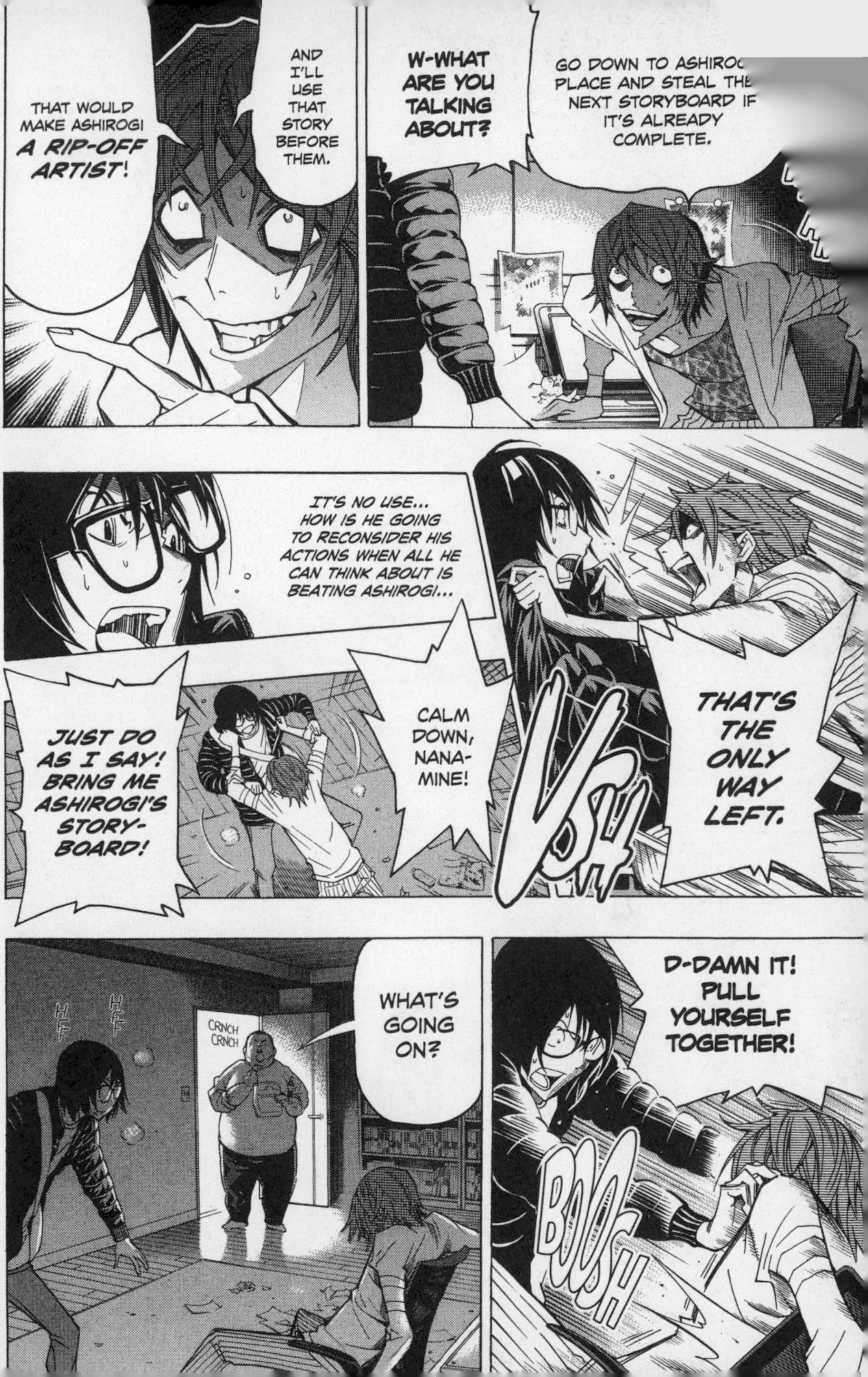

GO DOWN TO ASHIROG PLACE AND STEAL THE NEXT STORYBOARD IF IT'S ALREADY COMPLETE.
W-WHAT ARE YOU TALKING ABOUT?
AND I'LL USE THAT STORY BEFORE THEM.
THAT WOULD MAKE ASHIROGI A RIP-OFF ARTIST!
VSH
THAT'S THE ONLY WAY LEFT.
IT'S NO USE... HOW IS HE GOING TO RECONSIDER HIS ACTIONS WHEN ALL HE CAN THINK ABOUT IS BEATING ASHIROGI...
CALM DOWN, NANA-MINE!
JUST DO AS I SAY! BRING ME ASHIROGI'S STORY-BOARD!
D-DAMN IT! PULL YOURSELF TOGETHER!
BOOSH
WHAT'S GOING ON?
CRNCH CRNCH
HFF HFF

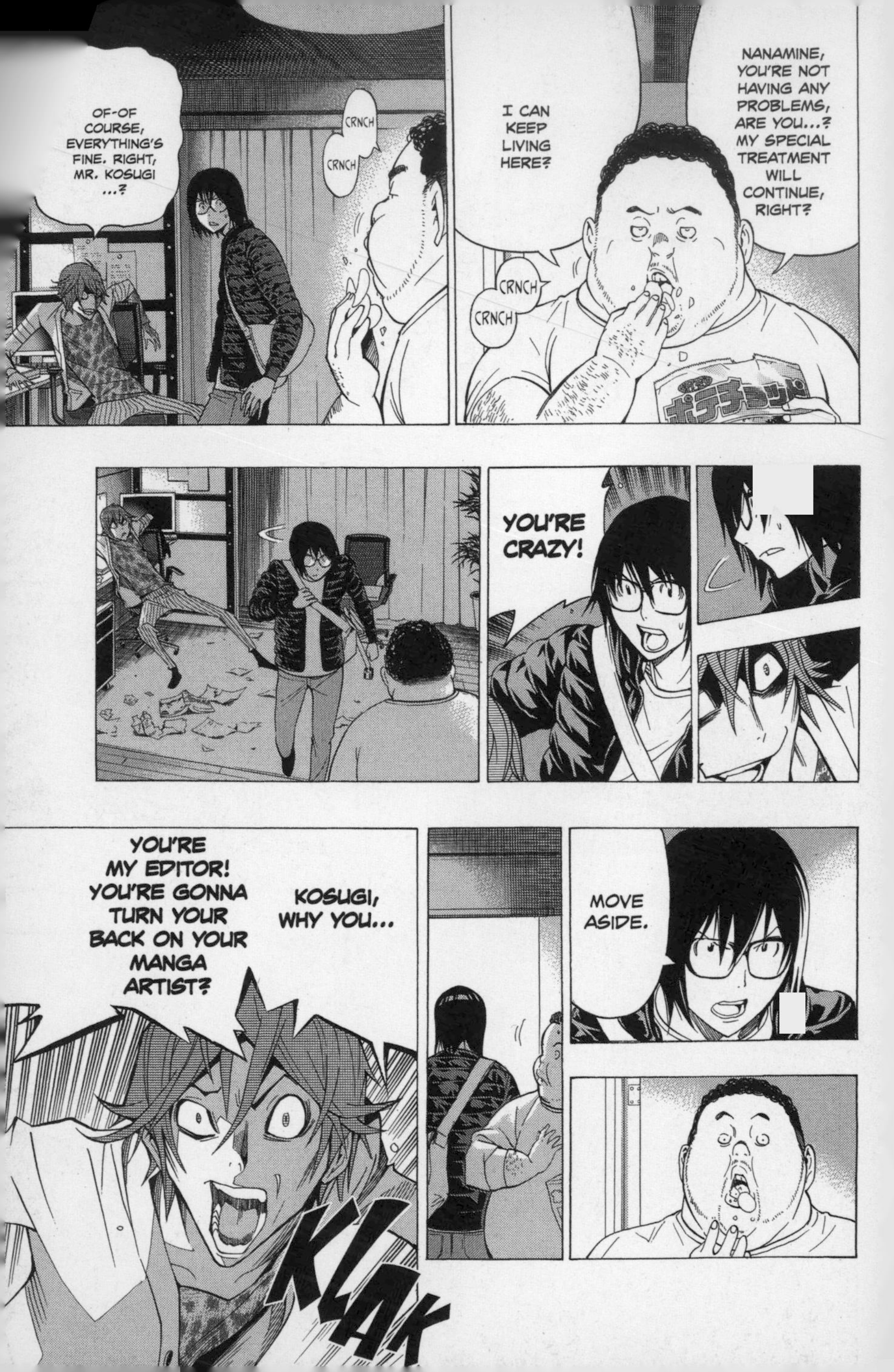
NANAMINE, YOU'RE NOT HAVING ANY PROBLEMS, ARE YOU...? MY SPECIAL TREATMENT WILL CONTINUE, RIGHT?
I CAN KEEP LIVING HERE?
CRNCH
CRNCH
CRNCH
CRNCH
OF-OF COURSE, EVERYTHING'S FINE. RIGHT, MR. KOSUGI ...?
YOU'RE CRAZY!
MOVE ASIDE.
KOSUGI, WHY YOU...
YOU'RE MY EDITOR! YOU'RE GONNA TURN YOUR BACK ON YOUR MANGA ARTIST?
KLAK

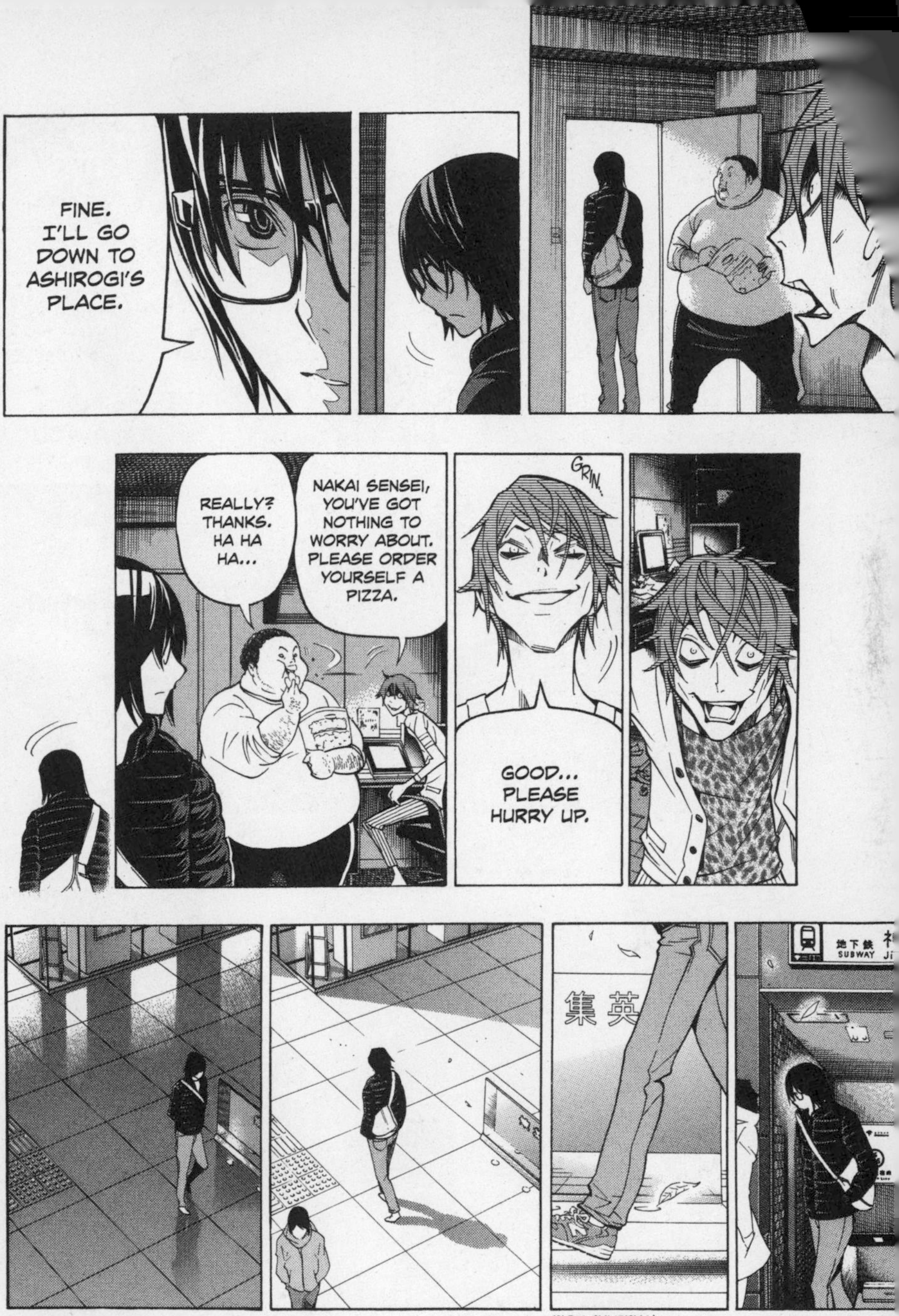
FINE. I'LL GO DOWN TO ASHIROGI'S PLACE.
GRIN...
GOOD... PLEASE HURRY UP.
NAKAI SENSEI, YOU'VE GOT NOTHING TO WORRY ABOUT. PLEASE ORDER YOURSELF A PIZZA.
REALLY? THANKS. HA HA HA...
地下鉄
SUBWAY
集英
(SIGN: SHUEISHA)

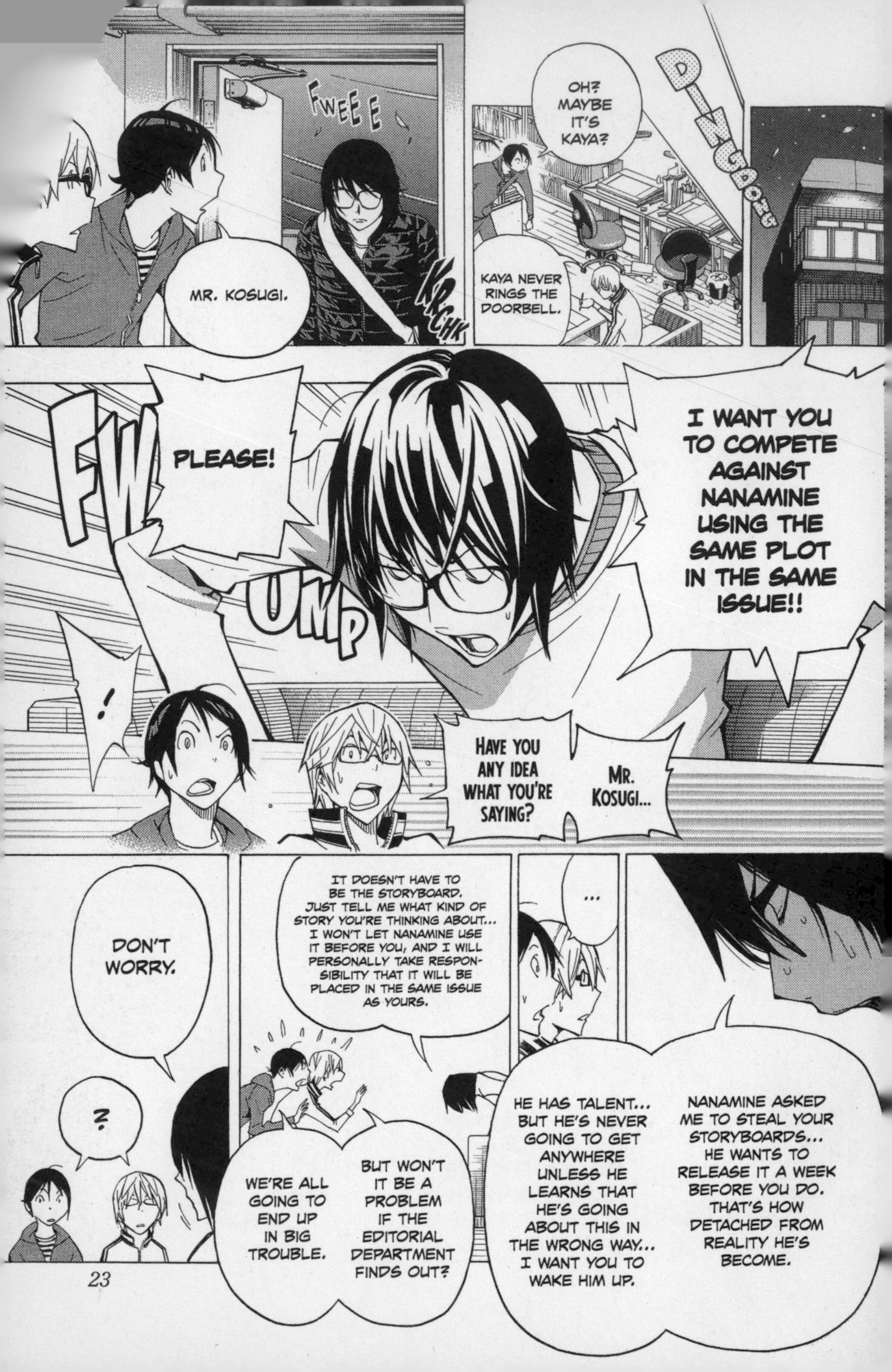
DINGDONG
OH? MAYBE IT'S KAYA?
KAYA NEVER RINGS THE DOORBELL.
FWEEE
KRCHK
MR. KOSUGI.
I WANT YOU TO COMPETE AGAINST NANAMINE USING THE SAME PLOT IN THE SAME ISSUE!!
PLEASE!
FWUMP
MR. KOSUGI...
HAVE YOU ANY IDEA WHAT YOU'RE SAYING?
!
NANAMINE ASKED ME TO STEAL YOUR STORYBOARDS... HE WANTS TO RELEASE IT A WEEK BEFORE YOU DO. THAT'S HOW DETACHED FROM REALITY HE'S BECOME.
HE HAS TALENT... BUT HE'S NEVER GOING TO GET ANYWHERE UNLESS HE LEARNS THAT HE'S GOING ABOUT THIS IN THE WRONG WAY... I WANT YOU TO WAKE HIM UP.
...
IT DOESN'T HAVE TO BE THE STORYBOARD. JUST TELL ME WHAT KIND OF STORY YOU'RE THINKING ABOUT... I WON'T LET NANAMINE USE IT BEFORE YOU, AND I WILL PERSONALLY TAKE RESPONSIBILITY THAT IT WILL BE PLACED IN THE SAME ISSUE AS YOURS.
BUT WON'T IT BE A PROBLEM IF THE EDITORIAL DEPARTMENT FINDS OUT?
WE'RE ALL GOING TO END UP IN BIG TROUBLE.
DON'T WORRY.
?

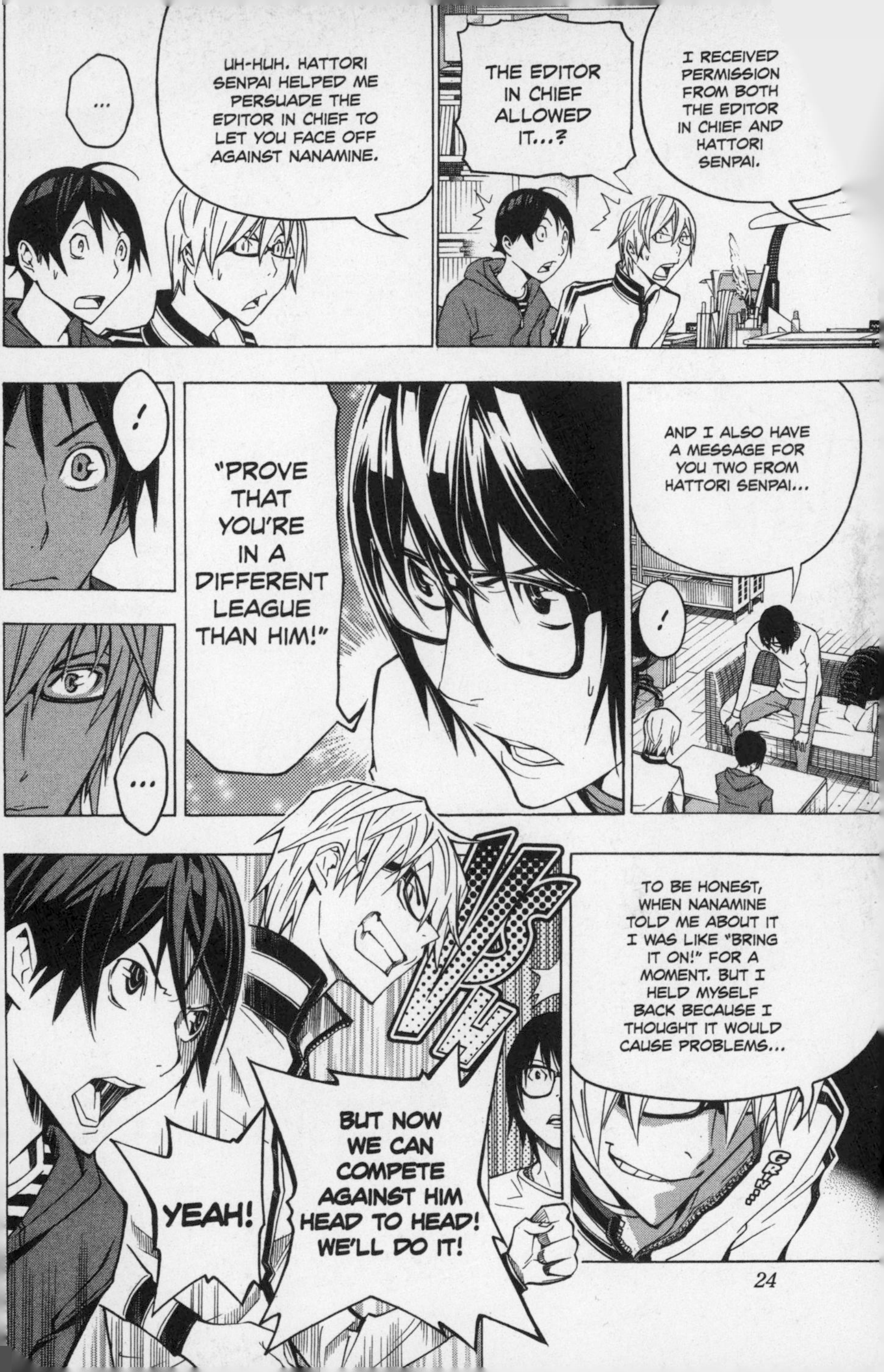
I RECEIVED PERMISSION FROM BOTH THE EDITOR IN CHIEF AND HATTORI SENPAI.
THE EDITOR IN CHIEF ALLOWED IT...?
UH-HUH. HATTORI SENPAI HELPED ME PERSUADE THE EDITOR IN CHIEF TO LET YOU FACE OFF AGAINST NANAMINE.
...
AND I ALSO HAVE A MESSAGE FOR YOU TWO FROM HATTORI SENPAI...
!
"PROVE THAT YOU'RE IN A DIFFERENT LEAGUE THAN HIM!"
!
...
TO BE HONEST, WHEN NANAMINE TOLD ME ABOUT IT I WAS LIKE "BRING IT ON!" FOR A MOMENT. BUT I HELD MYSELF BACK BECAUSE I THOUGHT IT WOULD CAUSE PROBLEMS...
BUT NOW WE CAN COMPETE AGAINST HIM HEAD TO HEAD! WE'LL DO IT!
YEAH!

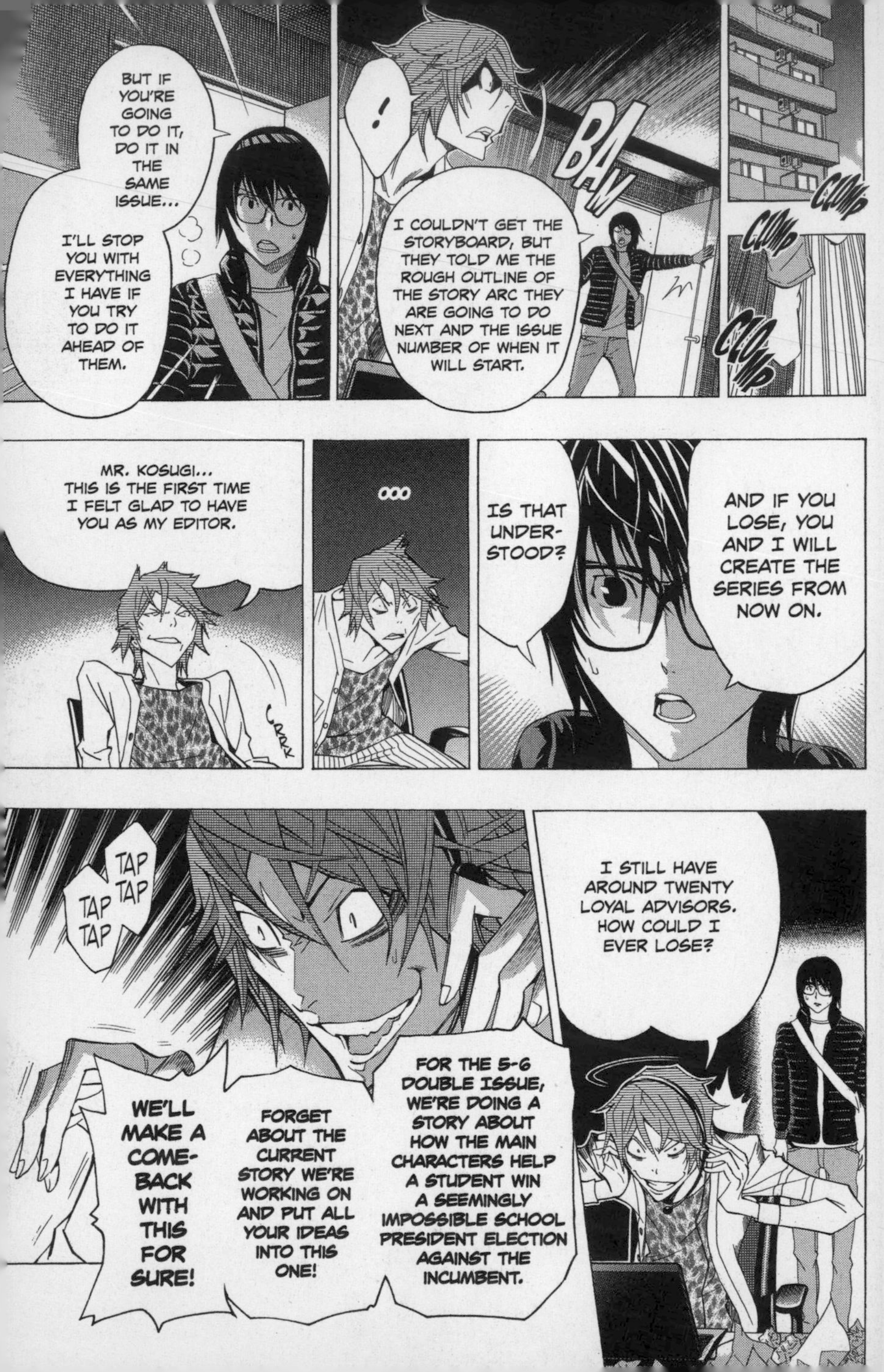
CLOMP
CLOMP
CLOMP
BAM
!
I COULDN'T GET THE STORYBOARD, BUT THEY TOLD ME THE ROUGH OUTLINE OF THE STORY ARC THEY ARE GOING TO DO NEXT AND THE ISSUE NUMBER OF WHEN IT WILL START.
BUT IF YOU'RE GOING TO DO IT, DO IT IN THE SAME ISSUE...
I'LL STOP YOU WITH EVERYTHING I HAVE IF YOU TRY TO DO IT AHEAD OF THEM.
AND IF YOU LOSE, YOU AND I WILL CREATE THE SERIES FROM NOW ON.
IS THAT UNDER-STOOD?
ooo
MR. KOSUGI... THIS IS THE FIRST TIME I FELT GLAD TO HAVE YOU AS MY EDITOR.
CRRK
I STILL HAVE AROUND TWENTY LOYAL ADVISORS. HOW COULD I EVER LOSE?
TAP TAP
TAP TAP
FOR THE 5-6 DOUBLE ISSUE, WE'RE DOING A STORY ABOUT HOW THE MAIN CHARACTERS HELP A STUDENT WIN A SEEMINGLY IMPOSSIBLE SCHOOL PRESIDENT ELECTION AGAINST THE INCUMBENT.
FORGET ABOUT THE CURRENT STORY WE'RE WORKING ON AND PUT ALL YOUR IDEAS INTO THIS ONE!
WE'LL MAKE A COME-BACK WITH THIS FOR SURE!

OHBA'S STORYBOARD

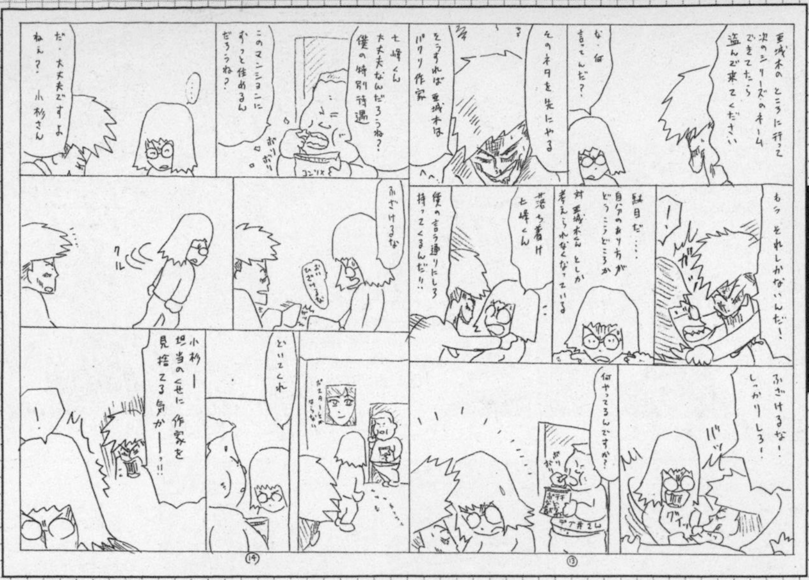
亜城木のところに行って 次のシリーズのネームできてたら盗んで来てください
な・何言ってんだ?
そのネタを先にやる
そうすれば亜城木はパクリ作家
七峰くん 大丈夫なんだろうね? 僕の特別待遇
このマンションにずっと住めるんだろうね?
ボリボリ
コンソメ
……
だ・大丈夫ですよねぇ? 小杉さん
もうそれしかないんだ!
!
駄目だ…… 自分のあり方がどうこうどころか 対亜城木さんとしか考えられなくなっている
落ち着け 七峰くん
僕の言う通りにしろ 持ってくるんだ!!
ふざけるな
クル
ふざけるな! しっかりしろ!
バッ
グイッ
何やってるんですか?
ボリボリ
どいてくれ
小杉ー 担当のくせに作家を見捨てる気かー!!
!

OBATA'S STORYBOARD

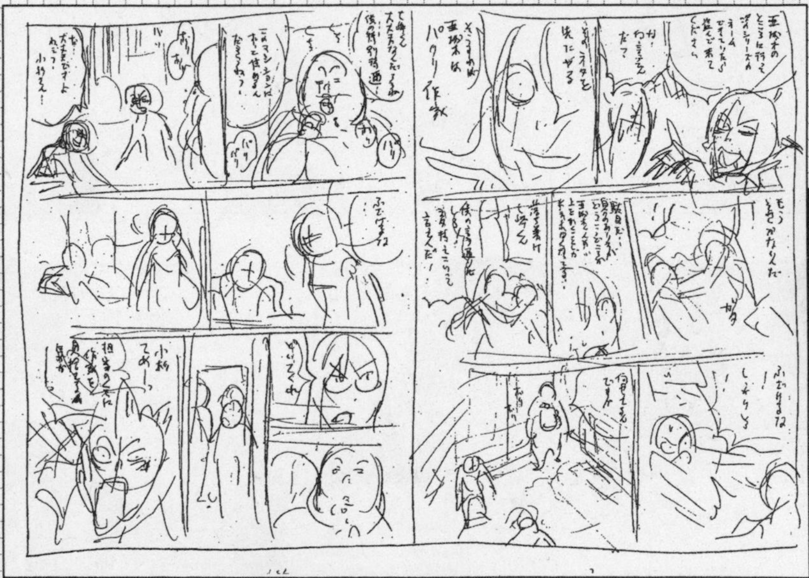

COMPLETE!

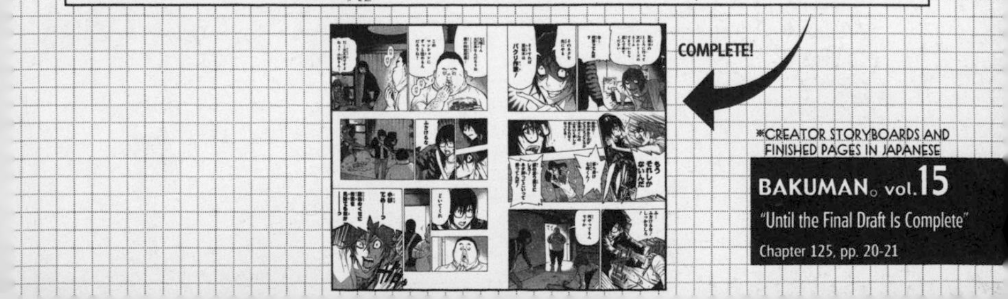

※CREATOR STORYBOARDS AND FINISHED PAGES IN JAPANESE

BAKUMAN。vol.15

"Until the Final Draft Is Complete"

Chapter 125, pp. 20-21

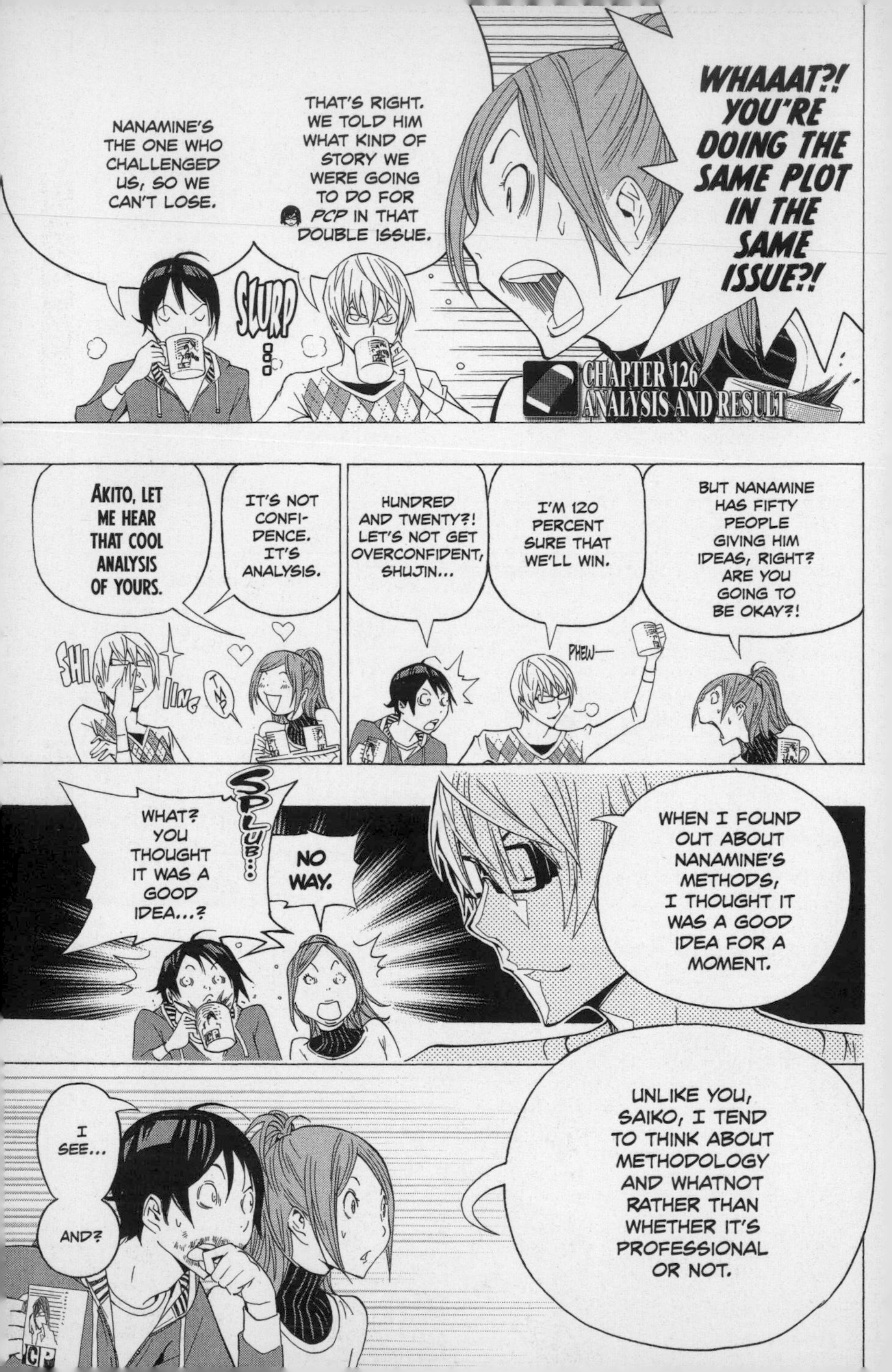
WHAAAT?! YOU'RE DOING THE SAME PLOT IN THE SAME ISSUE?!
CHAPTER 126
ANALYSIS AND RESULT
THAT'S RIGHT. WE TOLD HIM WHAT KIND OF STORY WE WERE GOING TO DO FOR PCP IN THAT DOUBLE ISSUE.
SLURP
NANAMINE'S THE ONE WHO CHALLENGED US, SO WE CAN'T LOSE.
BUT NANAMINE HAS FIFTY PEOPLE GIVING HIM IDEAS, RIGHT? ARE YOU GOING TO BE OKAY?!
I'M 120 PERCENT SURE THAT WE'LL WIN.
PHEW—
HUNDRED AND TWENTY?! LET'S NOT GET OVERCONFIDENT, SHUJIN...
IT'S NOT CONFIDENCE. IT'S ANALYSIS.
AKITO, LET ME HEAR THAT COOL ANALYSIS OF YOURS.
SHIIING
TMP
WHEN I FOUND OUT ABOUT NANAMINE'S METHODS, I THOUGHT IT WAS A GOOD IDEA FOR A MOMENT.
NO WAY.
SPLUB...
WHAT? YOU THOUGHT IT WAS A GOOD IDEA...?
UNLIKE YOU, SAIKO, I TEND TO THINK ABOUT METHODOLOGY AND WHATNOT RATHER THAN WHETHER IT'S PROFESSIONAL OR NOT.
I SEE...
AND?

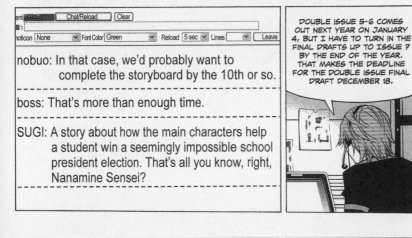

DOUBLE ISSUE 5-6 COMES OUT NEXT YEAR ON JANUARY 4, BUT I HAVE TO TURN IN THE FINAL DRAFTS UP TO ISSUE 7 BY THE END OF THE YEAR. THAT MAKES THE DEADLINE FOR THE DOUBLE ISSUE FINAL DRAFT DECEMBER 18.
Chat/Reload
Clear
None
Font Color
Green
Reload
5 sec
Lines
Leave
nobuo: In that case, we'd probably want to complete the storyboard by the 10th or so.
boss: That's more than enough time.
SUGI: A story about how the main characters help a student win a seemingly impossible school president election. That's all you know, right, Nanamine Sensei?
YES. BUT WE'RE TALKING ABOUT ASHIROGI HERE, SO I DOUBT THEY'LL DO SOME STORY ABOUT THE PCP MEMBERS REVEALING THE DARK SECRETS OF THE OTHER CANDIDATES TO BRING THEM DOWN.
boss: But this is going to be difficult since it's so stereotypical.
f-u: Yeah. After all, we're going to be using Ashirogi's framework of the story.
take20: We're all placing our ideas on the table because it's difficult, okay?
emo: How about a touching speech by that candidate and some kind of incident to back that up?
jj: We need a good manifesto that nobody could come up with.
nobuo: A front door approach is okay too, but I'd go with a big surprise ending.
kenchan: Right, Ashirogi may do that.
right: The important thing is for that student to have a cool and kick-ass victory.
I KNEW IT... THIS IS THE RIGHT AMOUNT OF PEOPLE... THE IDIOTS WHO WERE HERE OUT OF MERE CURIOSITY AND THE GUYS WHO COMPLAINED ALL THE TIME ARE GONE. THERE WERE ONLY FIVE PEOPLE INCLUDING ME WHEN I CREATED THE CLASSROOM OF TRUTH... FIFTY PEOPLE WERE TOO MANY...
THEY'RE ALL SERIOUSLY GIVING THEIR IDEAS. THIS WILL WORK.
THE RANK HAS BEEN FALLING SINCE CHAPTER 3 BUT I AM GOING TO RISE ABOVE PCP WITH CHAPTER 11 IN THE DOUBLE ISSUE.

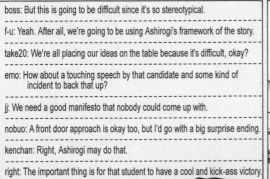

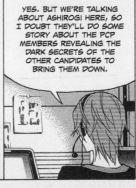

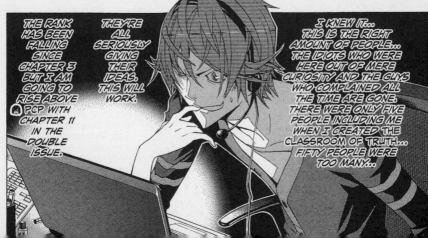

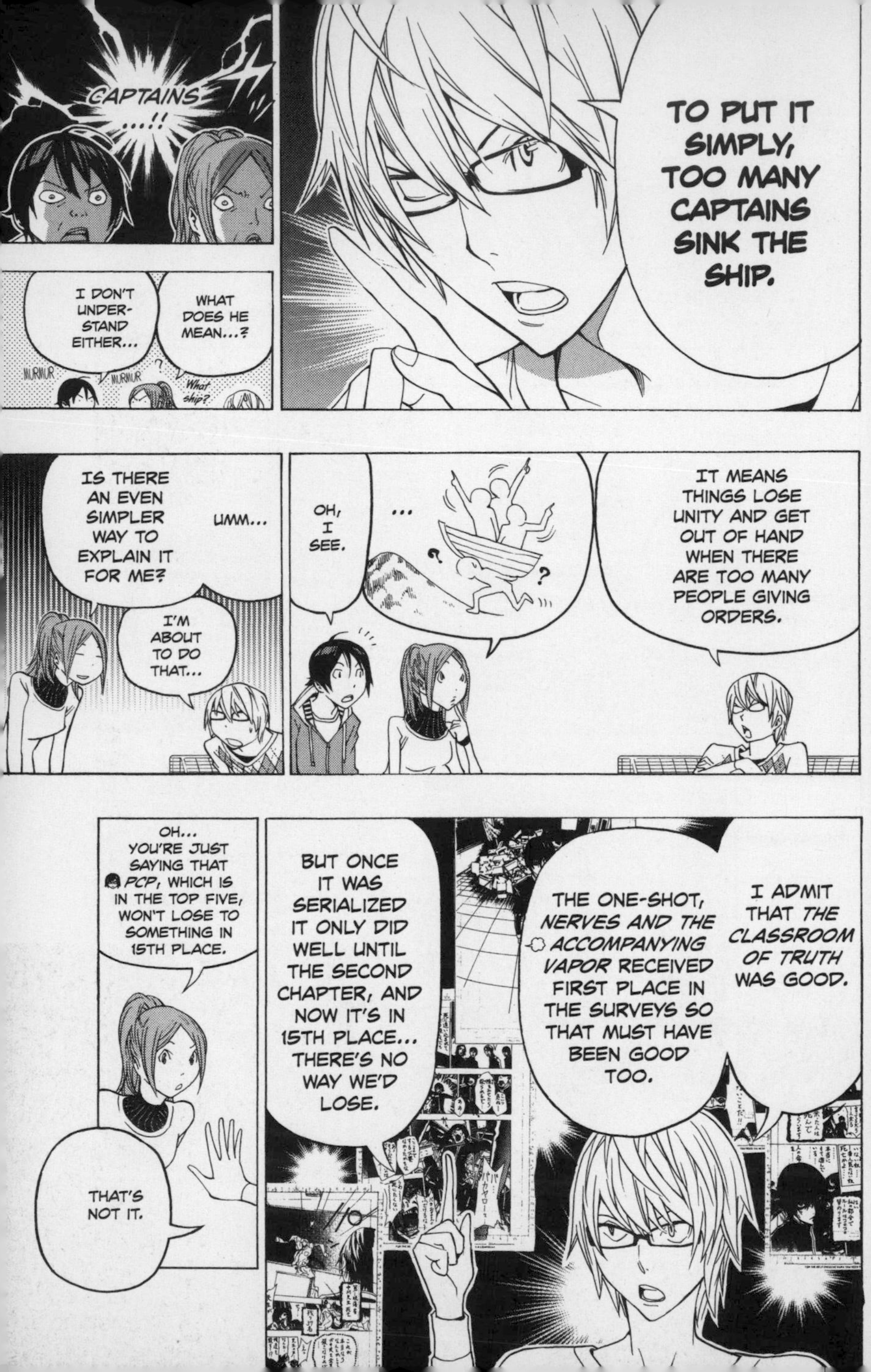
TO PUT IT SIMPLY, TOO MANY CAPTAINS SINK THE SHIP.
CAPTAINS ...!!
WHAT DOES HE MEAN...?
I DON'T UNDER-STAND EITHER...
MURMUR
MURMUR
What ship?
IT MEANS THINGS LOSE UNITY AND GET OUT OF HAND WHEN THERE ARE TOO MANY PEOPLE GIVING ORDERS.
...
OH, I SEE.
UMM...
IS THERE AN EVEN SIMPLER WAY TO EXPLAIN IT FOR ME?
I'M ABOUT TO DO THAT...
I ADMIT THAT *THE CLASSROOM OF TRUTH* WAS GOOD.
THE ONE-SHOT, *NERVES AND THE ACCOMPANYING VAPOR* RECEIVED FIRST PLACE IN THE SURVEYS SO THAT MUST HAVE BEEN GOOD TOO.
BUT ONCE IT WAS SERIALIZED IT ONLY DID WELL UNTIL THE SECOND CHAPTER, AND NOW IT'S IN 15TH PLACE... THERE'S NO WAY WE'D LOSE.
OH... YOU'RE JUST SAYING THAT *PCP*, WHICH IS IN THE TOP FIVE, WON'T LOSE TO SOMETHING IN 15TH PLACE.
THAT'S NOT IT.

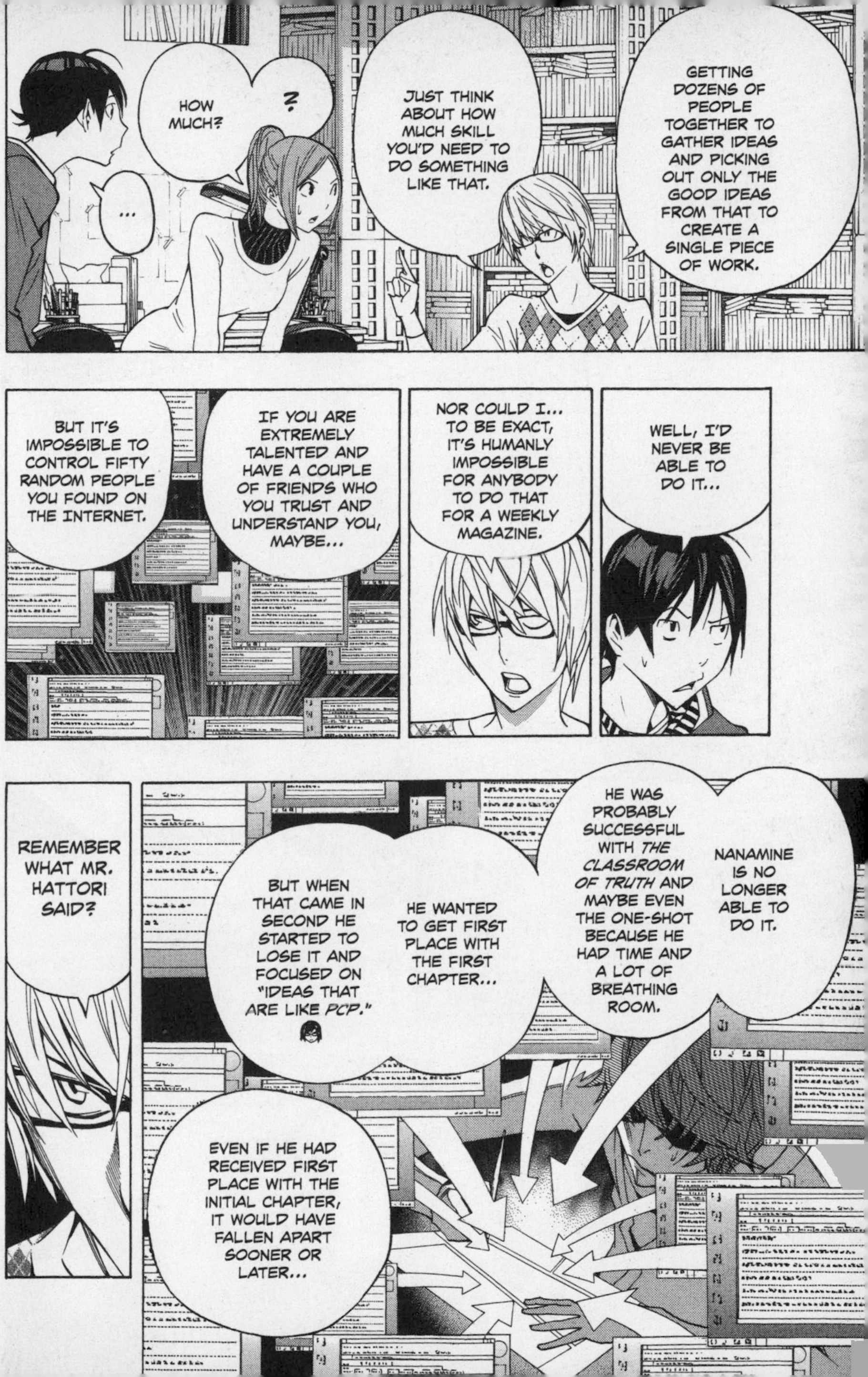
GETTING DOZENS OF PEOPLE TOGETHER TO GATHER IDEAS AND PICKING OUT ONLY THE GOOD IDEAS FROM THAT TO CREATE A SINGLE PIECE OF WORK.
JUST THINK ABOUT HOW MUCH SKILL YOU'D NEED TO DO SOMETHING LIKE THAT.
?
HOW MUCH?
...
WELL, I'D NEVER BE ABLE TO DO IT...
NOR COULD I... TO BE EXACT, IT'S HUMANLY IMPOSSIBLE FOR ANYBODY TO DO THAT FOR A WEEKLY MAGAZINE.
IF YOU ARE EXTREMELY TALENTED AND HAVE A COUPLE OF FRIENDS WHO YOU TRUST AND UNDERSTAND YOU, MAYBE...
BUT IT'S IMPOSSIBLE TO CONTROL FIFTY RANDOM PEOPLE YOU FOUND ON THE INTERNET.
NANAMINE IS NO LONGER ABLE TO DO IT.
HE WAS PROBABLY SUCCESSFUL WITH *THE CLASSROOM OF TRUTH* AND MAYBE EVEN THE ONE-SHOT BECAUSE HE HAD TIME AND A LOT OF BREATHING ROOM.
HE WANTED TO GET FIRST PLACE WITH THE FIRST CHAPTER...
BUT WHEN THAT CAME IN SECOND HE STARTED TO LOSE IT AND FOCUSED ON "IDEAS THAT ARE LIKE *PCP*."
EVEN IF HE HAD RECEIVED FIRST PLACE WITH THE INITIAL CHAPTER, IT WOULD HAVE FALLEN APART SOONER OR LATER...
REMEMBER WHAT MR. HATTORI SAID?

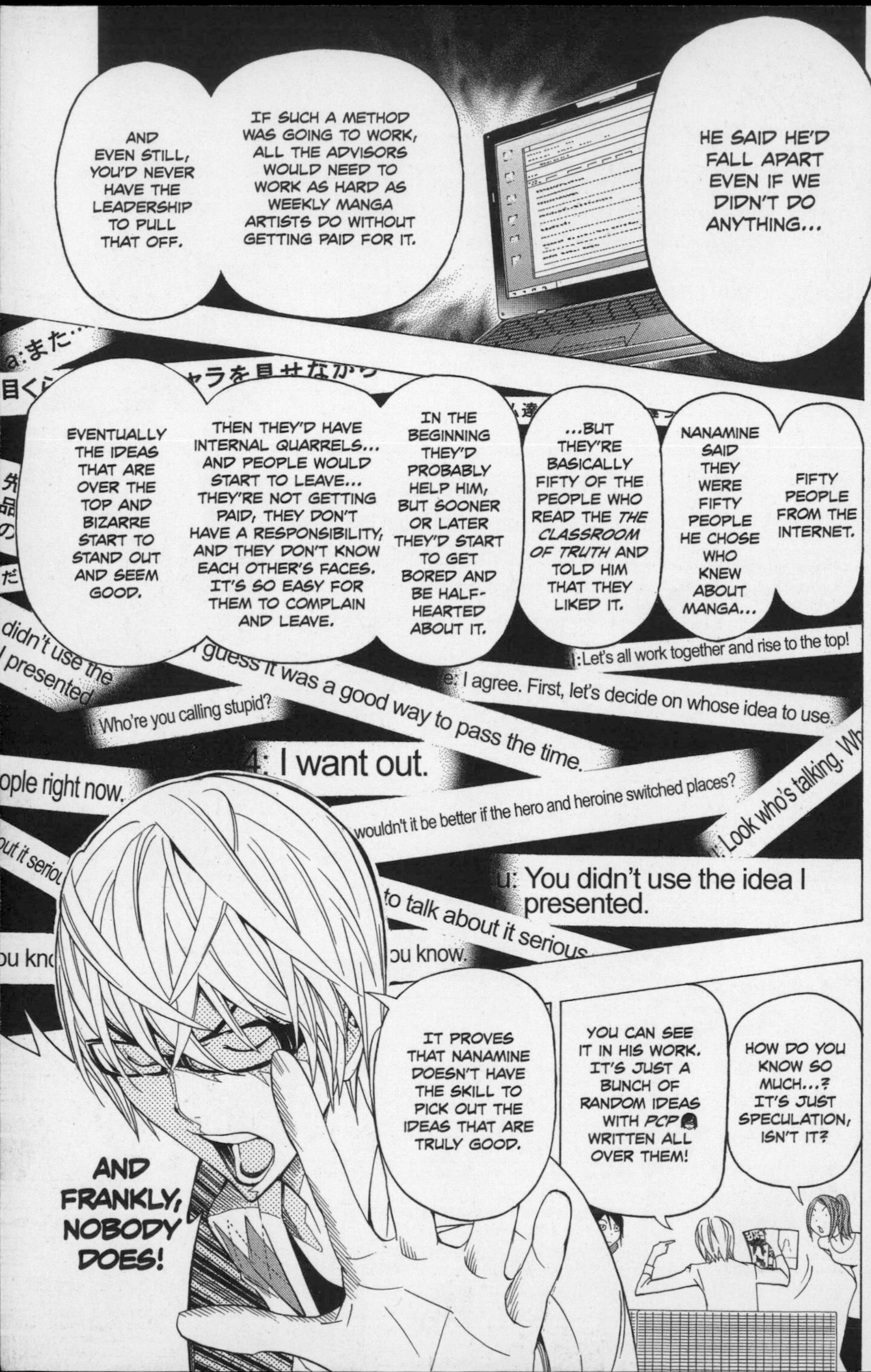
HE SAID HE'D FALL APART EVEN IF WE DIDN'T DO ANYTHING...
IF SUCH A METHOD WAS GOING TO WORK, ALL THE ADVISORS WOULD NEED TO WORK AS HARD AS WEEKLY MANGA ARTISTS DO WITHOUT GETTING PAID FOR IT.
AND EVEN STILL, YOU'D NEVER HAVE THE LEADERSHIP TO PULL THAT OFF.
FIFTY PEOPLE FROM THE INTERNET.
NANAMINE SAID THEY WERE FIFTY PEOPLE HE CHOSE WHO KNEW ABOUT MANGA...
...BUT THEY'RE BASICALLY FIFTY OF THE PEOPLE WHO READ THE *THE CLASSROOM OF TRUTH* AND TOLD HIM THAT THEY LIKED IT.
IN THE BEGINNING THEY'D PROBABLY HELP HIM, BUT SOONER OR LATER THEY'D START TO GET BORED AND BE HALF-HEARTED ABOUT IT.
THEN THEY'D HAVE INTERNAL QUARRELS... AND PEOPLE WOULD START TO LEAVE... THEY'RE NOT GETTING PAID, THEY DON'T HAVE A RESPONSIBILITY, AND THEY DON'T KNOW EACH OTHER'S FACES. IT'S SO EASY FOR THEM TO COMPLAIN AND LEAVE.
EVENTUALLY THE IDEAS THAT ARE OVER THE TOP AND BIZARRE START TO STAND OUT AND SEEM GOOD.
I:Let's all work together and rise to the top!
e: I agree. First, let's decide on whose idea to use.
guess it was a good way to pass the time.
Who're you calling stupid?
didn't use the
I presented
4: I want out.
ople right now.
wouldn't it be better if the hero and heroine switched places?
Look who's talking. Wh
u: You didn't use the idea I presented.
to talk about it serious
ou know.
HOW DO YOU KNOW SO MUCH...? IT'S JUST SPECULATION, ISN'T IT?
YOU CAN SEE IT IN HIS WORK. IT'S JUST A BUNCH OF RANDOM IDEAS WITH PCP WRITTEN ALL OVER THEM!
IT PROVES THAT NANAMINE DOESN'T HAVE THE SKILL TO PICK OUT THE IDEAS THAT ARE TRULY GOOD.
AND FRANKLY, NOBODY DOES!

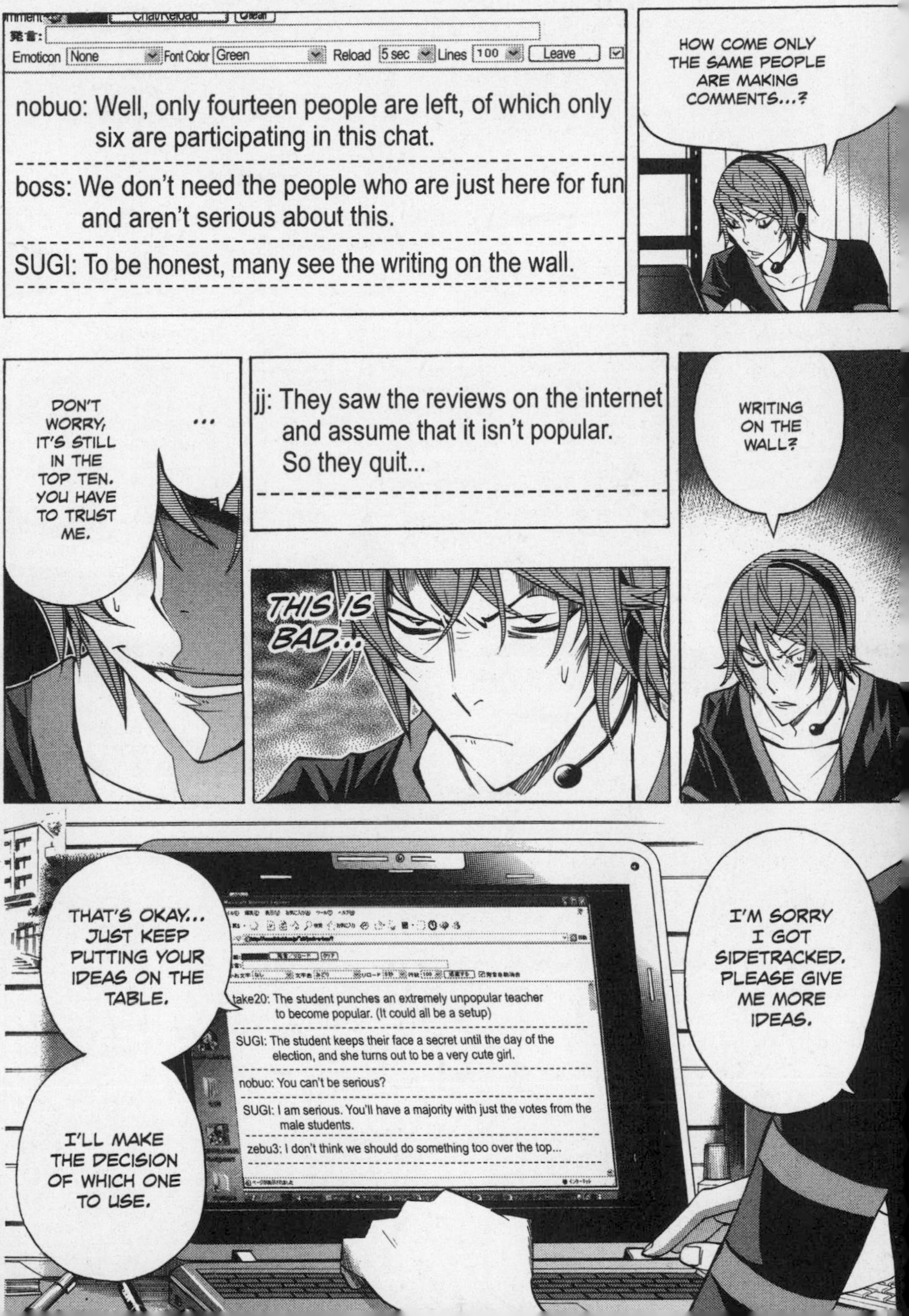
HOW COME ONLY THE SAME PEOPLE ARE MAKING COMMENTS...?
Emoticon None Font Color Green Reload 5 sec Lines 100 Leave
nobuo: Well, only fourteen people are left, of which only six are participating in this chat.
boss: We don't need the people who are just here for fun and aren't serious about this.
SUGI: To be honest, many see the writing on the wall.
WRITING ON THE WALL?
jj: They saw the reviews on the internet and assume that it isn't popular. So they quit...
THIS IS BAD...
...
DON'T WORRY, IT'S STILL IN THE TOP TEN. YOU HAVE TO TRUST ME.
I'M SORRY I GOT SIDETRACKED. PLEASE GIVE ME MORE IDEAS.
THAT'S OKAY... JUST KEEP PUTTING YOUR IDEAS ON THE TABLE.
take20: The student punches an extremely unpopular teacher to become popular. (It could all be a setup)
SUGI: The student keeps their face a secret until the day of the election, and she turns out to be a very cute girl.
nobuo: You can't be serious?
SUGI: I am serious. You'll have a majority with just the votes from the male students.
zebu3: I don't think we should do something too over the top...
I'LL MAKE THE DECISION OF WHICH ONE TO USE.

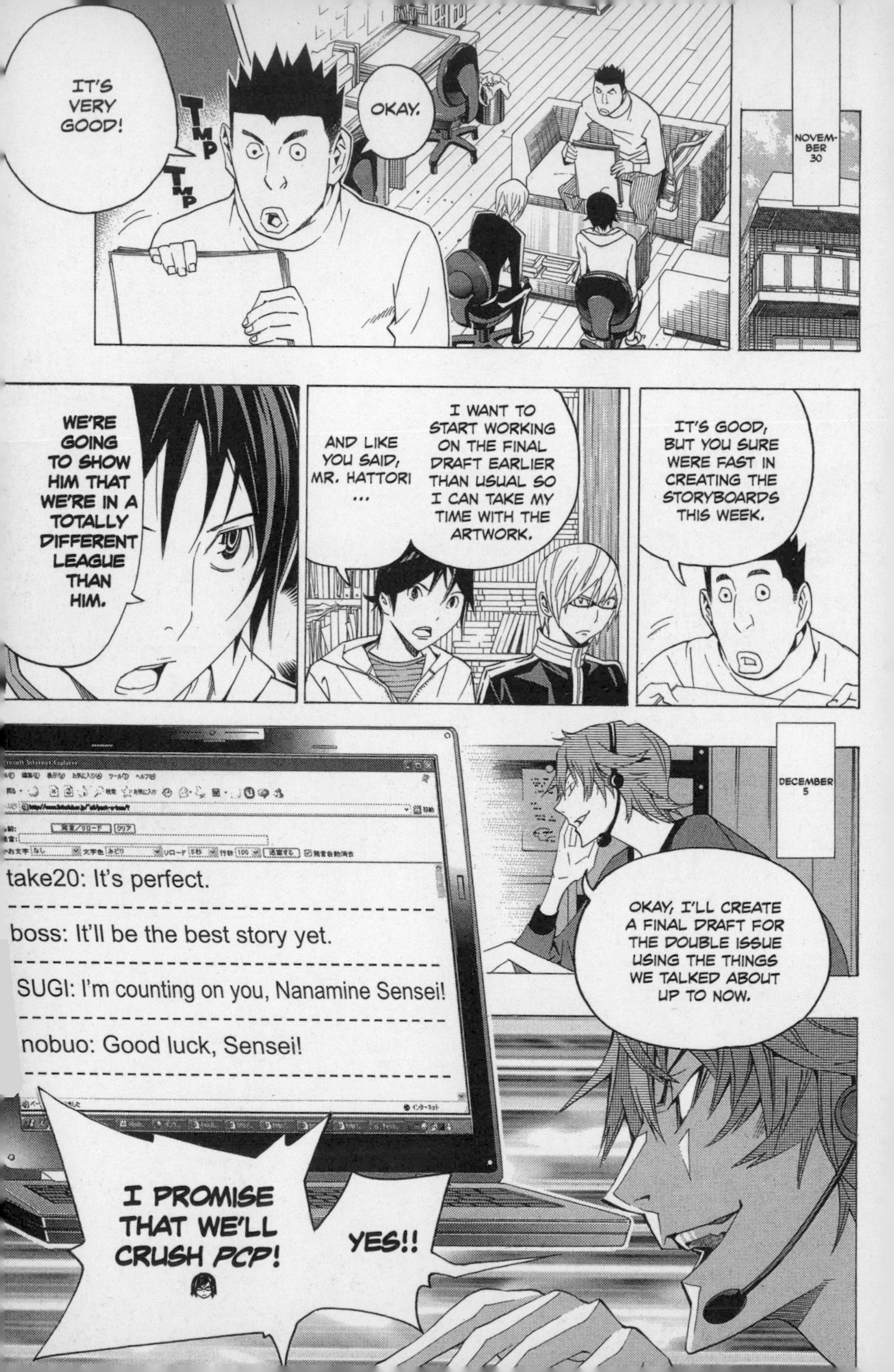
NOVEMBER 30
OKAY.
IT'S VERY GOOD!
TMP TMP
IT'S GOOD, BUT YOU SURE WERE FAST IN CREATING THE STORYBOARDS THIS WEEK.
I WANT TO START WORKING ON THE FINAL DRAFT EARLIER THAN USUAL SO I CAN TAKE MY TIME WITH THE ARTWORK.
AND LIKE YOU SAID, MR. HATTORI ...
WE'RE GOING TO SHOW HIM THAT WE'RE IN A TOTALLY DIFFERENT LEAGUE THAN HIM.
DECEMBER 5
OKAY, I'LL CREATE A FINAL DRAFT FOR THE DOUBLE ISSUE USING THE THINGS WE TALKED ABOUT UP TO NOW.
take20: It's perfect.
boss: It'll be the best story yet.
SUGI: I'm counting on you, Nanamine Sensei!
nobuo: Good luck, Sensei!
YES!!
I PROMISE THAT WE'LL CRUSH PCP!

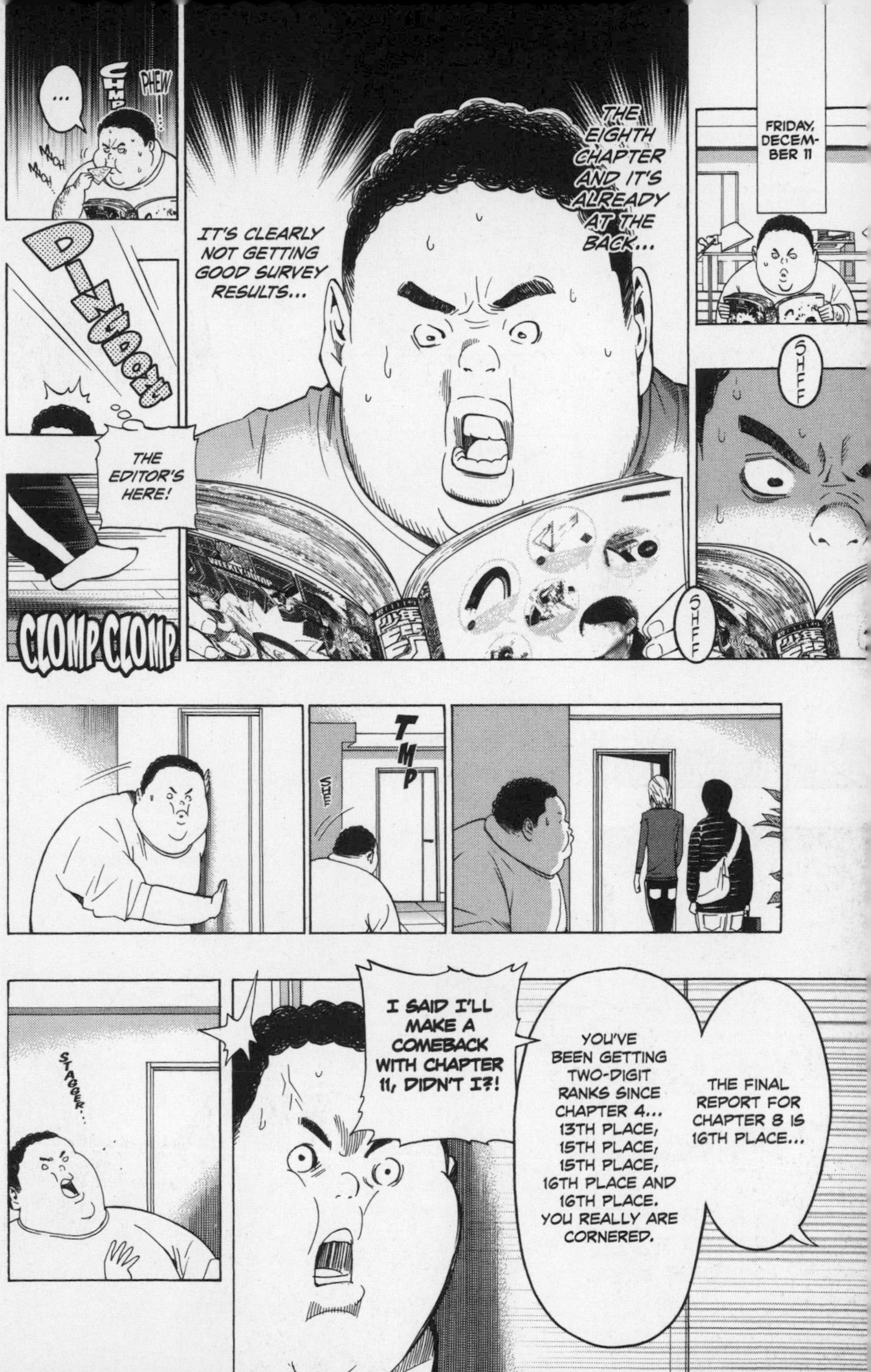
FRIDAY, DECEMBER 11
SHFF
SHFF
THE EIGHTH CHAPTER AND IT'S ALREADY AT THE BACK...
IT'S CLEARLY NOT GETTING GOOD SURVEY RESULTS...
PHEW
CHMP
...
MNCH MNCH
DINGDONG
THE EDITOR'S HERE!
CLOMP CLOMP
TMP
SHF
THE FINAL REPORT FOR CHAPTER 8 IS 16TH PLACE...
YOU'VE BEEN GETTING TWO-DIGIT RANKS SINCE CHAPTER 4... 13TH PLACE, 15TH PLACE, 15TH PLACE, 16TH PLACE AND 16TH PLACE. YOU REALLY ARE CORNERED.
I SAID I'LL MAKE A COMEBACK WITH CHAPTER 11, DIDN'T I?!
STAGGER...

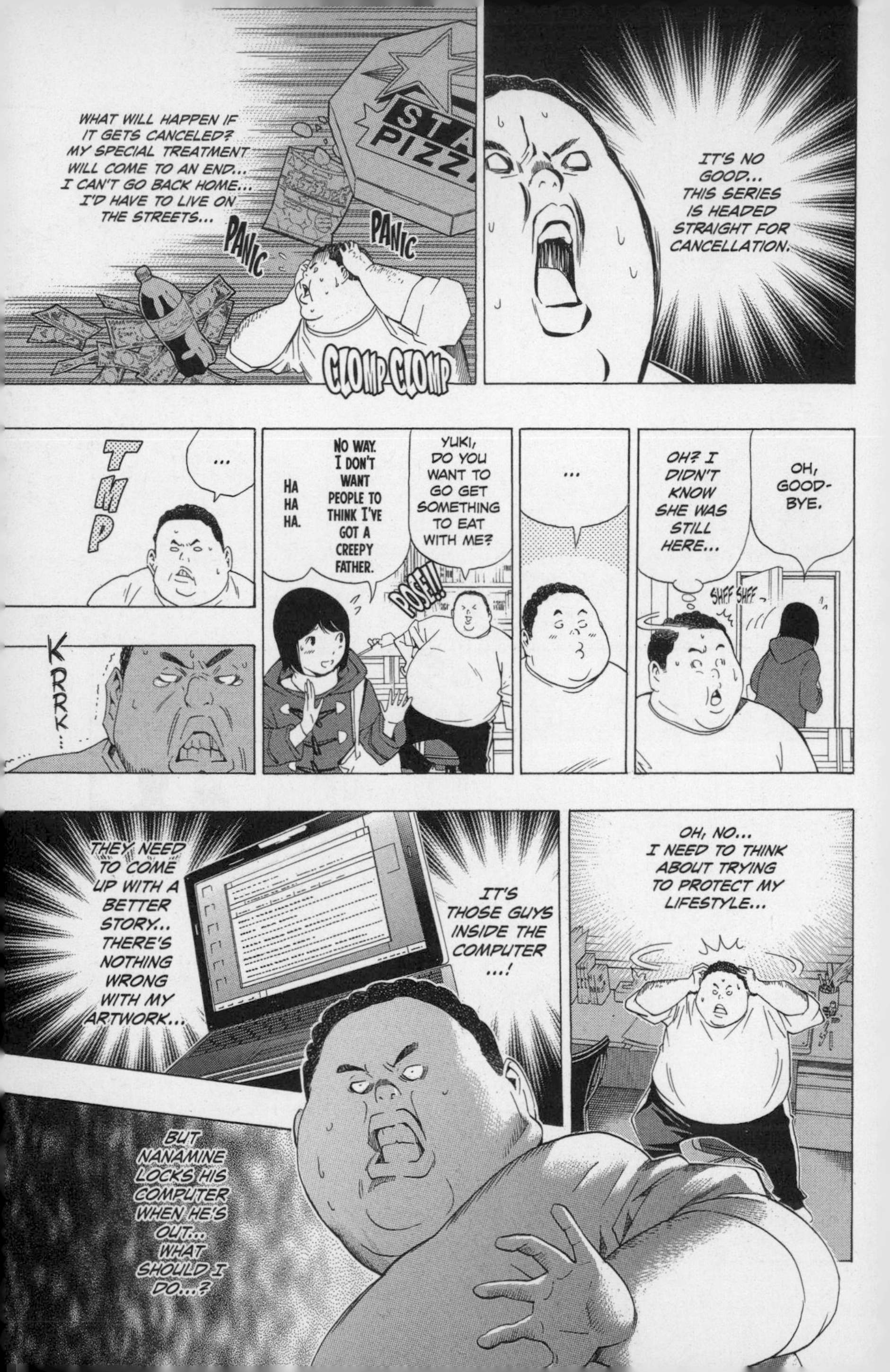
IT'S NO GOOD... THIS SERIES IS HEADED STRAIGHT FOR CANCELLATION.
WHAT WILL HAPPEN IF IT GETS CANCELED? MY SPECIAL TREATMENT WILL COME TO AN END... I CAN'T GO BACK HOME... I'D HAVE TO LIVE ON THE STREETS...
STA PIZZ
PANIC
PANIC
CLOMP CLOMP
OH, GOOD-BYE.
OH? I DIDN'T KNOW SHE WAS STILL HERE...
SHFF SHFF
...
YUKI, DO YOU WANT TO GO GET SOMETHING TO EAT WITH ME?
NO WAY. I DON'T WANT PEOPLE TO THINK I'VE GOT A CREEPY FATHER.
HA HA HA.
POSE!!
...
TMP
KRRK...
OH, NO... I NEED TO THINK ABOUT TRYING TO PROTECT MY LIFESTYLE...
IT'S THOSE GUYS INSIDE THE COMPUTER...!
THEY NEED TO COME UP WITH A BETTER STORY... THERE'S NOTHING WRONG WITH MY ARTWORK...
BUT NANAMINE LOCKS HIS COMPUTER WHEN HE'S OUT... WHAT SHOULD I DO...?

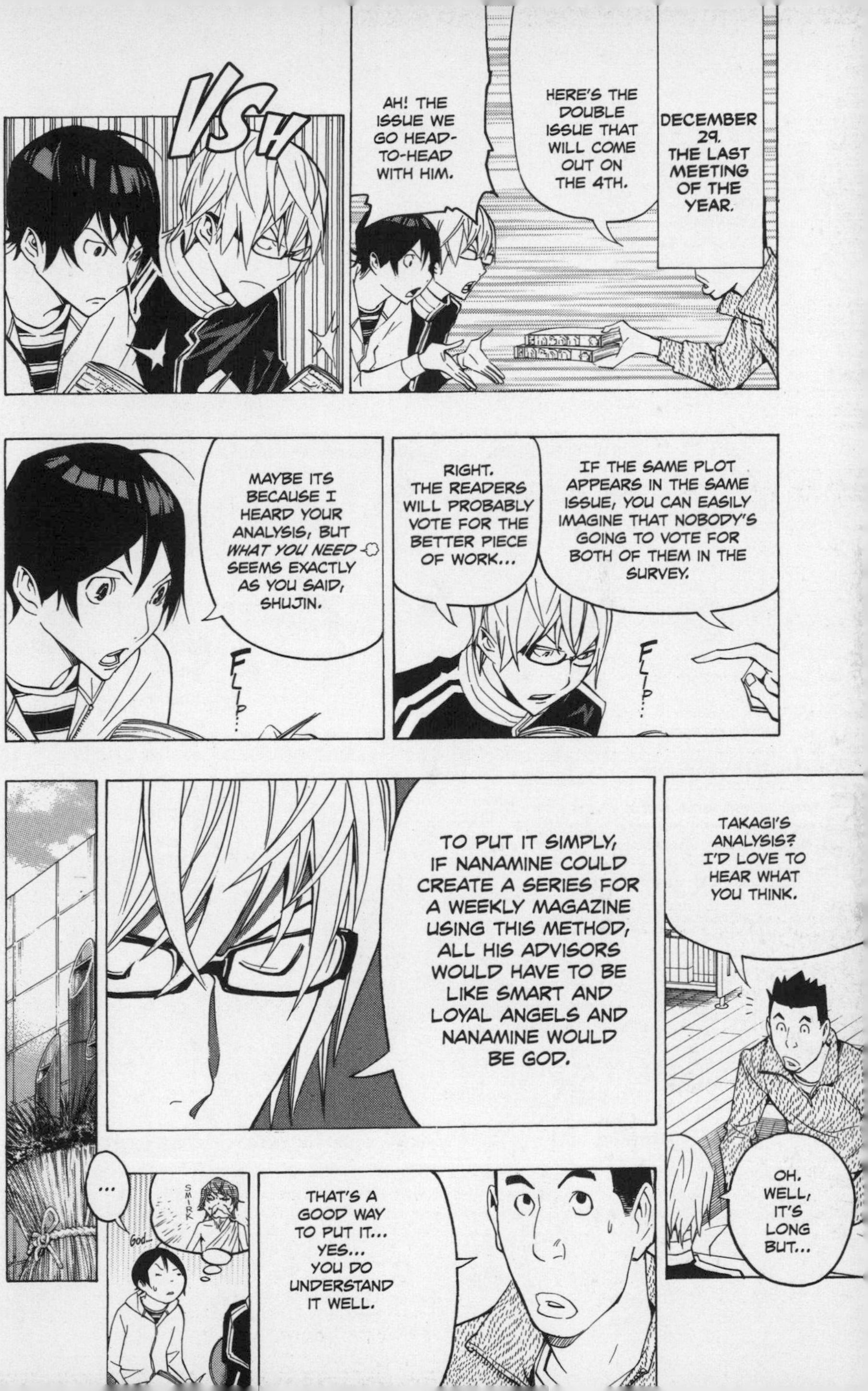
DECEMBER 29. THE LAST MEETING OF THE YEAR.
HERE'S THE DOUBLE ISSUE THAT WILL COME OUT ON THE 4TH.
AH! THE ISSUE WE GO HEAD-TO-HEAD WITH HIM.
VSH
IF THE SAME PLOT APPEARS IN THE SAME ISSUE, YOU CAN EASILY IMAGINE THAT NOBODY'S GOING TO VOTE FOR BOTH OF THEM IN THE SURVEY.
RIGHT. THE READERS WILL PROBABLY VOTE FOR THE BETTER PIECE OF WORK...
FLIP...
MAYBE ITS BECAUSE I HEARD YOUR ANALYSIS, BUT *WHAT YOU NEED* SEEMS EXACTLY AS YOU SAID, SHUJIN.
FLIP...
TAKAGI'S ANALYSIS? I'D LOVE TO HEAR WHAT YOU THINK.
OH. WELL, IT'S LONG BUT...
TO PUT IT SIMPLY, IF NANAMINE COULD CREATE A SERIES FOR A WEEKLY MAGAZINE USING THIS METHOD, ALL HIS ADVISORS WOULD HAVE TO BE LIKE SMART AND LOYAL ANGELS AND NANAMINE WOULD BE GOD.
THAT'S A GOOD WAY TO PUT IT... YES... YOU DO UNDERSTAND IT WELL.
SMIRK
God...
...

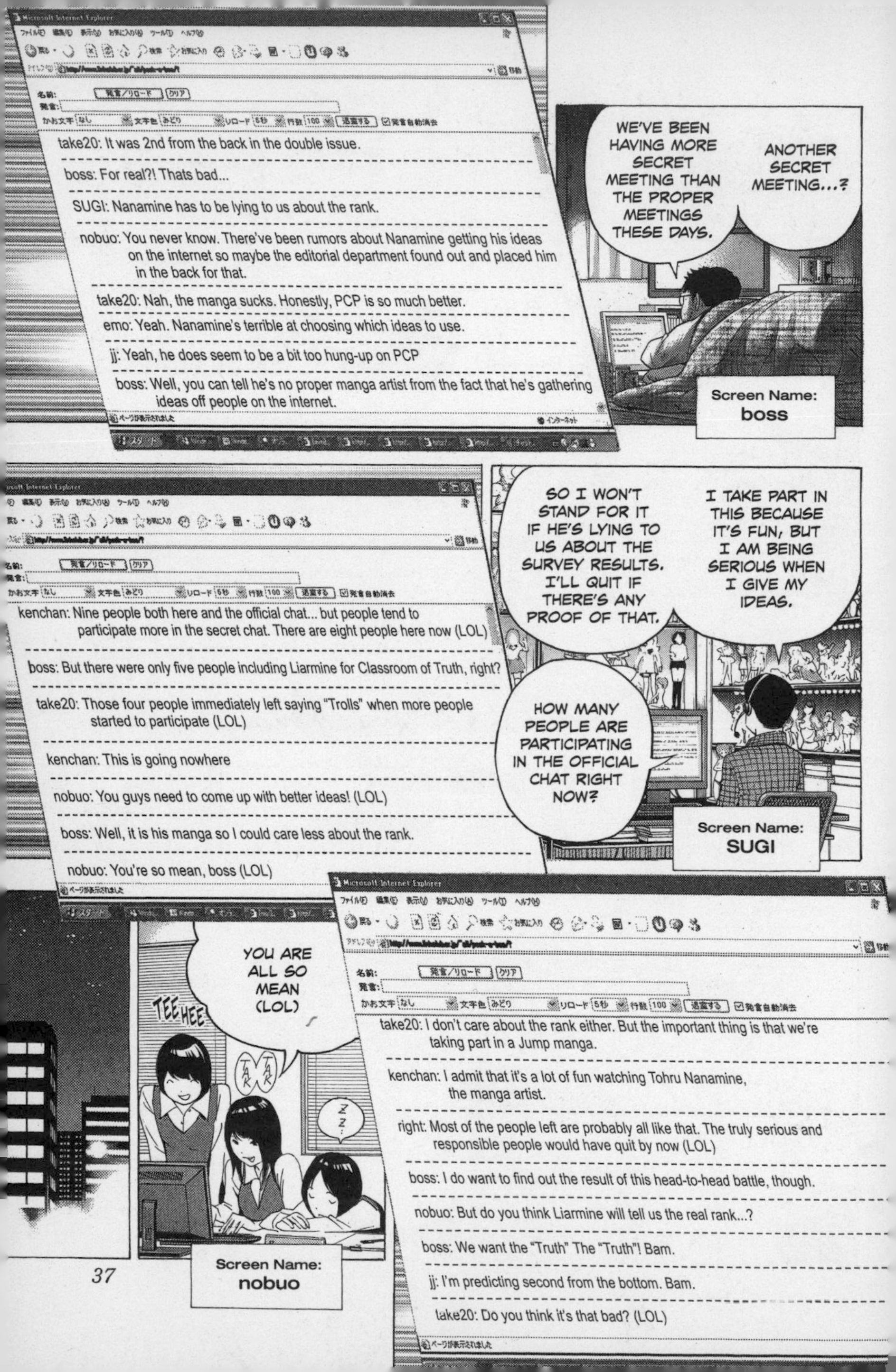
ANOTHER SECRET MEETING...?
WE'VE BEEN HAVING MORE SECRET MEETING THAN THE PROPER MEETINGS THESE DAYS.
Screen Name: boss
take20: It was 2nd from the back in the double issue.
boss: For real?! Thats bad...
SUGI: Nanamine has to be lying to us about the rank.
nobuo: You never know. There've been rumors about Nanamine getting his ideas on the internet so maybe the editorial department found out and placed him in the back for that.
take20: Nah, the manga sucks. Honestly, PCP is so much better.
emo: Yeah. Nanamine's terrible at choosing which ideas to use.
jj: Yeah, he does seem to be a bit too hung-up on PCP
boss: Well, you can tell he's no proper manga artist from the fact that he's gathering ideas off people on the internet.
I TAKE PART IN THIS BECAUSE IT'S FUN, BUT I AM BEING SERIOUS WHEN I GIVE MY IDEAS.
SO I WON'T STAND FOR IT IF HE'S LYING TO US ABOUT THE SURVEY RESULTS. I'LL QUIT IF THERE'S ANY PROOF OF THAT.
HOW MANY PEOPLE ARE PARTICIPATING IN THE OFFICIAL CHAT RIGHT NOW?
Screen Name: SUGI
kenchan: Nine people both here and the official chat... but people tend to participate more in the secret chat. There are eight people here now (LOL)
boss: But there were only five people including Liarmine for Classroom of Truth, right?
take20: Those four people immediately left saying "Trolls" when more people started to participate (LOL)
kenchan: This is going nowhere
nobuo: You guys need to come up with better ideas! (LOL)
boss: Well, it is his manga so I could care less about the rank.
nobuo: You're so mean, boss (LOL)
take20: I don't care about the rank either. But the important thing is that we're taking part in a Jump manga.
kenchan: I admit that it's a lot of fun watching Tohru Nanamine, the manga artist.
right: Most of the people left are probably all like that. The truly serious and responsible people would have quit by now (LOL)
boss: I do want to find out the result of this head-to-head battle, though.
nobuo: But do you think Liarmine will tell us the real rank...?
boss: We want the "Truth" The "Truth"! Bam.
jj: I'm predicting second from the bottom. Bam.
take20: Do you think it's that bad? (LOL)
YOU ARE ALL SO MEAN (LOL)
TEE HEE
Z Z
Screen Name: nobuo

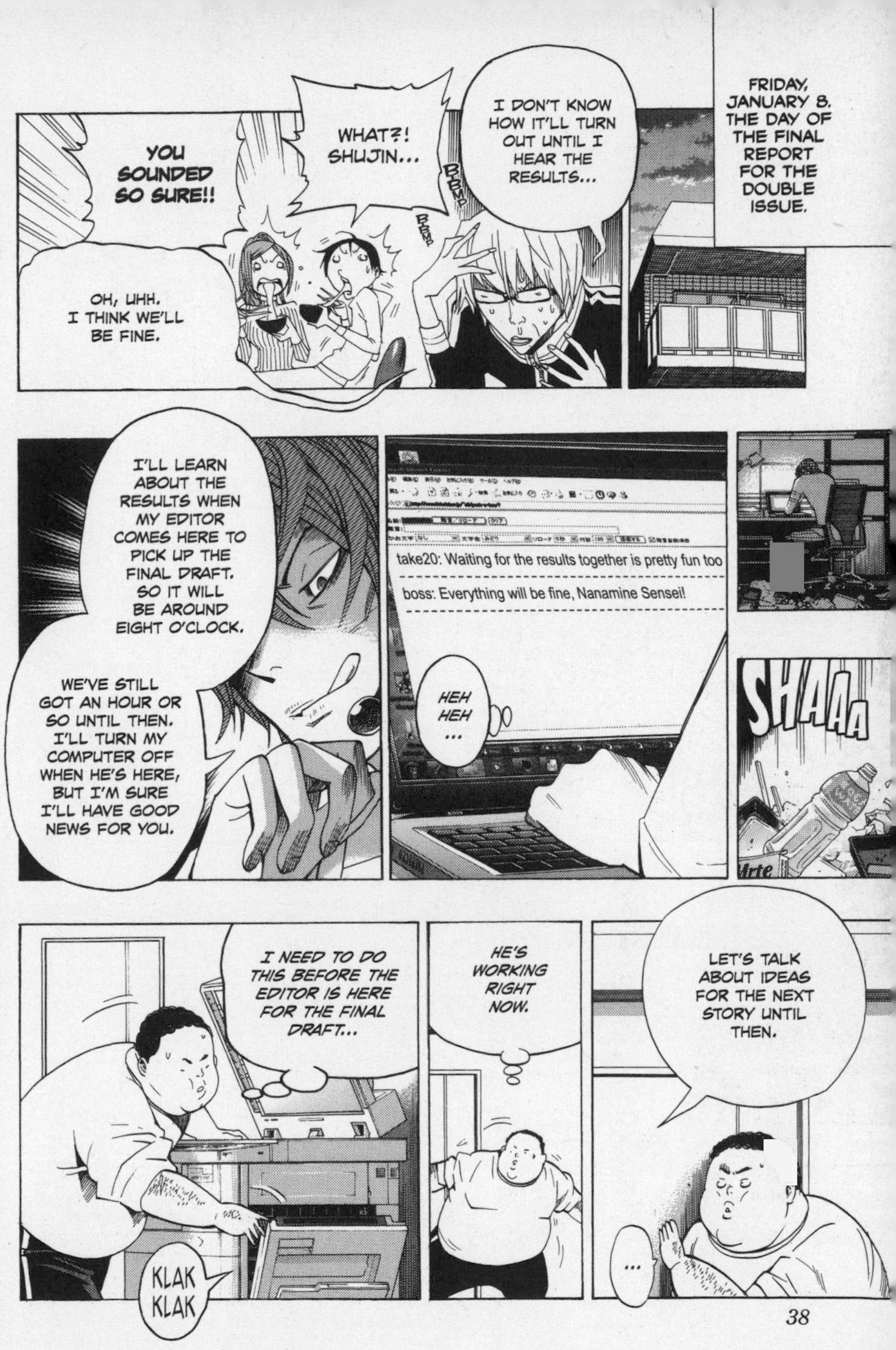
FRIDAY, JANUARY 8. THE DAY OF THE FINAL REPORT FOR THE DOUBLE ISSUE.
I DON'T KNOW HOW IT'LL TURN OUT UNTIL I HEAR THE RESULTS...
WHAT?! SHUJIN...
YOU SOUNDED SO SURE!!
OH, UHH. I THINK WE'LL BE FINE.
SHAAA
take20: Waiting for the results together is pretty fun too
boss: Everything will be fine, Nanamine Sensei!
HEH HEH ...
I'LL LEARN ABOUT THE RESULTS WHEN MY EDITOR COMES HERE TO PICK UP THE FINAL DRAFT. SO IT WILL BE AROUND EIGHT O'CLOCK.
WE'VE STILL GOT AN HOUR OR SO UNTIL THEN. I'LL TURN MY COMPUTER OFF WHEN HE'S HERE, BUT I'M SURE I'LL HAVE GOOD NEWS FOR YOU.
LET'S TALK ABOUT IDEAS FOR THE NEXT STORY UNTIL THEN.
...
HE'S WORKING RIGHT NOW.
I NEED TO DO THIS BEFORE THE EDITOR IS HERE FOR THE FINAL DRAFT...
KLAK KLAK

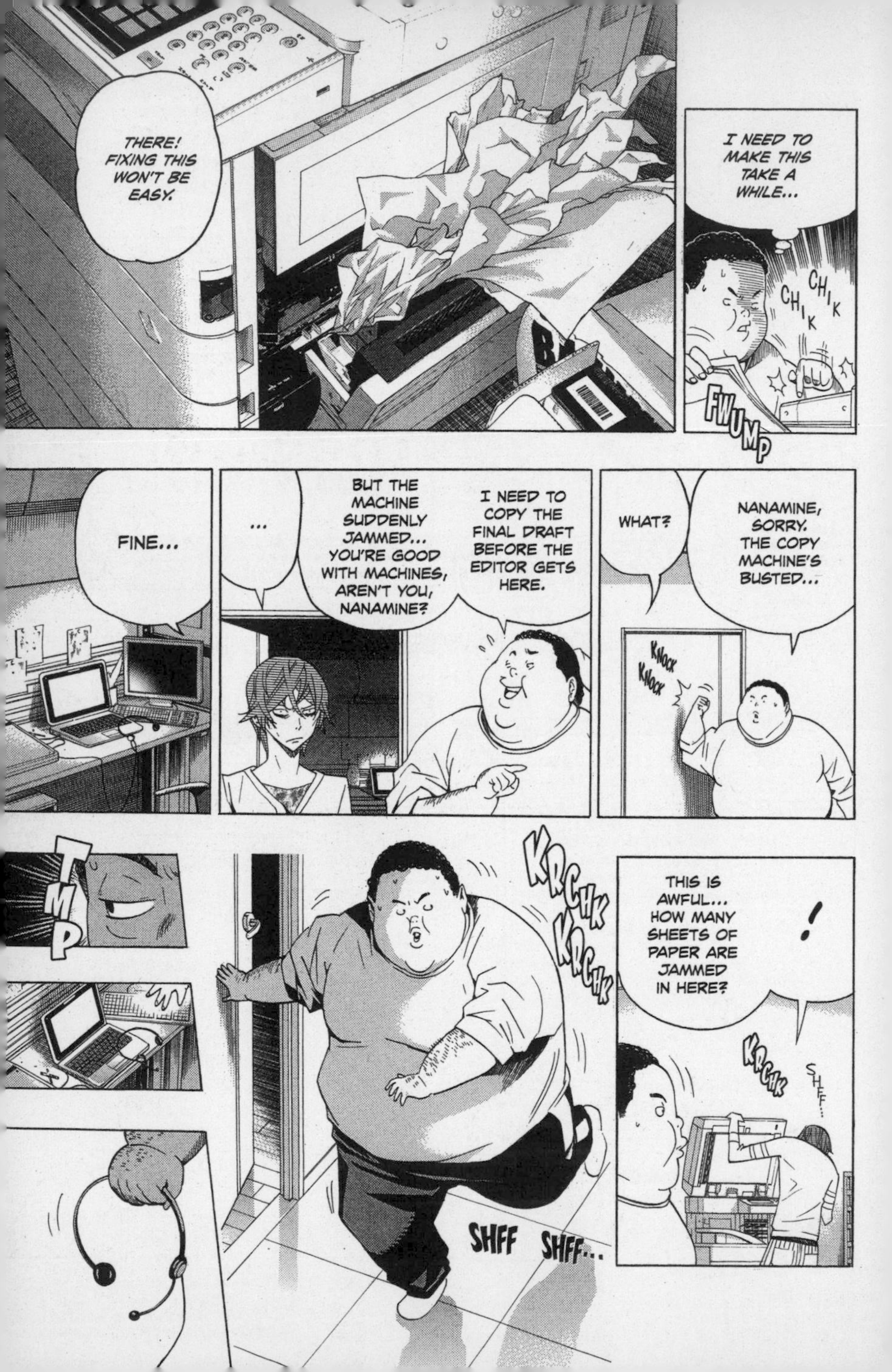

I NEED TO MAKE THIS TAKE A WHILE...
CHIK CHIK
FWUMP
THERE! FIXING THIS WON'T BE EASY.
NANAMINE, SORRY. THE COPY MACHINE'S BUSTED...
KNOCK KNOCK
WHAT?
I NEED TO COPY THE FINAL DRAFT BEFORE THE EDITOR GETS HERE.
BUT THE MACHINE SUDDENLY JAMMED... YOU'RE GOOD WITH MACHINES, AREN'T YOU, NANAMINE?
...
FINE...
THIS IS AWFUL... HOW MANY SHEETS OF PAPER ARE JAMMED IN HERE?
!
KRCHK
SHFF...
KRCHK KRCHK
SHFF SHFF...
TMP

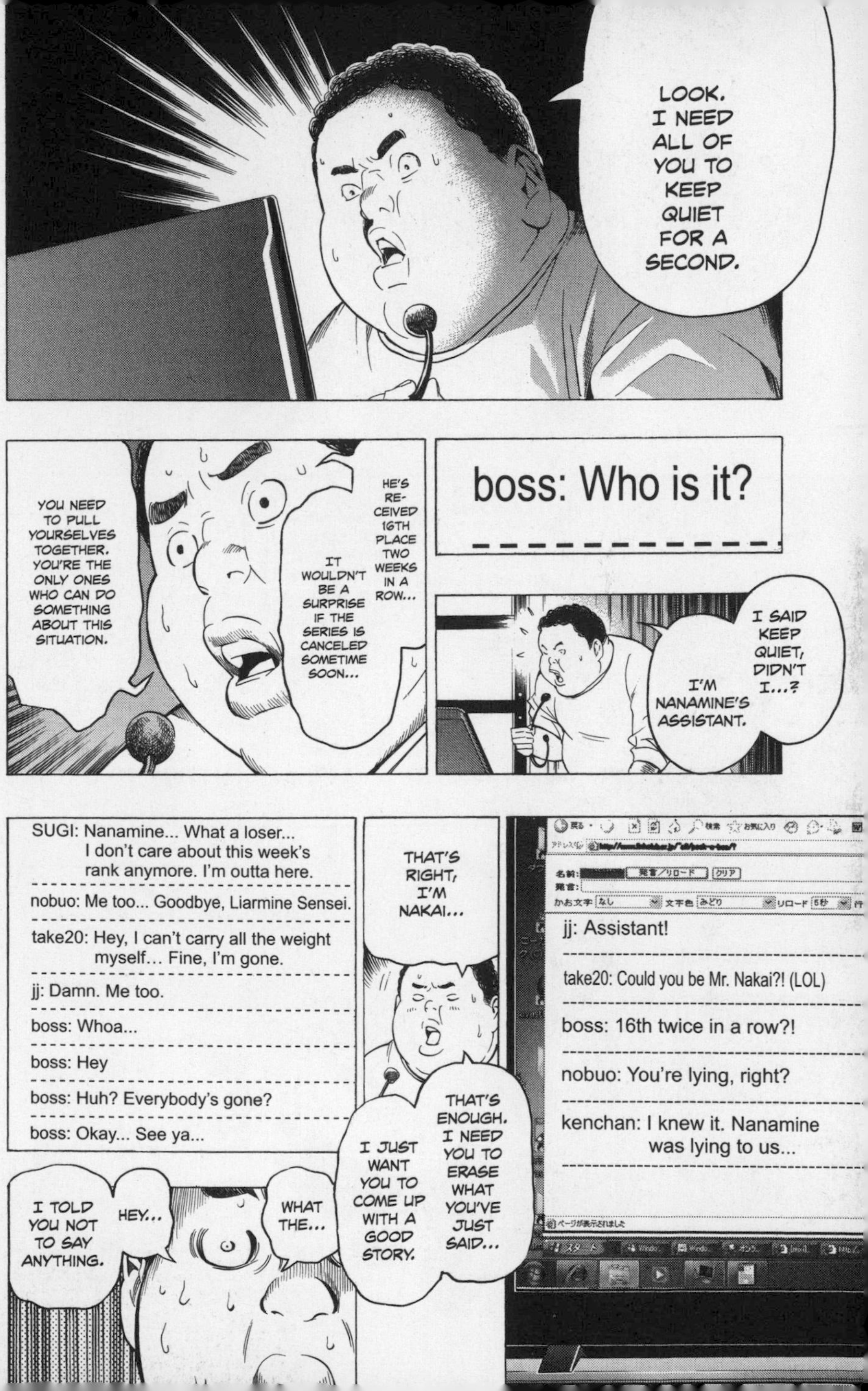
LOOK. I NEED ALL OF YOU TO KEEP QUIET FOR A SECOND.
boss: Who is it?
I SAID KEEP QUIET, DIDN'T I...?
I'M NANAMINE'S ASSISTANT.
HE'S RECEIVED 16TH PLACE TWO WEEKS IN A ROW...
IT WOULDN'T BE A SURPRISE IF THE SERIES IS CANCELED SOMETIME SOON...
YOU NEED TO PULL YOURSELVES TOGETHER. YOU'RE THE ONLY ONES WHO CAN DO SOMETHING ABOUT THIS SITUATION.
jj: Assistant!
take20: Could you be Mr. Nakai?! (LOL)
boss: 16th twice in a row?!
nobuo: You're lying, right?
kenchan: I knew it. Nanamine was lying to us...
THAT'S RIGHT, I'M NAKAI...
THAT'S ENOUGH. I NEED YOU TO ERASE WHAT YOU'VE JUST SAID...
I JUST WANT YOU TO COME UP WITH A GOOD STORY.
SUGI: Nanamine... What a loser... I don't care about this week's rank anymore. I'm outta here.
nobuo: Me too... Goodbye, Liarmine Sensei.
take20: Hey, I can't carry all the weight myself... Fine, I'm gone.
jj: Damn. Me too.
boss: Whoa...
boss: Hey
boss: Huh? Everybody's gone?
boss: Okay... See ya...
WHAT THE...
HEY...
I TOLD YOU NOT TO SAY ANYTHING.

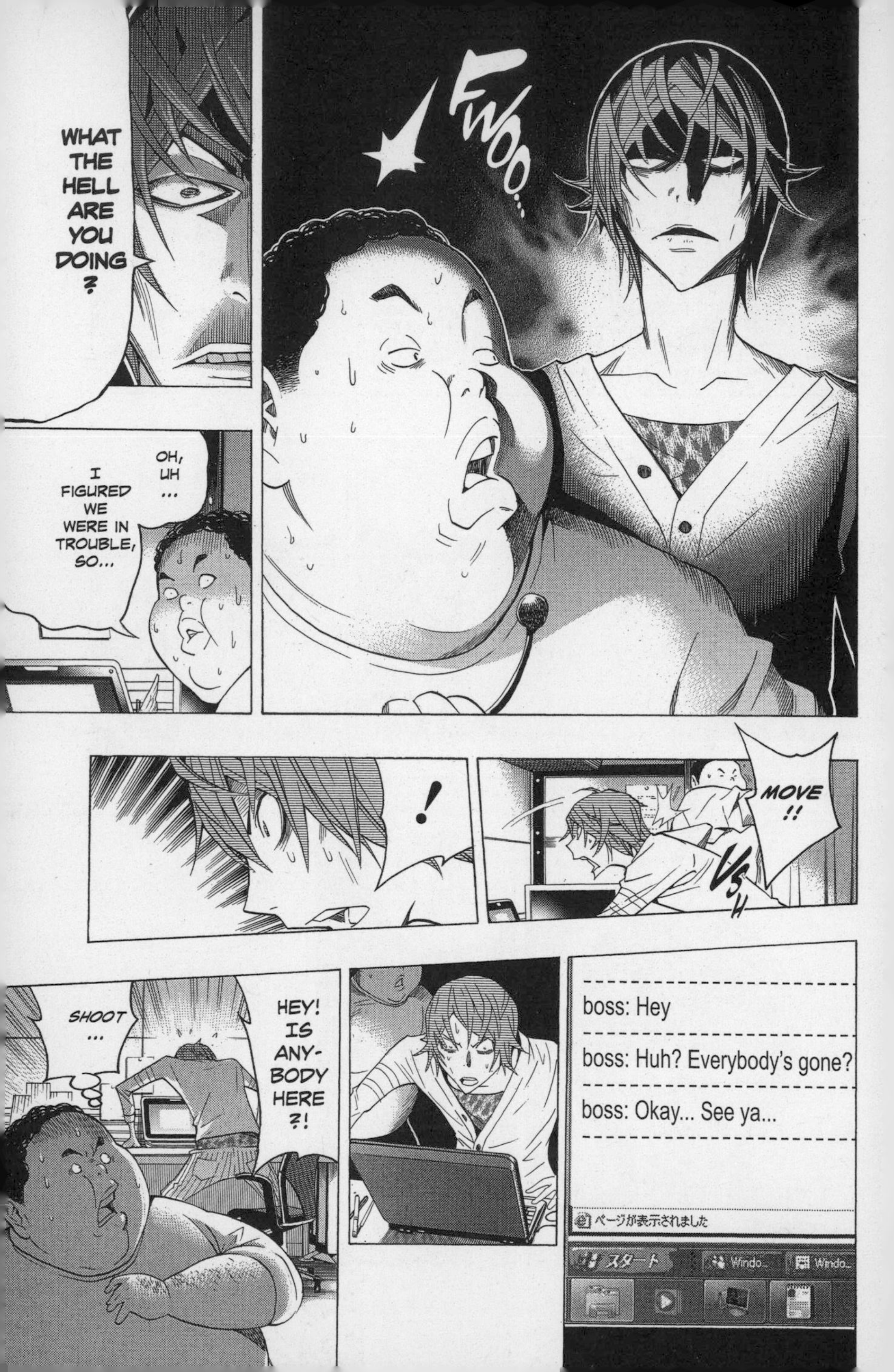
FWOO...
WHAT THE HELL ARE YOU DOING?
OH, UH...
I FIGURED WE WERE IN TROUBLE, SO...
MOVE!!
VSH
!
boss: Hey
boss: Huh? Everybody's gone?
boss: Okay... See ya...
ページが表示されました
スタート
Windo...
Windo...
HEY! IS ANYBODY HERE?!
SHOOT...

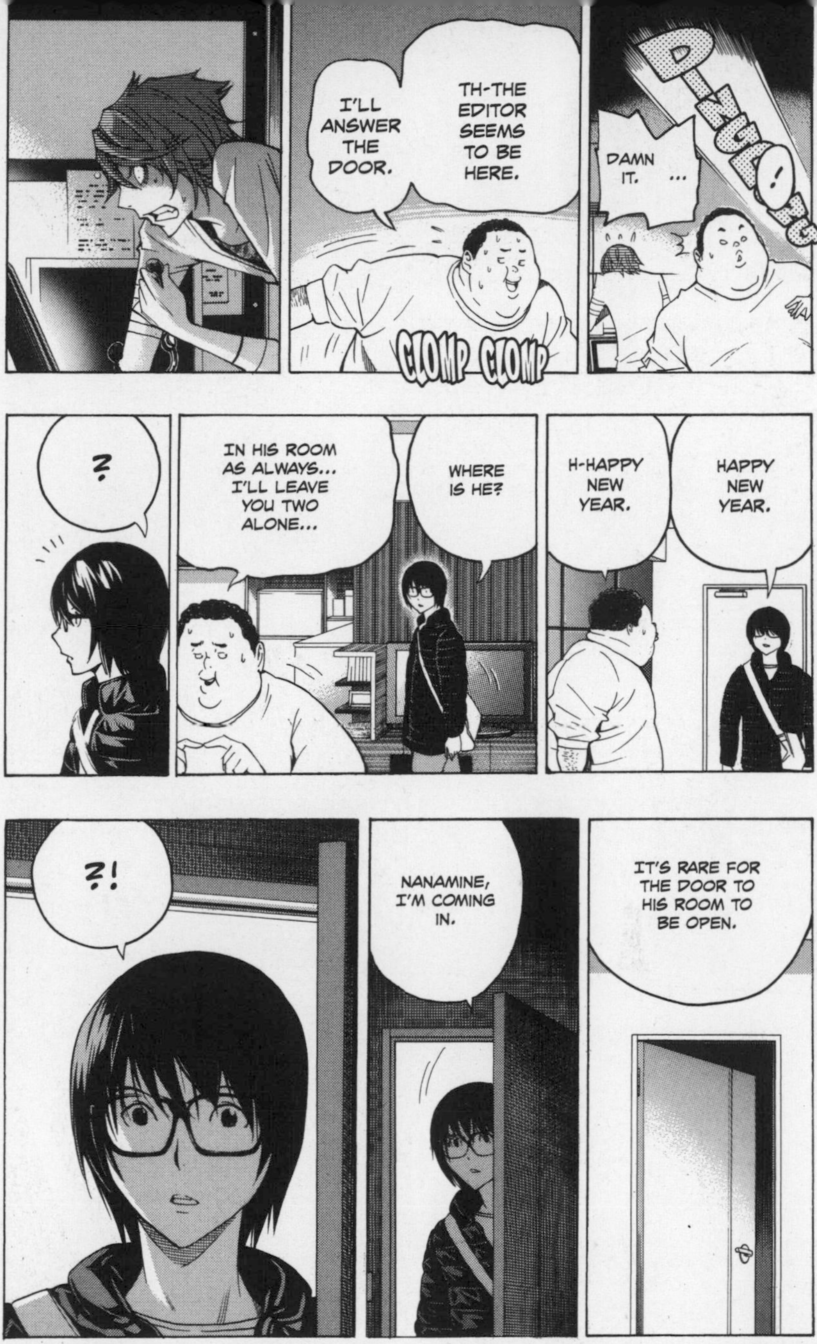
DING-DONG!
DAMN IT. ...
TH-THE EDITOR SEEMS TO BE HERE.
I'LL ANSWER THE DOOR.
CLOMP CLOMP
HAPPY NEW YEAR.
H-HAPPY NEW YEAR.
WHERE IS HE?
IN HIS ROOM AS ALWAYS... I'LL LEAVE YOU TWO ALONE...
?
IT'S RARE FOR THE DOOR TO HIS ROOM TO BE OPEN.
NANAMINE, I'M COMING IN.
?!

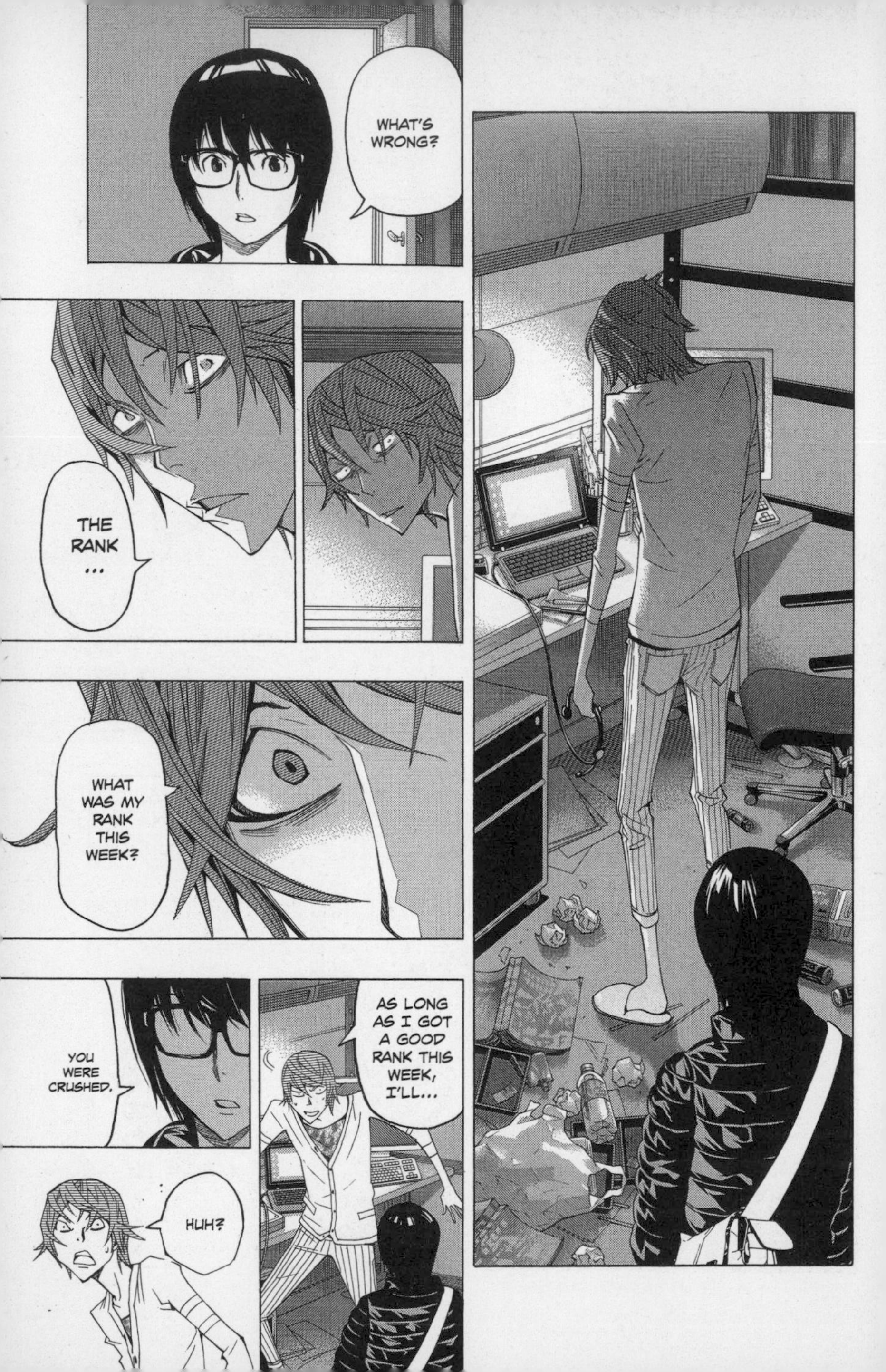
WHAT'S WRONG?
THE RANK ...
WHAT WAS MY RANK THIS WEEK?
AS LONG AS I GOT A GOOD RANK THIS WEEK, I'LL...
YOU WERE CRUSHED.
HUH?

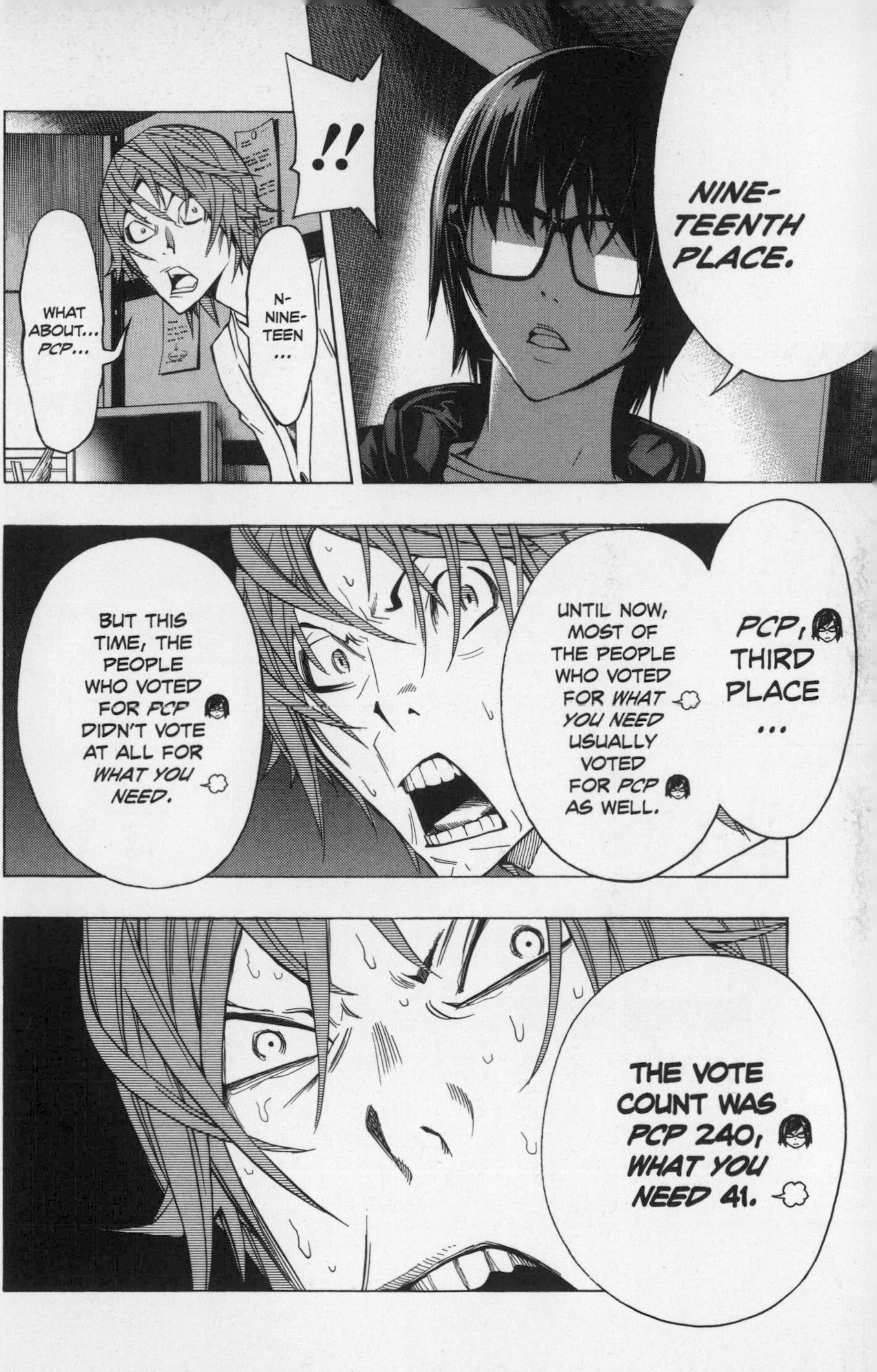
NINE-TEENTH PLACE.
!!
N-NINE-TEEN...
WHAT ABOUT... PCP...
PCP, THIRD PLACE...
UNTIL NOW, MOST OF THE PEOPLE WHO VOTED FOR WHAT YOU NEED USUALLY VOTED FOR PCP AS WELL.
BUT THIS TIME, THE PEOPLE WHO VOTED FOR PCP DIDN'T VOTE AT ALL FOR WHAT YOU NEED.
THE VOTE COUNT WAS PCP 240, WHAT YOU NEED 41.

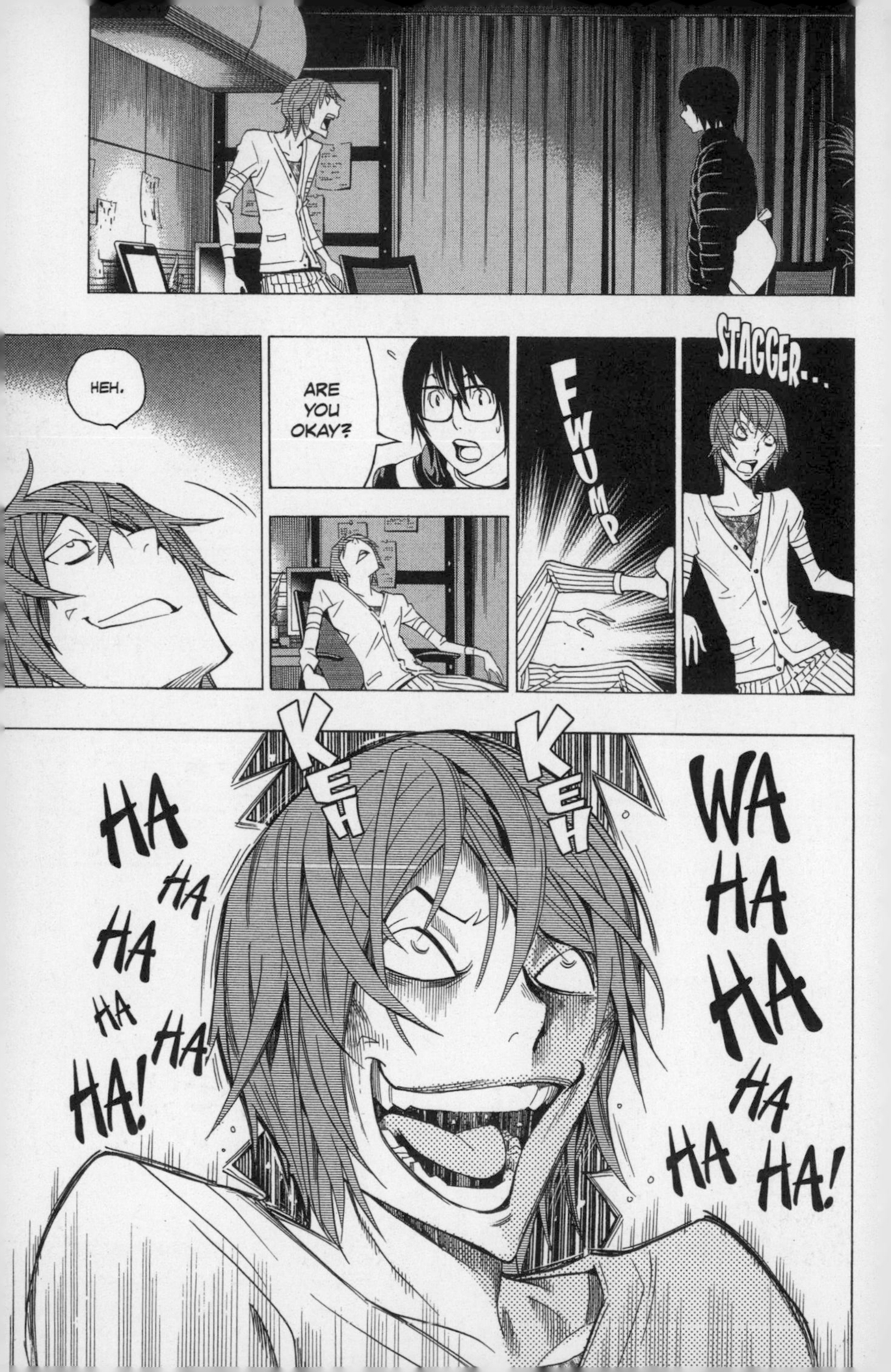
STAGGER...
FWUMP
ARE YOU OKAY?
HEH.
WA HA HA HA HA HA HA!
KEH
KEH
HA HA HA HA HA HA!

OHBA'S STORYBOARD

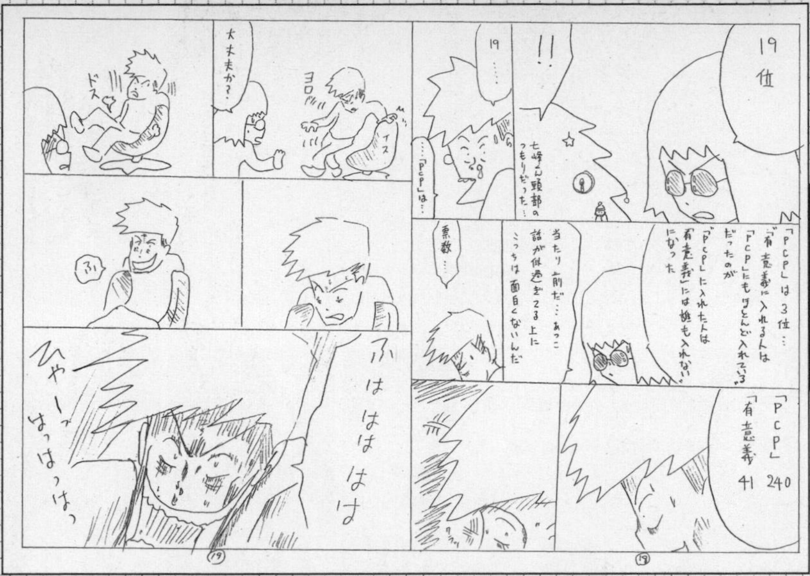
19位
!!
19……
七峰くん頭部のつもりだった…
…「PCP」は…
「PCP」は3位…「有意義」に入れる人は「PCP」にもほとんど入れている だったのが 「PCP」に入れた人は「有意義」には誰も入れない になった
当たり前だ…あっこ 話が似過ぎてる上に こっちは面白くないんだ
票数……
「PCP」240 「有意義」41
大丈夫か?
ヨロ
イス
ドス
ふ
ふははははは
ひゃーっはっはっはっ

OBATA'S STORYBOARD

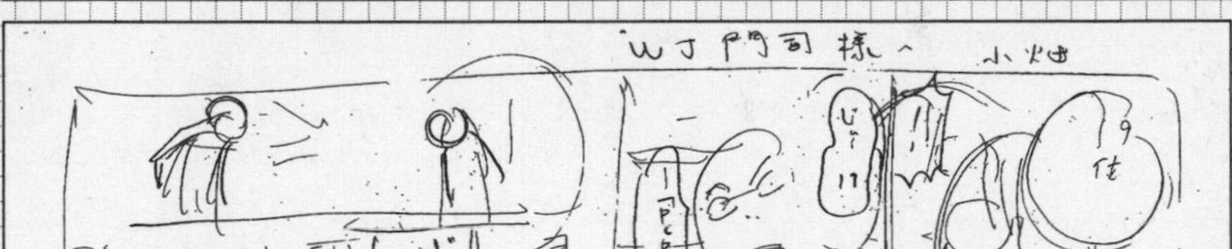
19位
!!
「PCP」は3位!!
票数 「PCP」240 「有意義」41
ふははははは

COMPLETE!

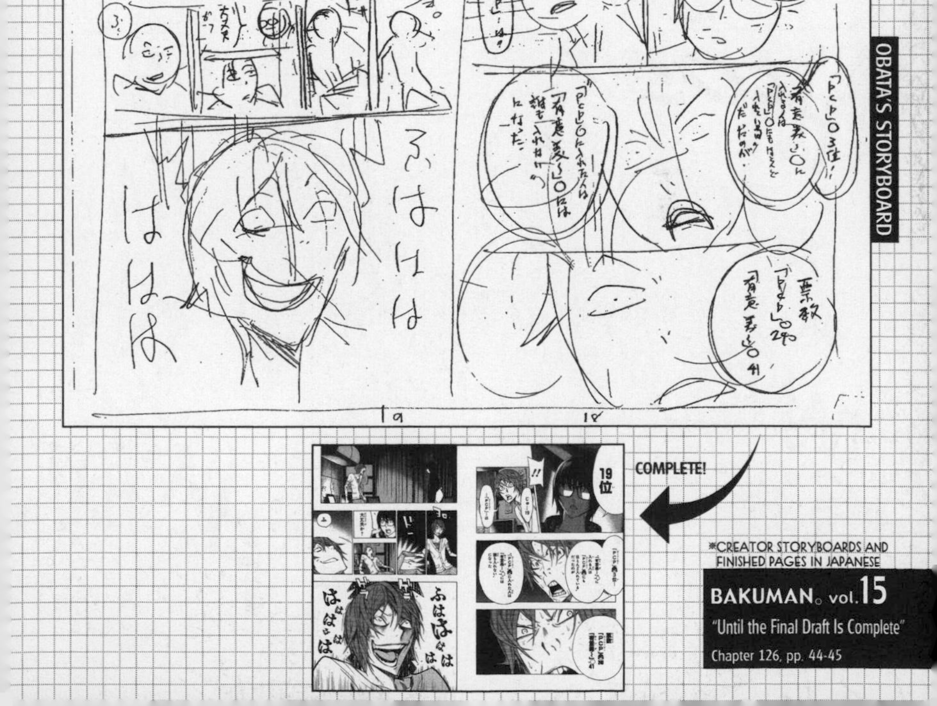
19位
!!
ふははははは

*CREATOR STORYBOARDS AND FINISHED PAGES IN JAPANESE

BAKUMAN。vol.15

"Until the Final Draft Is Complete"

Chapter 126, pp. 44-45

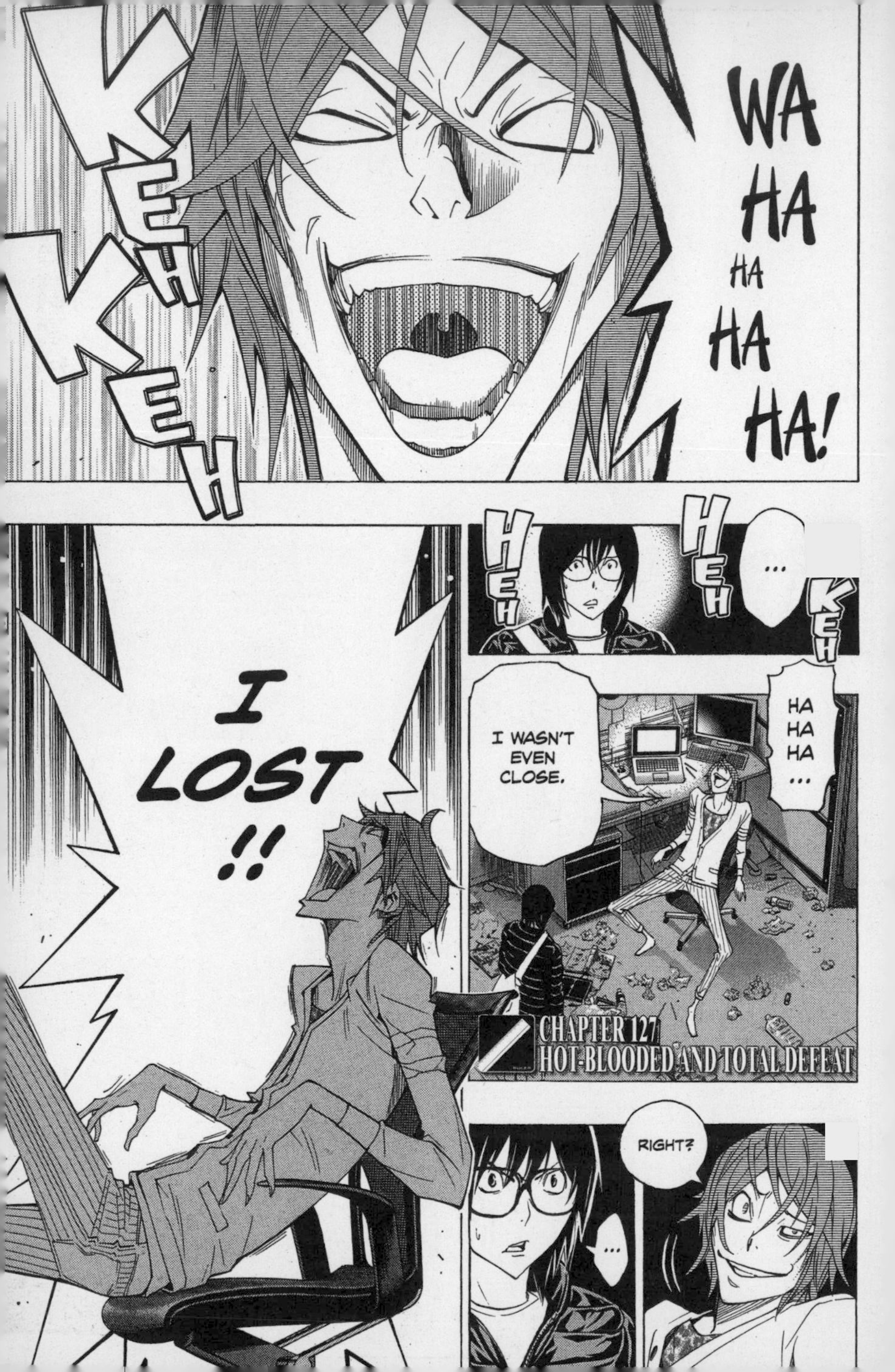
WA HA HA HA HA!
KEH KEH KEH
KEH
...
HEH HEH
HEH HEH
HA HA HA ...
I WASN'T EVEN CLOSE.
CHAPTER 127
HOT-BLOODED AND TOTAL DEFEAT
RIGHT?
...
I LOST!!

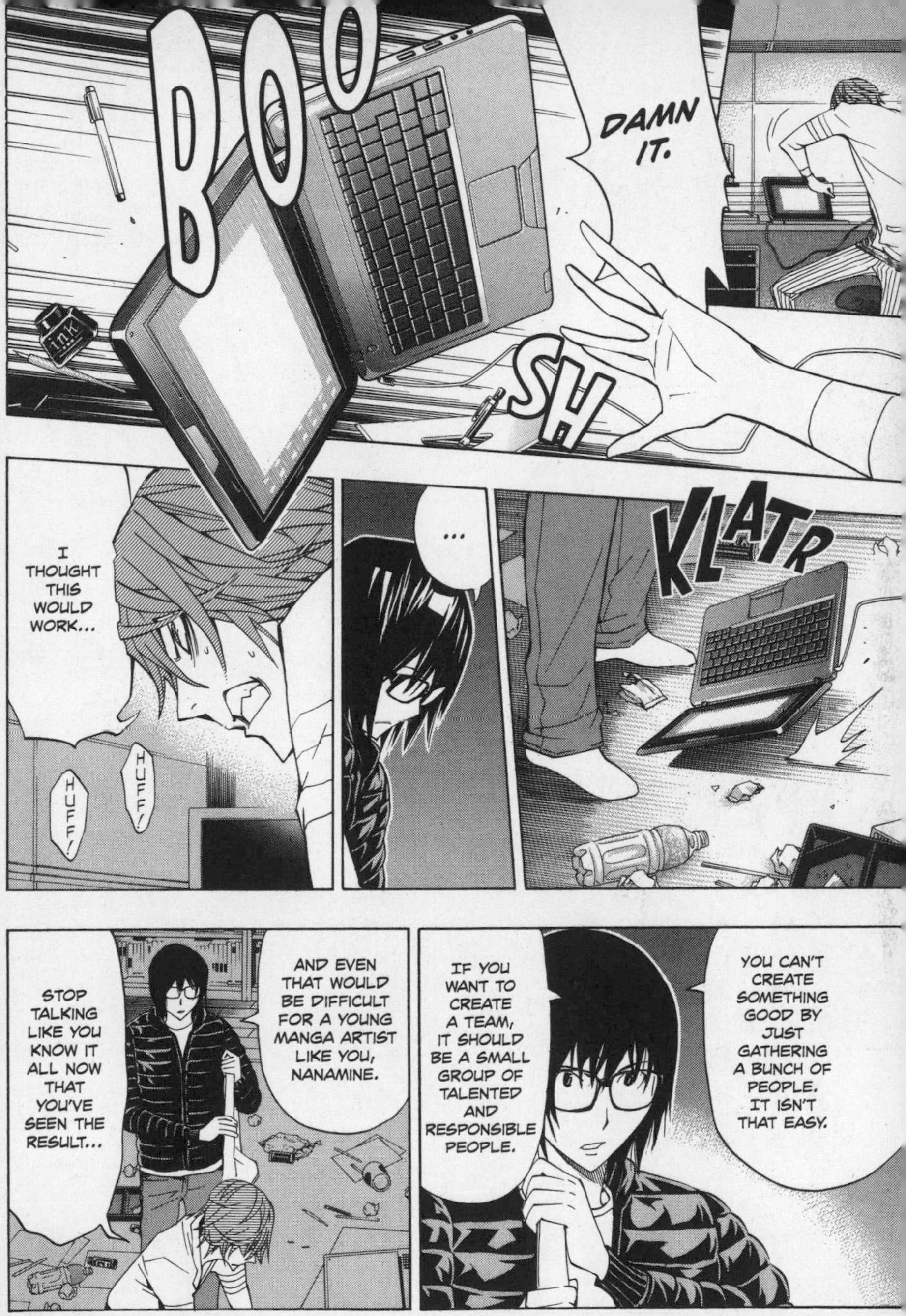
DAMN IT.
BOOO
SH
KLATR
...
I THOUGHT THIS WOULD WORK...
HUFF!
HUFF!
YOU CAN'T CREATE SOMETHING GOOD BY JUST GATHERING A BUNCH OF PEOPLE. IT ISN'T THAT EASY.
IF YOU WANT TO CREATE A TEAM, IT SHOULD BE A SMALL GROUP OF TALENTED AND RESPONSIBLE PEOPLE.
AND EVEN THAT WOULD BE DIFFICULT FOR A YOUNG MANGA ARTIST LIKE YOU, NANAMINE.
STOP TALKING LIKE YOU KNOW IT ALL NOW THAT YOU'VE SEEN THE RESULT...

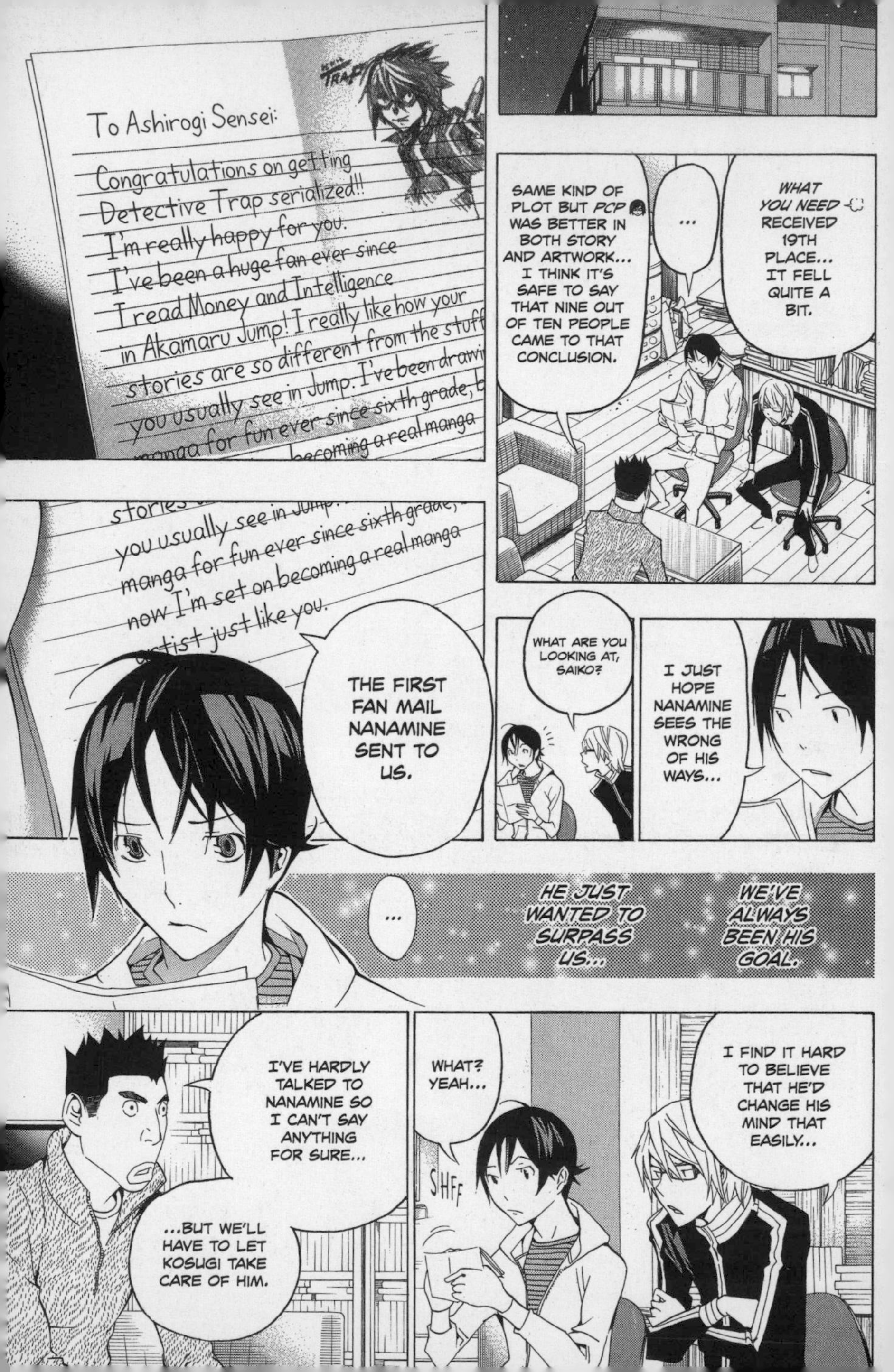
WHAT YOU NEED RECEIVED 19TH PLACE... IT FELL QUITE A BIT.
...
SAME KIND OF PLOT BUT PCP WAS BETTER IN BOTH STORY AND ARTWORK... I THINK IT'S SAFE TO SAY THAT NINE OUT OF TEN PEOPLE CAME TO THAT CONCLUSION.
To Ashirogi Sensei:
Congratulations on getting Detective Trap serialized!! I'm really happy for you. I've been a huge fan ever since I read Money and Intelligence in Akamaru Jump! I really like how your stories are so different from the stuff you usually see in Jump. I've been drawi manga for fun ever since sixth grade, b becoming a real manga
I JUST HOPE NANAMINE SEES THE WRONG OF HIS WAYS...
WHAT ARE YOU LOOKING AT, SAIKO?
you usually see in Jump. manga for fun ever since sixth grade, now I'm set on becoming a real manga artist just like you.
THE FIRST FAN MAIL NANAMINE SENT TO US.
WE'VE ALWAYS BEEN HIS GOAL.
HE JUST WANTED TO SURPASS US...
...
I FIND IT HARD TO BELIEVE THAT HE'D CHANGE HIS MIND THAT EASILY...
WHAT? YEAH...
SHFF
I'VE HARDLY TALKED TO NANAMINE SO I CAN'T SAY ANYTHING FOR SURE...
...BUT WE'LL HAVE TO LET KOSUGI TAKE CARE OF HIM.

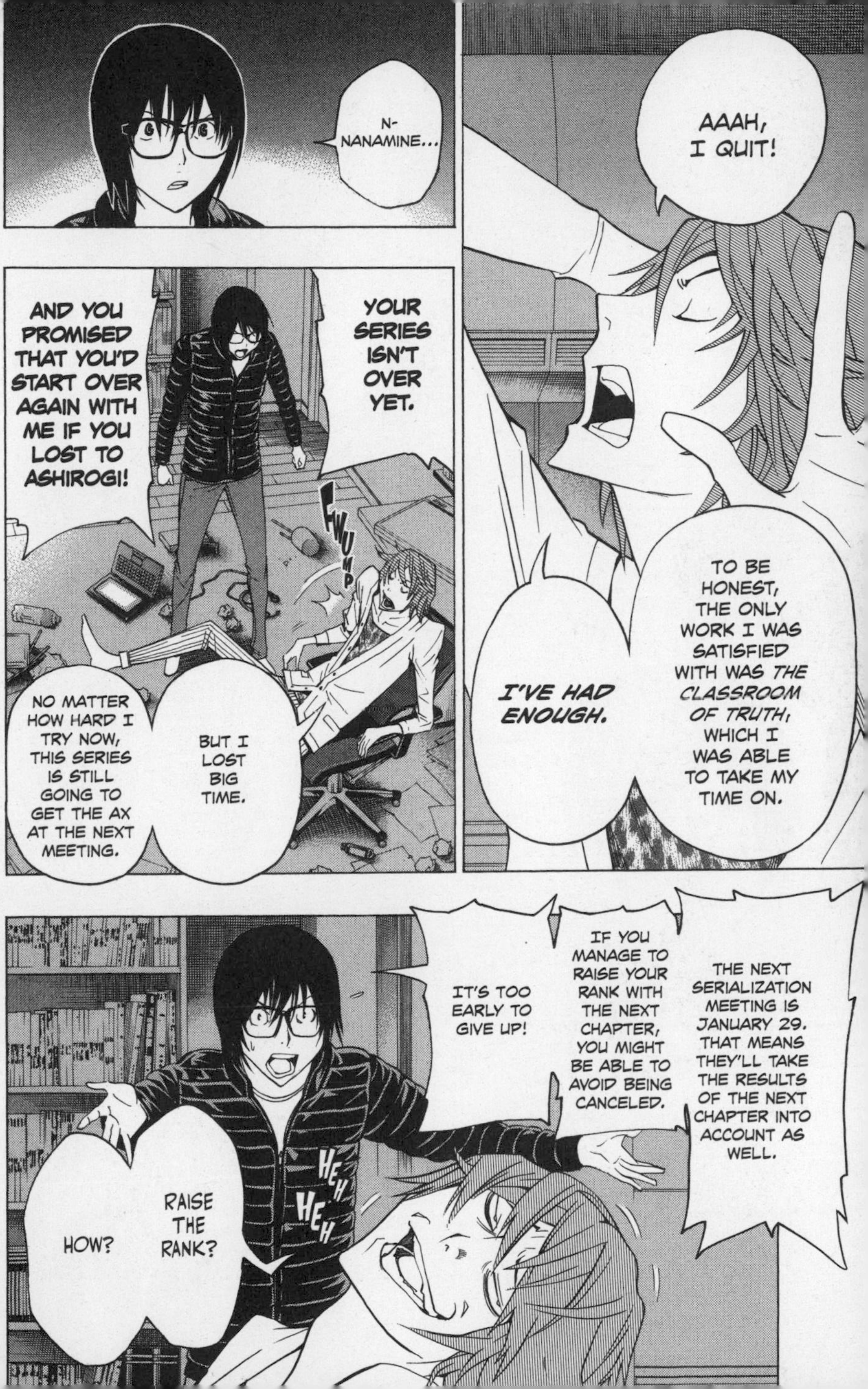
AAAH, I QUIT!
TO BE HONEST, THE ONLY WORK I WAS SATISFIED WITH WAS *THE CLASSROOM OF TRUTH*, WHICH I WAS ABLE TO TAKE MY TIME ON.
I'VE HAD ENOUGH.
N- NANAMINE...
YOUR SERIES ISN'T OVER YET.
AND YOU PROMISED THAT YOU'D START OVER AGAIN WITH ME IF YOU LOST TO ASHIROGI!
FWUMP
BUT I LOST BIG TIME.
NO MATTER HOW HARD I TRY NOW, THIS SERIES IS STILL GOING TO GET THE AX AT THE NEXT MEETING.
THE NEXT SERIALIZATION MEETING IS JANUARY 29. THAT MEANS THEY'LL TAKE THE RESULTS OF THE NEXT CHAPTER INTO ACCOUNT AS WELL.
IF YOU MANAGE TO RAISE YOUR RANK WITH THE NEXT CHAPTER, YOU MIGHT BE ABLE TO AVOID BEING CANCELED.
IT'S TOO EARLY TO GIVE UP!
HEH HEH
RAISE THE RANK?
HOW?

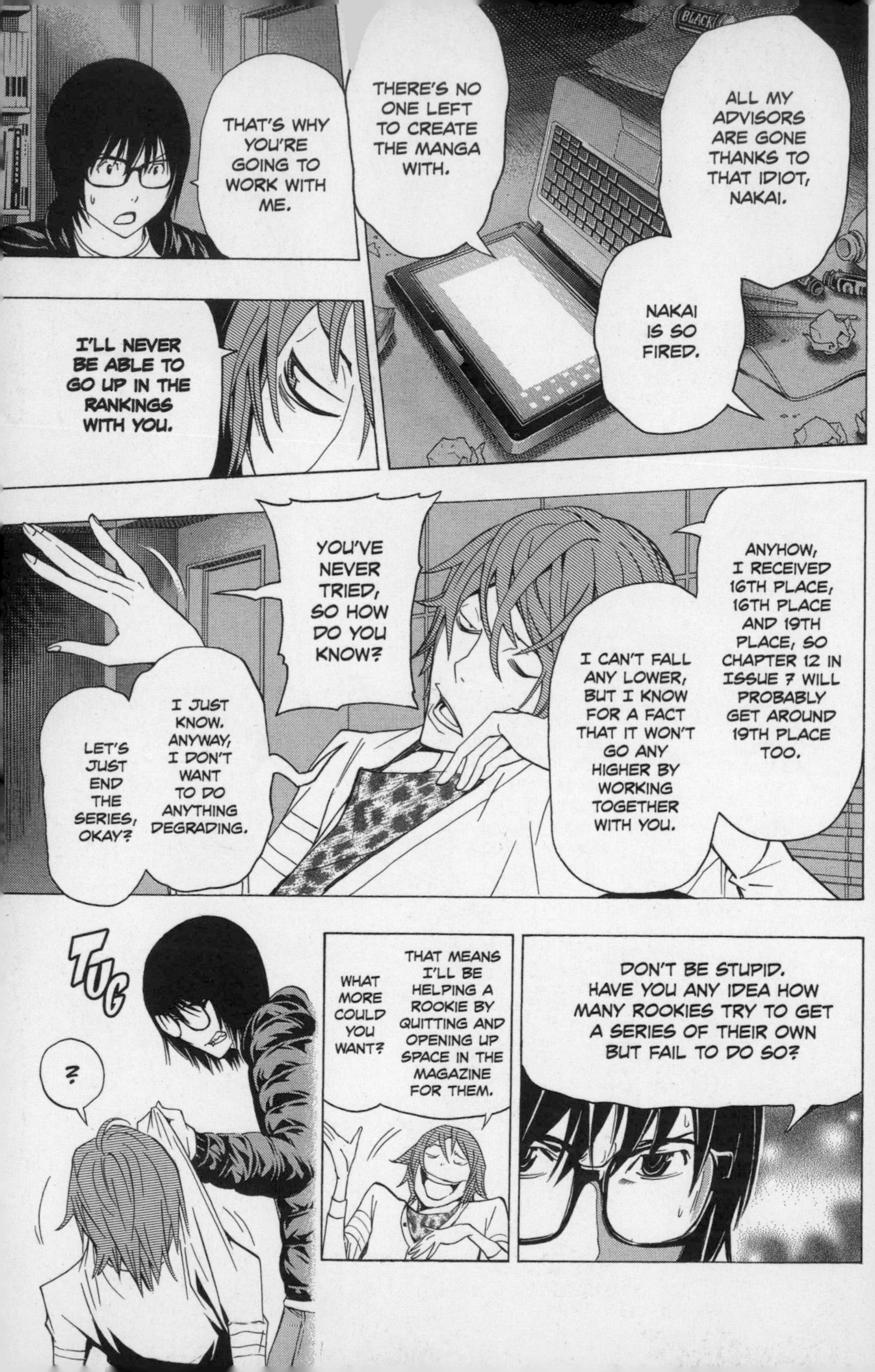
ALL MY ADVISORS ARE GONE THANKS TO THAT IDIOT, NAKAI.
THERE'S NO ONE LEFT TO CREATE THE MANGA WITH.
NAKAI IS SO FIRED.
THAT'S WHY YOU'RE GOING TO WORK WITH ME.
I'LL NEVER BE ABLE TO GO UP IN THE RANKINGS WITH YOU.
ANYHOW, I RECEIVED 16TH PLACE, 16TH PLACE AND 19TH PLACE, SO CHAPTER 12 IN ISSUE 7 WILL PROBABLY GET AROUND 19TH PLACE TOO.
I CAN'T FALL ANY LOWER, BUT I KNOW FOR A FACT THAT IT WON'T GO ANY HIGHER BY WORKING TOGETHER WITH YOU.
YOU'VE NEVER TRIED, SO HOW DO YOU KNOW?
I JUST KNOW. ANYWAY, I DON'T WANT TO DO ANYTHING DEGRADING.
LET'S JUST END THE SERIES, OKAY?
DON'T BE STUPID. HAVE YOU ANY IDEA HOW MANY ROOKIES TRY TO GET A SERIES OF THEIR OWN BUT FAIL TO DO SO?
THAT MEANS I'LL BE HELPING A ROOKIE BY QUITTING AND OPENING UP SPACE IN THE MAGAZINE FOR THEM.
WHAT MORE COULD YOU WANT?
TUG
?

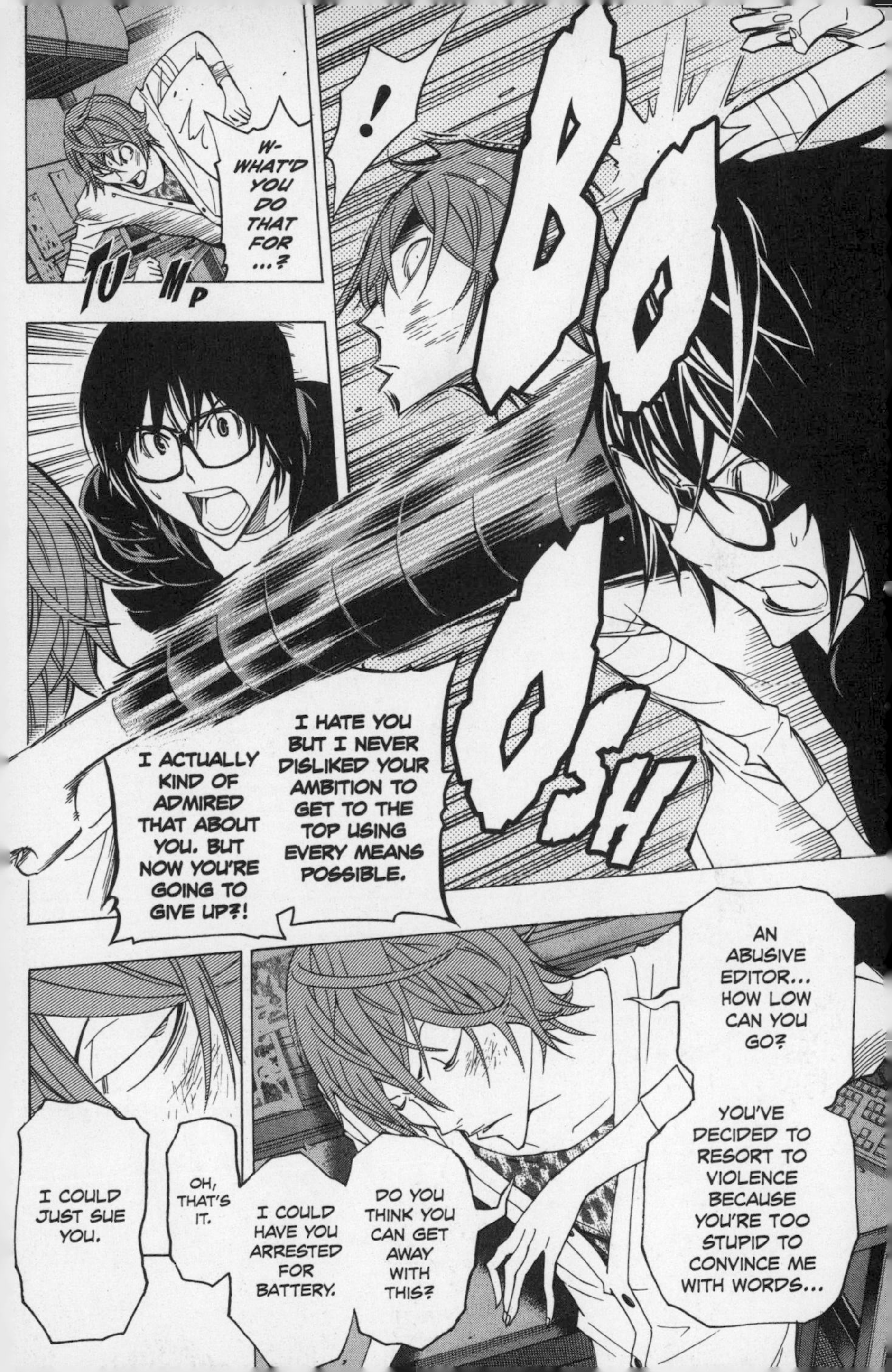
!
BOOSH
W-WHAT'D YOU DO THAT FOR...?
TUMP
I HATE YOU BUT I NEVER DISLIKED YOUR AMBITION TO GET TO THE TOP USING EVERY MEANS POSSIBLE.
I ACTUALLY KIND OF ADMIRED THAT ABOUT YOU. BUT NOW YOU'RE GOING TO GIVE UP?!
AN ABUSIVE EDITOR... HOW LOW CAN YOU GO?
YOU'VE DECIDED TO RESORT TO VIOLENCE BECAUSE YOU'RE TOO STUPID TO CONVINCE ME WITH WORDS...
DO YOU THINK YOU CAN GET AWAY WITH THIS?
I COULD HAVE YOU ARRESTED FOR BATTERY.
OH, THAT'S IT.
I COULD JUST SUE YOU.

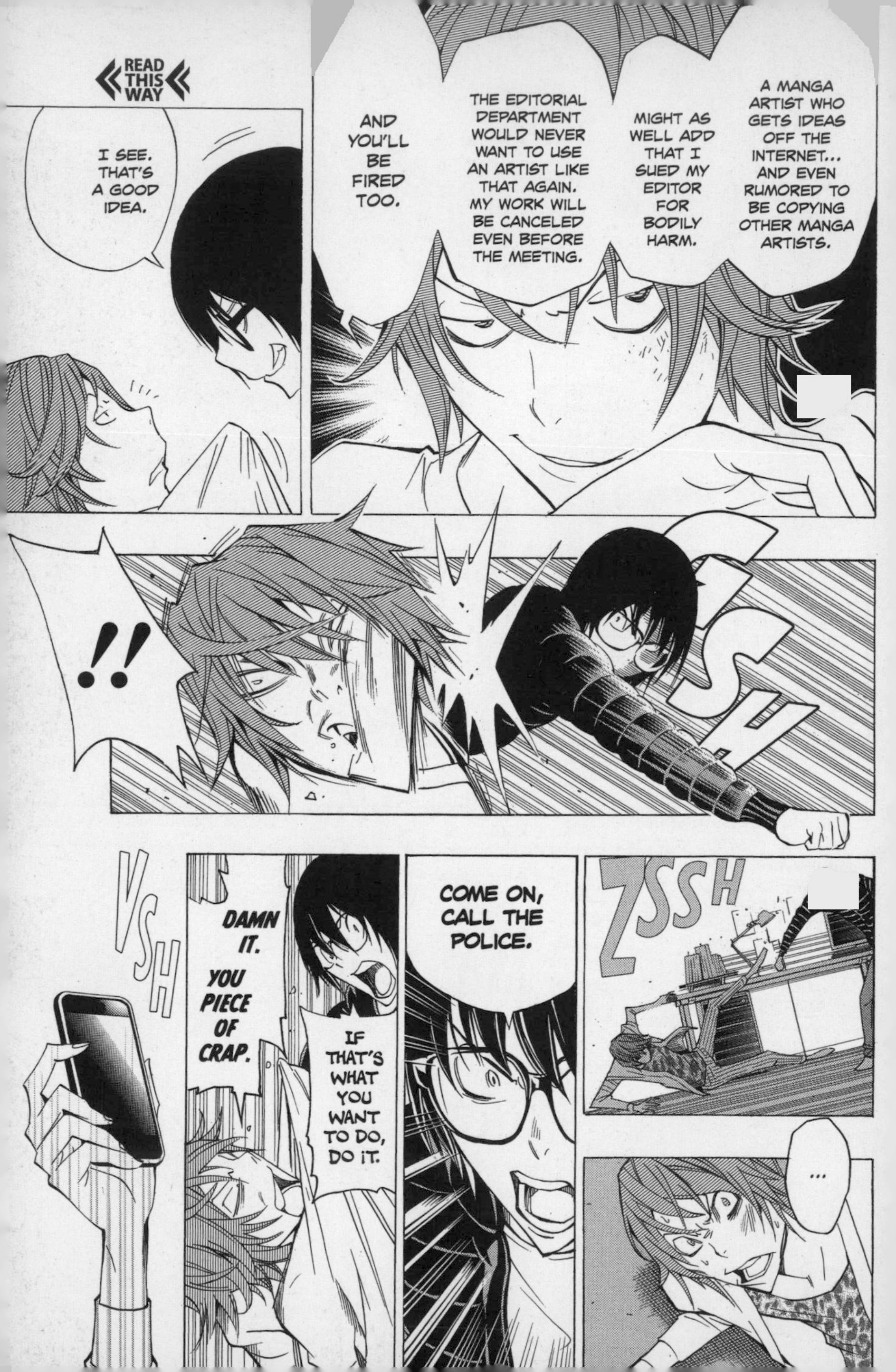
READ THIS WAY
A MANGA ARTIST WHO GETS IDEAS OFF THE INTERNET... AND EVEN RUMORED TO BE COPYING OTHER MANGA ARTISTS.
MIGHT AS WELL ADD THAT I SUED MY EDITOR FOR BODILY HARM.
THE EDITORIAL DEPARTMENT WOULD NEVER WANT TO USE AN ARTIST LIKE THAT AGAIN. MY WORK WILL BE CANCELED EVEN BEFORE THE MEETING.
AND YOU'LL BE FIRED TOO.
I SEE. THAT'S A GOOD IDEA.
SH
!!
ZSSH
...
COME ON, CALL THE POLICE.
IF THAT'S WHAT YOU WANT TO DO, DO IT.
DAMN IT.
YOU PIECE OF CRAP.
VSH

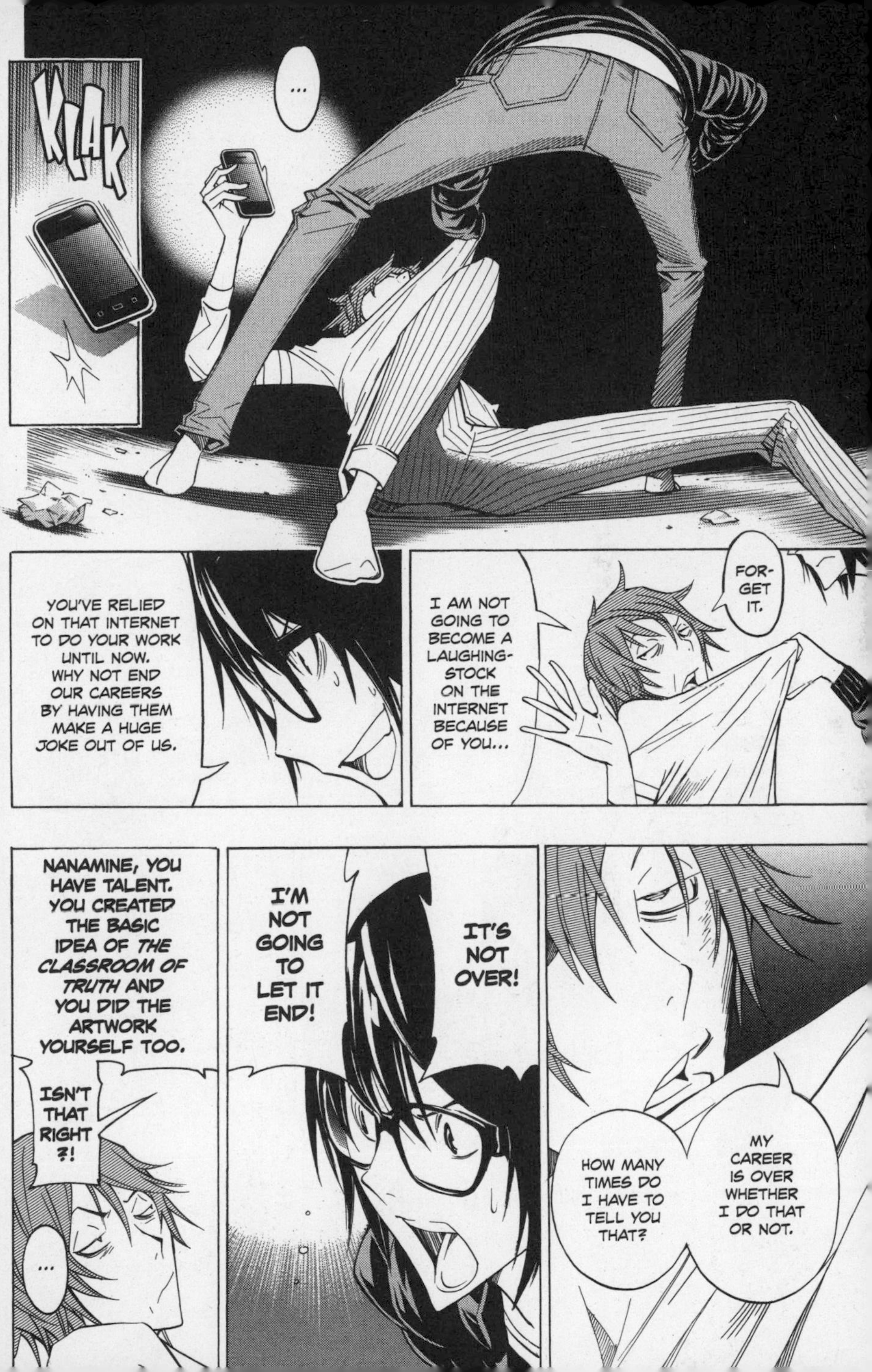
...
KLAK
FOR-GET IT.
I AM NOT GOING TO BECOME A LAUGHING-STOCK ON THE INTERNET BECAUSE OF YOU...
YOU'VE RELIED ON THAT INTERNET TO DO YOUR WORK UNTIL NOW. WHY NOT END OUR CAREERS BY HAVING THEM MAKE A HUGE JOKE OUT OF US.
MY CAREER IS OVER WHETHER I DO THAT OR NOT.
HOW MANY TIMES DO I HAVE TO TELL YOU THAT?
IT'S NOT OVER!
I'M NOT GOING TO LET IT END!
NANAMINE, YOU HAVE TALENT. YOU CREATED THE BASIC IDEA OF *THE CLASSROOM OF TRUTH* AND YOU DID THE ARTWORK YOURSELF TOO.
ISN'T THAT RIGHT ?!
...

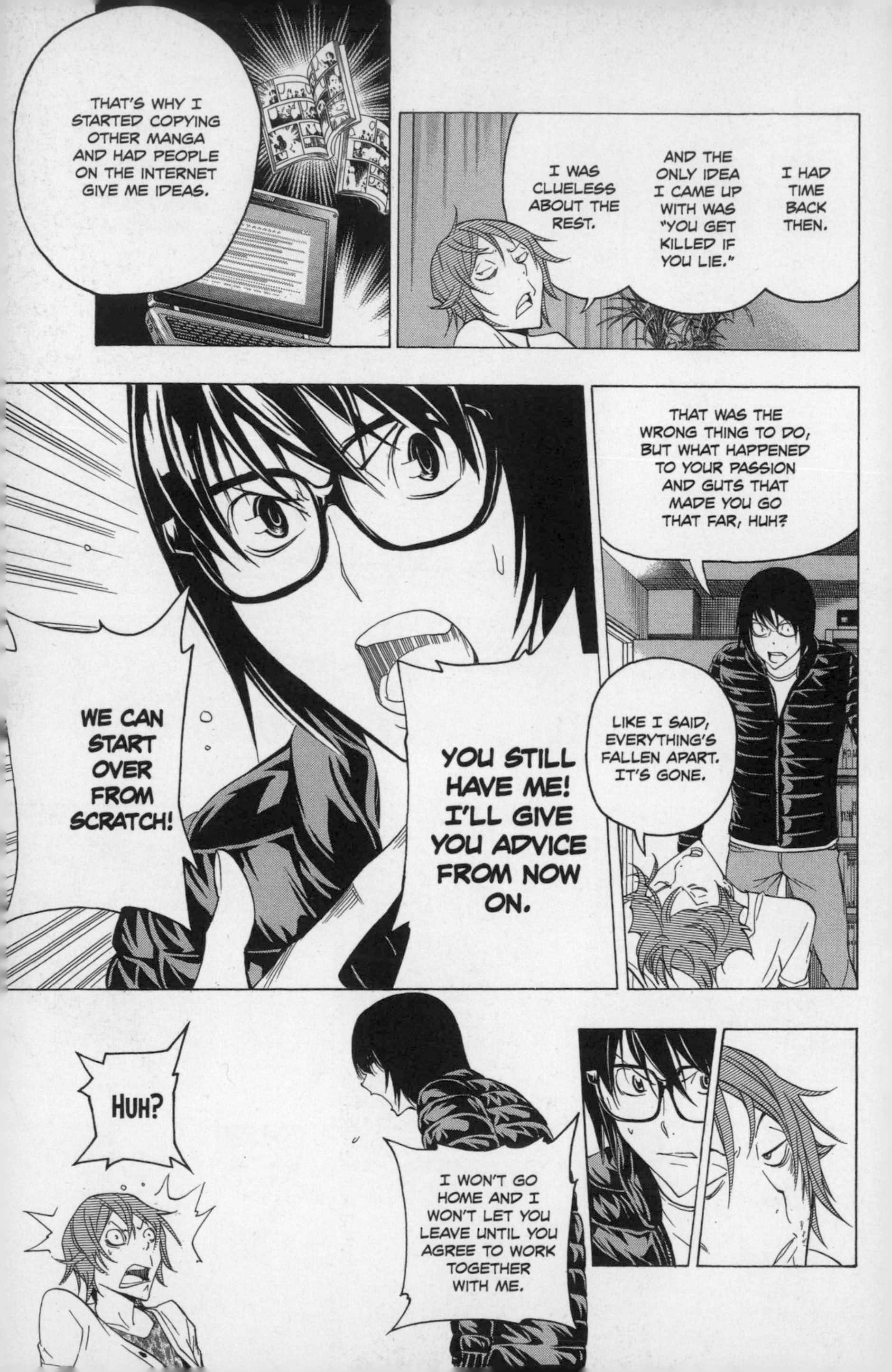
I HAD TIME BACK THEN.
AND THE ONLY IDEA I CAME UP WITH WAS "YOU GET KILLED IF YOU LIE."
I WAS CLUELESS ABOUT THE REST.
THAT'S WHY I STARTED COPYING OTHER MANGA AND HAD PEOPLE ON THE INTERNET GIVE ME IDEAS.
THAT WAS THE WRONG THING TO DO, BUT WHAT HAPPENED TO YOUR PASSION AND GUTS THAT MADE YOU GO THAT FAR, HUH?
LIKE I SAID, EVERYTHING'S FALLEN APART. IT'S GONE.
YOU STILL HAVE ME! I'LL GIVE YOU ADVICE FROM NOW ON.
WE CAN START OVER FROM SCRATCH!
I WON'T GO HOME AND I WON'T LET YOU LEAVE UNTIL YOU AGREE TO WORK TOGETHER WITH ME.
HUH?

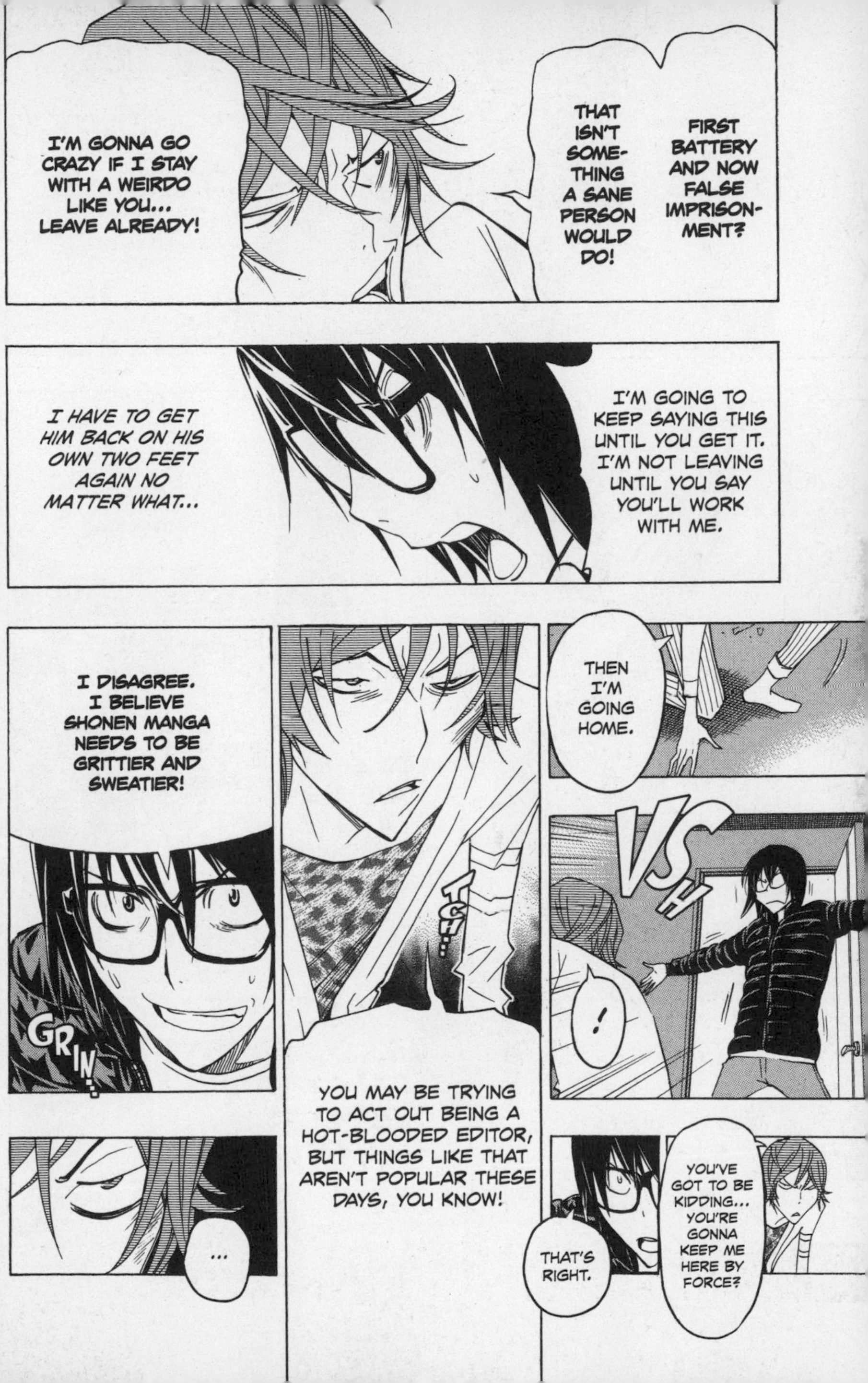
FIRST BATTERY AND NOW FALSE IMPRISONMENT?
THAT ISN'T SOMETHING A SANE PERSON WOULD DO!
I'M GONNA GO CRAZY IF I STAY WITH A WEIRDO LIKE YOU... LEAVE ALREADY!
I'M GOING TO KEEP SAYING THIS UNTIL YOU GET IT. I'M NOT LEAVING UNTIL YOU SAY YOU'LL WORK WITH ME.
I HAVE TO GET HIM BACK ON HIS OWN TWO FEET AGAIN NO MATTER WHAT...
THEN I'M GOING HOME.
VSH
!
YOU'VE GOT TO BE KIDDING... YOU'RE GONNA KEEP ME HERE BY FORCE?
THAT'S RIGHT.
TCH...
YOU MAY BE TRYING TO ACT OUT BEING A HOT-BLOODED EDITOR, BUT THINGS LIKE THAT AREN'T POPULAR THESE DAYS, YOU KNOW!
I DISAGREE. I BELIEVE SHONEN MANGA NEEDS TO BE GRITTIER AND SWEATIER!
GRIN...
...

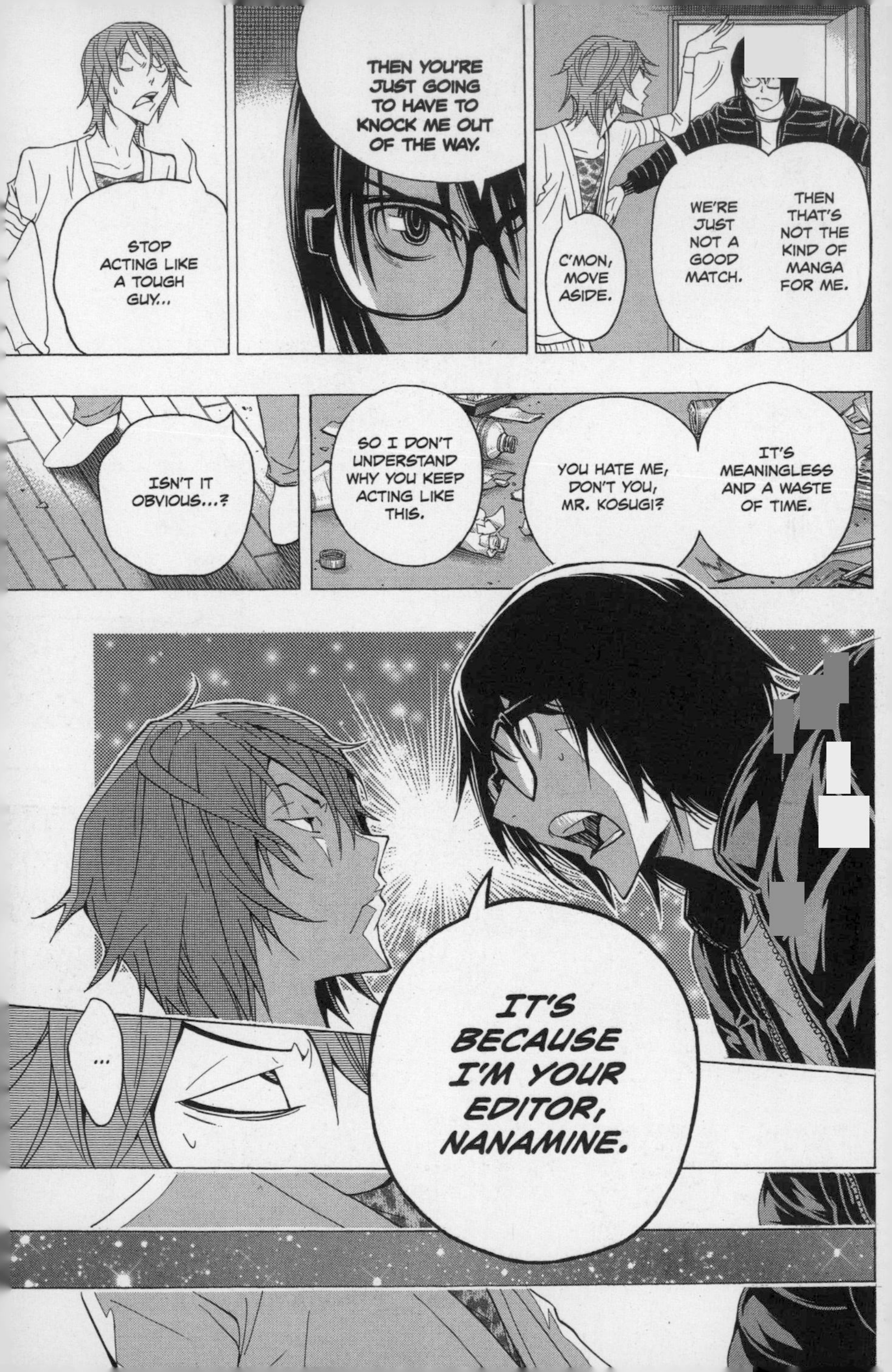
THEN THAT'S NOT THE KIND OF MANGA FOR ME.
WE'RE JUST NOT A GOOD MATCH.
C'MON, MOVE ASIDE.
THEN YOU'RE JUST GOING TO HAVE TO KNOCK ME OUT OF THE WAY.
STOP ACTING LIKE A TOUGH GUY...
IT'S MEANINGLESS AND A WASTE OF TIME.
YOU HATE ME, DON'T YOU, MR. KOSUGI?
SO I DON'T UNDERSTAND WHY YOU KEEP ACTING LIKE THIS.
ISN'T IT OBVIOUS...?
IT'S BECAUSE I'M YOUR EDITOR, NANAMINE.
...

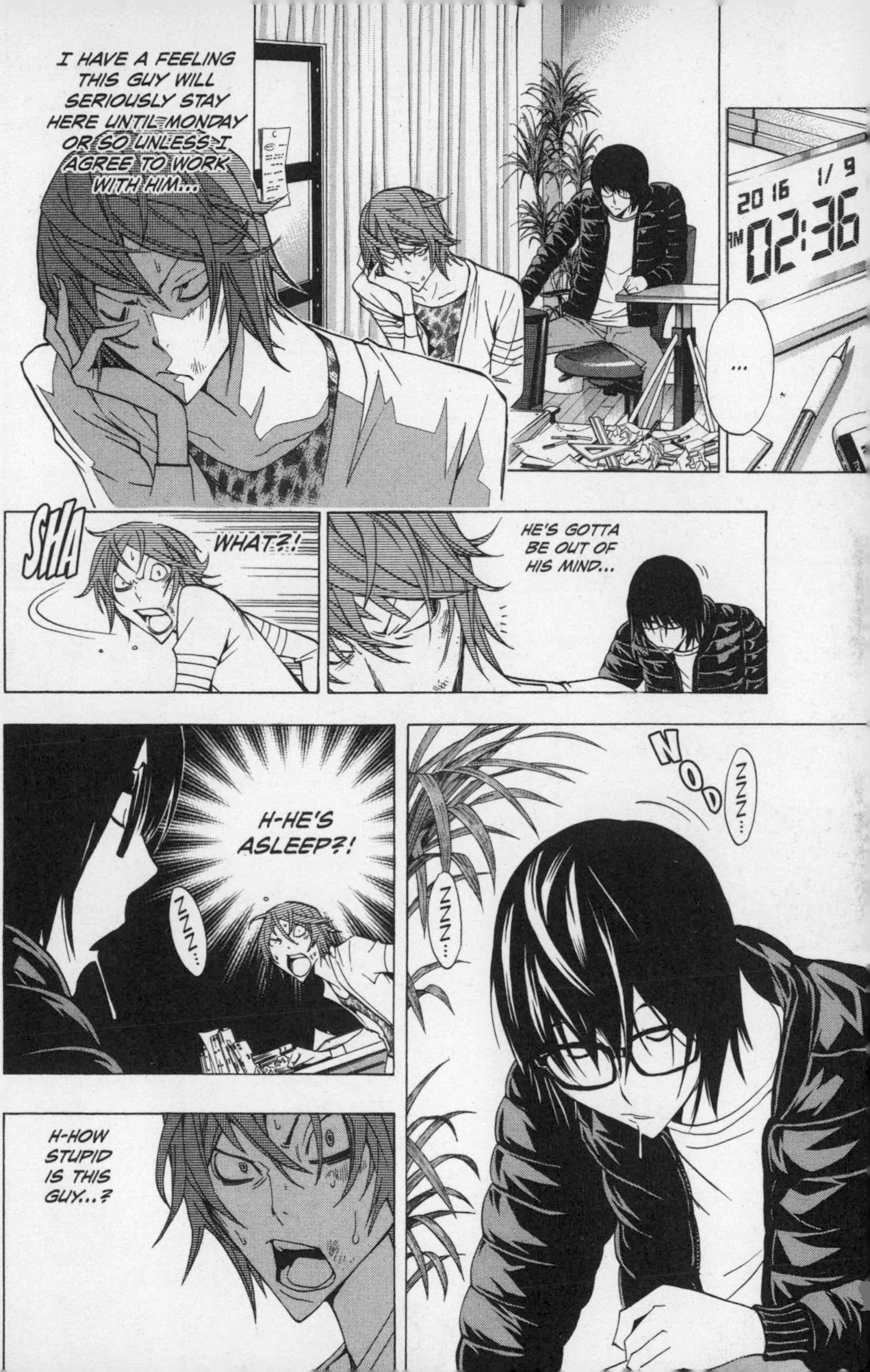
2016 1/ 9
AM 02:36
...
I HAVE A FEELING THIS GUY WILL SERIOUSLY STAY HERE UNTIL MONDAY OR SO UNLESS I AGREE TO WORK WITH HIM...
HE'S GOTTA BE OUT OF HIS MIND...
SHA
WHAT?!
NOD
ZZZ...
ZZZ...
H-HE'S ASLEEP?!
ZZZ...
H-HOW STUPID IS THIS GUY...?

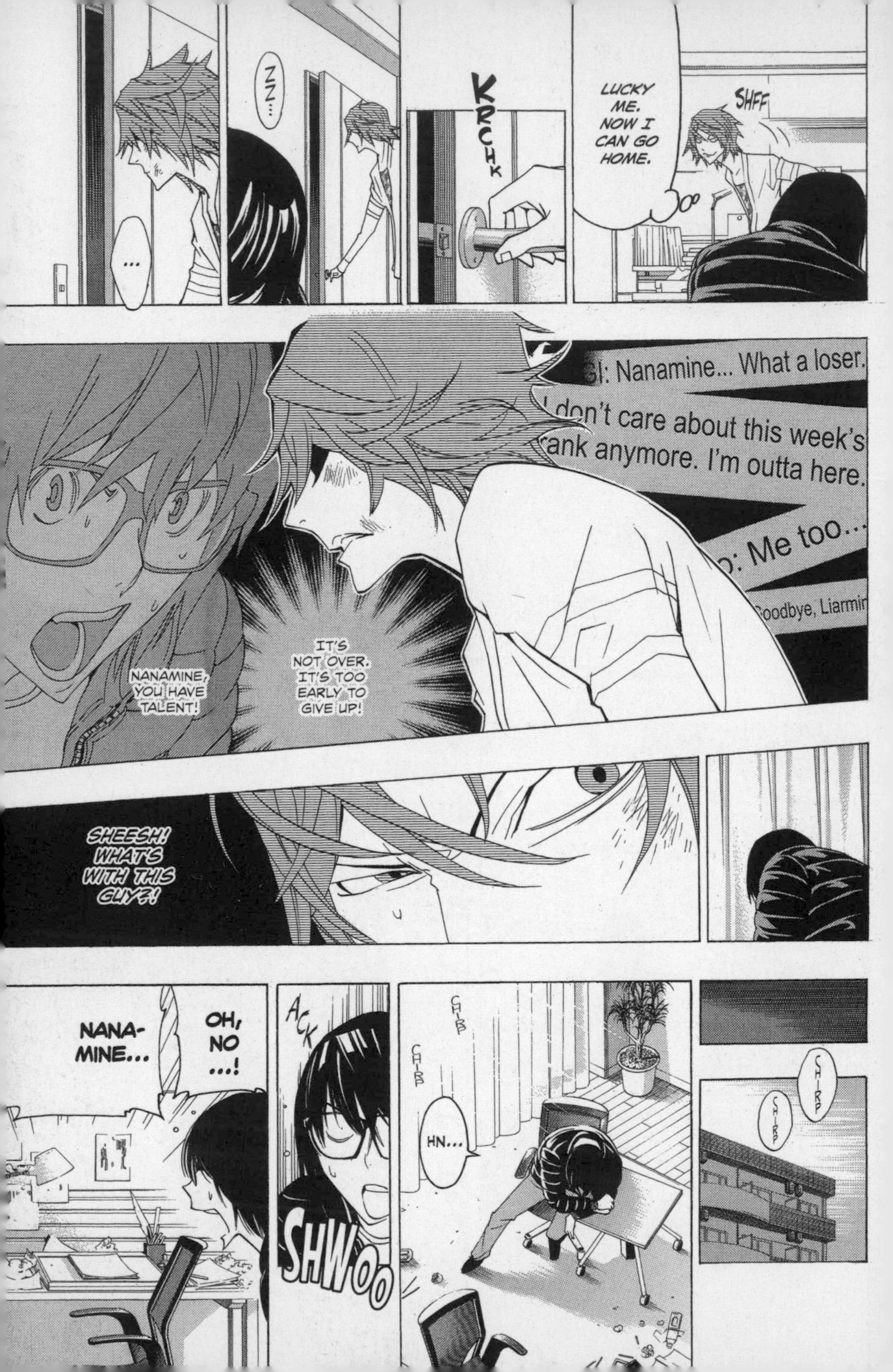
SHFF
LUCKY ME. NOW I CAN GO HOME.
KRCHK
ZZ...
...
I: Nanamine... What a loser.
I don't care about this week's rank anymore. I'm outta here.
: Me too...
Goodbye, Liarmin
IT'S NOT OVER. IT'S TOO EARLY TO GIVE UP!
NANAMINE, YOU HAVE TALENT!
SHEESH! WHAT'S WITH THIS GUY?!
CHIRP
CHIRP
CHIRP
CHIRP
HN...
ACK
SHWOO
OH, NO ...!
NANA-MINE...

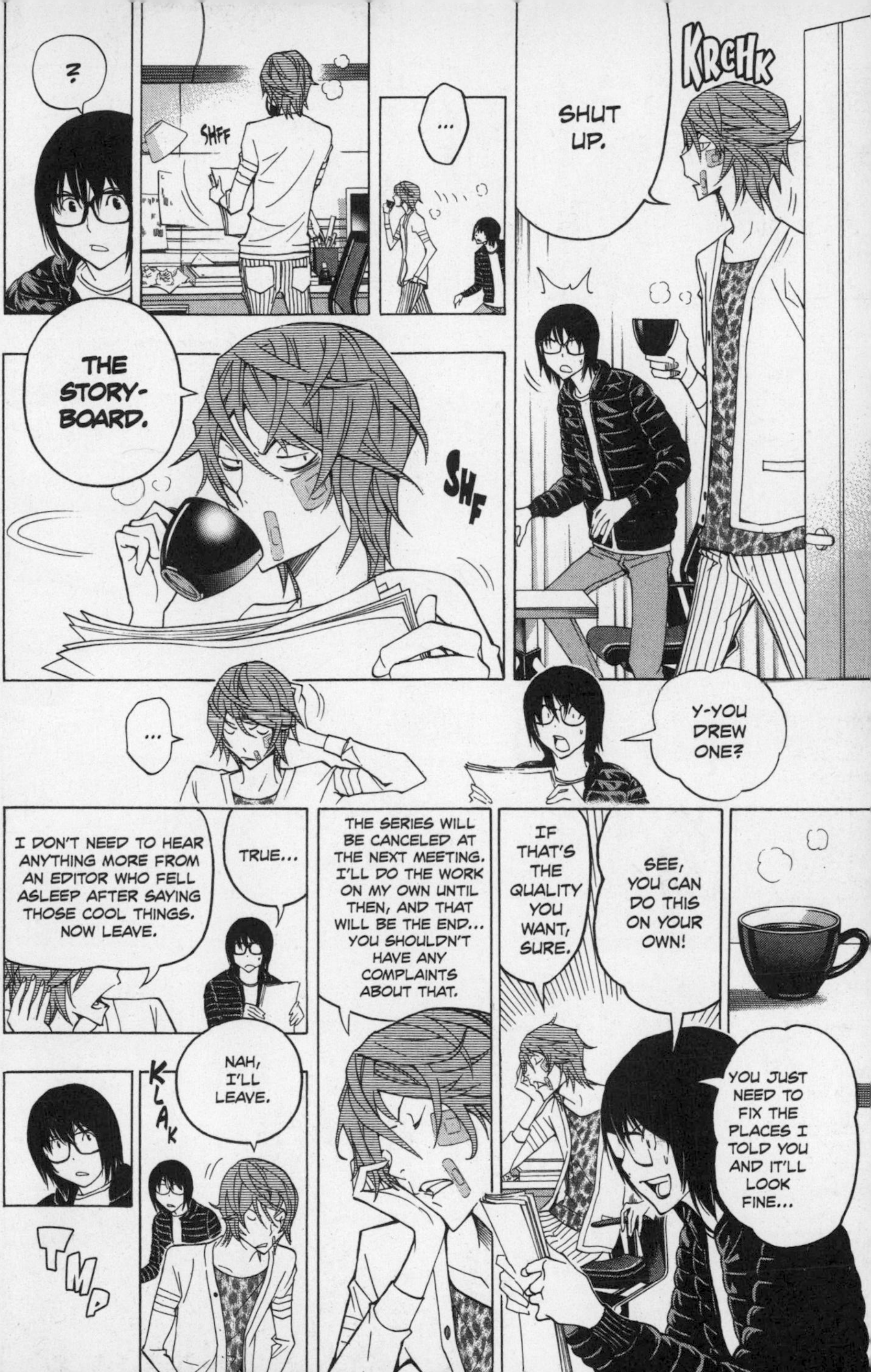
KRCHK
SHUT UP.
...
SHFF
?
THE STORY-BOARD.
SHF
Y-YOU DREW ONE?
...
SEE, YOU CAN DO THIS ON YOUR OWN!
IF THAT'S THE QUALITY YOU WANT, SURE.
THE SERIES WILL BE CANCELED AT THE NEXT MEETING. I'LL DO THE WORK ON MY OWN UNTIL THEN, AND THAT WILL BE THE END... YOU SHOULDN'T HAVE ANY COMPLAINTS ABOUT THAT.
TRUE...
I DON'T NEED TO HEAR ANYTHING MORE FROM AN EDITOR WHO FELL ASLEEP AFTER SAYING THOSE COOL THINGS. NOW LEAVE.
YOU JUST NEED TO FIX THE PLACES I TOLD YOU AND IT'LL LOOK FINE...
NAH, I'LL LEAVE.
KLAK
TMP

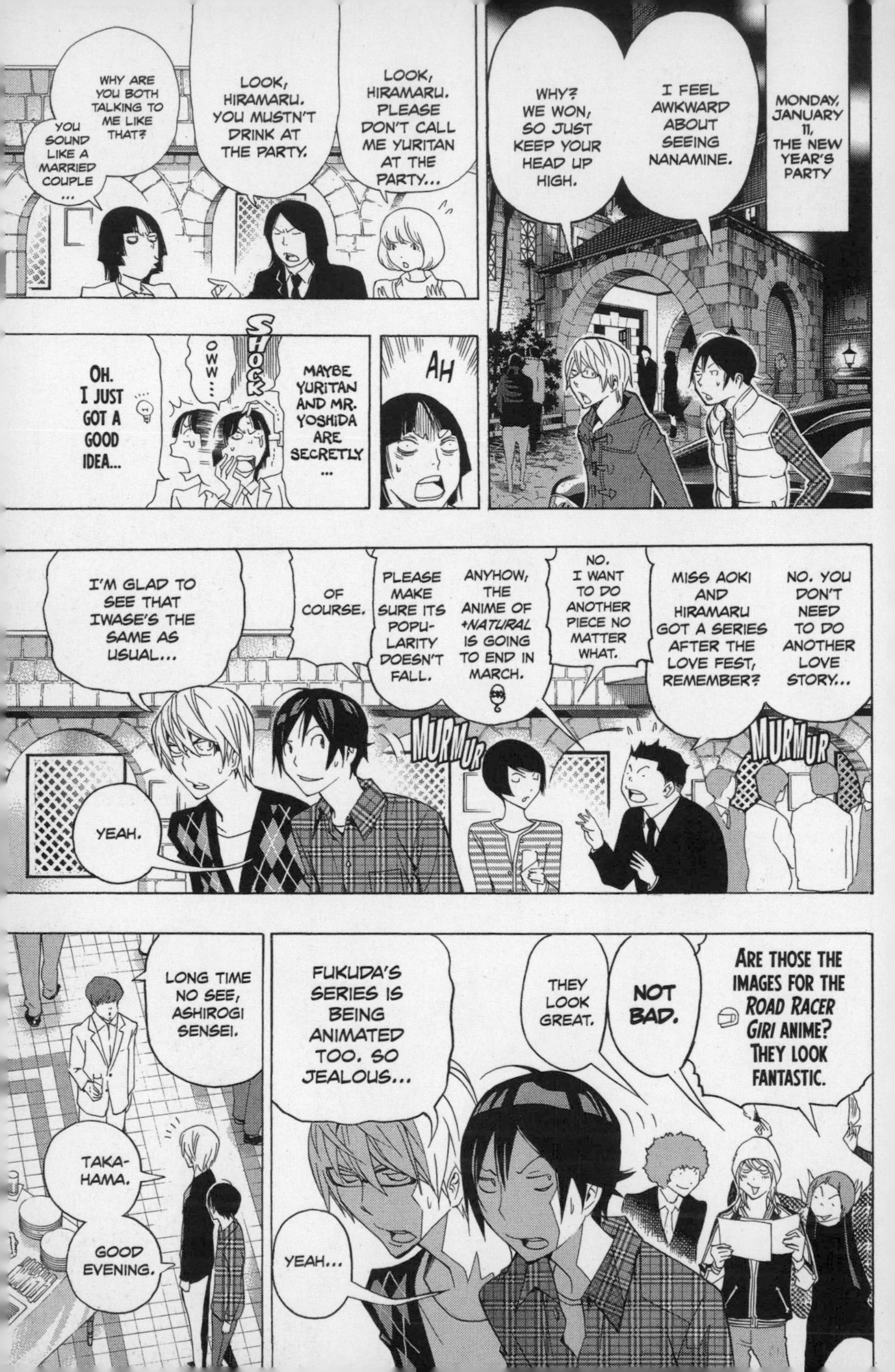
MONDAY, JANUARY 11, THE NEW YEAR'S PARTY
I FEEL AWKWARD ABOUT SEEING NANAMINE.
WHY? WE WON, SO JUST KEEP YOUR HEAD UP HIGH.
LOOK, HIRAMARU. PLEASE DON'T CALL ME YURITAN AT THE PARTY...
LOOK, HIRAMARU. YOU MUSTN'T DRINK AT THE PARTY.
WHY ARE YOU BOTH TALKING TO ME LIKE THAT?
YOU SOUND LIKE A MARRIED COUPLE ...
AH
MAYBE YURITAN AND MR. YOSHIDA ARE SECRETLY ...
SHOCK
OWW...
OH. I JUST GOT A GOOD IDEA...
NO. YOU DON'T NEED TO DO ANOTHER LOVE STORY...
MISS AOKI AND HIRAMARU GOT A SERIES AFTER THE LOVE FEST, REMEMBER?
MURMUR
NO. I WANT TO DO ANOTHER PIECE NO MATTER WHAT.
ANYHOW, THE ANIME OF +NATURAL IS GOING TO END IN MARCH.
PLEASE MAKE SURE ITS POPULARITY DOESN'T FALL.
OF COURSE.
MURMUR
I'M GLAD TO SEE THAT IWASE'S THE SAME AS USUAL...
YEAH.
ARE THOSE THE IMAGES FOR THE ROAD RACER GIRI ANIME? THEY LOOK FANTASTIC.
NOT BAD.
THEY LOOK GREAT.
FUKUDA'S SERIES IS BEING ANIMATED TOO. SO JEALOUS...
YEAH...
LONG TIME NO SEE, ASHIROGI SENSEI.
TAKA-HAMA.
GOOD EVENING.

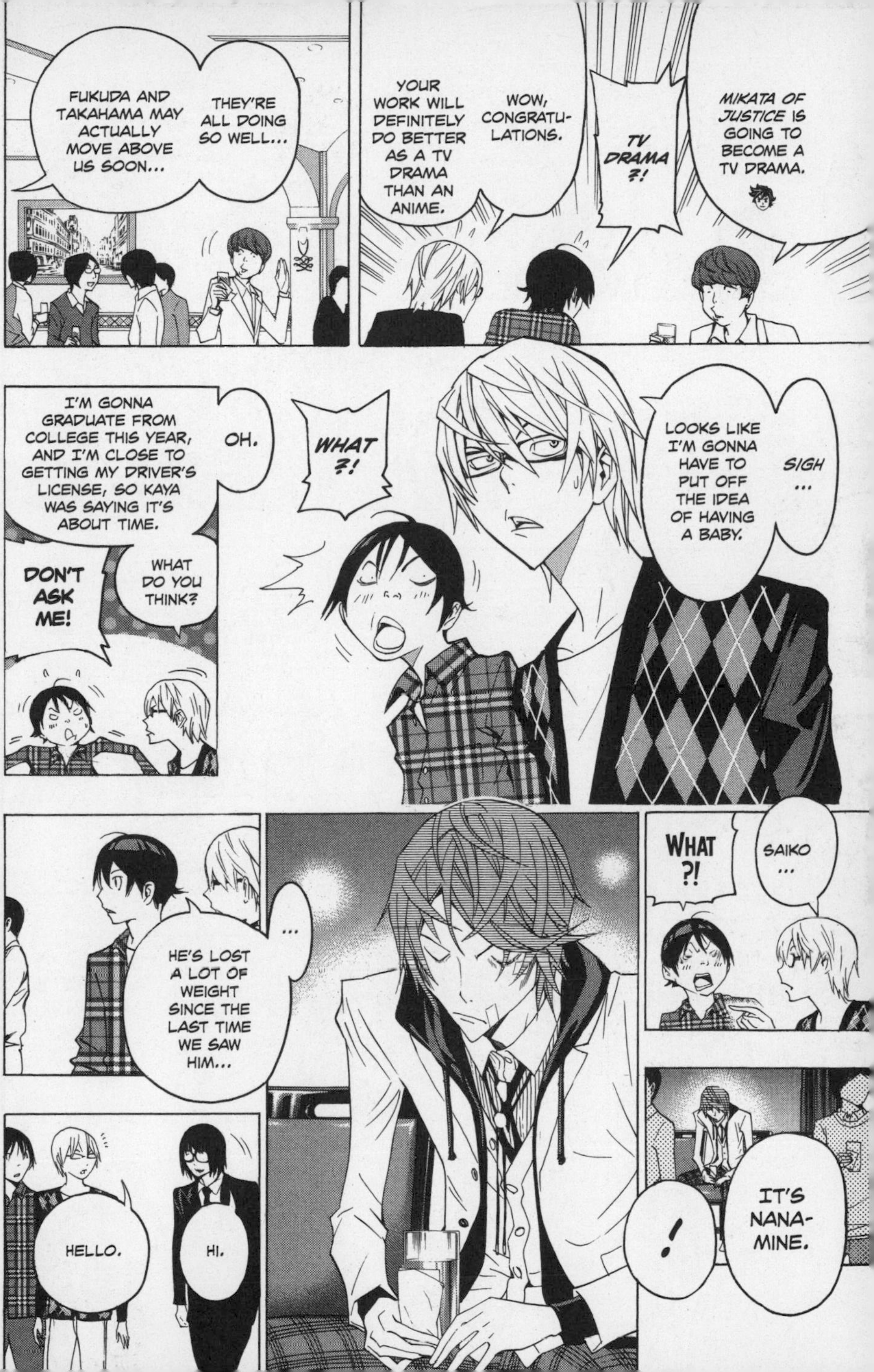
MIKATA OF JUSTICE IS GOING TO BECOME A TV DRAMA.
TV DRAMA?!
WOW, CONGRATULATIONS.
YOUR WORK WILL DEFINITELY DO BETTER AS A TV DRAMA THAN AN ANIME.
THEY'RE ALL DOING SO WELL...
FUKUDA AND TAKAHAMA MAY ACTUALLY MOVE ABOVE US SOON...
SIGH...
LOOKS LIKE I'M GONNA HAVE TO PUT OFF THE IDEA OF HAVING A BABY.
WHAT?!
OH.
I'M GONNA GRADUATE FROM COLLEGE THIS YEAR, AND I'M CLOSE TO GETTING MY DRIVER'S LICENSE, SO KAYA WAS SAYING IT'S ABOUT TIME.
WHAT DO YOU THINK?
DON'T ASK ME!
SAIKO...
WHAT?!
IT'S NANAMINE.
!
...
HE'S LOST A LOT OF WEIGHT SINCE THE LAST TIME WE SAW HIM...
HI.
HELLO.

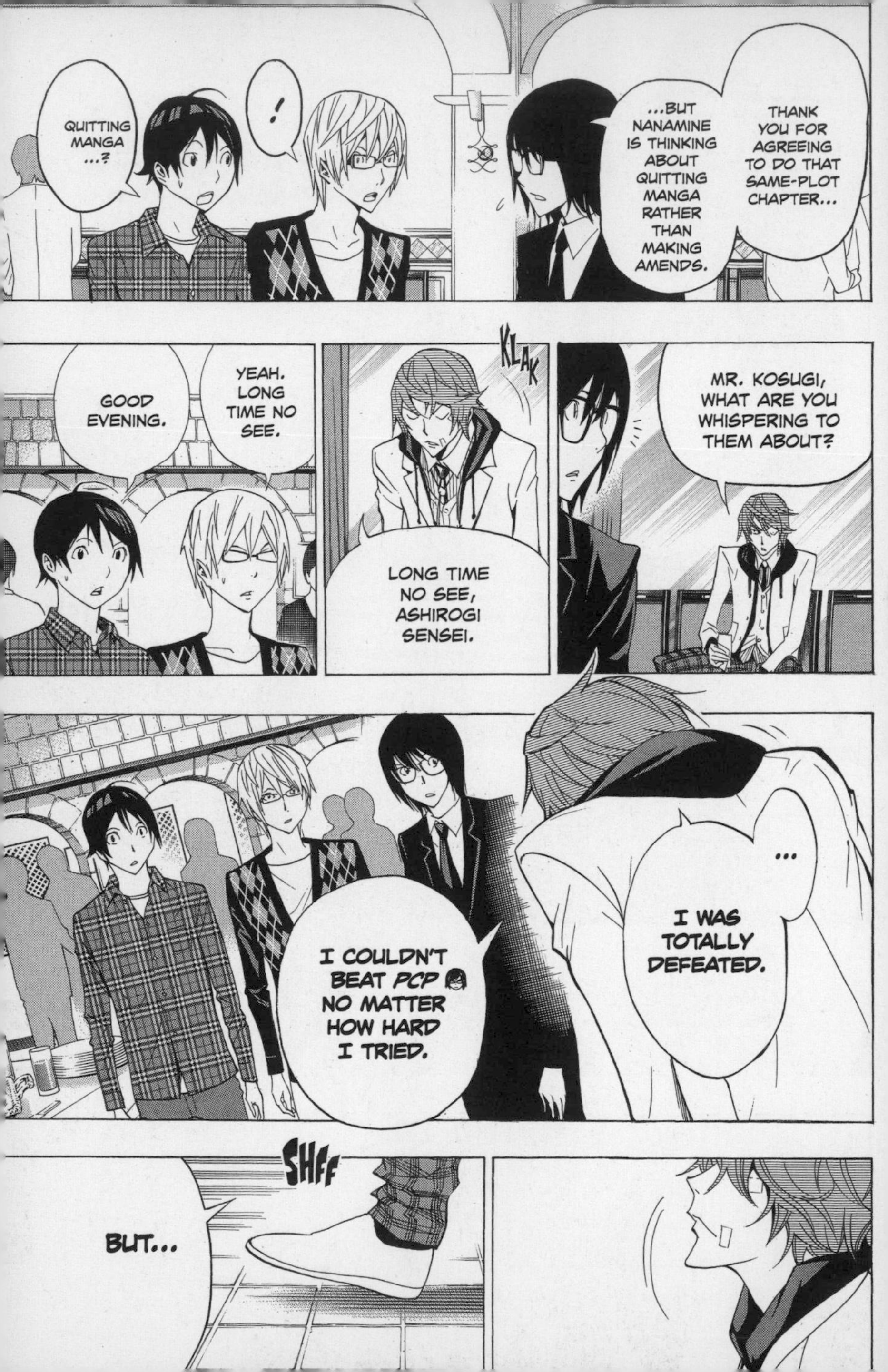
THANK YOU FOR AGREEING TO DO THAT SAME-PLOT CHAPTER...
...BUT NANAMINE IS THINKING ABOUT QUITTING MANGA RATHER THAN MAKING AMENDS.
!
QUITTING MANGA ...?
MR. KOSUGI, WHAT ARE YOU WHISPERING TO THEM ABOUT?
KLAK
LONG TIME NO SEE, ASHIROGI SENSEI.
YEAH. LONG TIME NO SEE.
GOOD EVENING.
...
I WAS TOTALLY DEFEATED.
I COULDN'T BEAT PCP NO MATTER HOW HARD I TRIED.
SHFF
BUT...

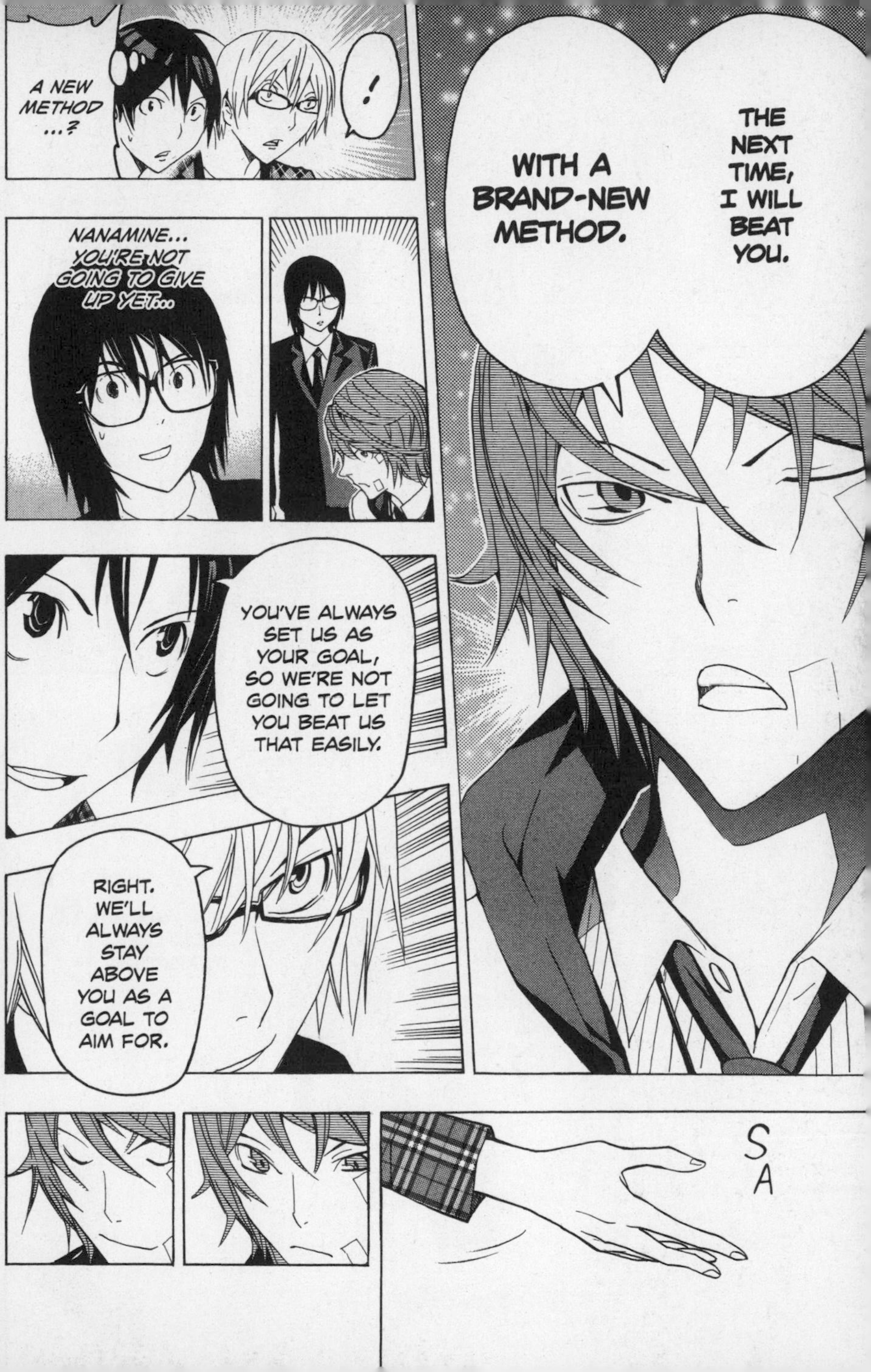
THE NEXT TIME, I WILL BEAT YOU.
WITH A BRAND-NEW METHOD.
!
A NEW METHOD ...?
NANAMINE... YOU'RE NOT GOING TO GIVE UP YET...
YOU'VE ALWAYS SET US AS YOUR GOAL, SO WE'RE NOT GOING TO LET YOU BEAT US THAT EASILY.
RIGHT. WE'LL ALWAYS STAY ABOVE YOU AS A GOAL TO AIM FOR.
SA

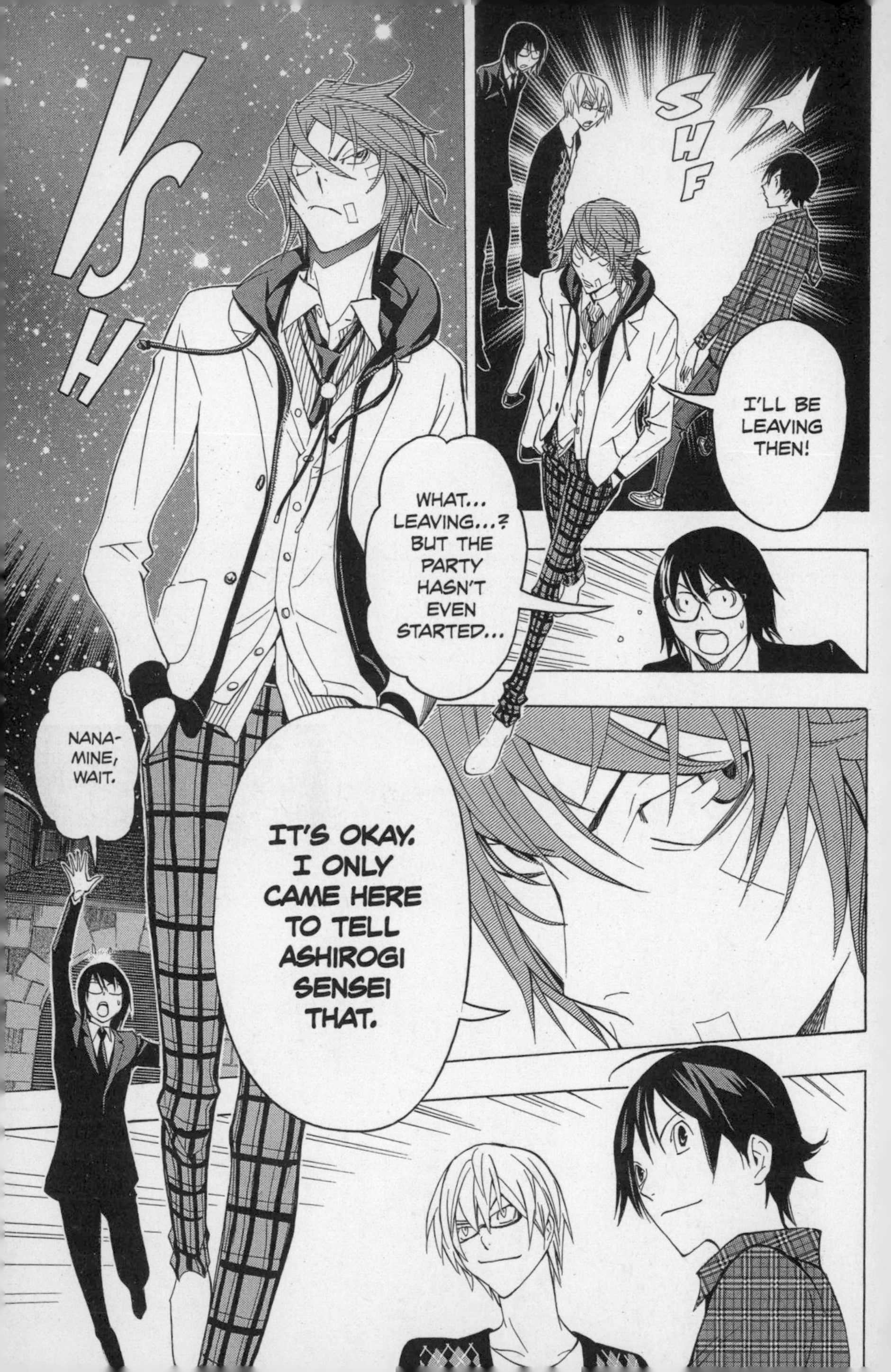
SHF
I'LL BE LEAVING THEN!
WHAT... LEAVING...? BUT THE PARTY HASN'T EVEN STARTED...
VSH
NANA-MINE, WAIT.
IT'S OKAY. I ONLY CAME HERE TO TELL ASHIROGI SENSEI THAT.

OHBA'S STORYBOARD

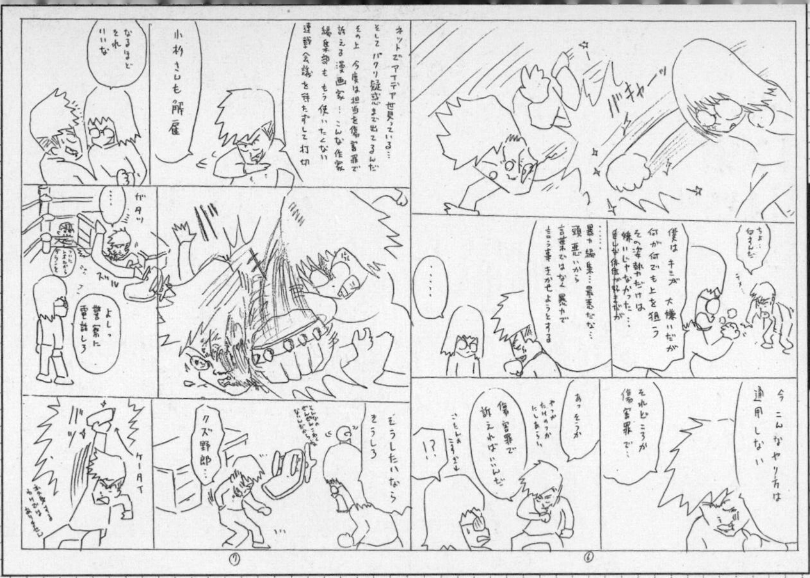
バキャーッ
僕はキミが大嫌いだが 何が何でも上を狙う その姿勢だけは嫌いじゃなかった…
……
今こんなやり方は通用しない
それどころか傷害罪で…
あっそうか
傷害罪で訴えればいいんだ
!?
ネットでアイデア見ている… そして パクリ疑惑まで出てるんだ その上 今度は担当を傷害罪で訴える漫画家…こんな作家 編集部も もう使いたくない 連載会議を待たずして打切
小杉さんも解雇
なるほど それいいな
ガタッ
……
よし、警察に電話しろ
そうしたいならそうしろ
クズ野郎…
ケータイ

OBATA'S STORYBOARD

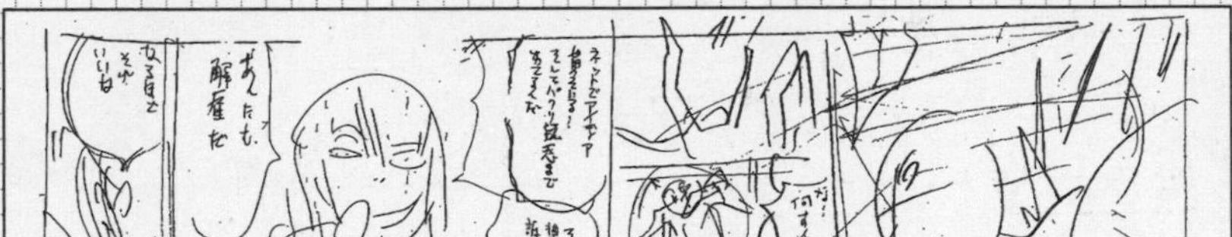

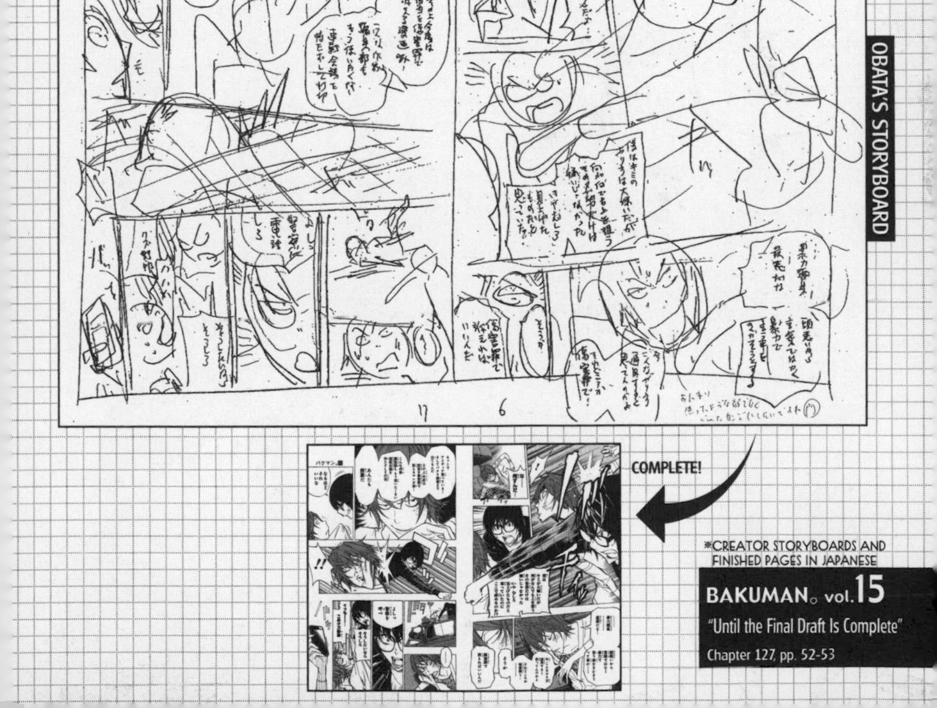

COMPLETE!

※CREATOR STORYBOARDS AND FINISHED PAGES IN JAPANESE

BAKUMAN。vol.15

"Until the Final Draft Is Complete"

Chapter 127, pp. 52-53

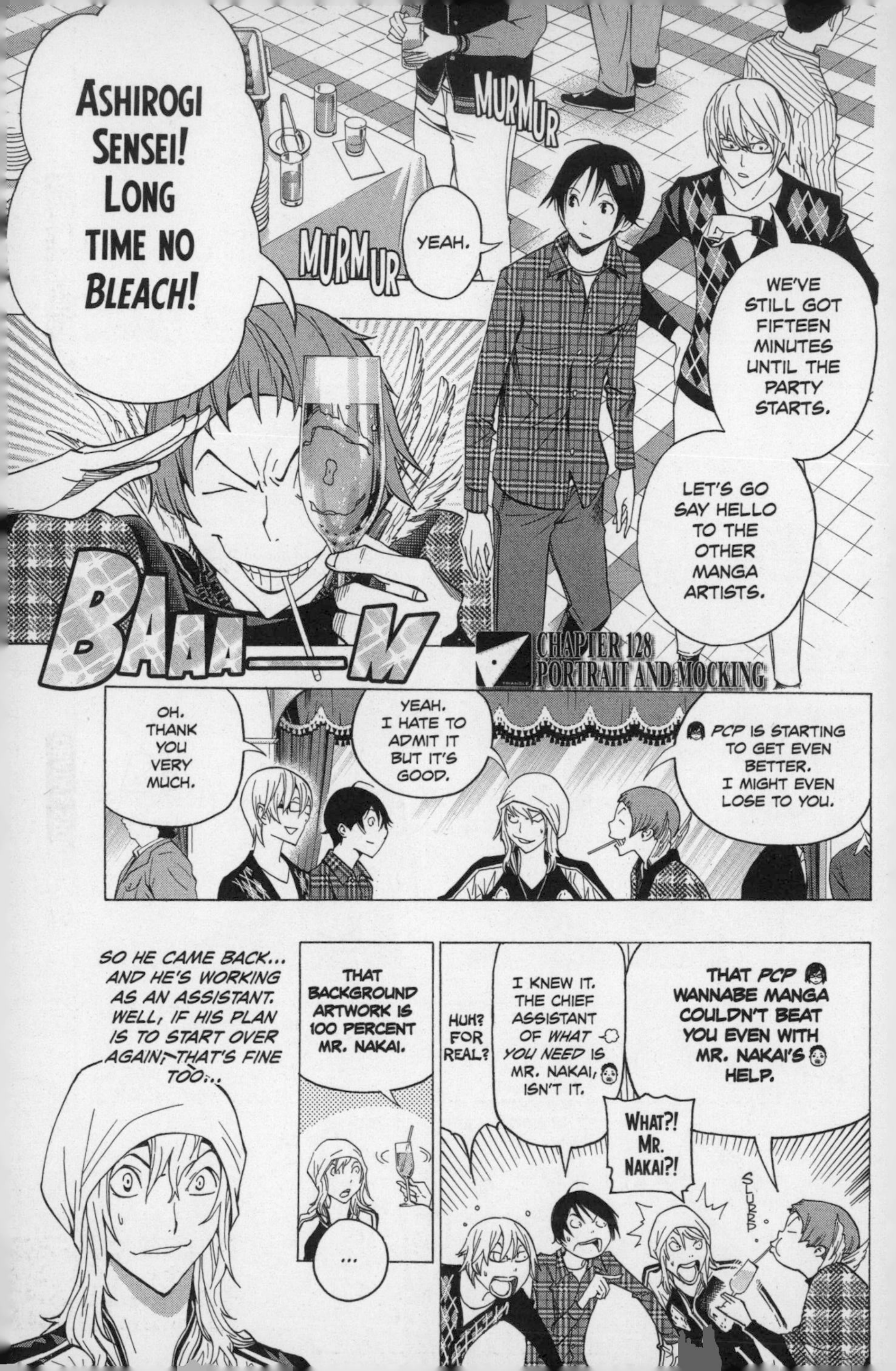

WE'VE STILL GOT FIFTEEN MINUTES UNTIL THE PARTY STARTS.
LET'S GO SAY HELLO TO THE OTHER MANGA ARTISTS.
MURMUR
YEAH.
MURMUR
ASHIROGI SENSEI! LONG TIME NO BLEACH!
BAAA—N
CHAPTER 128 PORTRAIT AND MOCKING
PCP IS STARTING TO GET EVEN BETTER. I MIGHT EVEN LOSE TO YOU.
YEAH. I HATE TO ADMIT IT BUT IT'S GOOD.
OH. THANK YOU VERY MUCH.
THAT PCP WANNABE MANGA COULDN'T BEAT YOU EVEN WITH MR. NAKAI'S HELP.
I KNEW IT. THE CHIEF ASSISTANT OF WHAT YOU NEED IS MR. NAKAI, ISN'T IT.
HUH? FOR REAL?
WHAT?! MR. NAKAI?!
SLURRP
THAT BACKGROUND ARTWORK IS 100 PERCENT MR. NAKAI.
...
SO HE CAME BACK... AND HE'S WORKING AS AN ASSISTANT. WELL, IF HIS PLAN IS TO START OVER AGAIN, THAT'S FINE TOO...

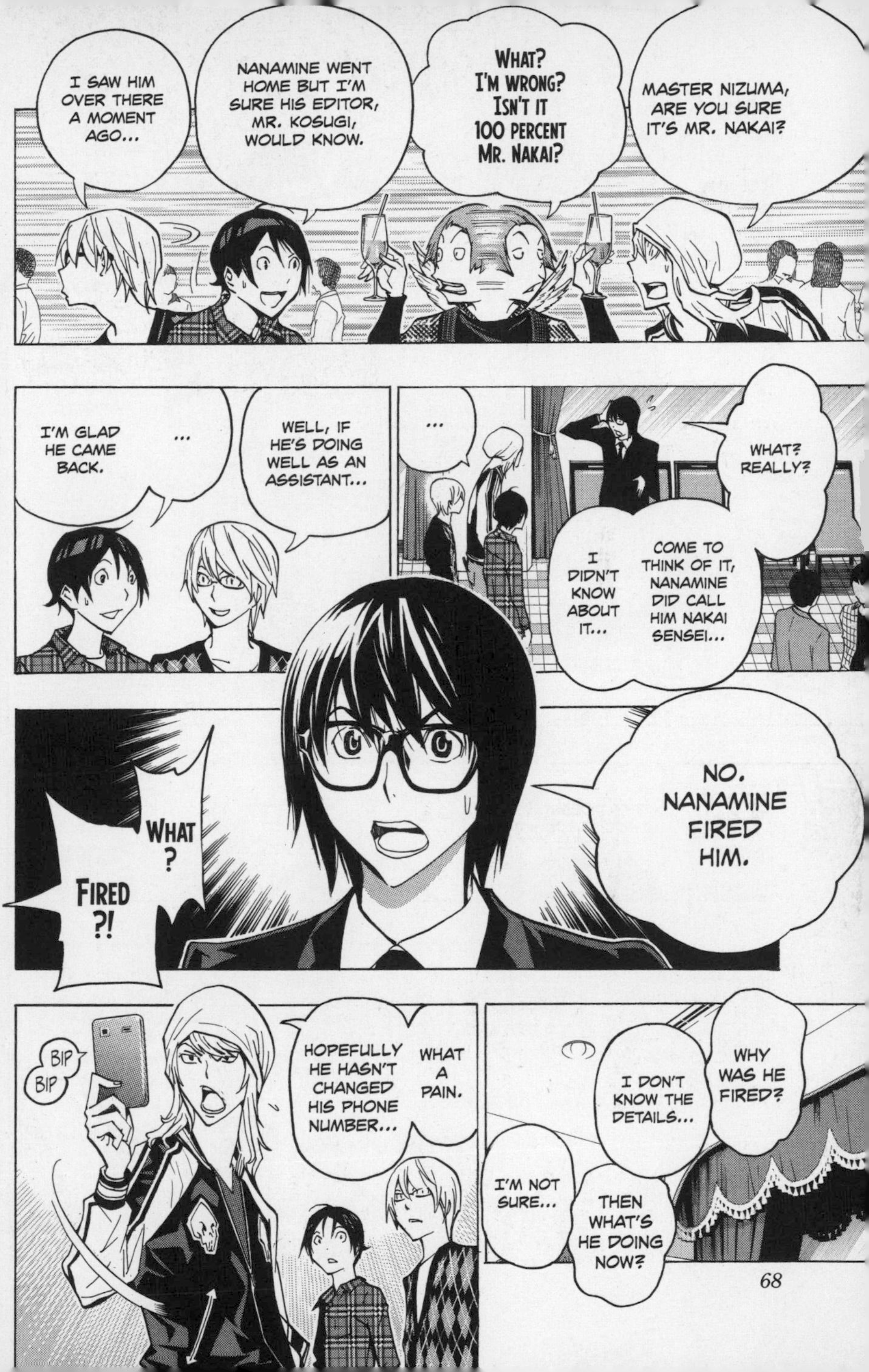

MASTER NIZUMA, ARE YOU SURE IT'S MR. NAKAI?
WHAT? I'M WRONG? ISN'T IT 100 PERCENT MR. NAKAI?
NANAMINE WENT HOME BUT I'M SURE HIS EDITOR, MR. KOSUGI, WOULD KNOW.
I SAW HIM OVER THERE A MOMENT AGO...
WHAT? REALLY?
COME TO THINK OF IT, NANAMINE DID CALL HIM NAKAI SENSEI...
I DIDN'T KNOW ABOUT IT...
...
WELL, IF HE'S DOING WELL AS AN ASSISTANT...
...
I'M GLAD HE CAME BACK.
NO. NANAMINE FIRED HIM.
WHAT?
FIRED?!
WHY WAS HE FIRED?
I DON'T KNOW THE DETAILS...
THEN WHAT'S HE DOING NOW?
I'M NOT SURE...
WHAT A PAIN.
HOPEFULLY HE HASN'T CHANGED HIS PHONE NUMBER...
BIP BIP

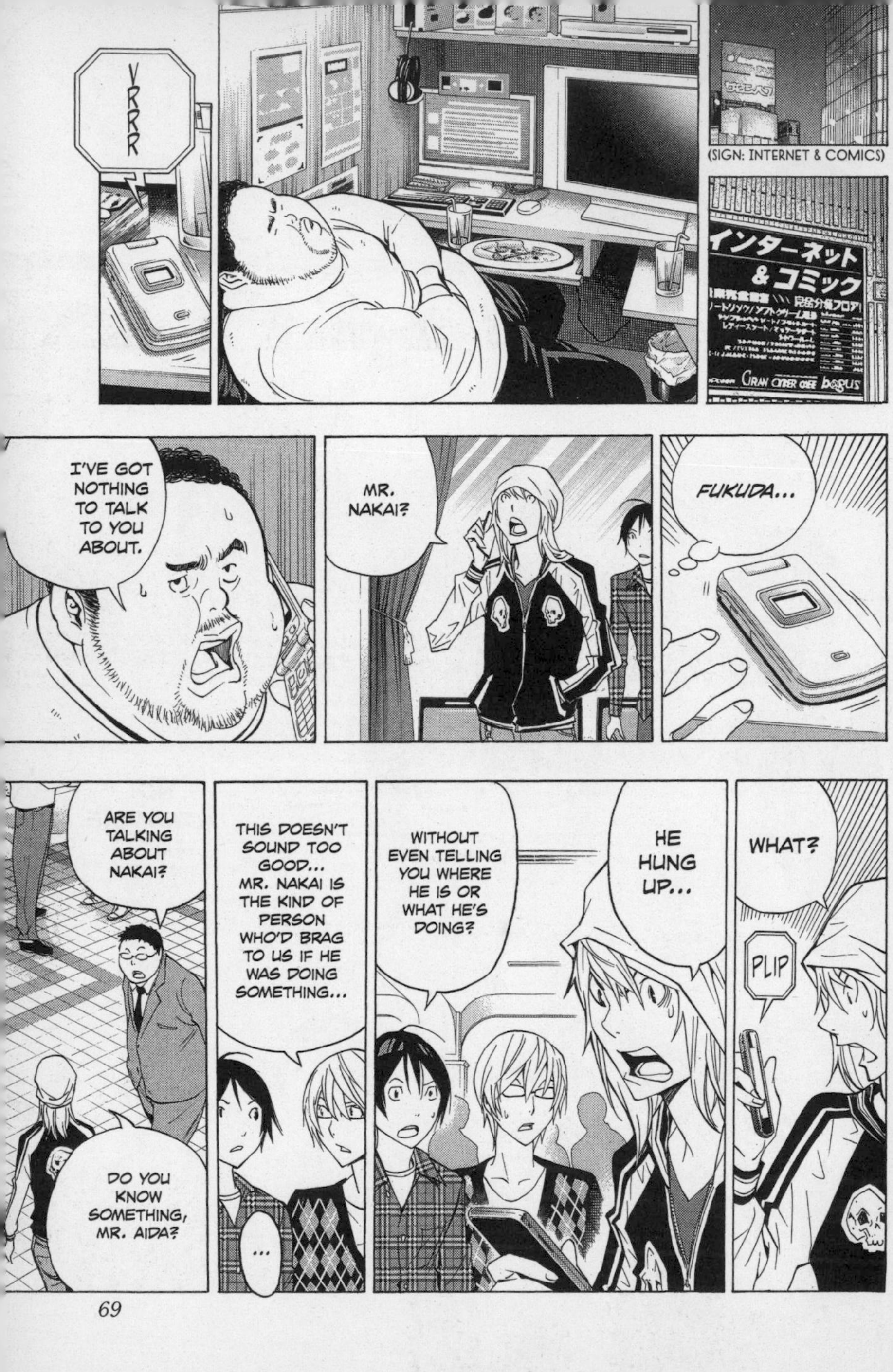
(SIGN: INTERNET & COMICS)
インターネット
&コミック
GRAN CYBER CAFE bagus
VRRR
FUKUDA...
MR. NAKAI?
I'VE GOT NOTHING TO TALK TO YOU ABOUT.
WHAT?
PLIP
HE HUNG UP...
WITHOUT EVEN TELLING YOU WHERE HE IS OR WHAT HE'S DOING?
THIS DOESN'T SOUND TOO GOOD... MR. NAKAI IS THE KIND OF PERSON WHO'D BRAG TO US IF HE WAS DOING SOMETHING...
...
ARE YOU TALKING ABOUT NAKAI?
DO YOU KNOW SOMETHING, MR. AIDA?

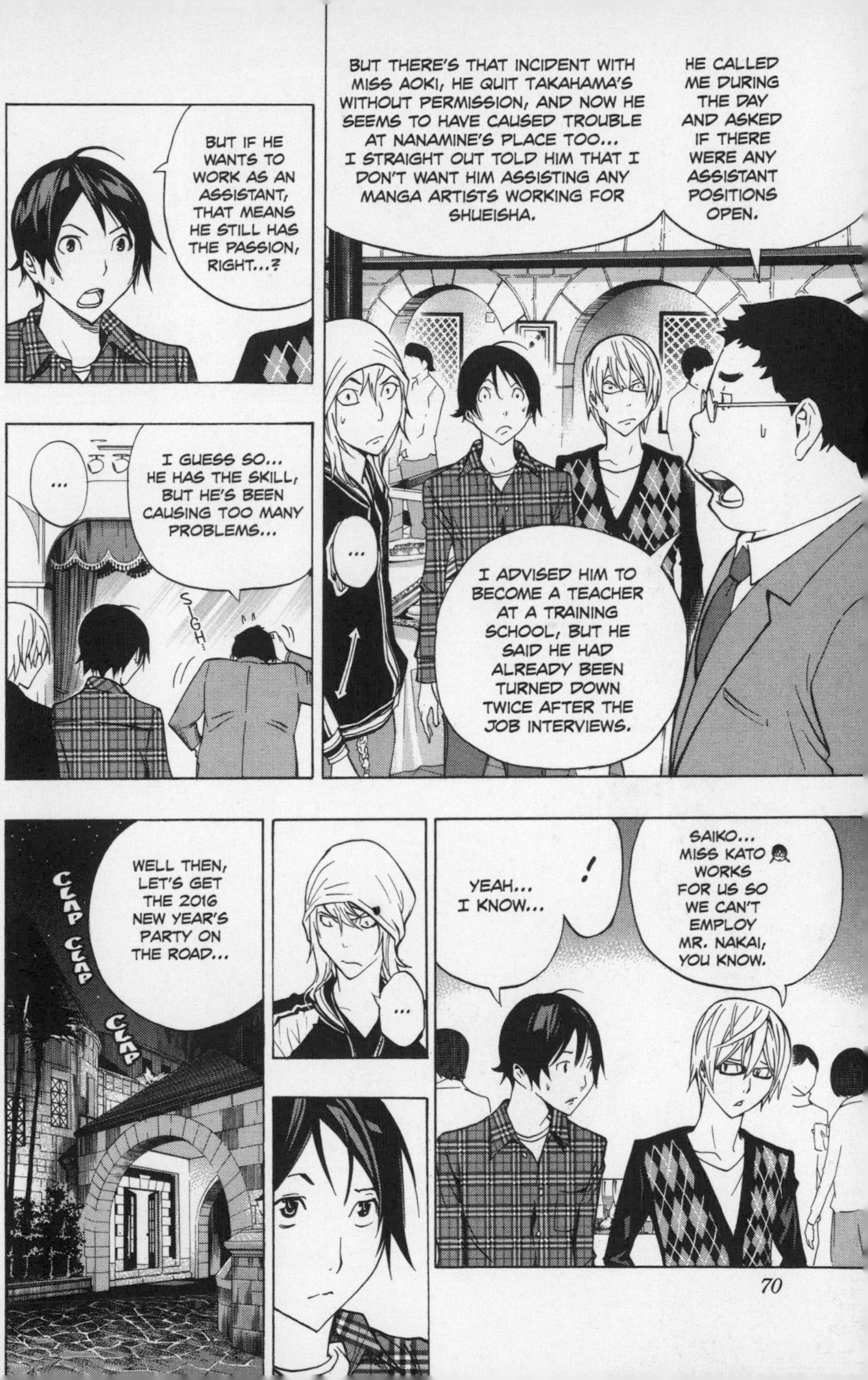
HE CALLED ME DURING THE DAY AND ASKED IF THERE WERE ANY ASSISTANT POSITIONS OPEN.
BUT THERE'S THAT INCIDENT WITH MISS AOKI, HE QUIT TAKAHAMA'S WITHOUT PERMISSION, AND NOW HE SEEMS TO HAVE CAUSED TROUBLE AT NANAMINE'S PLACE TOO... I STRAIGHT OUT TOLD HIM THAT I DON'T WANT HIM ASSISTING ANY MANGA ARTISTS WORKING FOR SHUEISHA.
I ADVISED HIM TO BECOME A TEACHER AT A TRAINING SCHOOL, BUT HE SAID HE HAD ALREADY BEEN TURNED DOWN TWICE AFTER THE JOB INTERVIEWS.
...
BUT IF HE WANTS TO WORK AS AN ASSISTANT, THAT MEANS HE STILL HAS THE PASSION, RIGHT...?
I GUESS SO... HE HAS THE SKILL, BUT HE'S BEEN CAUSING TOO MANY PROBLEMS...
...
SIGH...
SAIKO... MISS KATO WORKS FOR US SO WE CAN'T EMPLOY MR. NAKAI, YOU KNOW.
!
YEAH... I KNOW...
...
WELL THEN, LET'S GET THE 2016 NEW YEAR'S PARTY ON THE ROAD...
CLAP
CLAP
CLAP

READ THIS WAY

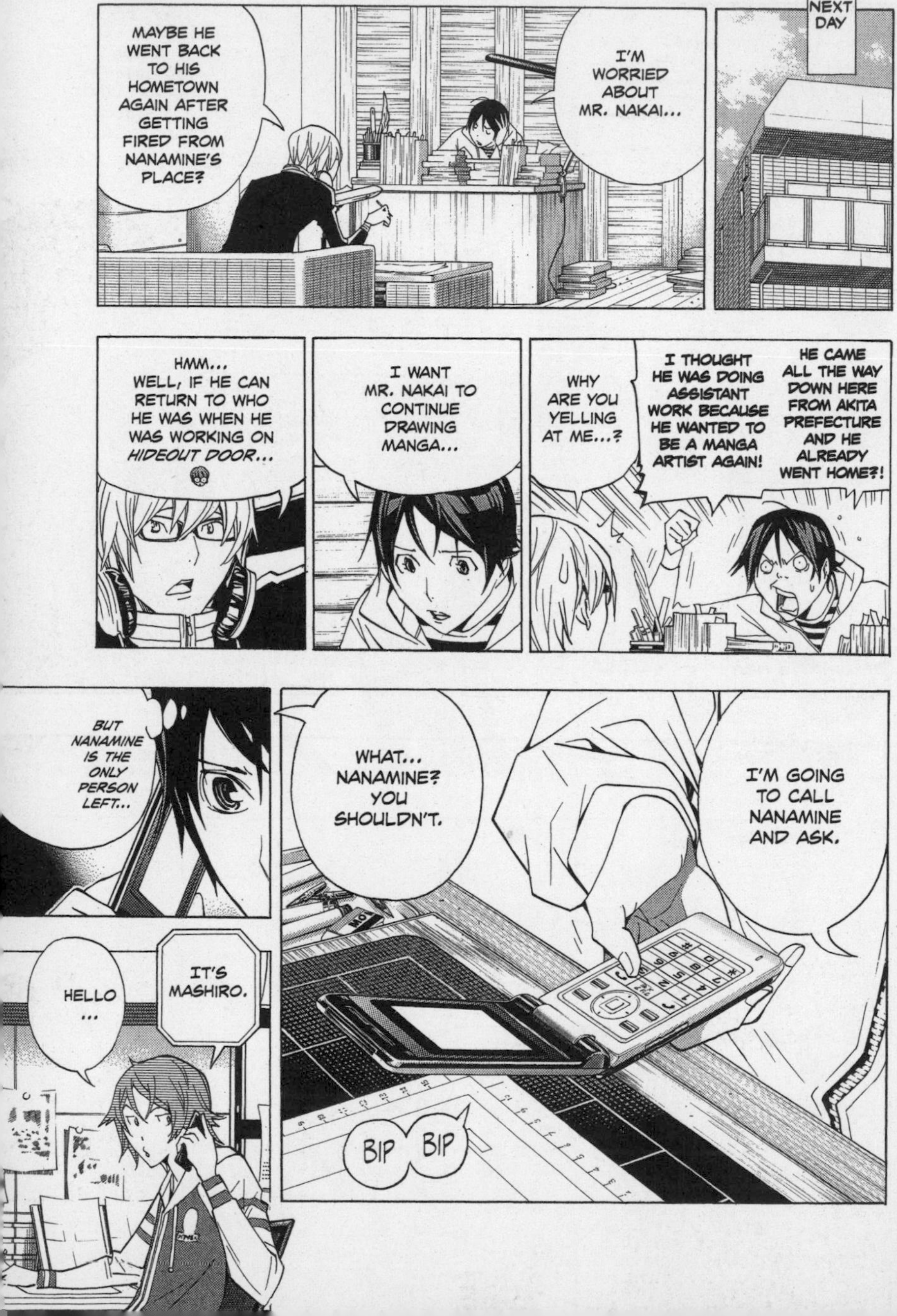
THE NEXT DAY
I'M WORRIED ABOUT MR. NAKAI...
MAYBE HE WENT BACK TO HIS HOMETOWN AGAIN AFTER GETTING FIRED FROM NANAMINE'S PLACE?
HE CAME ALL THE WAY DOWN HERE FROM AKITA PREFECTURE AND HE ALREADY WENT HOME?!
I THOUGHT HE WAS DOING ASSISTANT WORK BECAUSE HE WANTED TO BE A MANGA ARTIST AGAIN!
WHY ARE YOU YELLING AT ME...?
I WANT MR. NAKAI TO CONTINUE DRAWING MANGA...
HMM... WELL, IF HE CAN RETURN TO WHO HE WAS WHEN HE WAS WORKING ON *HIDEOUT DOOR*...
I'M GOING TO CALL NANAMINE AND ASK.
WHAT... NANAMINE? YOU SHOULDN'T.
BIP BIP
BUT NANAMINE IS THE ONLY PERSON LEFT...
IT'S MASHIRO.
HELLO ...

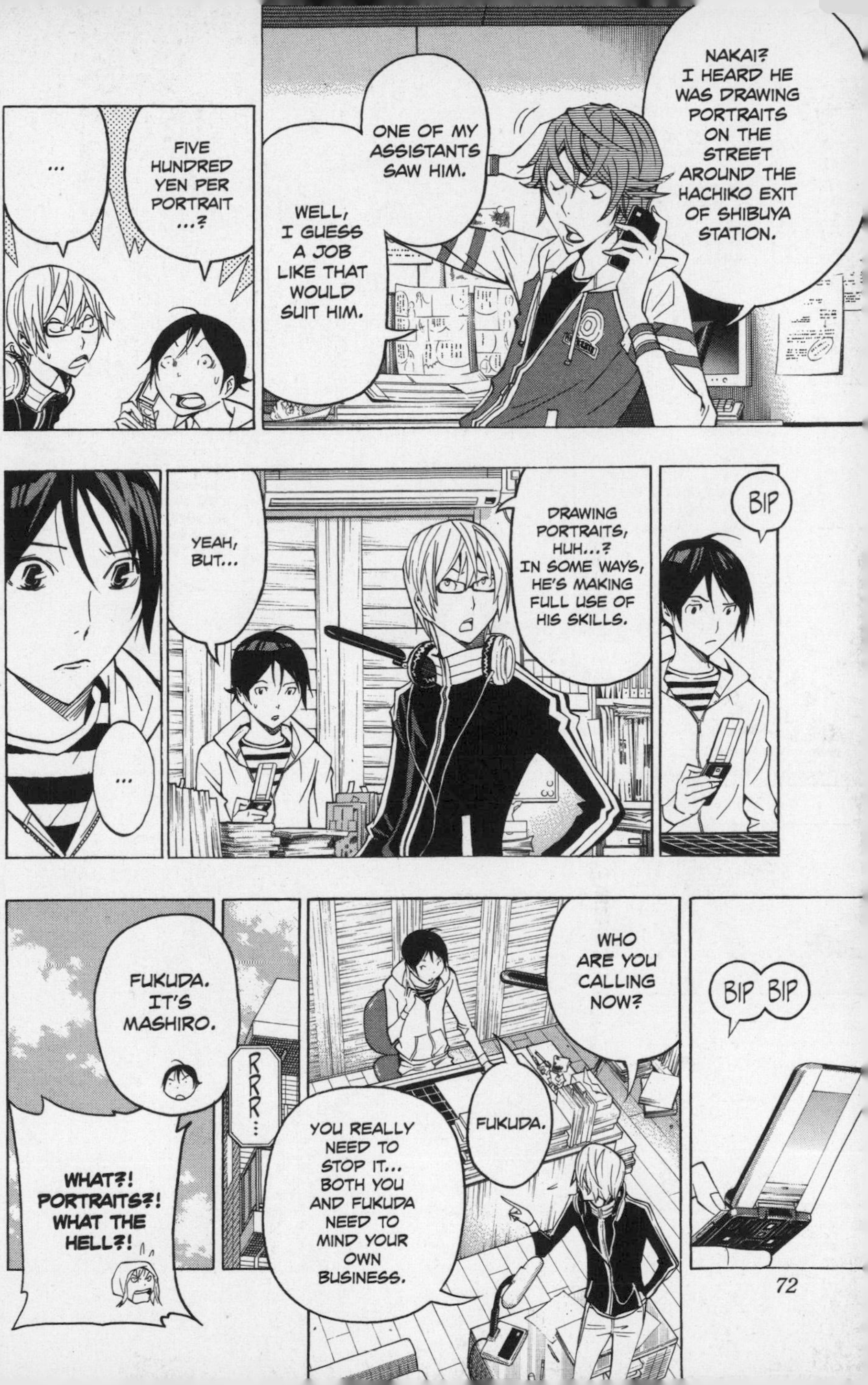
NAKAI? I HEARD HE WAS DRAWING PORTRAITS ON THE STREET AROUND THE HACHIKO EXIT OF SHIBUYA STATION.
ONE OF MY ASSISTANTS SAW HIM.
WELL, I GUESS A JOB LIKE THAT WOULD SUIT HIM.
FIVE HUNDRED YEN PER PORTRAIT ...?
...
BIP
DRAWING PORTRAITS, HUH...? IN SOME WAYS, HE'S MAKING FULL USE OF HIS SKILLS.
YEAH, BUT...
...
BIP BIP
WHO ARE YOU CALLING NOW?
FUKUDA.
YOU REALLY NEED TO STOP IT... BOTH YOU AND FUKUDA NEED TO MIND YOUR OWN BUSINESS.
FUKUDA. IT'S MASHIRO.
RRR...
WHAT?! PORTRAITS?! WHAT THE HELL?!

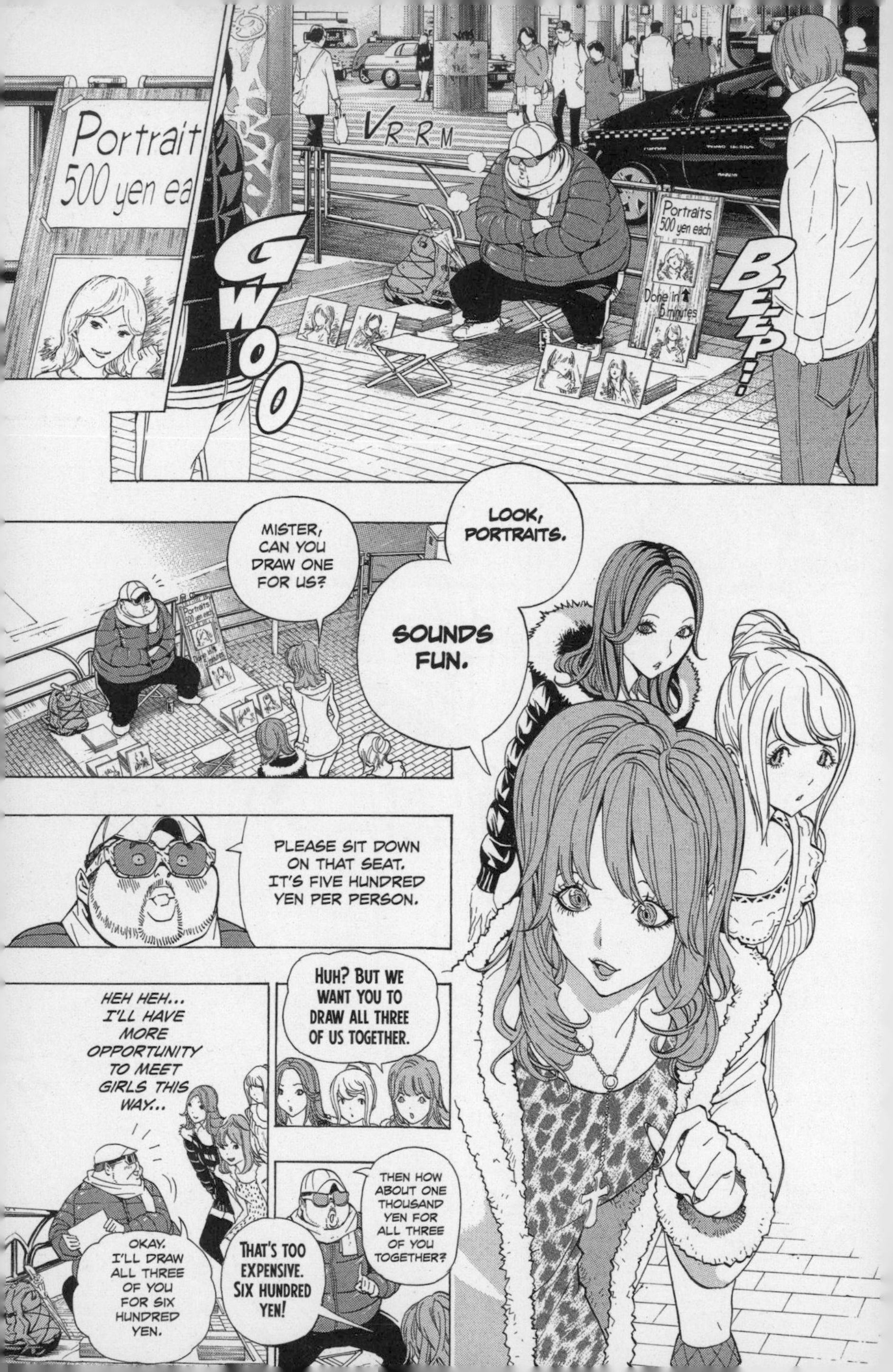
BEEP!!
Portraits
500 yen each
Done in
5 minutes
VRRM
GWOO
Portrait
500 yen ea
LOOK, PORTRAITS.
SOUNDS FUN.
MISTER, CAN YOU DRAW ONE FOR US?
PLEASE SIT DOWN ON THAT SEAT. IT'S FIVE HUNDRED YEN PER PERSON.
HUH? BUT WE WANT YOU TO DRAW ALL THREE OF US TOGETHER.
HEH HEH... I'LL HAVE MORE OPPORTUNITY TO MEET GIRLS THIS WAY...
THEN HOW ABOUT ONE THOUSAND YEN FOR ALL THREE OF YOU TOGETHER?
THAT'S TOO EXPENSIVE. SIX HUNDRED YEN!
OKAY. I'LL DRAW ALL THREE OF YOU FOR SIX HUNDRED YEN.

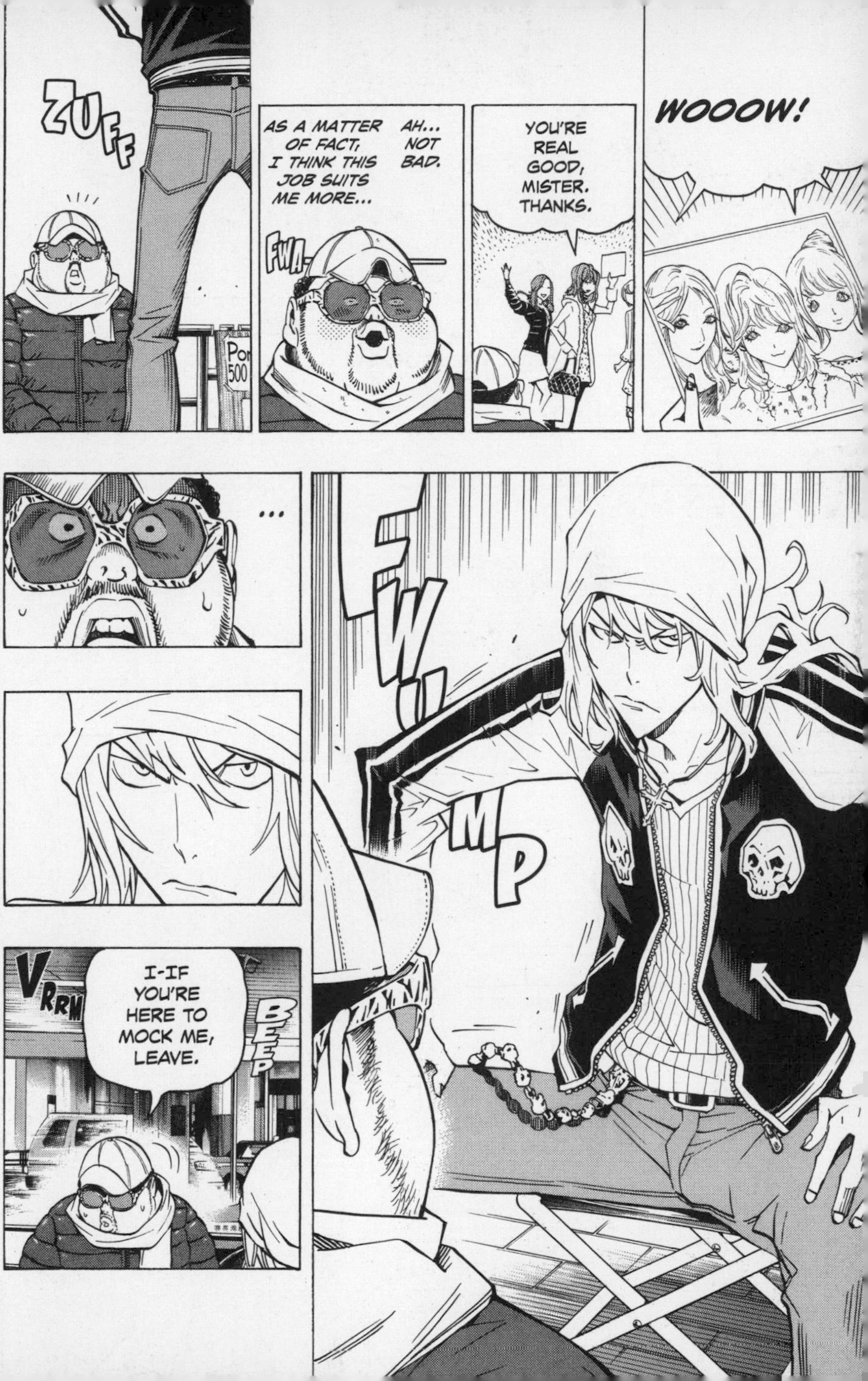
WOOOW!
YOU'RE REAL GOOD, MISTER. THANKS.
AH... NOT BAD.
AS A MATTER OF FACT, I THINK THIS JOB SUITS ME MORE...
FWA
ZUFF
FWUMP
...
I-IF YOU'RE HERE TO MOCK ME, LEAVE.
BEEP
VRRM

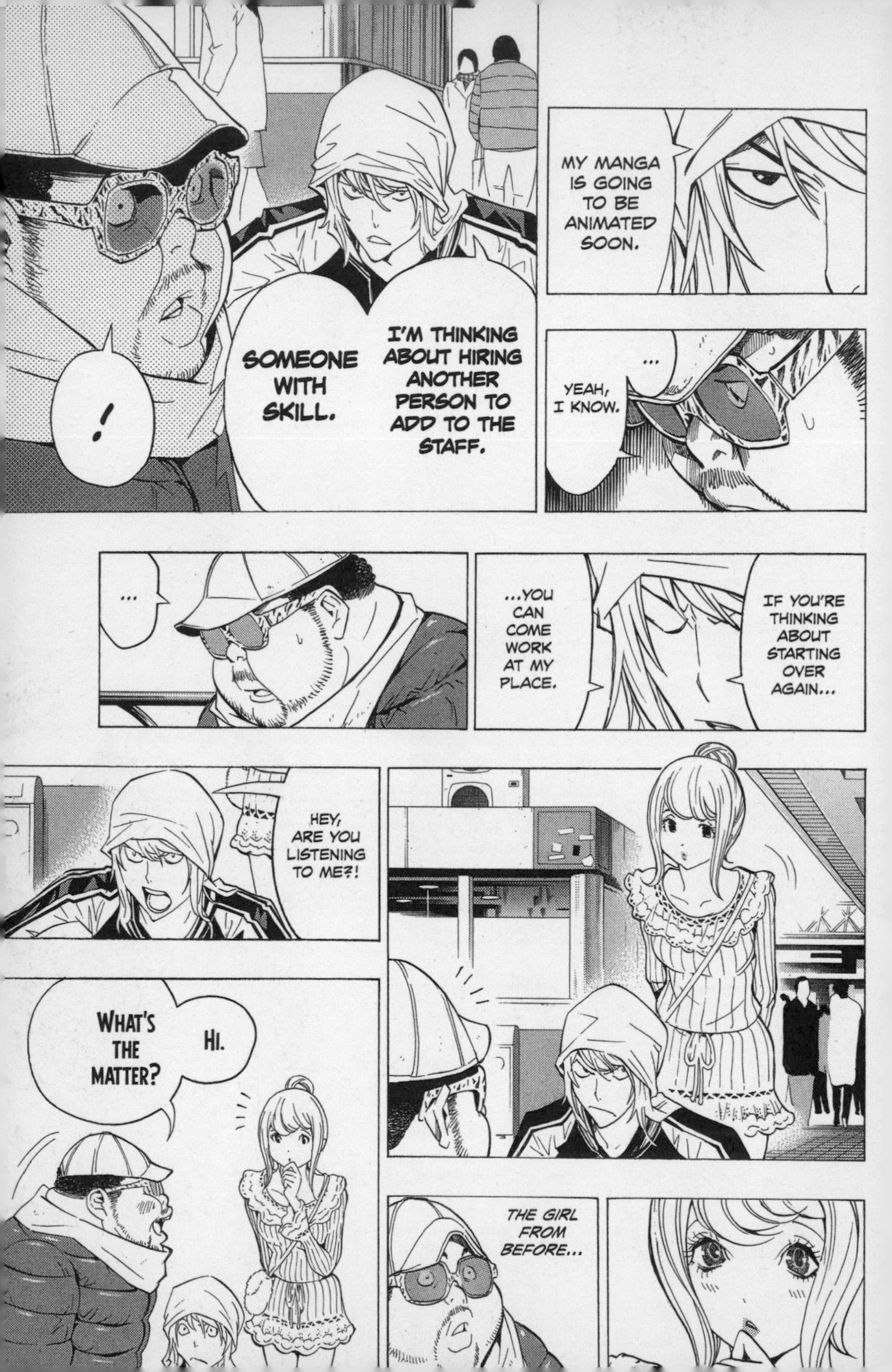
MY MANGA IS GOING TO BE ANIMATED SOON.
...
YEAH, I KNOW.
I'M THINKING ABOUT HIRING ANOTHER PERSON TO ADD TO THE STAFF.
SOMEONE WITH SKILL.
!
IF YOU'RE THINKING ABOUT STARTING OVER AGAIN...
...YOU CAN COME WORK AT MY PLACE.
...
HEY, ARE YOU LISTENING TO ME?!
HI.
WHAT'S THE MATTER?
THE GIRL FROM BEFORE...

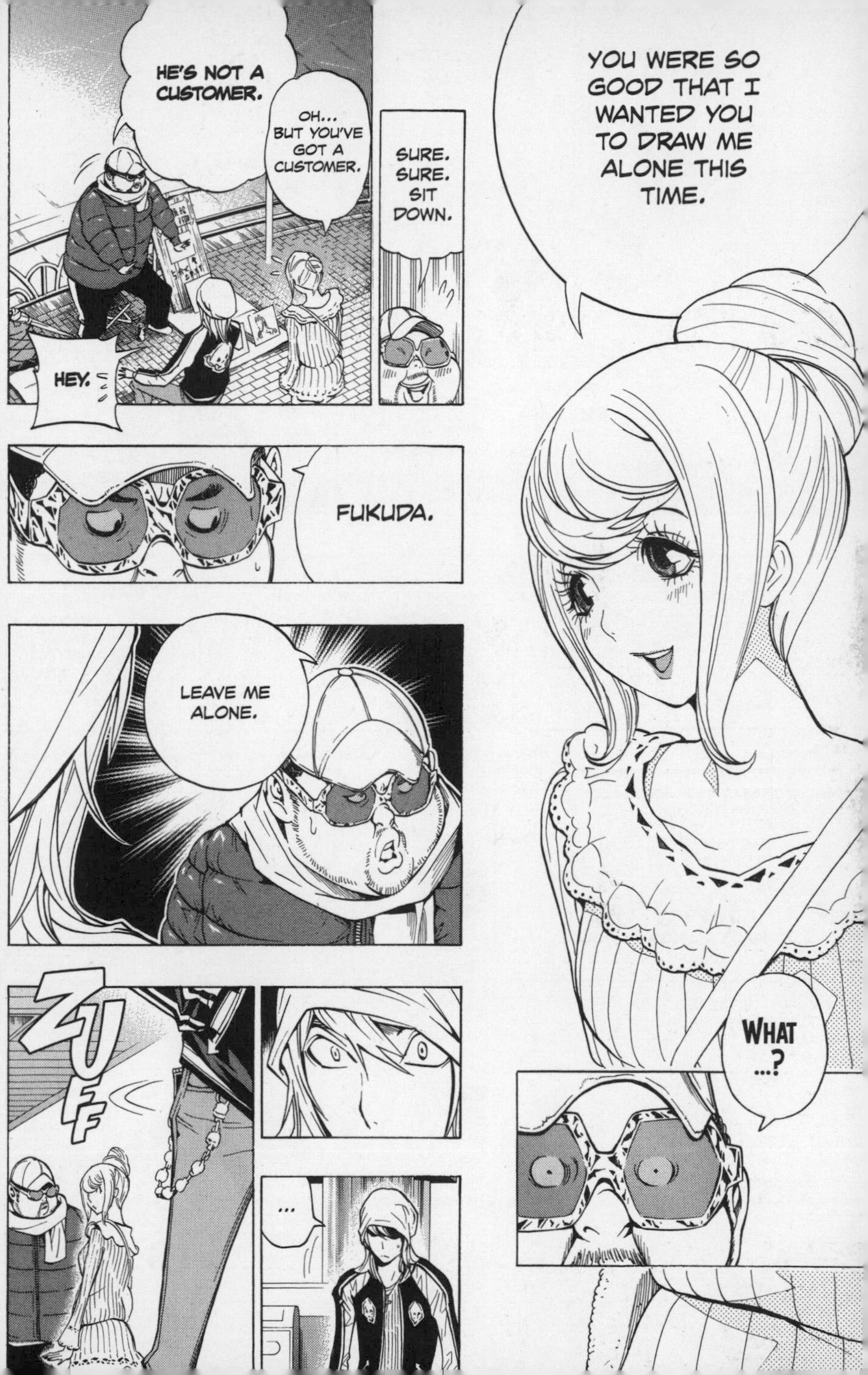
YOU WERE SO GOOD THAT I WANTED YOU TO DRAW ME ALONE THIS TIME.
WHAT ...?
SURE. SURE. SIT DOWN.
OH... BUT YOU'VE GOT A CUSTOMER.
HE'S NOT A CUSTOMER.
HEY.
FUKUDA.
LEAVE ME ALONE.
ZUFF
...

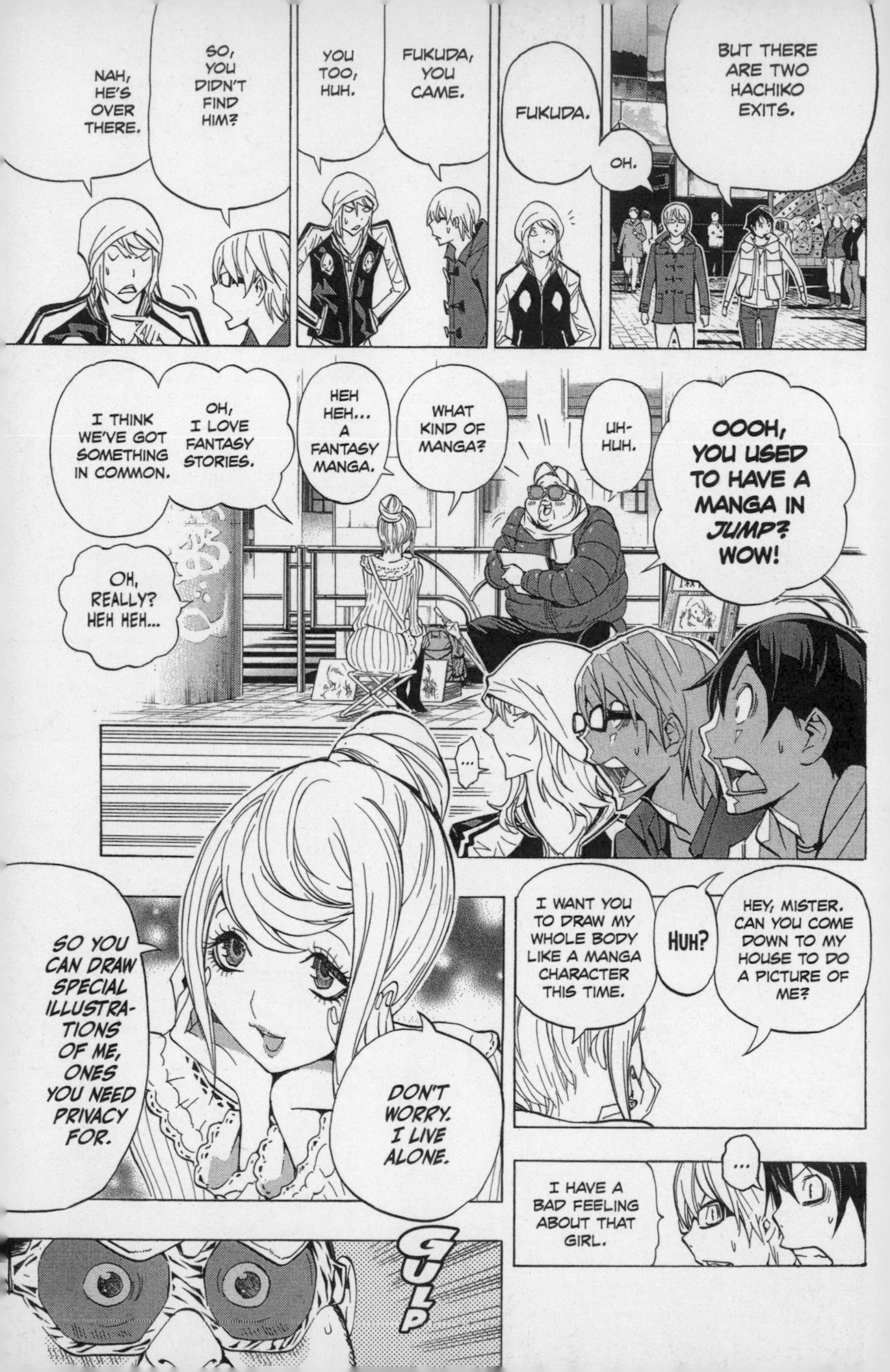
BUT THERE ARE TWO HACHIKO EXITS.
FUKUDA.
OH.
FUKUDA, YOU CAME.
YOU TOO, HUH.
SO, YOU DIDN'T FIND HIM?
NAH, HE'S OVER THERE.
OOOH, YOU USED TO HAVE A MANGA IN *JUMP*? WOW!
UH-HUH.
WHAT KIND OF MANGA?
HEH HEH... A FANTASY MANGA.
OH, I LOVE FANTASY STORIES.
I THINK WE'VE GOT SOMETHING IN COMMON.
OH, REALLY? HEH HEH...
...
HEY, MISTER. CAN YOU COME DOWN TO MY HOUSE TO DO A PICTURE OF ME?
HUH?
I WANT YOU TO DRAW MY WHOLE BODY LIKE A MANGA CHARACTER THIS TIME.
...
I HAVE A BAD FEELING ABOUT THAT GIRL.
SO YOU CAN DRAW SPECIAL ILLUSTRATIONS OF ME, ONES YOU NEED PRIVACY FOR.
DON'T WORRY. I LIVE ALONE.
GULP

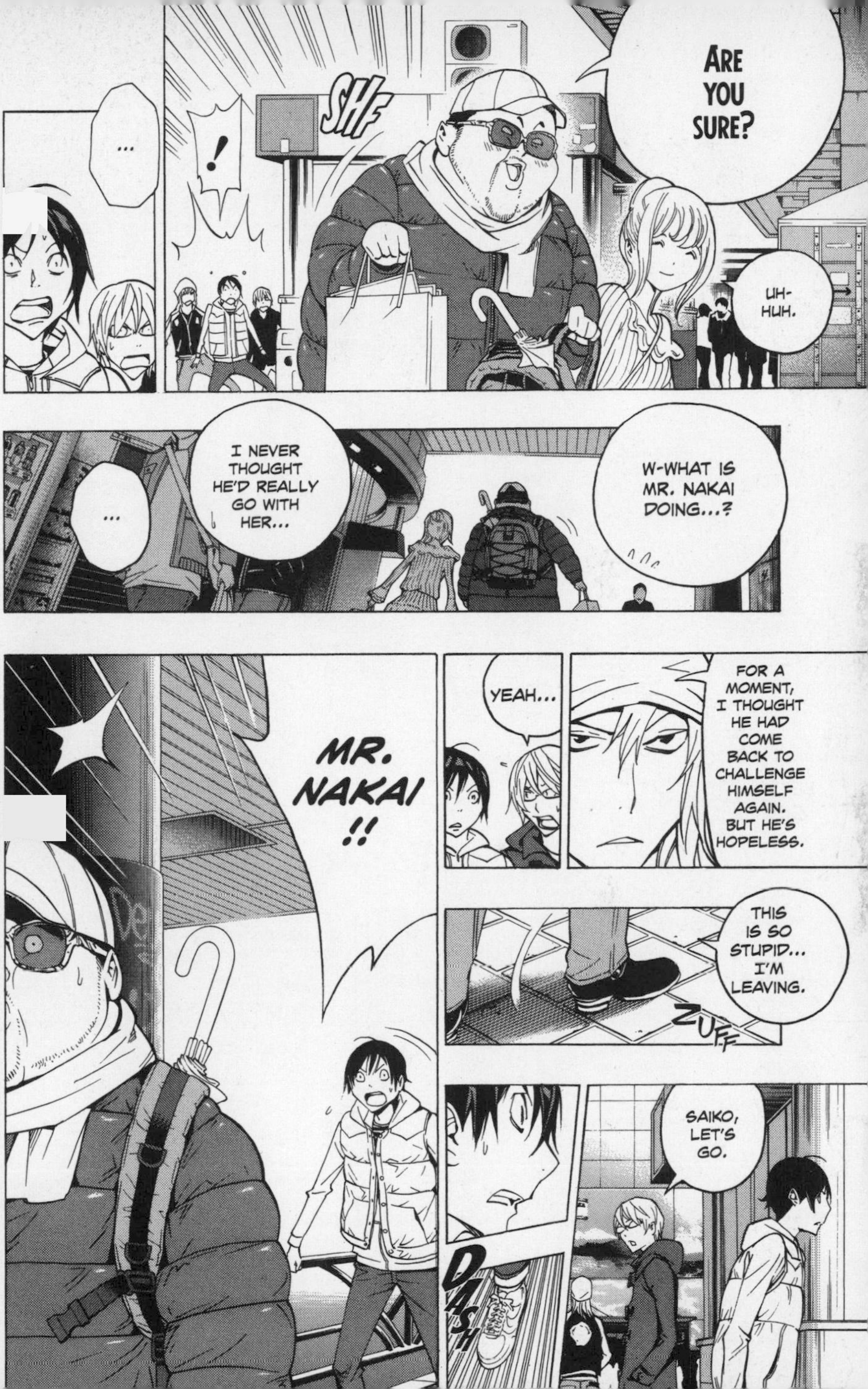
ARE YOU SURE?
SHF
UH-HUH.
!
...
W-WHAT IS MR. NAKAI DOING...?
I NEVER THOUGHT HE'D REALLY GO WITH HER...
...
FOR A MOMENT, I THOUGHT HE HAD COME BACK TO CHALLENGE HIMSELF AGAIN. BUT HE'S HOPELESS.
YEAH...
THIS IS SO STUPID... I'M LEAVING.
ZUFF
SAIKO, LET'S GO.
DASH
MR. NAKAI !!

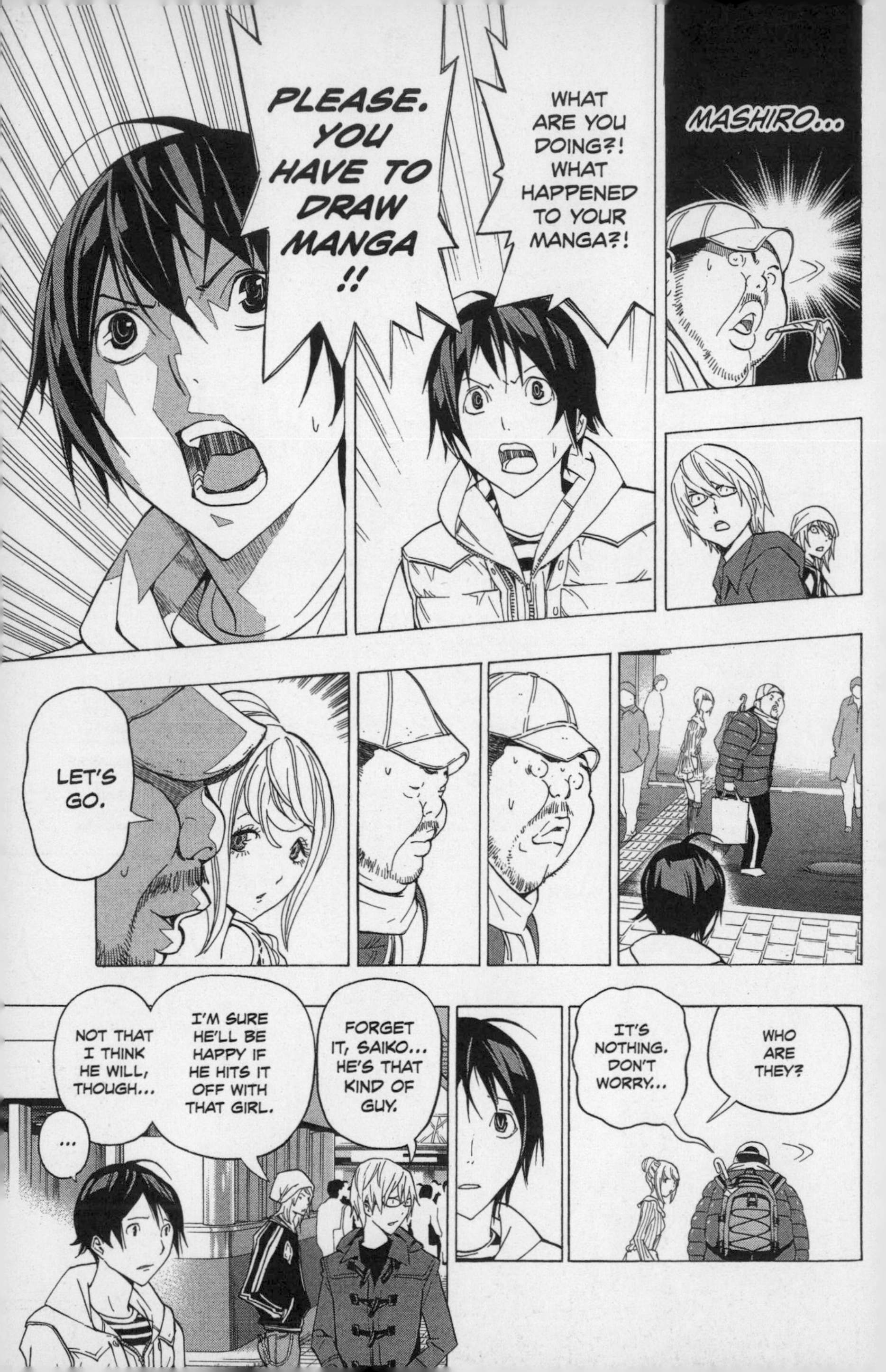
MASHIRO...
WHAT ARE YOU DOING?! WHAT HAPPENED TO YOUR MANGA?!
PLEASE. YOU HAVE TO DRAW MANGA!!
LET'S GO.
WHO ARE THEY?
IT'S NOTHING. DON'T WORRY...
FORGET IT, SAIKO... HE'S THAT KIND OF GUY.
I'M SURE HE'LL BE HAPPY IF HE HITS IT OFF WITH THAT GIRL.
NOT THAT I THINK HE WILL, THOUGH...
...

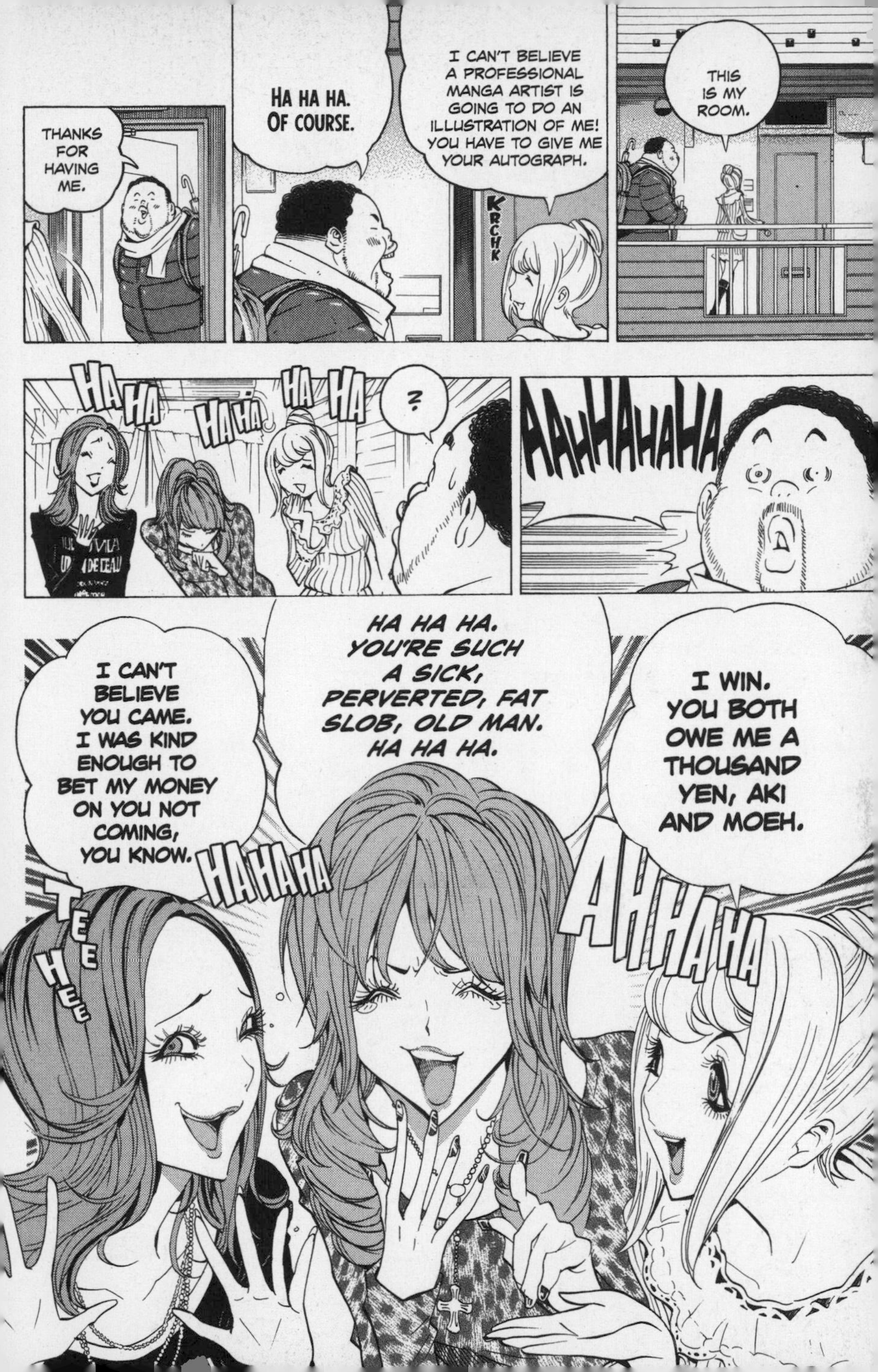
THIS IS MY ROOM.
I CAN'T BELIEVE A PROFESSIONAL MANGA ARTIST IS GOING TO DO AN ILLUSTRATION OF ME! YOU HAVE TO GIVE ME YOUR AUTOGRAPH.
KRCHK
HA HA HA. OF COURSE.
THANKS FOR HAVING ME.
AAHHAHAHAHA
?
HA HA
HA HA
HA HA
I WIN. YOU BOTH OWE ME A THOUSAND YEN, AKI AND MOEH.
AHHAHAHA
HA HA HA. YOU'RE SUCH A SICK, PERVERTED, FAT SLOB, OLD MAN. HA HA HA.
HAHAHA
I CAN'T BELIEVE YOU CAME. I WAS KIND ENOUGH TO BET MY MONEY ON YOU NOT COMING, YOU KNOW.
TEE HEE

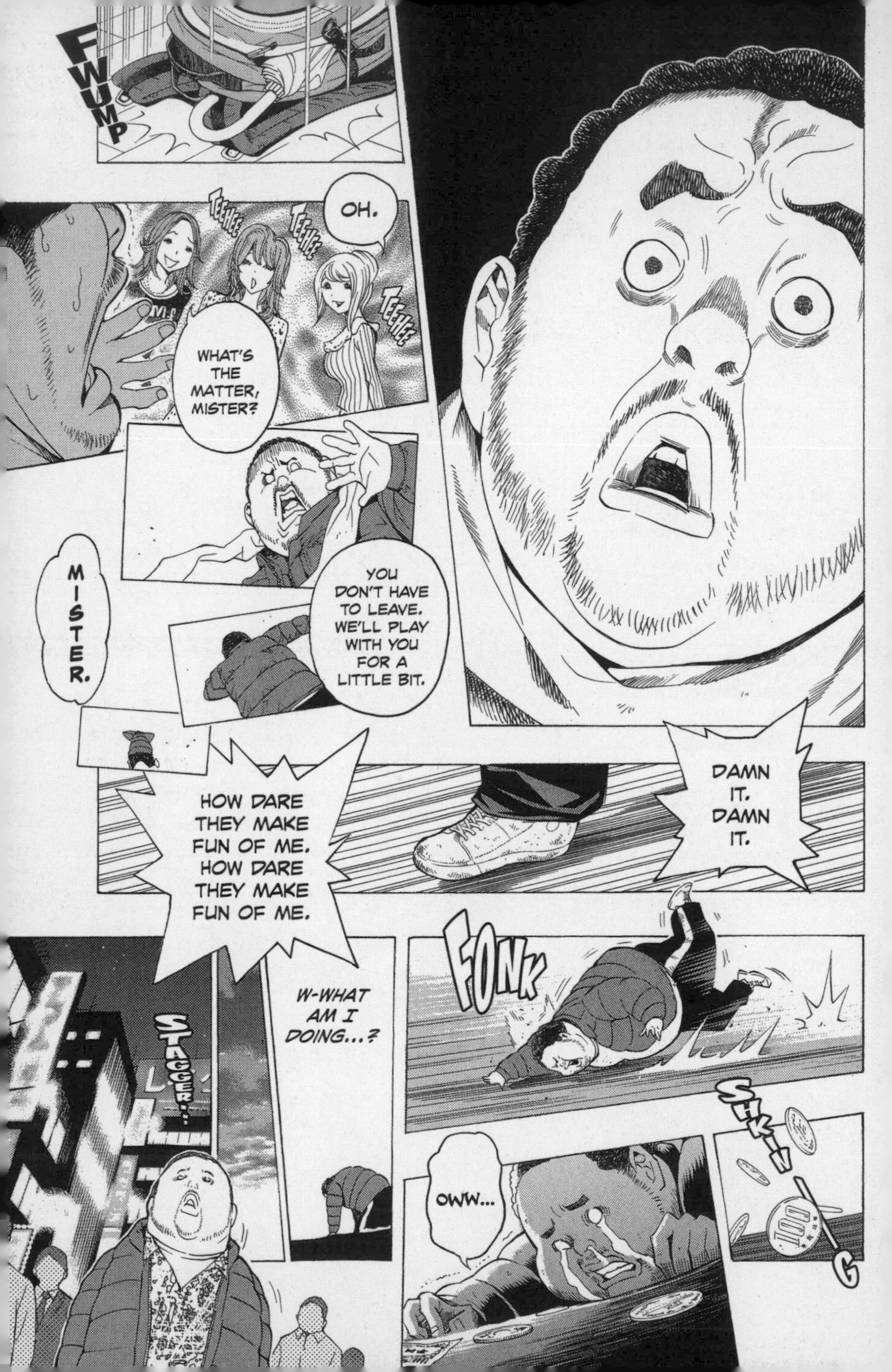
FWUMP
OH.
TEEHEE
TEEHEE
TEEHEE
WHAT'S THE MATTER, MISTER?
MISTER.
YOU DON'T HAVE TO LEAVE. WE'LL PLAY WITH YOU FOR A LITTLE BIT.
DAMN IT. DAMN IT.
HOW DARE THEY MAKE FUN OF ME. HOW DARE THEY MAKE FUN OF ME.
FONK
SHKING
OWW...
W-WHAT AM I DOING...?
STAGGER...

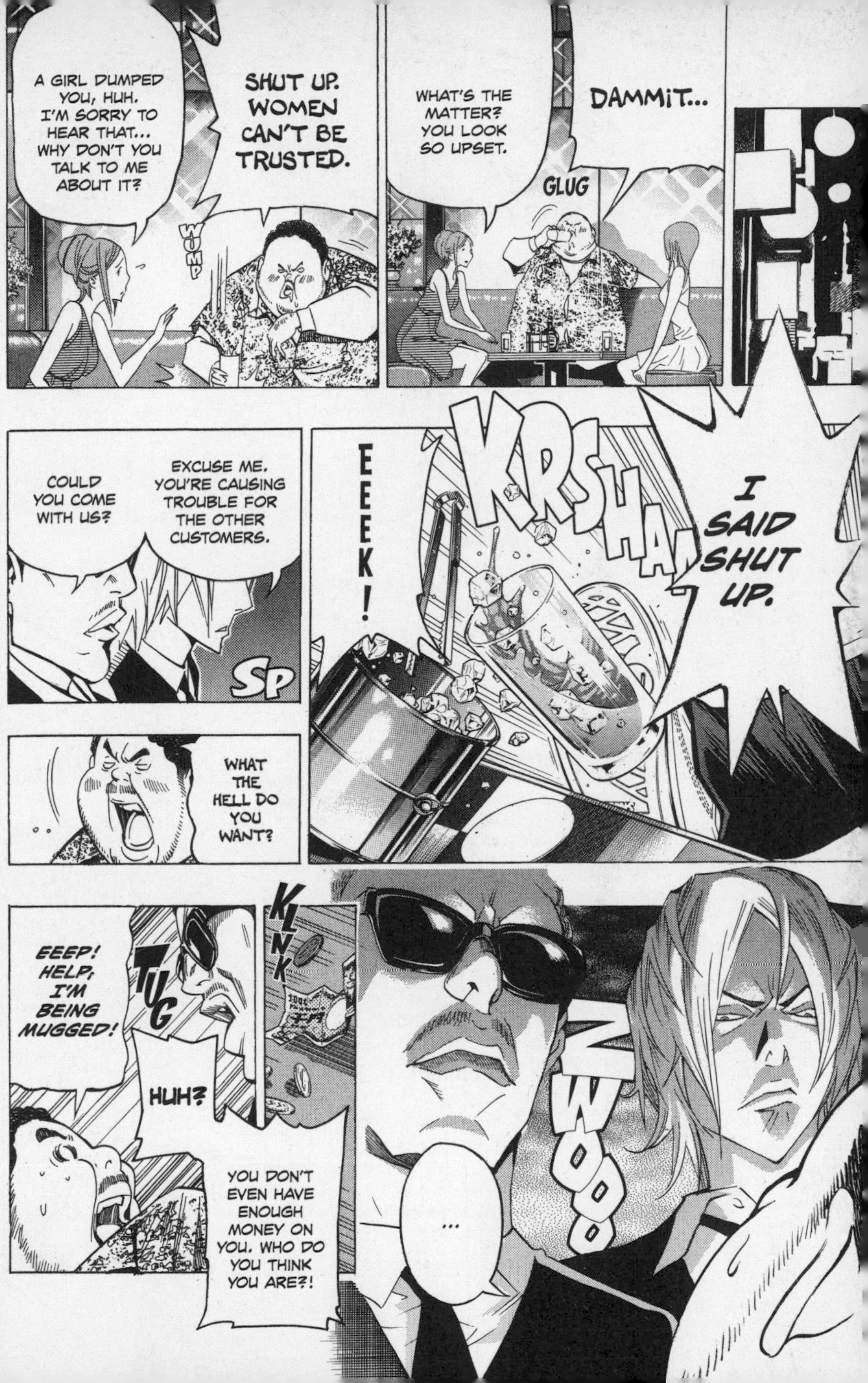
DAMMIT...
WHAT'S THE MATTER? YOU LOOK SO UPSET.
GLUG
SHUT UP. WOMEN CAN'T BE TRUSTED.
A GIRL DUMPED YOU, HUH. I'M SORRY TO HEAR THAT... WHY DON'T YOU TALK TO ME ABOUT IT?
WUMP
I SAID SHUT UP.
KRSHAN
EEEK!
EXCUSE ME. YOU'RE CAUSING TROUBLE FOR THE OTHER CUSTOMERS.
COULD YOU COME WITH US?
SP
WHAT THE HELL DO YOU WANT?
ZWOOO
...
KLINK
TUG
EEEP! HELP, I'M BEING MUGGED!
HUH?
YOU DON'T EVEN HAVE ENOUGH MONEY ON YOU. WHO DO YOU THINK YOU ARE?!

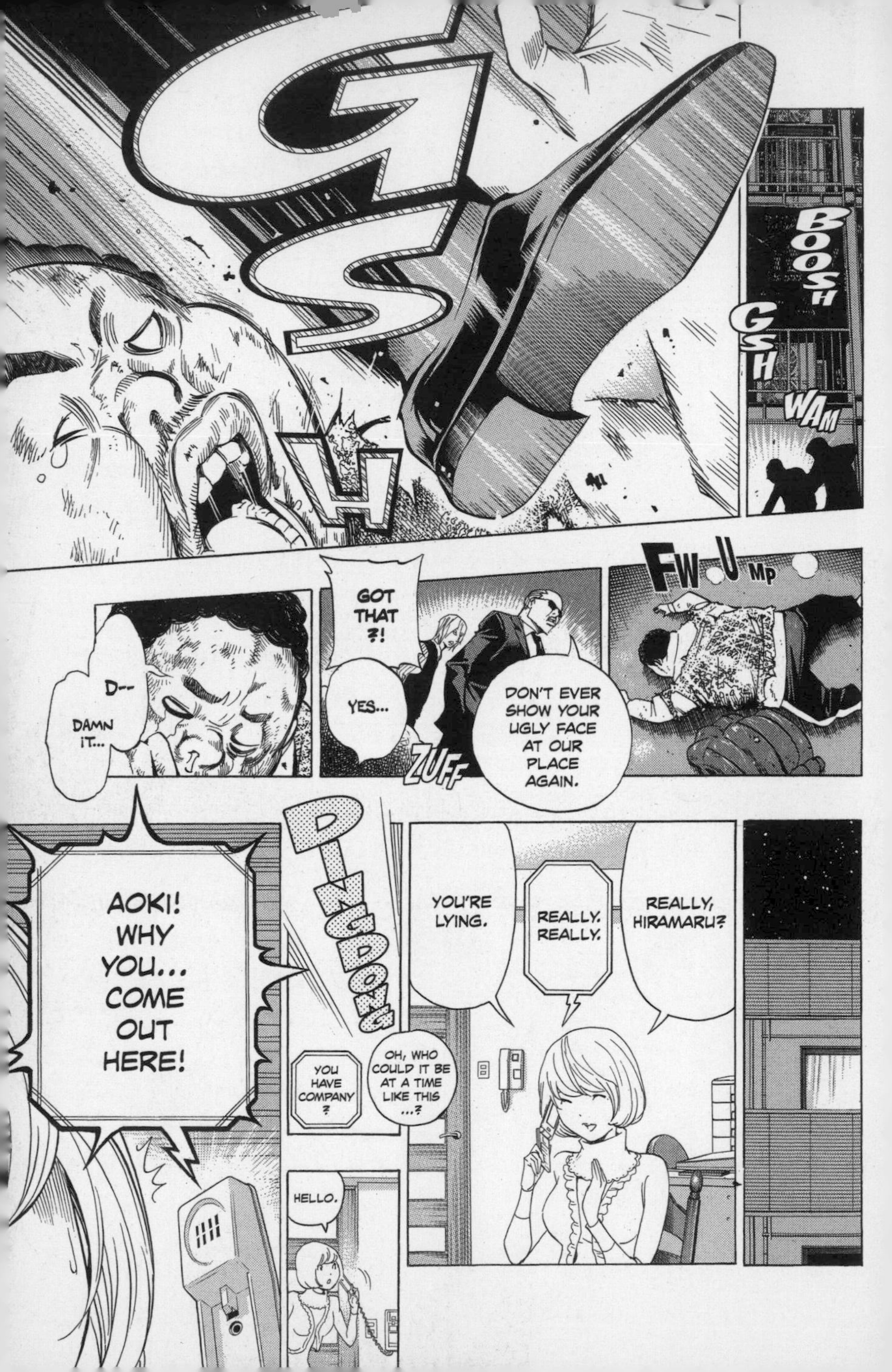
BOOSH
GSH
WAM
GSH!
FWUMP
DON'T EVER SHOW YOUR UGLY FACE AT OUR PLACE AGAIN.
GOT THAT?!
YES...
ZUFF
D--
DAMN IT...
REALLY, HIRAMARU?
REALLY. REALLY.
YOU'RE LYING.
DINGDONG
OH, WHO COULD IT BE AT A TIME LIKE THIS...?
YOU HAVE COMPANY?
HELLO.
AOKI! WHY YOU... COME OUT HERE!

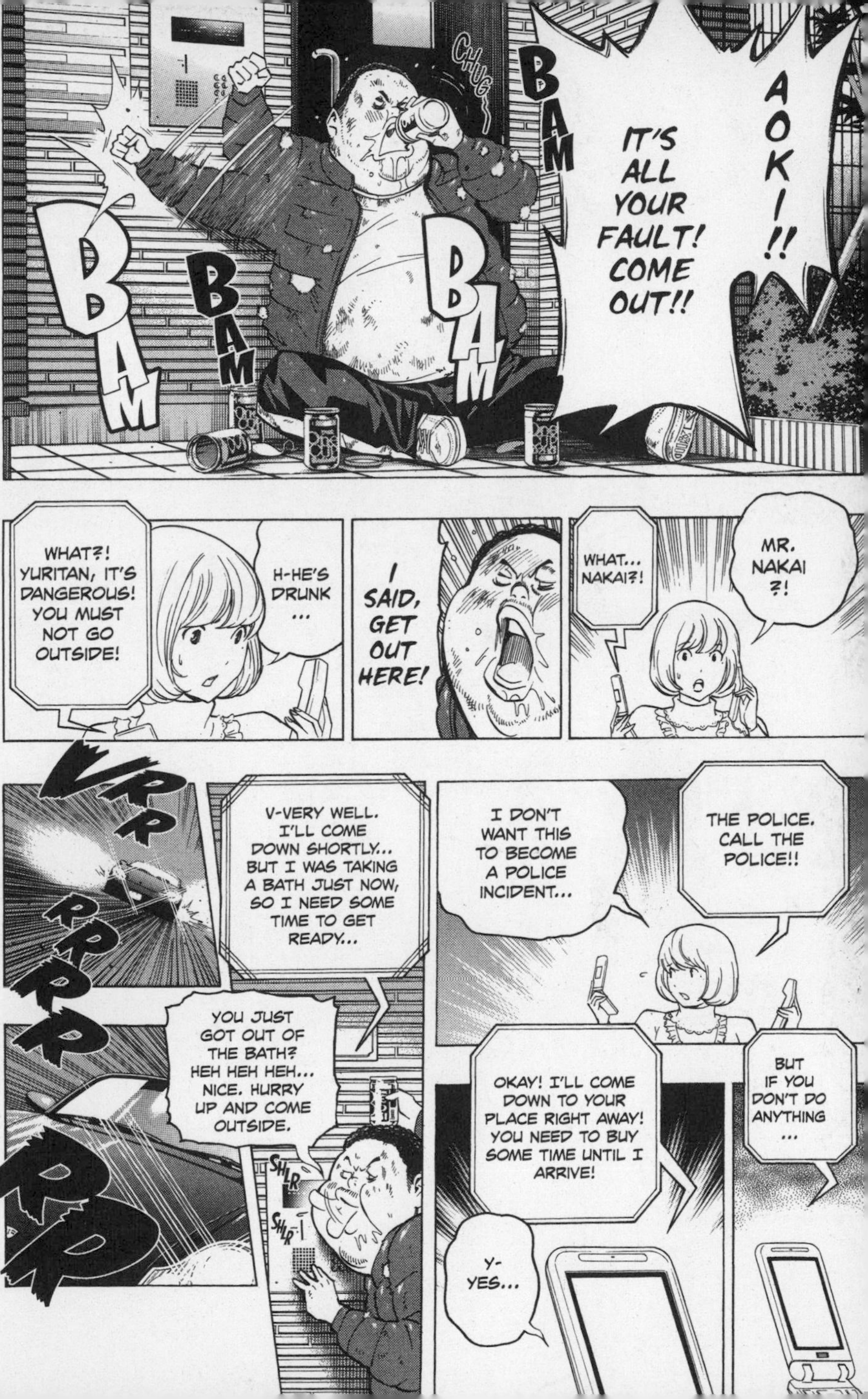
AOKI!!
IT'S ALL YOUR FAULT! COME OUT!!
BAM
CHUG~
BAM
BAM
BAM
MR. NAKAI?!
WHAT... NAKAI?!
I SAID, GET OUT HERE!
H-HE'S DRUNK...
WHAT?! YURITAN, IT'S DANGEROUS! YOU MUST NOT GO OUTSIDE!
THE POLICE. CALL THE POLICE!!
I DON'T WANT THIS TO BECOME A POLICE INCIDENT...
BUT IF YOU DON'T DO ANYTHING...
OKAY! I'LL COME DOWN TO YOUR PLACE RIGHT AWAY! YOU NEED TO BUY SOME TIME UNTIL I ARRIVE!
Y-YES...
V-VERY WELL. I'LL COME DOWN SHORTLY... BUT I WAS TAKING A BATH JUST NOW, SO I NEED SOME TIME TO GET READY...
VRRRRRRR
YOU JUST GOT OUT OF THE BATH? HEH HEH HEH... NICE. HURRY UP AND COME OUTSIDE.
SHLR
SHLR

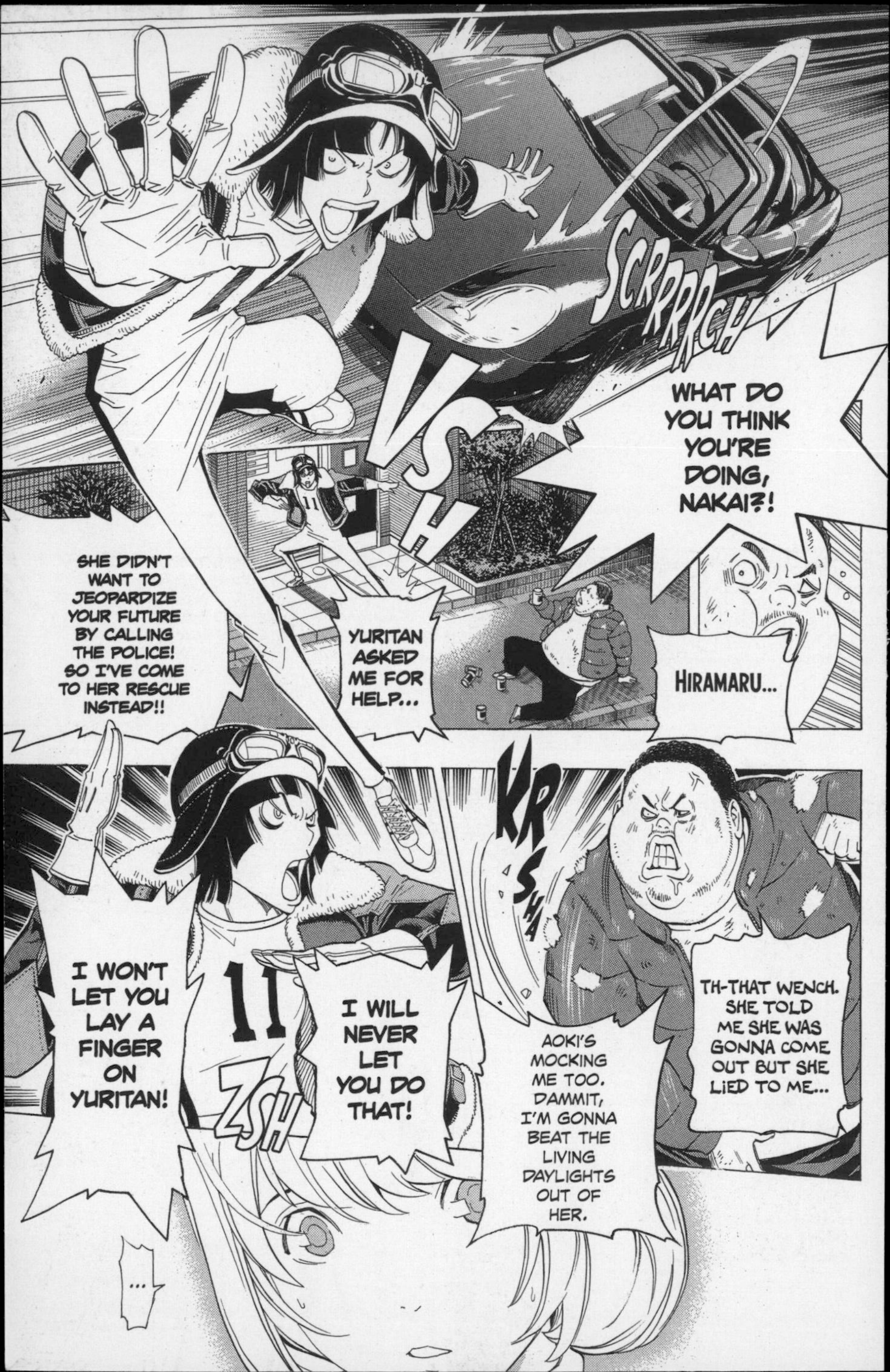
SCRRRCH
VSH
WHAT DO YOU THINK YOU'RE DOING, NAKAI?!
HIRAMARU...
YURITAN ASKED ME FOR HELP...
SHE DIDN'T WANT TO JEOPARDIZE YOUR FUTURE BY CALLING THE POLICE! SO I'VE COME TO HER RESCUE INSTEAD!!
KRSHA
TH-THAT WENCH. SHE TOLD ME SHE WAS GONNA COME OUT BUT SHE LIED TO ME...
AOKI'S MOCKING ME TOO. DAMMIT, I'M GONNA BEAT THE LIVING DAYLIGHTS OUT OF HER.
I WILL NEVER LET YOU DO THAT!
I WON'T LET YOU LAY A FINGER ON YURITAN!
ZSH
...

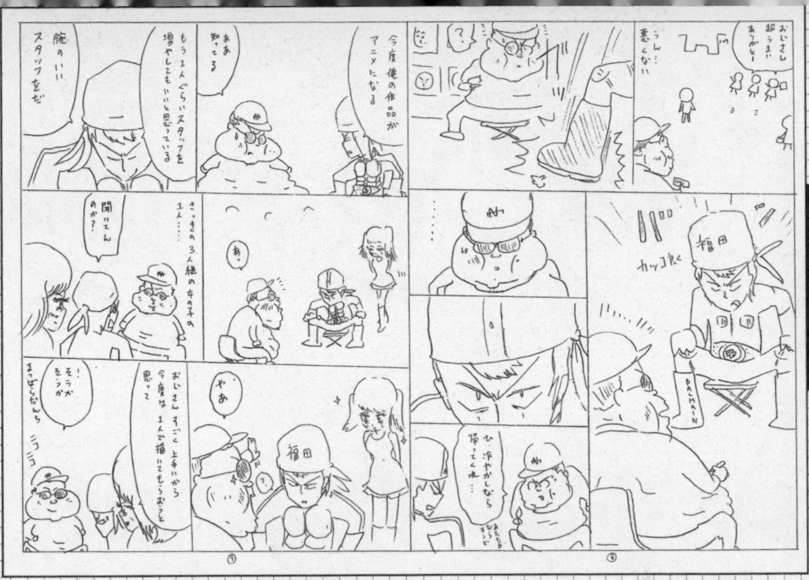
ワッ
おじさん超うまいありがとー
うん…悪くない
今度俺の作品がアニメになる
ああ知ってる
もう2人ぐらいスタッフを増やしてもいいと思っている
腕のいいスタッフをだ
カッコ良く
福田
BALMAIN
聞いてんのか?
あっ
ひ、冷やかしなら帰ってくれ…
おじさん すごく上手いから 今度は2人で描いてもらおうと思って
やあ
!そうかそうか

OHBA'S STORYBOARD

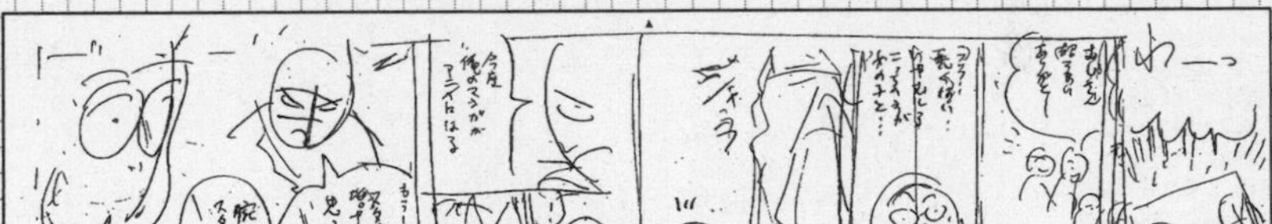

OBATA'S STORYBOARD

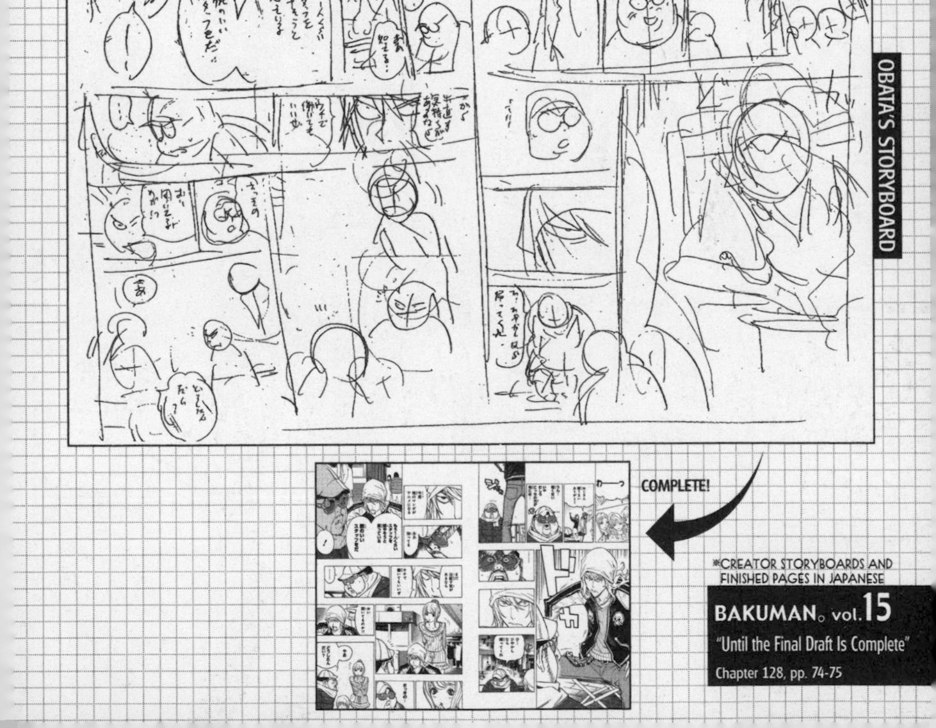

COMPLETE!

※CREATOR STORYBOARDS AND FINISHED PAGES IN JAPANESE

BAKUMAN。 vol.15

"Until the Final Draft Is Complete"

Chapter 128, pp. 74-75

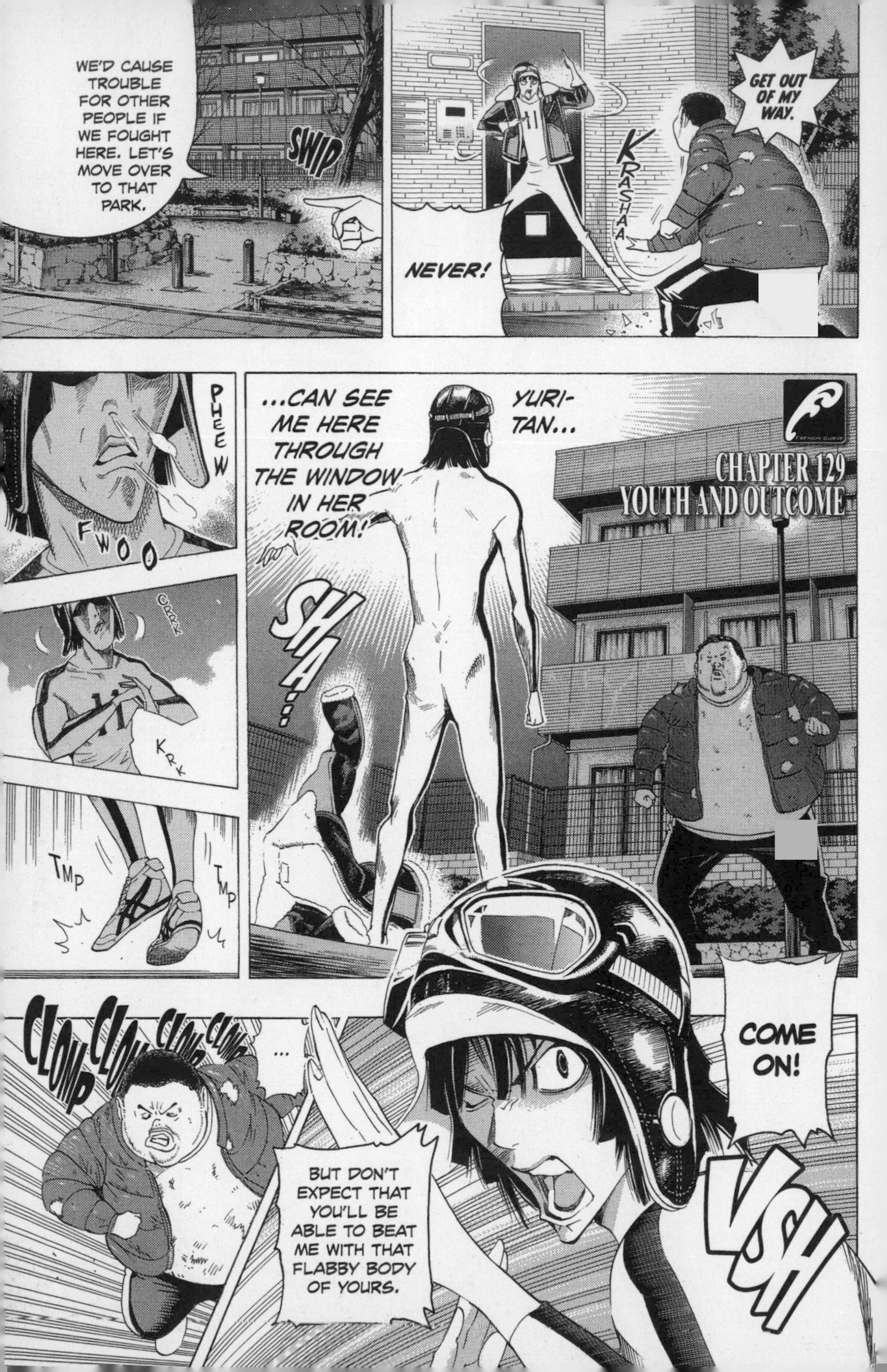

GET OUT OF MY WAY.
KRASHAA
NEVER!
WE'D CAUSE TROUBLE FOR OTHER PEOPLE IF WE FOUGHT HERE. LET'S MOVE OVER TO THAT PARK.
SWIP
CHAPTER 129
YOUTH AND OUTCOME
YURI-TAN...
...CAN SEE ME HERE THROUGH THE WINDOW IN HER ROOM!
SHA...
PHEEW
FWOO
KRK
TMP
TMP
COME ON!
VSH
BUT DON'T EXPECT THAT YOU'LL BE ABLE TO BEAT ME WITH THAT FLABBY BODY OF YOURS.
...
CLOMP CLOMP CLOMP CLOMP

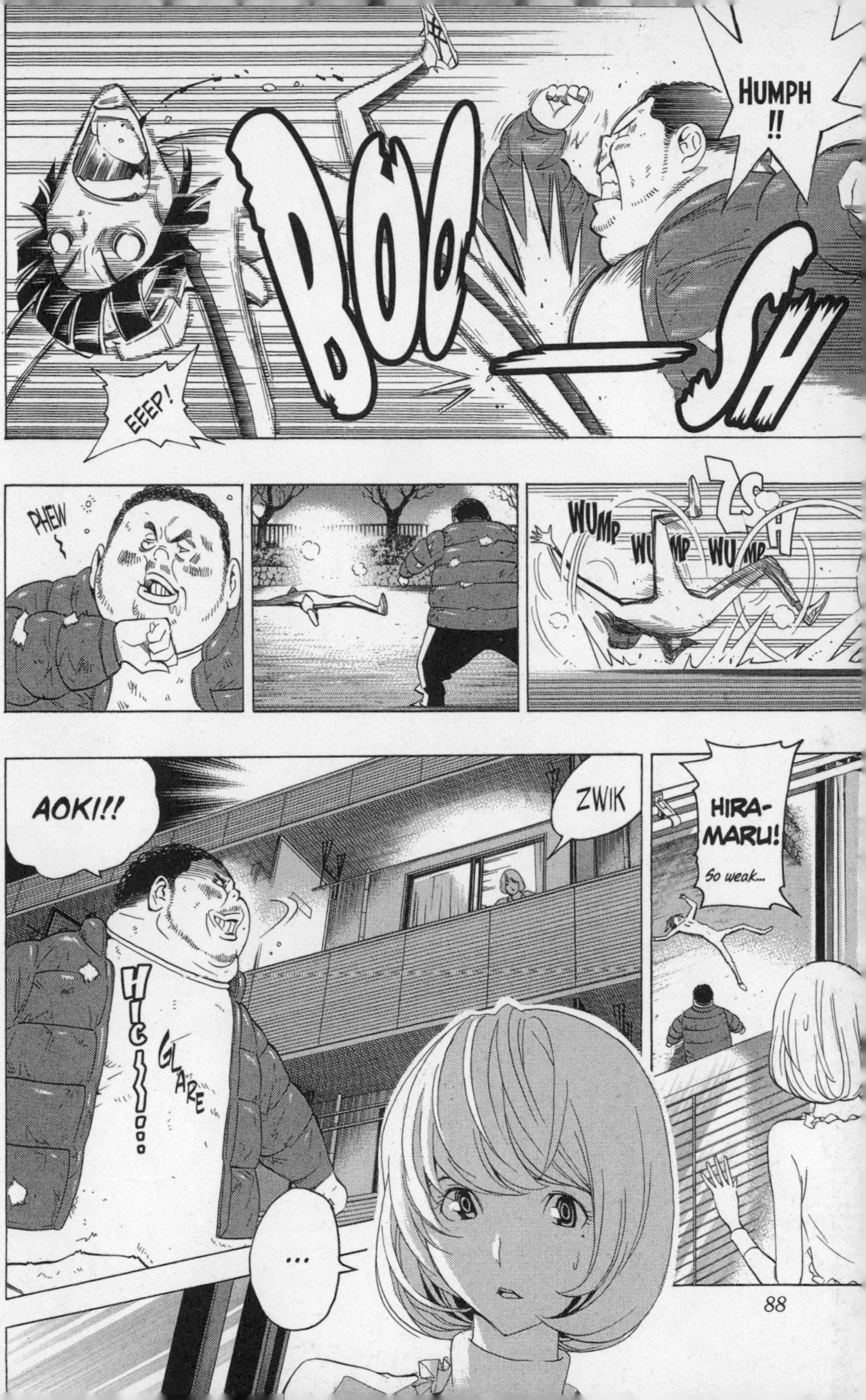
HUMPH !!
BOOSH
EEEP!
ZSH
WUMP WUMP WUMP
PHEW
HIRA-MARU!
So weak...
ZWIK
AOKI!!
GLARE
HIC...
...

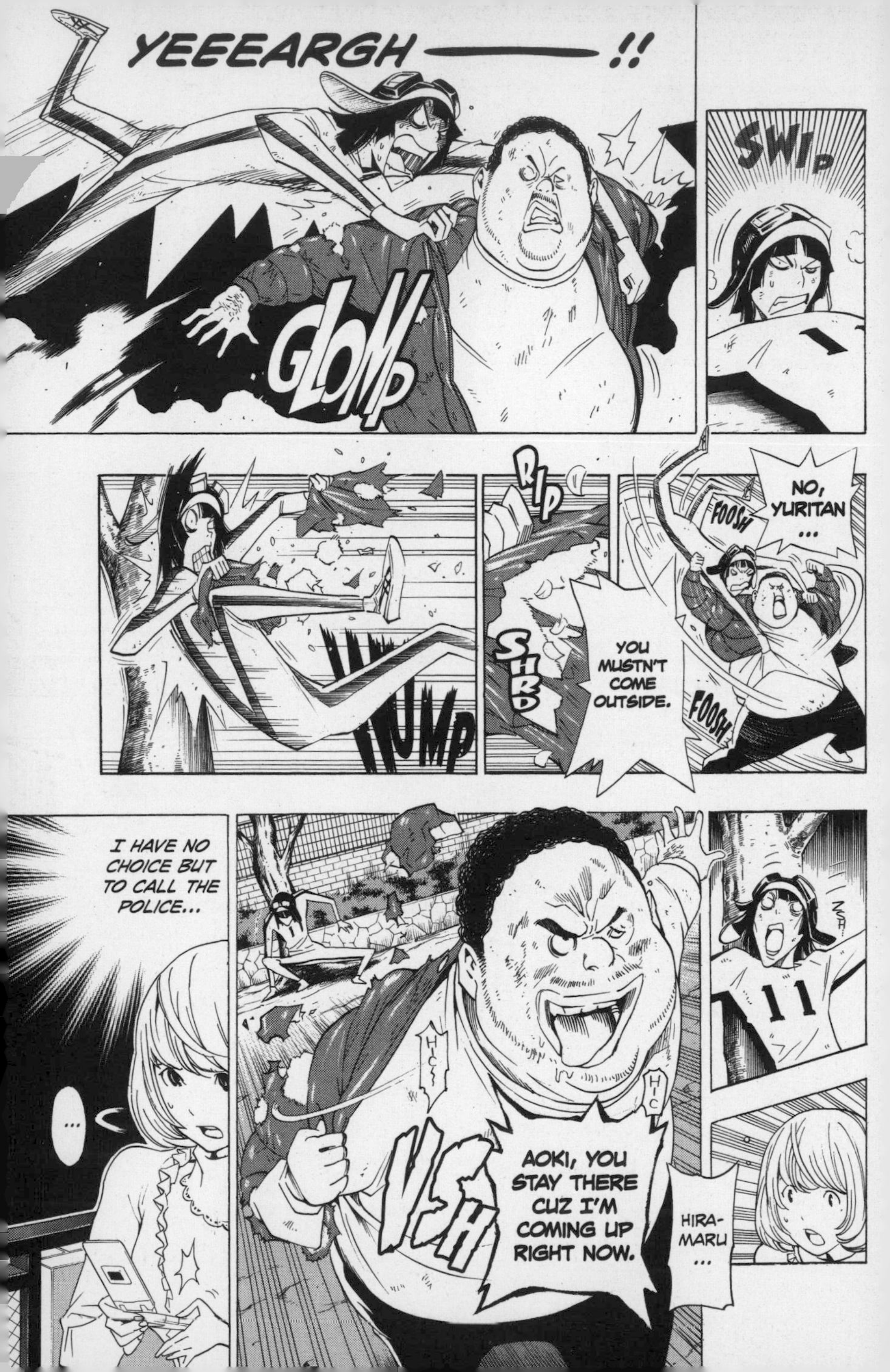
SWIP
YEEEARGH——!!
GLOMP
NO, YURITAN...
FOOSH
FOOSH
RIP
SHRD
YOU MUSTN'T COME OUTSIDE.
WHUMP
ZSH...
HIRA-MARU...
HIC
HIC
AOKI, YOU STAY THERE CUZ I'M COMING UP RIGHT NOW.
I HAVE NO CHOICE BUT TO CALL THE POLICE...
...

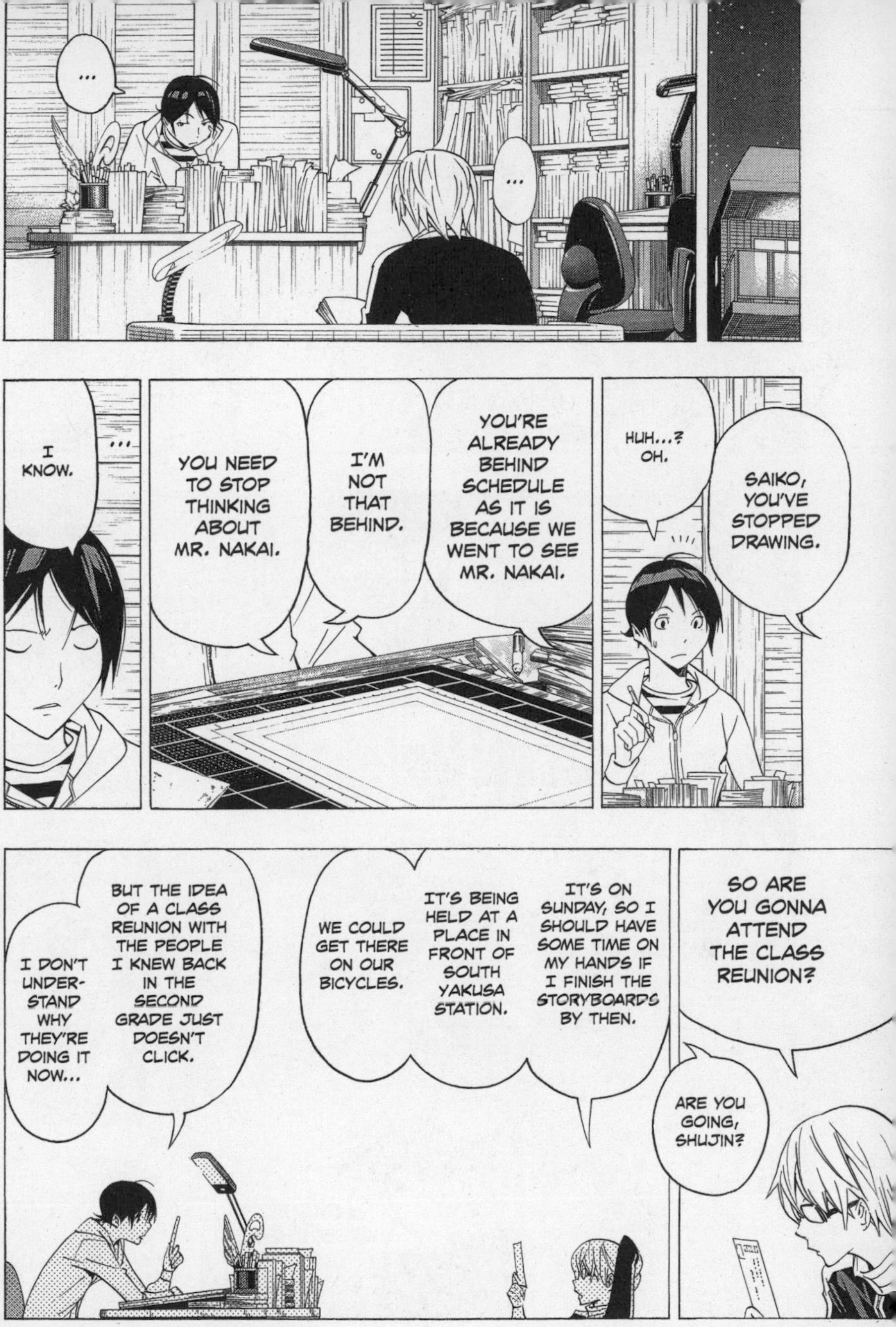
...
...
SAIKO, YOU'VE STOPPED DRAWING.
HUH...? OH.
YOU'RE ALREADY BEHIND SCHEDULE AS IT IS BECAUSE WE WENT TO SEE MR. NAKAI.
I'M NOT THAT BEHIND.
YOU NEED TO STOP THINKING ABOUT MR. NAKAI.
...
I KNOW.
SO ARE YOU GONNA ATTEND THE CLASS REUNION?
ARE YOU GOING, SHUJIN?
IT'S ON SUNDAY, SO I SHOULD HAVE SOME TIME ON MY HANDS IF I FINISH THE STORYBOARDS BY THEN.
IT'S BEING HELD AT A PLACE IN FRONT OF SOUTH YAKUSA STATION.
WE COULD GET THERE ON OUR BICYCLES.
BUT THE IDEA OF A CLASS REUNION WITH THE PEOPLE I KNEW BACK IN THE SECOND GRADE JUST DOESN'T CLICK.
I DON'T UNDERSTAND WHY THEY'RE DOING IT NOW...

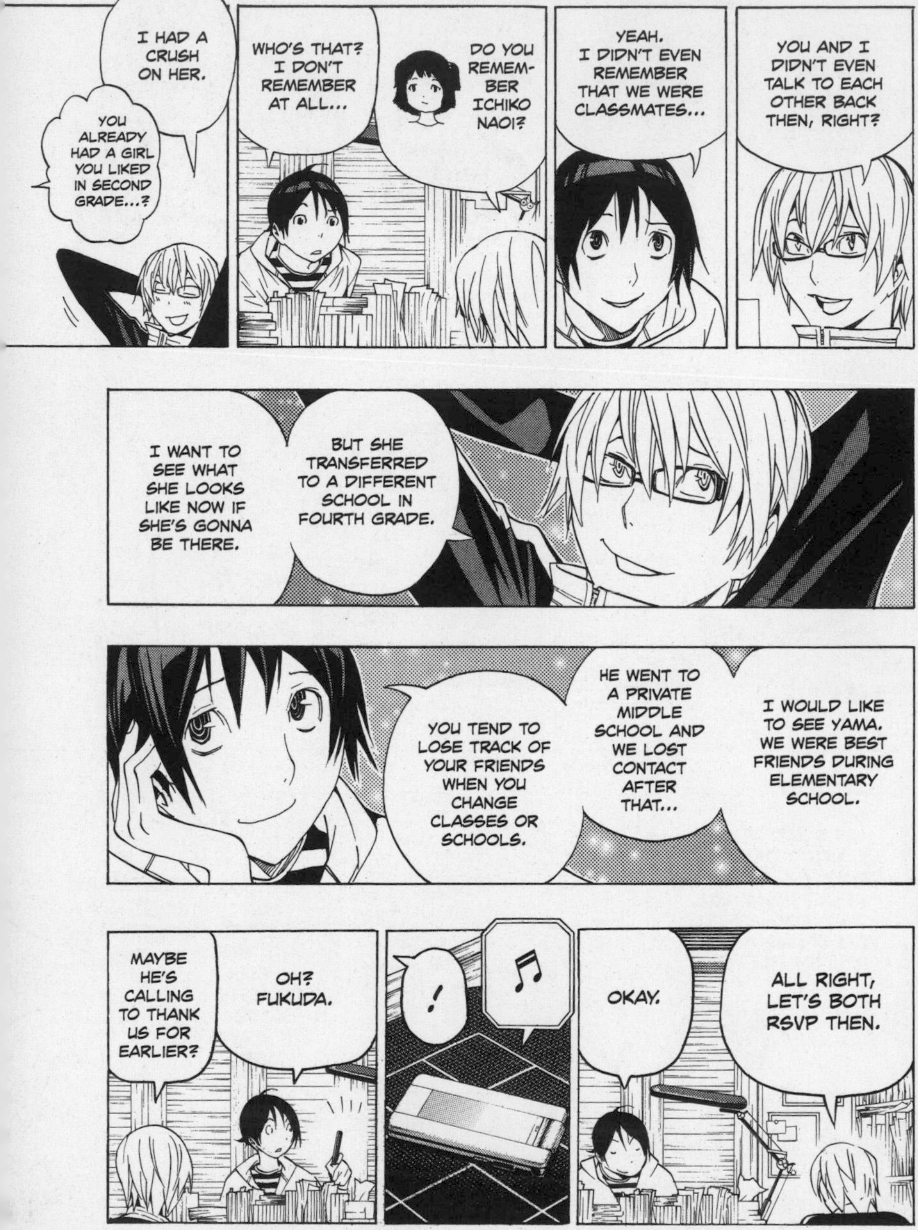
YOU AND I DIDN'T EVEN TALK TO EACH OTHER BACK THEN, RIGHT?
YEAH. I DIDN'T EVEN REMEMBER THAT WE WERE CLASSMATES...
DO YOU REMEMBER ICHIKO NAOI?
WHO'S THAT? I DON'T REMEMBER AT ALL...
I HAD A CRUSH ON HER.
YOU ALREADY HAD A GIRL YOU LIKED IN SECOND GRADE...?
BUT SHE TRANSFERRED TO A DIFFERENT SCHOOL IN FOURTH GRADE.
I WANT TO SEE WHAT SHE LOOKS LIKE NOW IF SHE'S GONNA BE THERE.
I WOULD LIKE TO SEE YAMA. WE WERE BEST FRIENDS DURING ELEMENTARY SCHOOL.
HE WENT TO A PRIVATE MIDDLE SCHOOL AND WE LOST CONTACT AFTER THAT...
YOU TEND TO LOSE TRACK OF YOUR FRIENDS WHEN YOU CHANGE CLASSES OR SCHOOLS.
ALL RIGHT, LET'S BOTH RSVP THEN.
OKAY.
♪
!
OH? FUKUDA.
MAYBE HE'S CALLING TO THANK US FOR EARLIER?

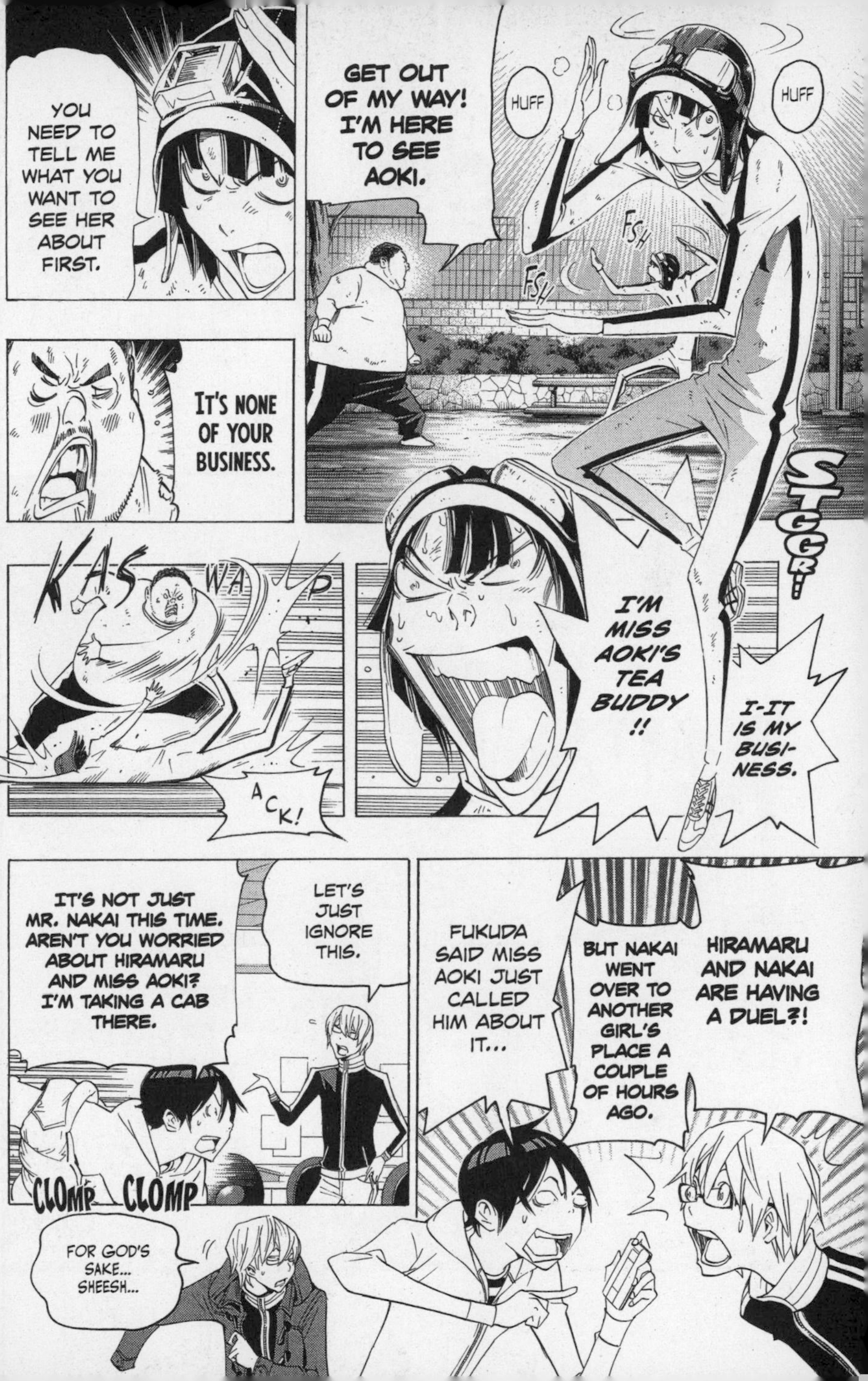
HUFF
HUFF
GET OUT OF MY WAY! I'M HERE TO SEE AOKI.
FSH
FSH
YOU NEED TO TELL ME WHAT YOU WANT TO SEE HER ABOUT FIRST.
IT'S NONE OF YOUR BUSINESS.
STGGR...
I-IT IS MY BUSI-NESS.
I'M MISS AOKI'S TEA BUDDY!!
KAS WAP
ACK!
HIRAMARU AND NAKAI ARE HAVING A DUEL?!
BUT NAKAI WENT OVER TO ANOTHER GIRL'S PLACE A COUPLE OF HOURS AGO.
FUKUDA SAID MISS AOKI JUST CALLED HIM ABOUT IT...
FOR GOD'S SAKE... SHEESH...
LET'S JUST IGNORE THIS.
IT'S NOT JUST MR. NAKAI THIS TIME. AREN'T YOU WORRIED ABOUT HIRAMARU AND MISS AOKI? I'M TAKING A CAB THERE.
CLOMP CLOMP

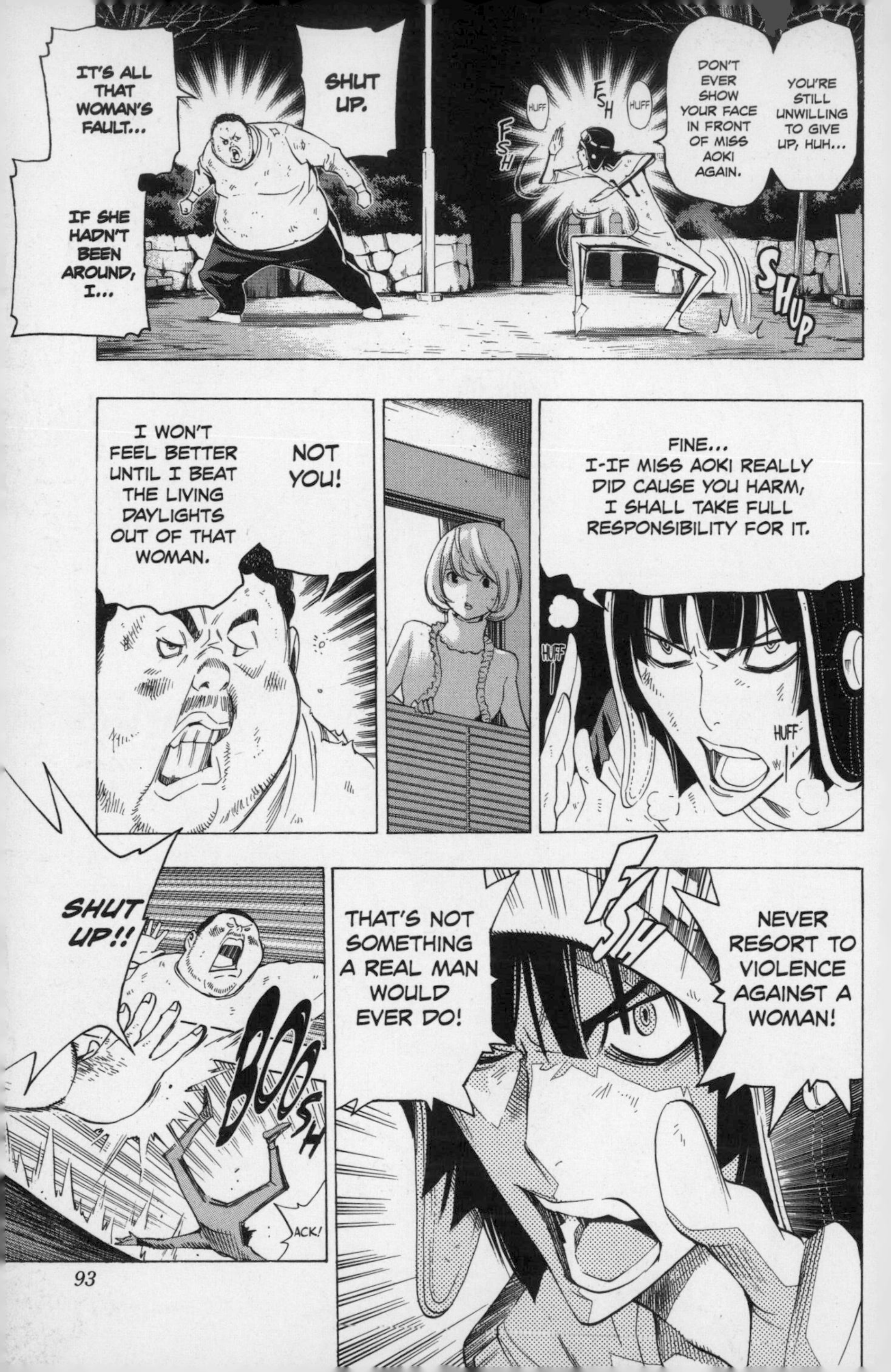
YOU'RE STILL UNWILLING TO GIVE UP, HUH...
DON'T EVER SHOW YOUR FACE IN FRONT OF MISS AOKI AGAIN.
HUFF
FSH
HUFF
FSH
SHUP
SHUT UP.
IT'S ALL THAT WOMAN'S FAULT...
IF SHE HADN'T BEEN AROUND, I...
FINE...
I-IF MISS AOKI REALLY DID CAUSE YOU HARM, I SHALL TAKE FULL RESPONSIBILITY FOR IT.
HUFF
HUFF
NOT YOU!
I WON'T FEEL BETTER UNTIL I BEAT THE LIVING DAYLIGHTS OUT OF THAT WOMAN.
NEVER RESORT TO VIOLENCE AGAINST A WOMAN!
THAT'S NOT SOMETHING A REAL MAN WOULD EVER DO!
FSH
SHUT UP!!
BOOSH
ACK!

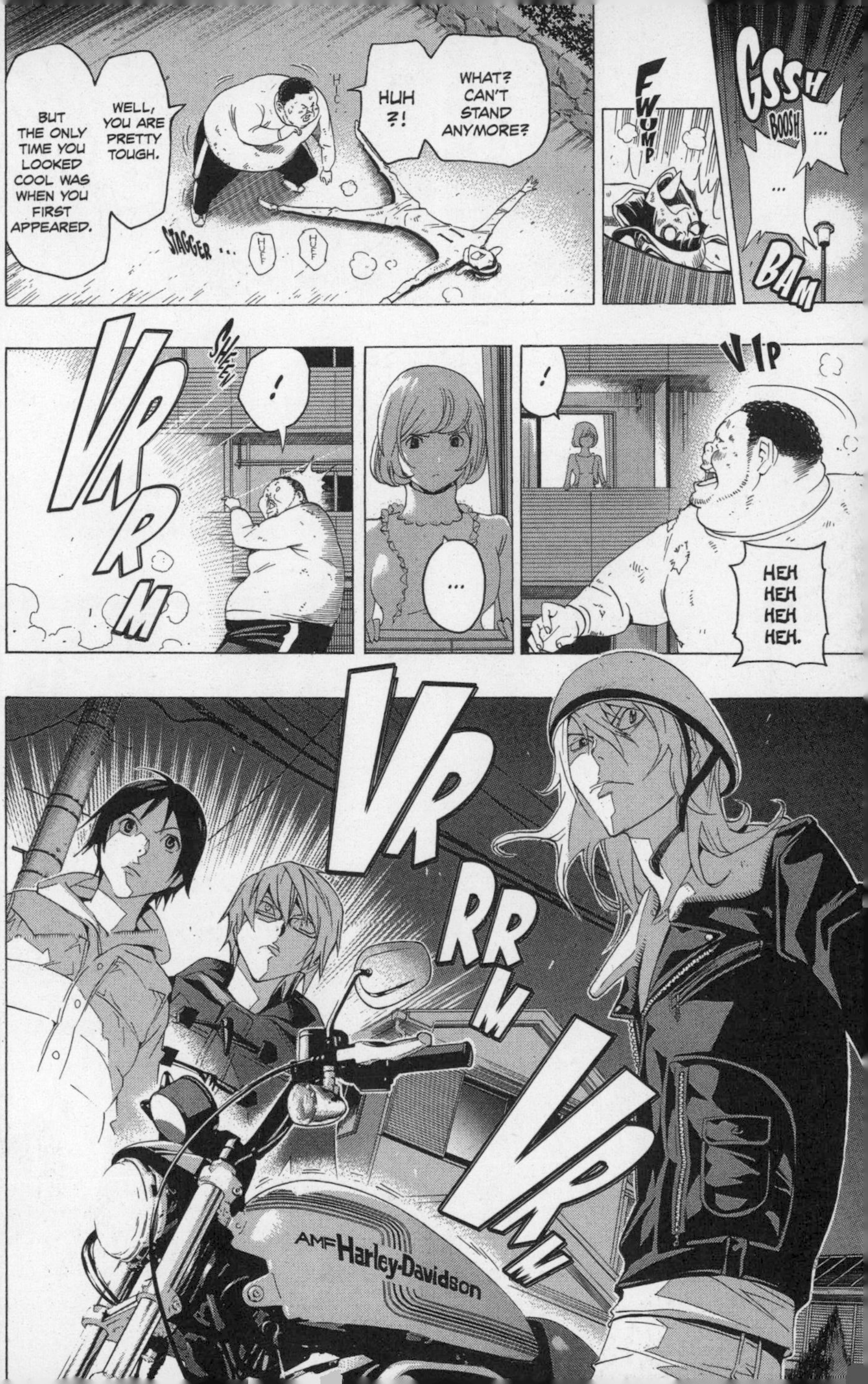
GSSH
BOOSH
...
...
BAM
FWUMP
WHAT? CAN'T STAND ANYMORE?
HUH ?!
HIC
WELL, YOU ARE PRETTY TOUGH.
BUT THE ONLY TIME YOU LOOKED COOL WAS WHEN YOU FIRST APPEARED.
STAGGER ...
HUF
HUF
VIP
!
HEH HEH HEH HEH.
...
SHEEN
!
VRRM
VRRRM
VRRM
AMF Harley-Davidson

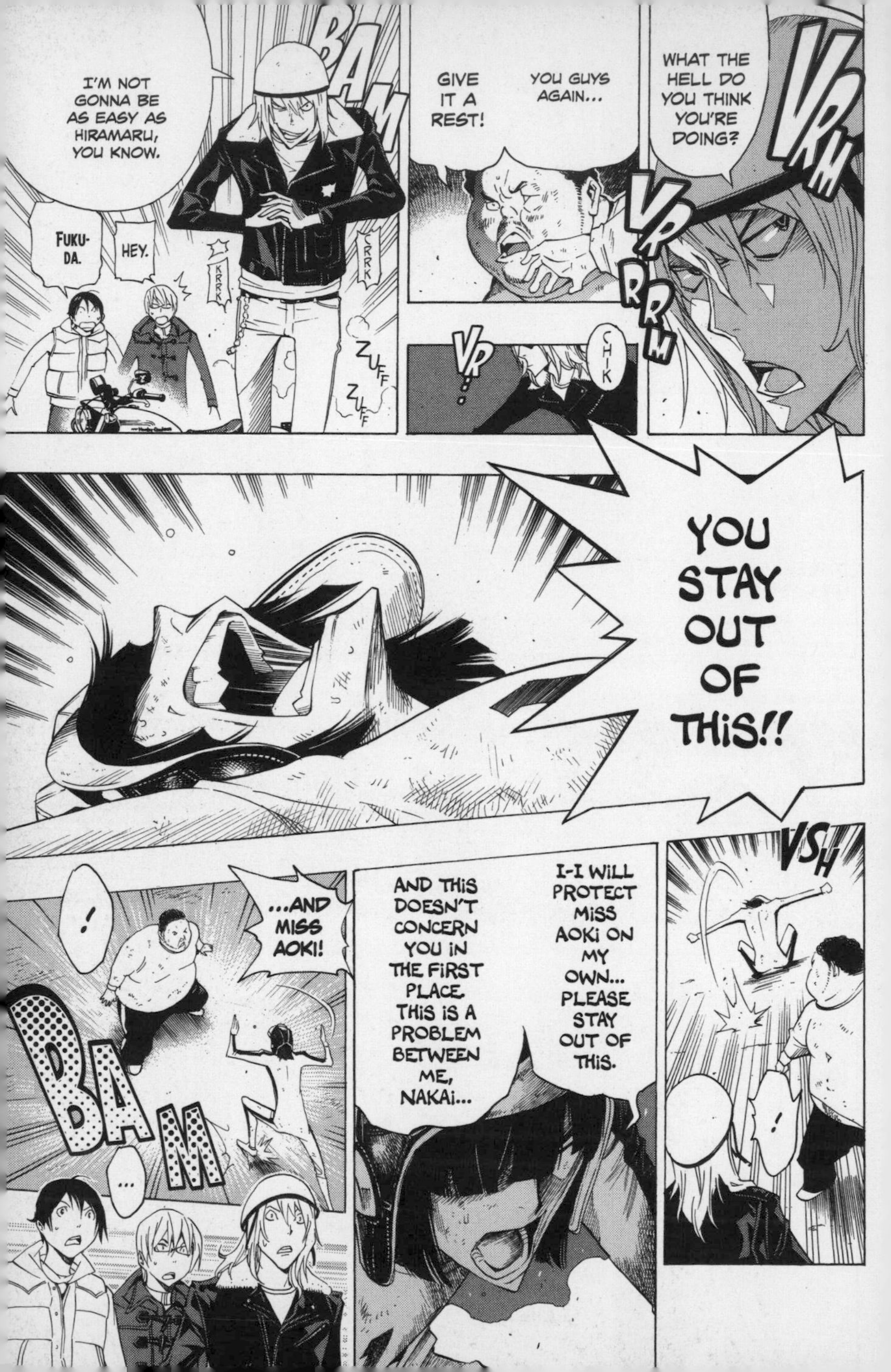
VRM
WHAT THE HELL DO YOU THINK YOU'RE DOING?
VRRRM
YOU GUYS AGAIN...
GIVE IT A REST!
CHIK
VR
BAM
I'M NOT GONNA BE AS EASY AS HIRAMARU, YOU KNOW.
CRRK
KRRK
HEY.
FUKU-DA.
ZUFF
ZUFF
YOU STAY OUT OF THIS!!
VSH
!
I-I WILL PROTECT MISS AOKI ON MY OWN... PLEASE STAY OUT OF THIS.
AND THIS DOESN'T CONCERN YOU IN THE FIRST PLACE. THIS IS A PROBLEM BETWEEN ME, NAKAI...
...AND MISS AOKI!
!
BAM
...

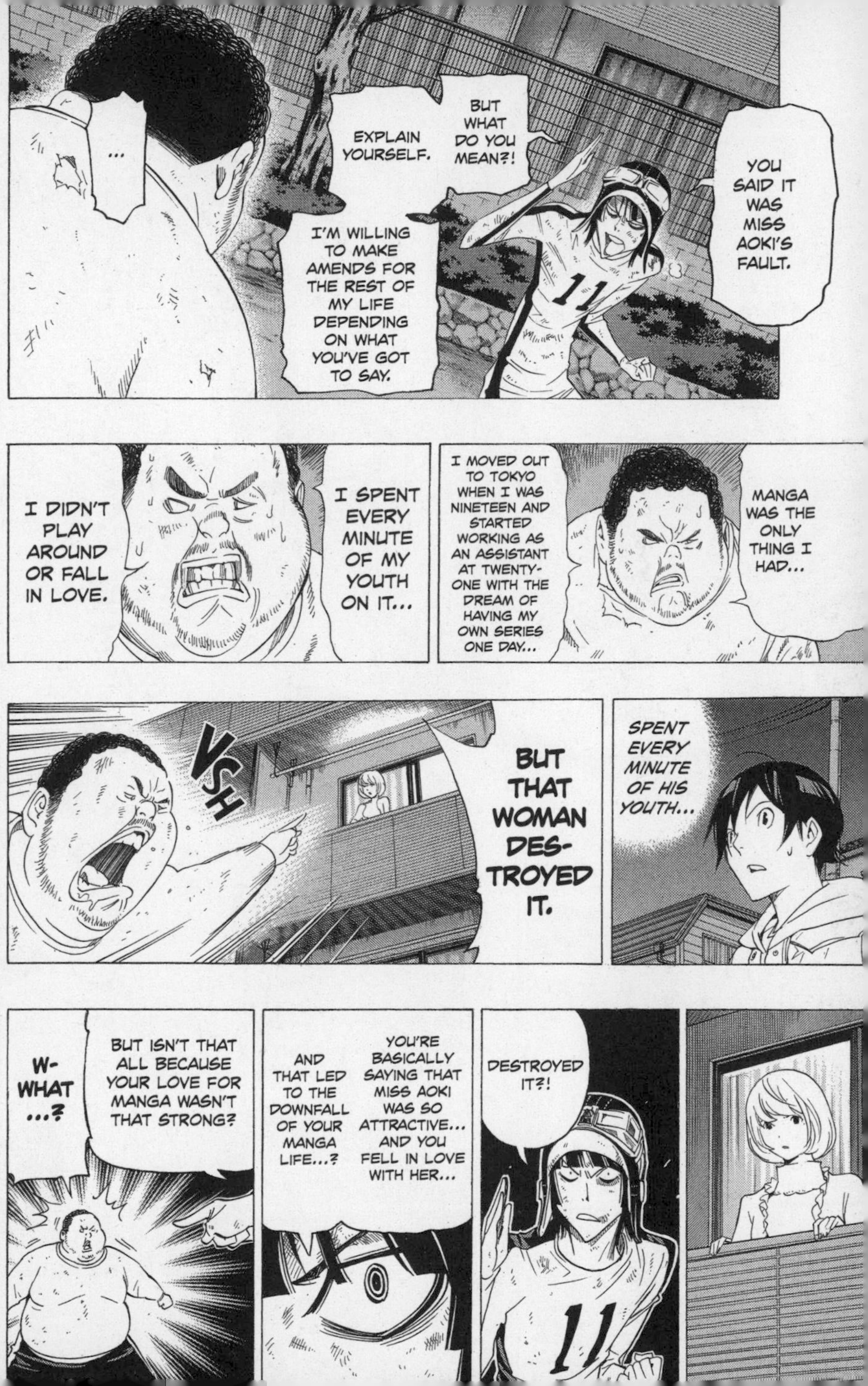
YOU SAID IT WAS MISS AOKI'S FAULT.
BUT WHAT DO YOU MEAN?!
EXPLAIN YOURSELF.
I'M WILLING TO MAKE AMENDS FOR THE REST OF MY LIFE DEPENDING ON WHAT YOU'VE GOT TO SAY.
...
MANGA WAS THE ONLY THING I HAD...
I MOVED OUT TO TOKYO WHEN I WAS NINETEEN AND STARTED WORKING AS AN ASSISTANT AT TWENTY-ONE WITH THE DREAM OF HAVING MY OWN SERIES ONE DAY...
I SPENT EVERY MINUTE OF MY YOUTH ON IT...
I DIDN'T PLAY AROUND OR FALL IN LOVE.
SPENT EVERY MINUTE OF HIS YOUTH...
BUT THAT WOMAN DES-TROYED IT.
VSH
DESTROYED IT?!
YOU'RE BASICALLY SAYING THAT MISS AOKI WAS SO ATTRACTIVE... AND YOU FELL IN LOVE WITH HER...
AND THAT LED TO THE DOWNFALL OF YOUR MANGA LIFE...?
BUT ISN'T THAT ALL BECAUSE YOUR LOVE FOR MANGA WASN'T THAT STRONG?
W-WHAT...?

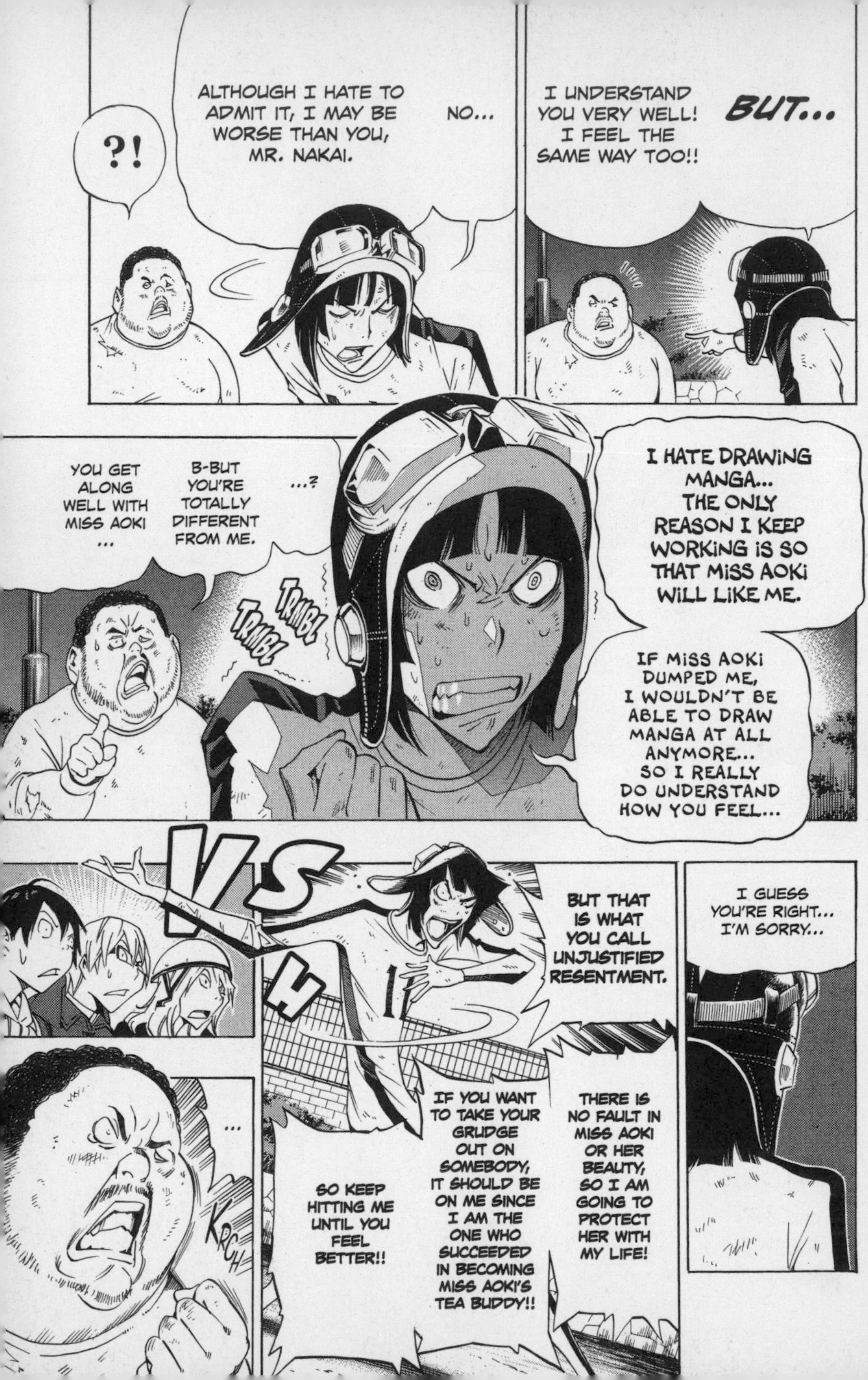
BUT...
I UNDERSTAND YOU VERY WELL! I FEEL THE SAME WAY TOO!!
NO...
ALTHOUGH I HATE TO ADMIT IT, I MAY BE WORSE THAN YOU, MR. NAKAI.
?!
I HATE DRAWING MANGA... THE ONLY REASON I KEEP WORKING IS SO THAT MISS AOKI WILL LIKE ME.
IF MISS AOKI DUMPED ME, I WOULDN'T BE ABLE TO DRAW MANGA AT ALL ANYMORE... SO I REALLY DO UNDERSTAND HOW YOU FEEL...
...?
B-BUT YOU'RE TOTALLY DIFFERENT FROM ME.
YOU GET ALONG WELL WITH MISS AOKI ...
TRMBL
TRMBL
I GUESS YOU'RE RIGHT... I'M SORRY...
BUT THAT IS WHAT YOU CALL UNJUSTIFIED RESENTMENT.
THERE IS NO FAULT IN MISS AOKI OR HER BEAUTY, SO I AM GOING TO PROTECT HER WITH MY LIFE!
IF YOU WANT TO TAKE YOUR GRUDGE OUT ON SOMEBODY, IT SHOULD BE ON ME SINCE I AM THE ONE WHO SUCCEEDED IN BECOMING MISS AOKI'S TEA BUDDY!!
SO KEEP HITTING ME UNTIL YOU FEEL BETTER!!
...
KRCH

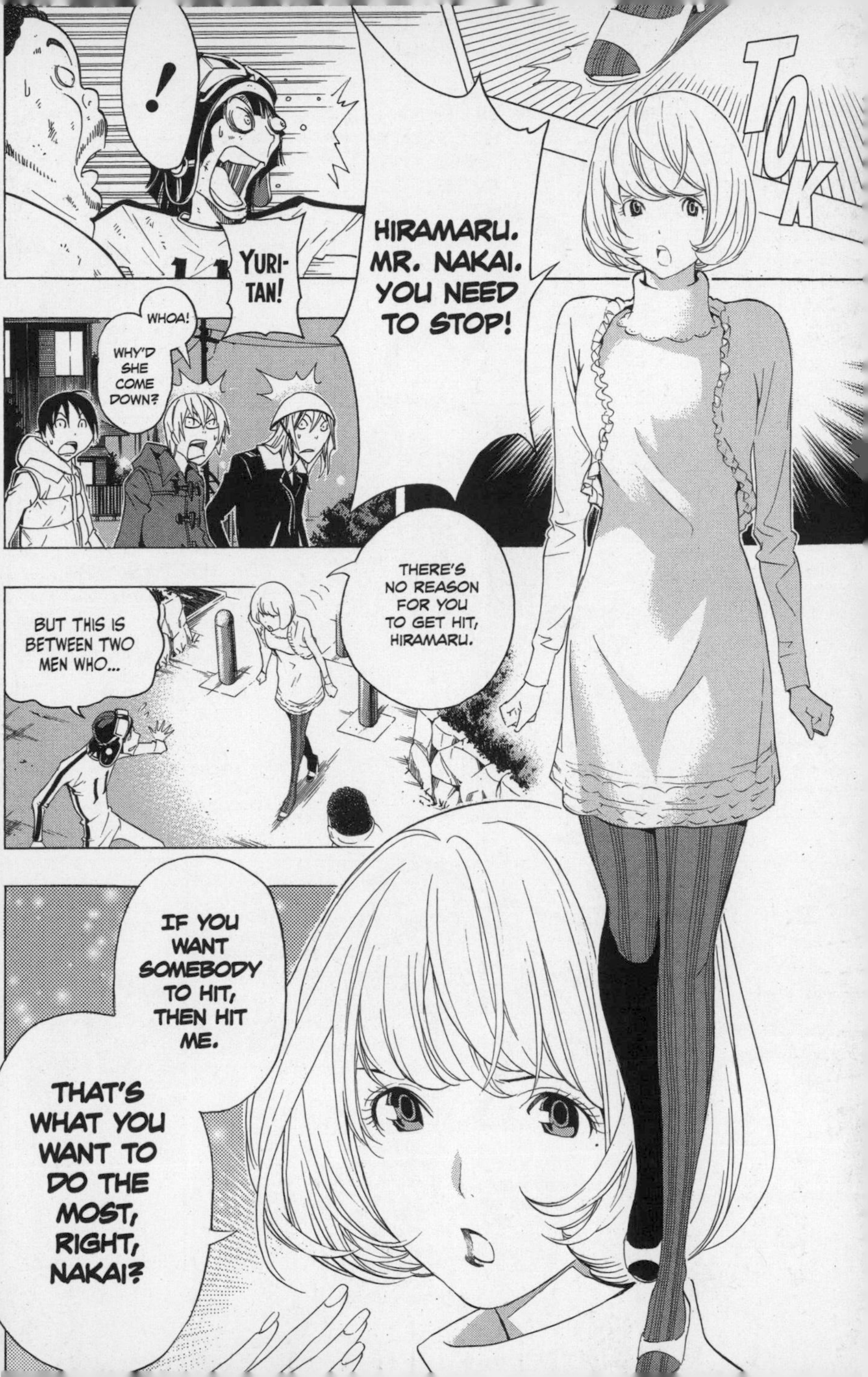
TOK
HIRAMARU. MR. NAKAI. YOU NEED TO STOP!
!
YURI-TAN!
WHOA!
WHY'D SHE COME DOWN?
THERE'S NO REASON FOR YOU TO GET HIT, HIRAMARU.
BUT THIS IS BETWEEN TWO MEN WHO...
IF YOU WANT SOMEBODY TO HIT, THEN HIT ME.
THAT'S WHAT YOU WANT TO DO THE MOST, RIGHT, NAKAI?

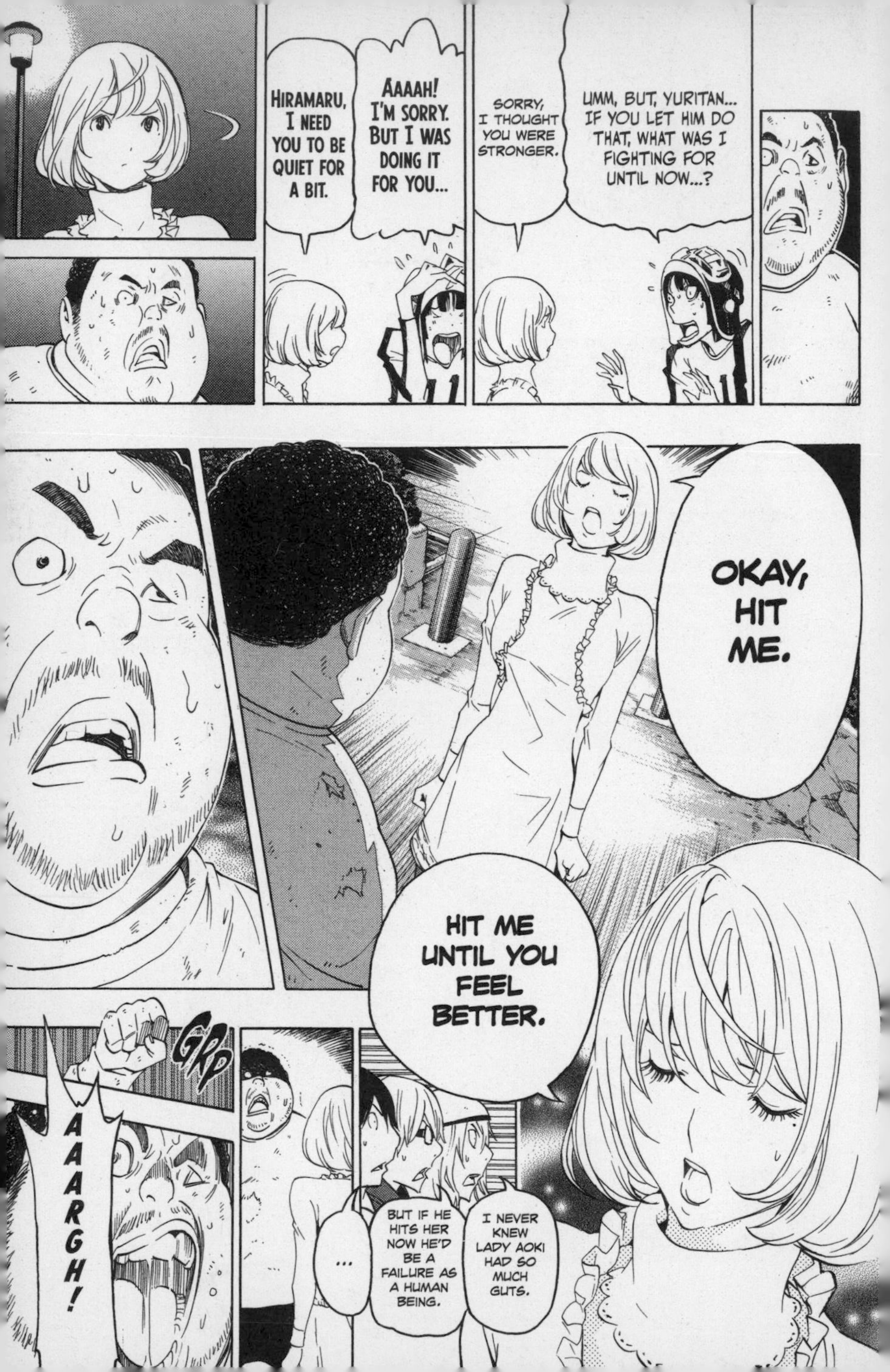
UMM, BUT, YURITAN... IF YOU LET HIM DO THAT, WHAT WAS I FIGHTING FOR UNTIL NOW...?
SORRY, I THOUGHT YOU WERE STRONGER.
AAAAH! I'M SORRY. BUT I WAS DOING IT FOR YOU...
HIRAMARU, I NEED YOU TO BE QUIET FOR A BIT.
OKAY, HIT ME.
HIT ME UNTIL YOU FEEL BETTER.
I NEVER KNEW LADY AOKI HAD SO MUCH GUTS.
BUT IF HE HITS HER NOW HE'D BE A FAILURE AS A HUMAN BEING.
...
GRP
AAAARGH!

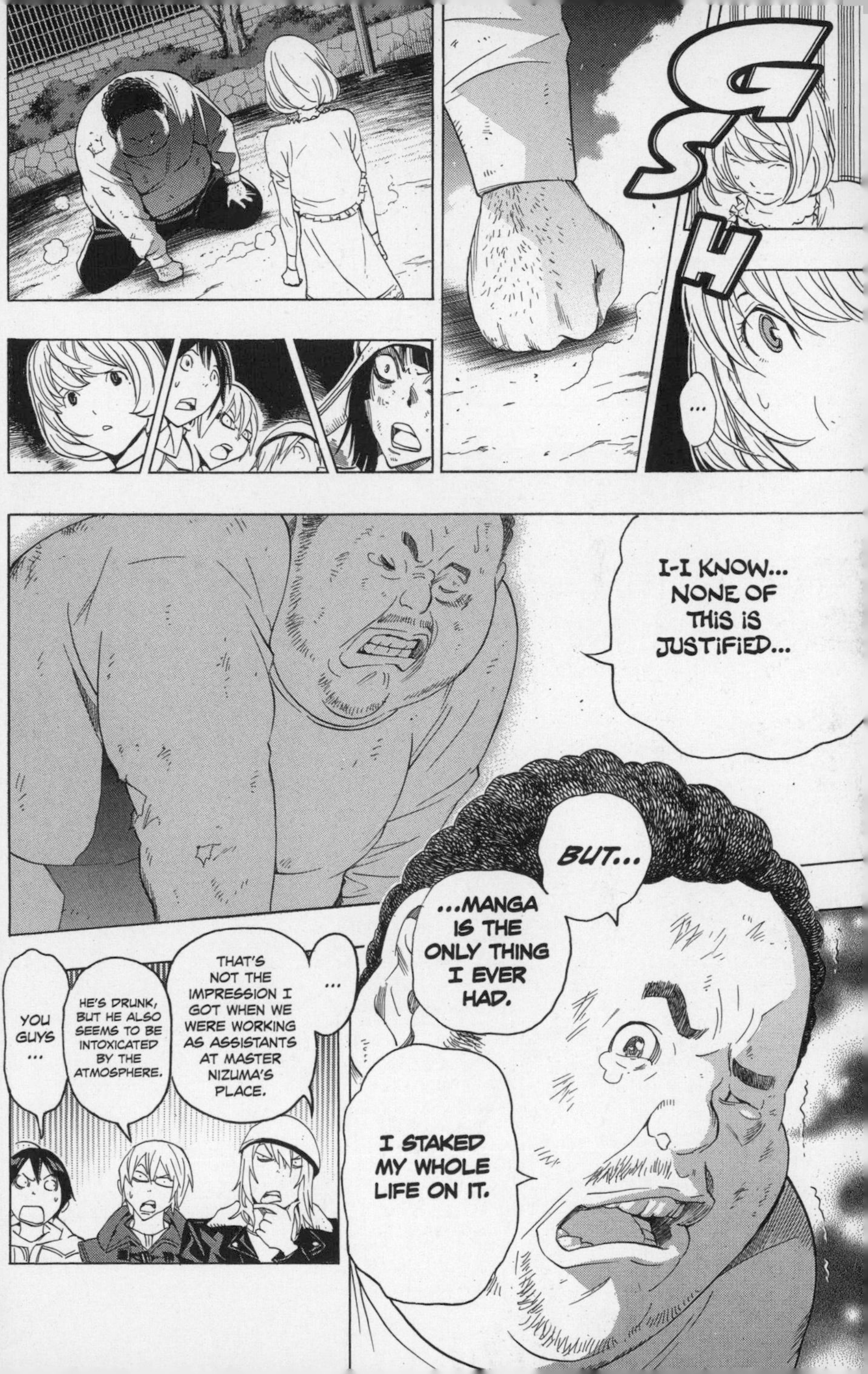
GSH
...
I-I KNOW... NONE OF THIS IS JUSTIFIED...
BUT...
...MANGA IS THE ONLY THING I EVER HAD.
I STAKED MY WHOLE LIFE ON IT.
...
THAT'S NOT THE IMPRESSION I GOT WHEN WE WERE WORKING AS ASSISTANTS AT MASTER NIZUMA'S PLACE.
HE'S DRUNK, BUT HE ALSO SEEMS TO BE INTOXICATED BY THE ATMOSPHERE.
YOU GUYS ...

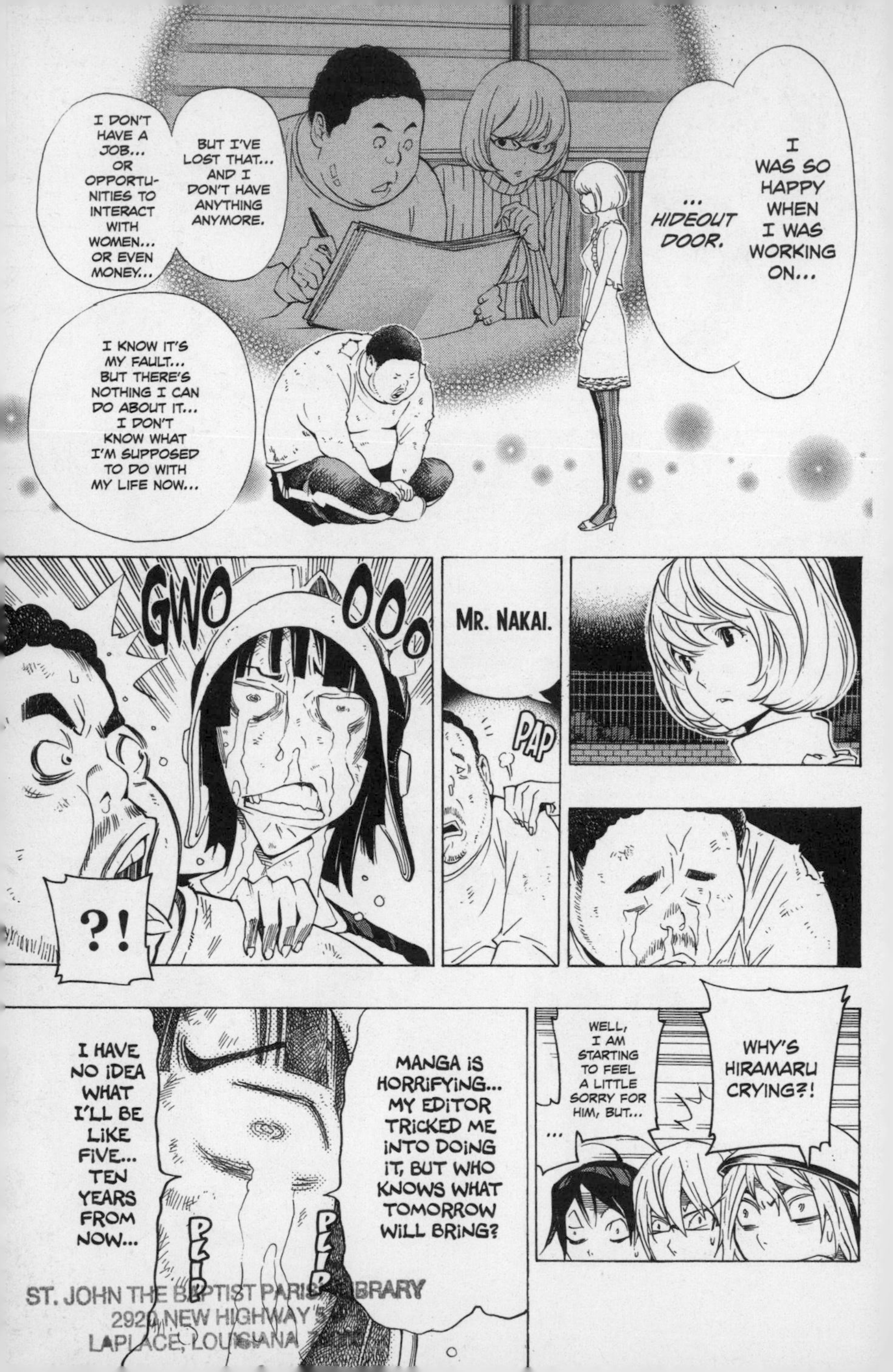
I WAS SO HAPPY WHEN I WAS WORKING ON...
... HIDEOUT DOOR.
BUT I'VE LOST THAT... AND I DON'T HAVE ANYTHING ANYMORE.
I DON'T HAVE A JOB... OR OPPORTUNITIES TO INTERACT WITH WOMEN... OR EVEN MONEY...
I KNOW IT'S MY FAULT... BUT THERE'S NOTHING I CAN DO ABOUT IT... I DON'T KNOW WHAT I'M SUPPOSED TO DO WITH MY LIFE NOW...
MR. NAKAI.
PAP
GWO OOO
?!
WHY'S HIRAMARU CRYING?!
WELL, I AM STARTING TO FEEL A LITTLE SORRY FOR HIM, BUT...
...
MANGA IS HORRIFYING... MY EDITOR TRICKED ME INTO DOING IT, BUT WHO KNOWS WHAT TOMORROW WILL BRING?
I HAVE NO IDEA WHAT I'LL BE LIKE FIVE... TEN YEARS FROM NOW...
PLIP
PLIP

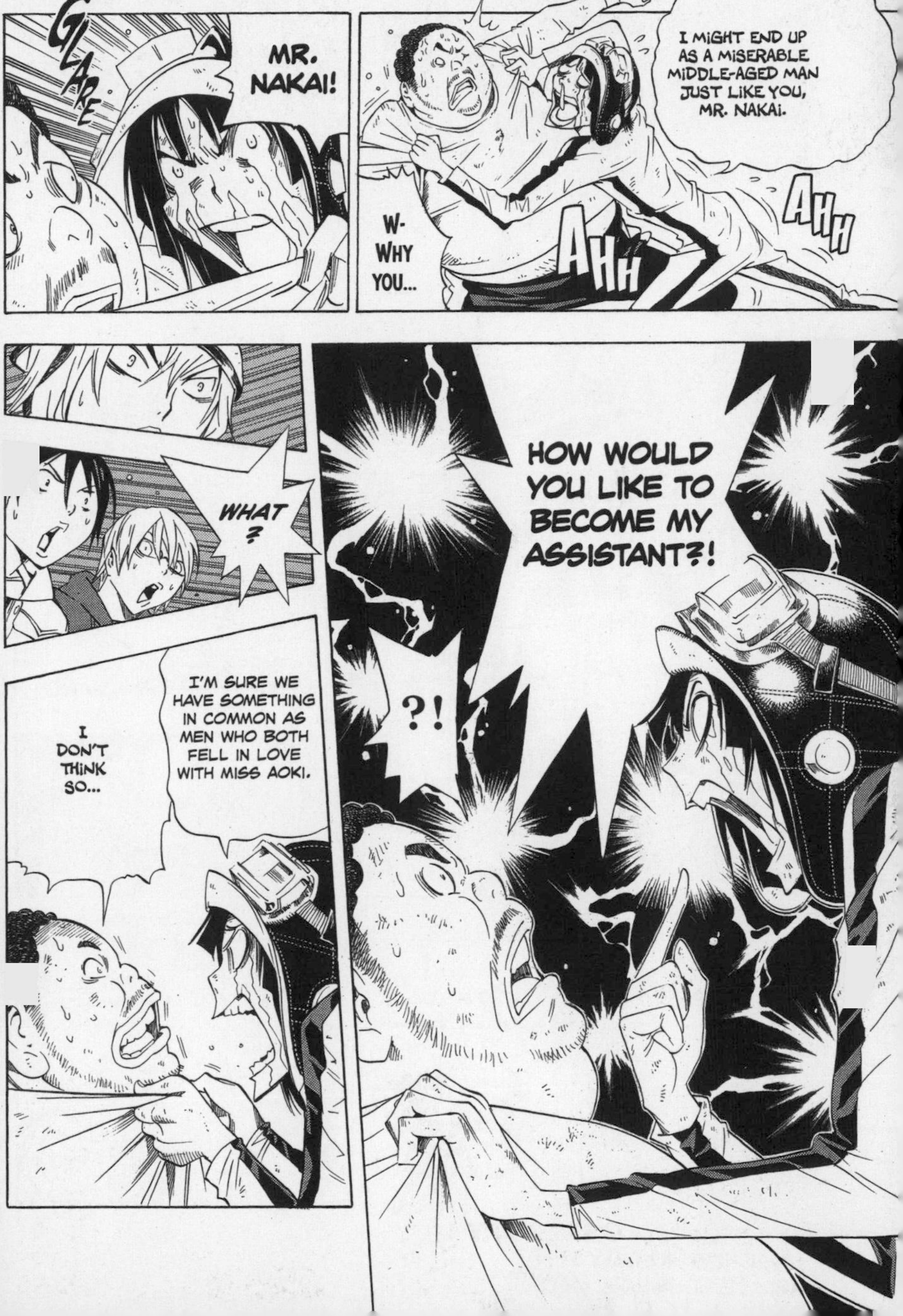
I MIGHT END UP AS A MISERABLE MIDDLE-AGED MAN JUST LIKE YOU, MR. NAKAI.
AHH
AHH
W-WHY YOU...
GLARE
MR. NAKAI!
HOW WOULD YOU LIKE TO BECOME MY ASSISTANT?!
?!
WHAT?
I'M SURE WE HAVE SOMETHING IN COMMON AS MEN WHO BOTH FELL IN LOVE WITH MISS AOKI.
I DON'T THINK SO...

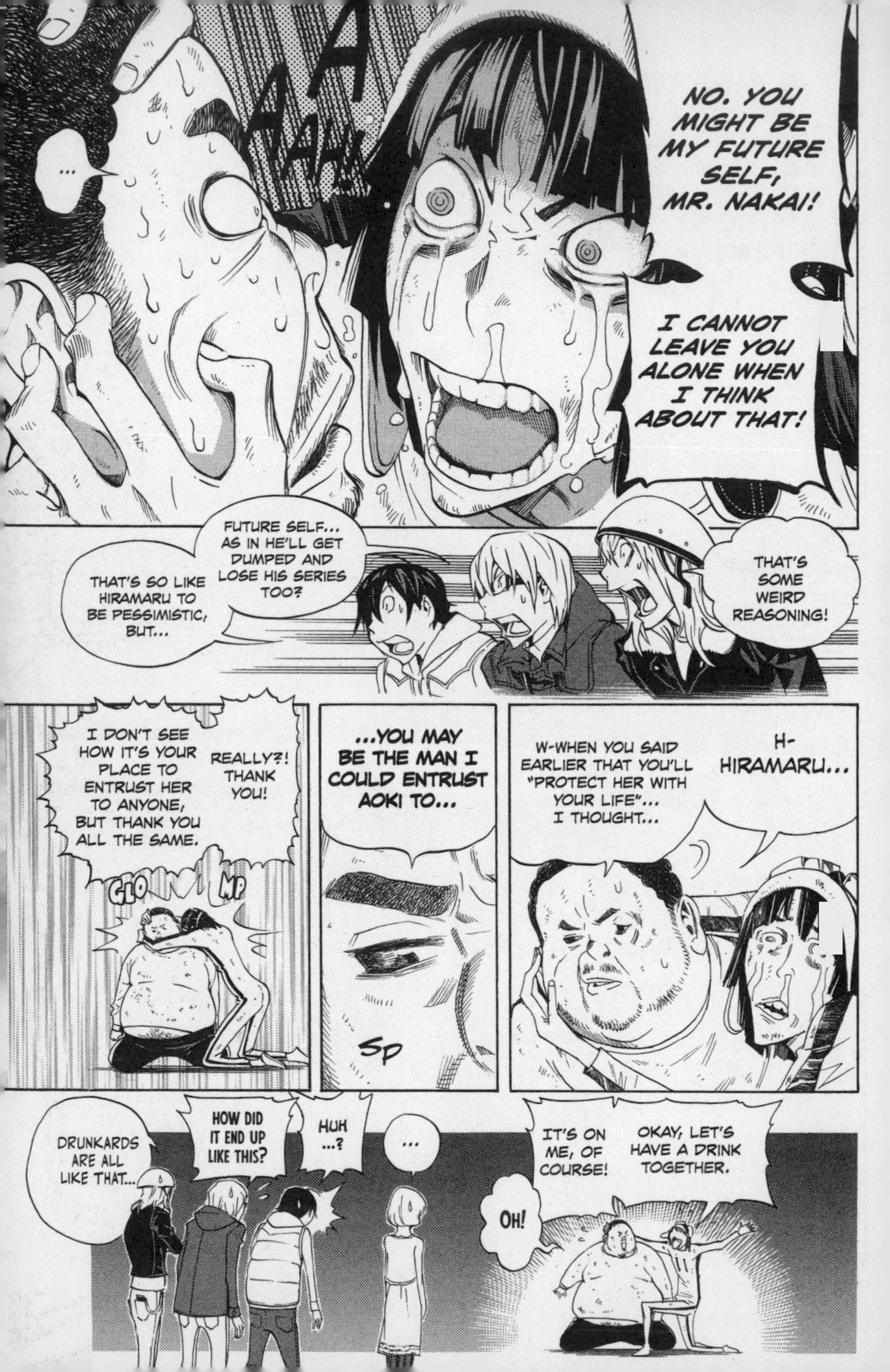
NO. YOU MIGHT BE MY FUTURE SELF, MR. NAKAI!
I CANNOT LEAVE YOU ALONE WHEN I THINK ABOUT THAT!
AAAH!!
...
THAT'S SOME WEIRD REASONING!
FUTURE SELF... AS IN HE'LL GET DUMPED AND LOSE HIS SERIES TOO?
THAT'S SO LIKE HIRAMARU TO BE PESSIMISTIC, BUT...
H- HIRAMARU...
W-WHEN YOU SAID EARLIER THAT YOU'LL "PROTECT HER WITH YOUR LIFE"... I THOUGHT...
...YOU MAY BE THE MAN I COULD ENTRUST AOKI TO...
SP
REALLY?! THANK YOU!
I DON'T SEE HOW IT'S YOUR PLACE TO ENTRUST HER TO ANYONE, BUT THANK YOU ALL THE SAME.
GLOMP
OKAY, LET'S HAVE A DRINK TOGETHER.
IT'S ON ME, OF COURSE!
OH!
...
HUH ...?
HOW DID IT END UP LIKE THIS?
DRUNKARDS ARE ALL LIKE THAT...

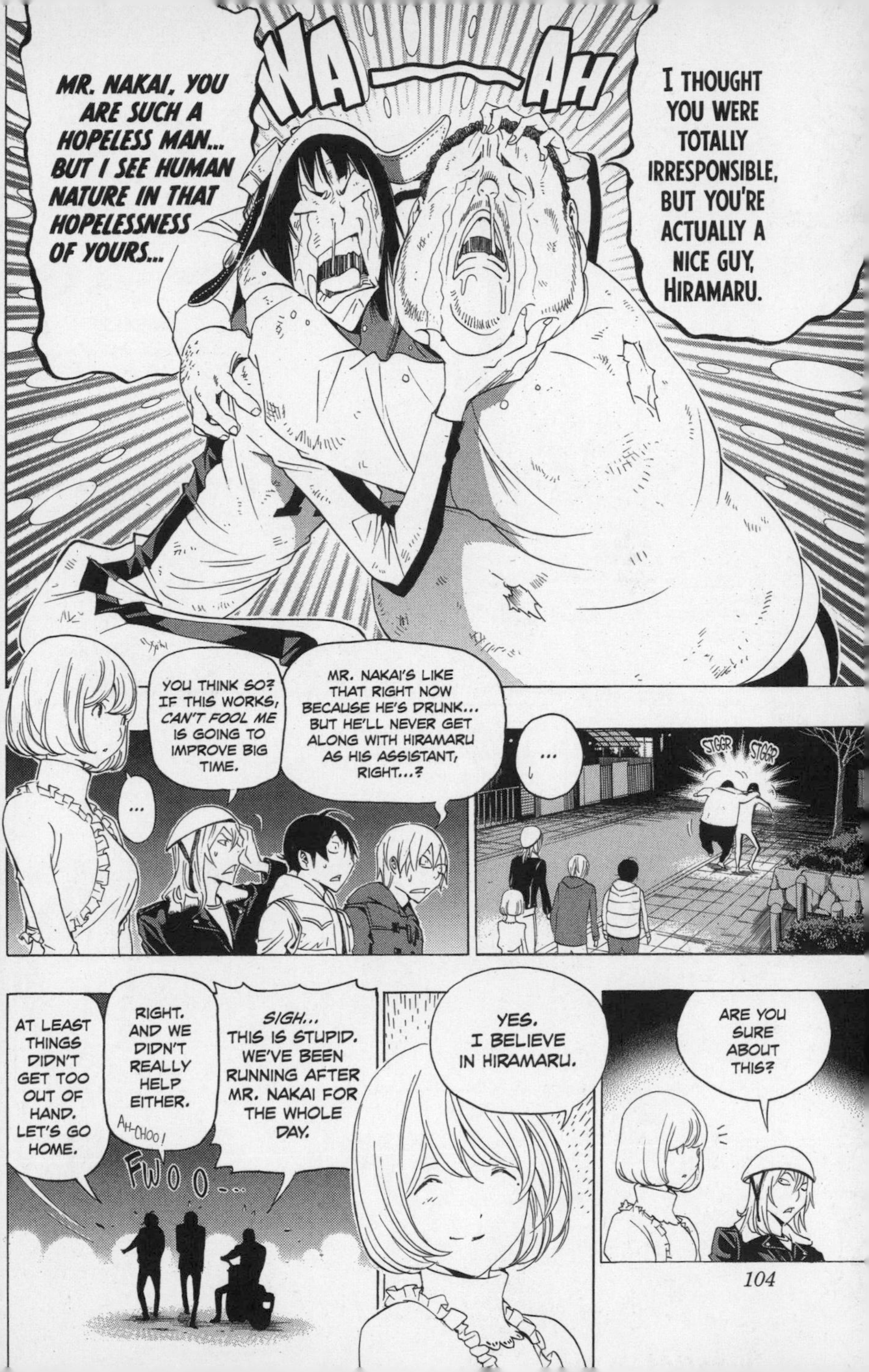

I THOUGHT YOU WERE TOTALLY IRRESPONSIBLE, BUT YOU'RE ACTUALLY A NICE GUY, HIRAMARU.
NA——AH
MR. NAKAI, YOU ARE SUCH A HOPELESS MAN... BUT I SEE HUMAN NATURE IN THAT HOPELESSNESS OF YOURS...
STGGR
STGGR
...
MR. NAKAI'S LIKE THAT RIGHT NOW BECAUSE HE'S DRUNK... BUT HE'LL NEVER GET ALONG WITH HIRAMARU AS HIS ASSISTANT, RIGHT...?
YOU THINK SO? IF THIS WORKS, *CAN'T FOOL ME* IS GOING TO IMPROVE BIG TIME.
...
ARE YOU SURE ABOUT THIS?
YES. I BELIEVE IN HIRAMARU.
SIGH... THIS IS STUPID. WE'VE BEEN RUNNING AFTER MR. NAKAI FOR THE WHOLE DAY.
RIGHT. AND WE DIDN'T REALLY HELP EITHER.
AT LEAST THINGS DIDN'T GET TOO OUT OF HAND. LET'S GO HOME.
AH-CHOO!
FWOO O...

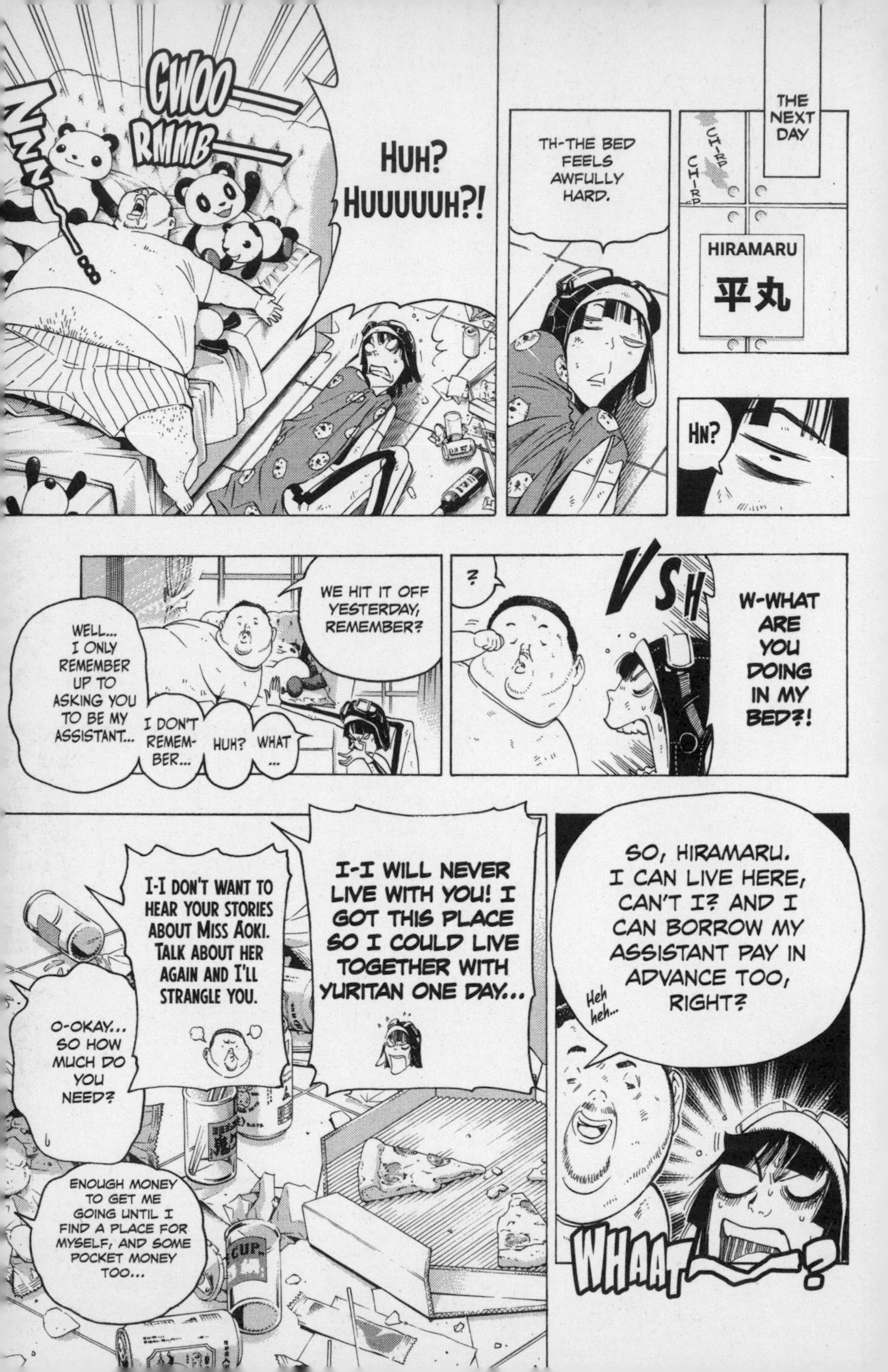
THE NEXT DAY
CHIRP
CHIRP
HIRAMARU
平丸
HN?
TH-THE BED FEELS AWFULLY HARD.
HUH? HUUUUUH?!
GWOO RMMB
VSH
W-WHAT ARE YOU DOING IN MY BED?!
?
WE HIT IT OFF YESTERDAY, REMEMBER?
WHAT...
HUH?
I DON'T REMEMBER...
WELL... I ONLY REMEMBER UP TO ASKING YOU TO BE MY ASSISTANT...
SO, HIRAMARU. I CAN LIVE HERE, CAN'T I? AND I CAN BORROW MY ASSISTANT PAY IN ADVANCE TOO, RIGHT?
Heh heh...
WHAAT—?
I-I WILL NEVER LIVE WITH YOU! I GOT THIS PLACE SO I COULD LIVE TOGETHER WITH YURITAN ONE DAY...
I-I DON'T WANT TO HEAR YOUR STORIES ABOUT MISS AOKI. TALK ABOUT HER AGAIN AND I'LL STRANGLE YOU.
O-OKAY... SO HOW MUCH DO YOU NEED?
ENOUGH MONEY TO GET ME GOING UNTIL I FIND A PLACE FOR MYSELF, AND SOME POCKET MONEY TOO...

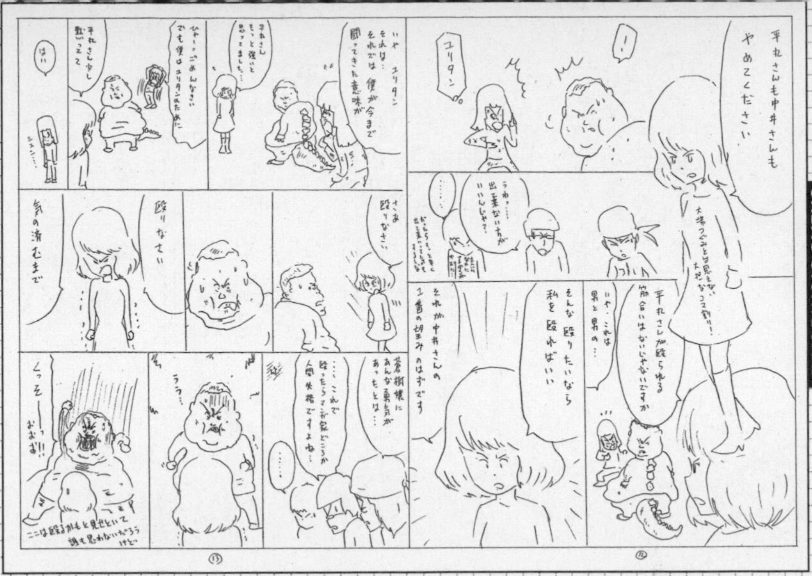
平丸さんも中井さんも やめてください
!
ユリタン
平丸さんが殴られる筋合いはないじゃないですか
いや、これは男と男の…
そんな殴りたいなら私を殴ればいい
それが中井さんの1番の望みのはずです
いや ユリタン それでは 僕が今まで 闘ってきた意味が
平丸さん もっと強いと思ってました…
ひゃーっ ごめんなさい でも僕はユリタンのために
平丸さん少し黙ってて
はい
さあ 殴りなさい
殴りなさい
気の済むまで
蒼樹嬢に あんな勇気が あったとは…
…これで 殴ったら ご飯どころか 人間失格ですよね…
くっそ…おおお!!

OHBA'S STORYBOARD

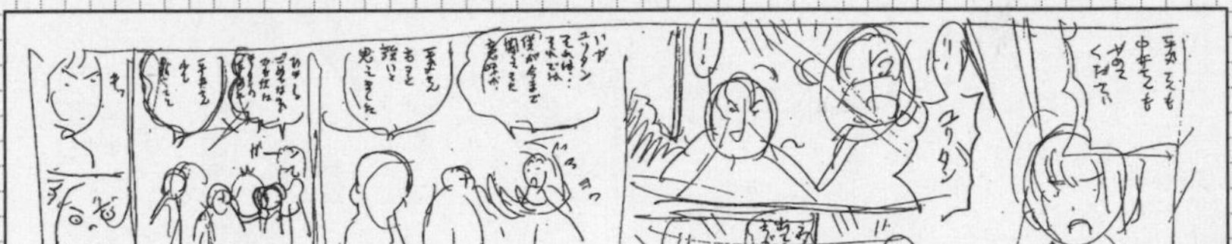

OBATA'S STORYBOARD

COMPLETE!

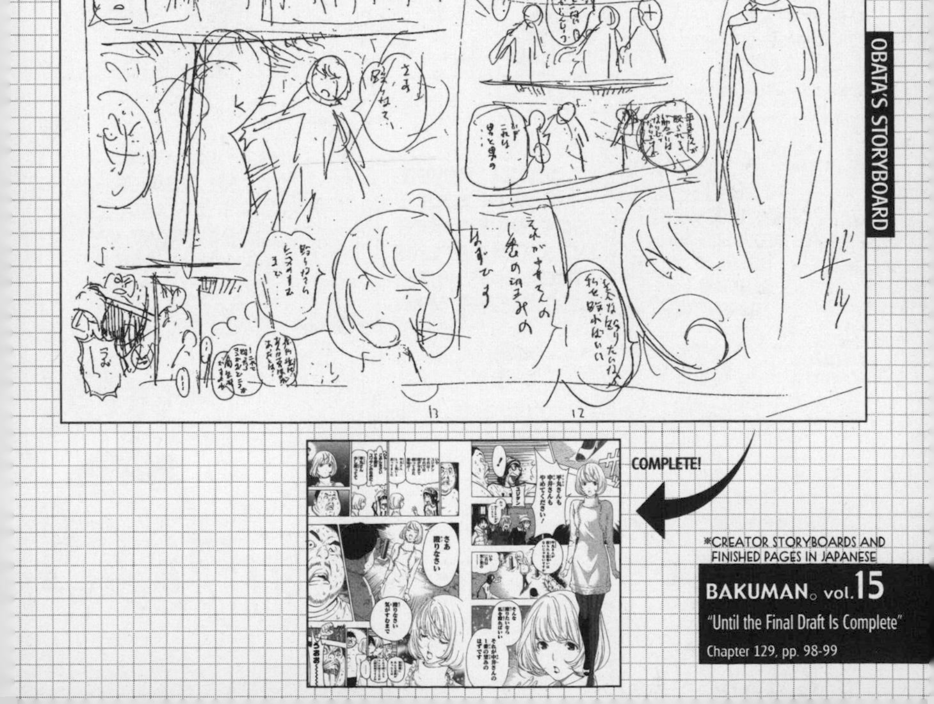

※CREATOR STORYBOARDS AND FINISHED PAGES IN JAPANESE

BAKUMAN。 vol. 15

"Until the Final Draft Is Complete"

Chapter 129, pp. 98-99

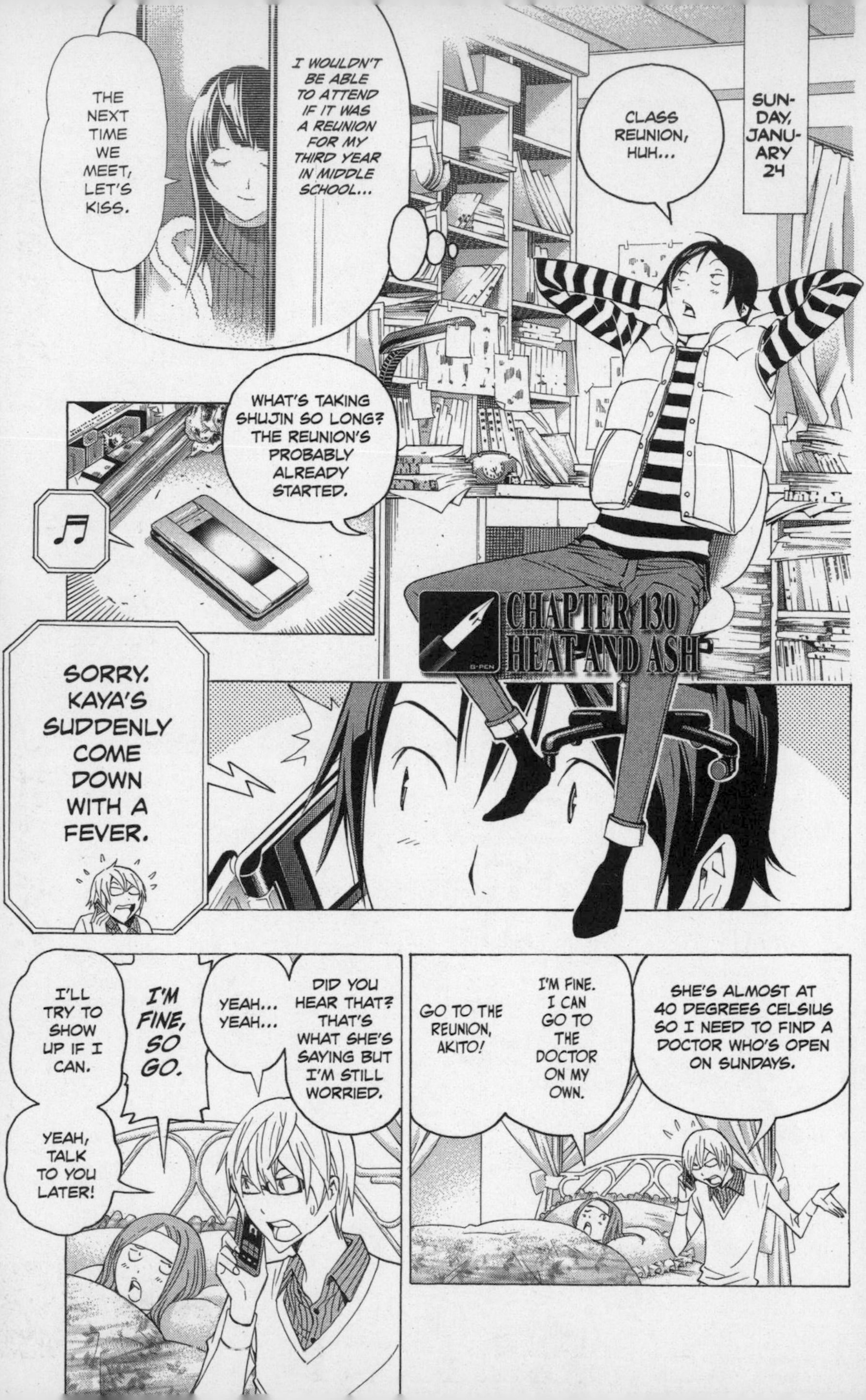
SUNDAY, JANUARY 24
CLASS REUNION, HUH...
I WOULDN'T BE ABLE TO ATTEND IF IT WAS A REUNION FOR MY THIRD YEAR IN MIDDLE SCHOOL...
THE NEXT TIME WE MEET, LET'S KISS.
WHAT'S TAKING SHUJIN SO LONG? THE REUNION'S PROBABLY ALREADY STARTED.
♬
CHAPTER 130
HEAT AND ASH
SORRY. KAYA'S SUDDENLY COME DOWN WITH A FEVER.
SHE'S ALMOST AT 40 DEGREES CELSIUS SO I NEED TO FIND A DOCTOR WHO'S OPEN ON SUNDAYS.
I'M FINE. I CAN GO TO THE DOCTOR ON MY OWN.
GO TO THE REUNION, AKITO!
DID YOU HEAR THAT? THAT'S WHAT SHE'S SAYING BUT I'M STILL WORRIED.
YEAH... YEAH...
I'M FINE, SO GO.
I'LL TRY TO SHOW UP IF I CAN.
YEAH, TALK TO YOU LATER!

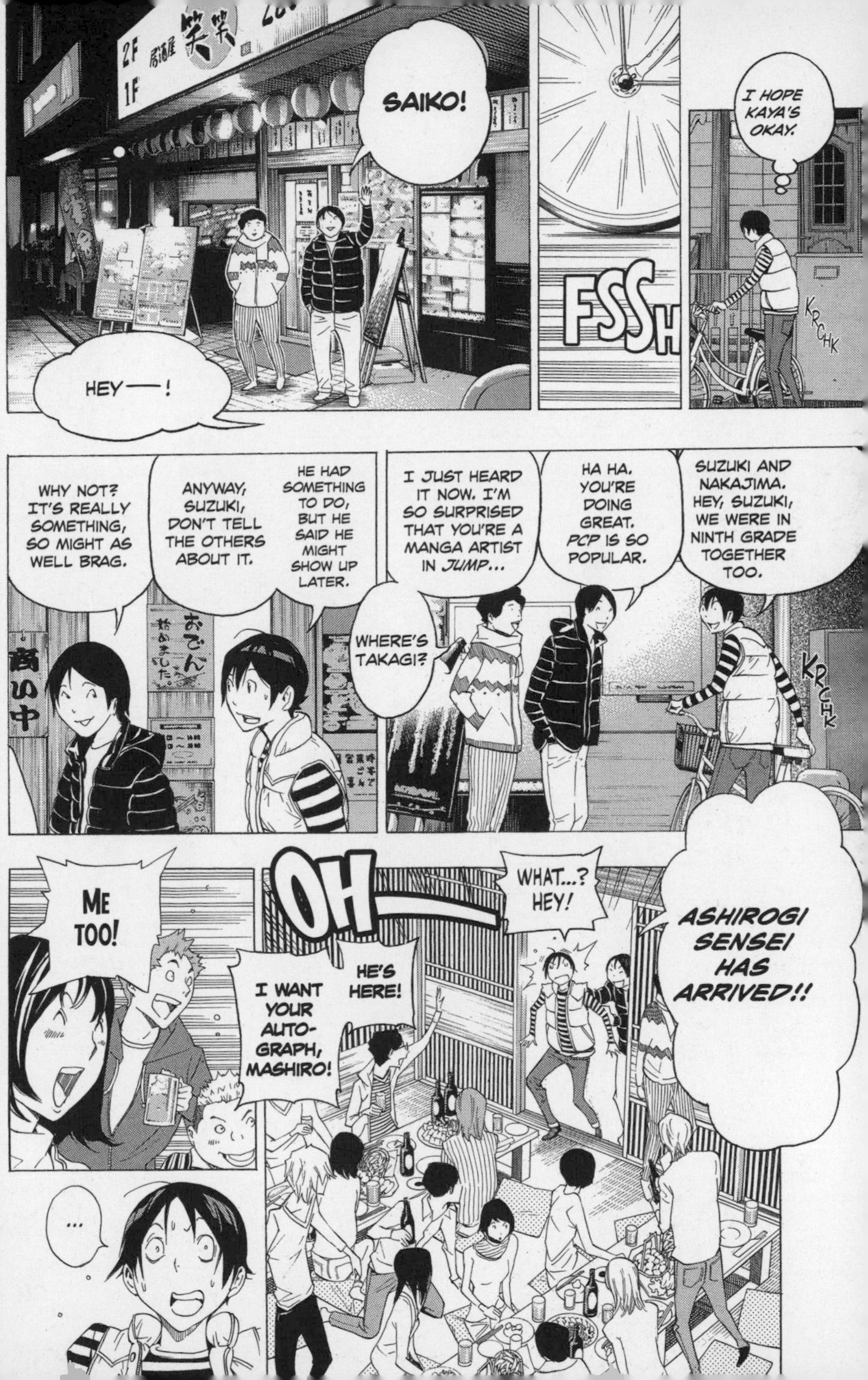

I HOPE KAYA'S OKAY.
KRCHK
FSSH
SAIKO!
HEY—!
SUZUKI AND NAKAJIMA. HEY, SUZUKI, WE WERE IN NINTH GRADE TOGETHER TOO.
HA HA. YOU'RE DOING GREAT. *PCP* IS SO POPULAR.
I JUST HEARD IT NOW. I'M SO SURPRISED THAT YOU'RE A MANGA ARTIST IN *JUMP*...
WHERE'S TAKAGI?
KRCHK
HE HAD SOMETHING TO DO, BUT HE SAID HE MIGHT SHOW UP LATER.
ANYWAY, SUZUKI, DON'T TELL THE OTHERS ABOUT IT.
WHY NOT? IT'S REALLY SOMETHING, SO MIGHT AS WELL BRAG.
ASHIROGI SENSEI HAS ARRIVED!!
WHAT...? HEY!
OH—
HE'S HERE!
I WANT YOUR AUTO-GRAPH, MASHIRO!
ME TOO!
...

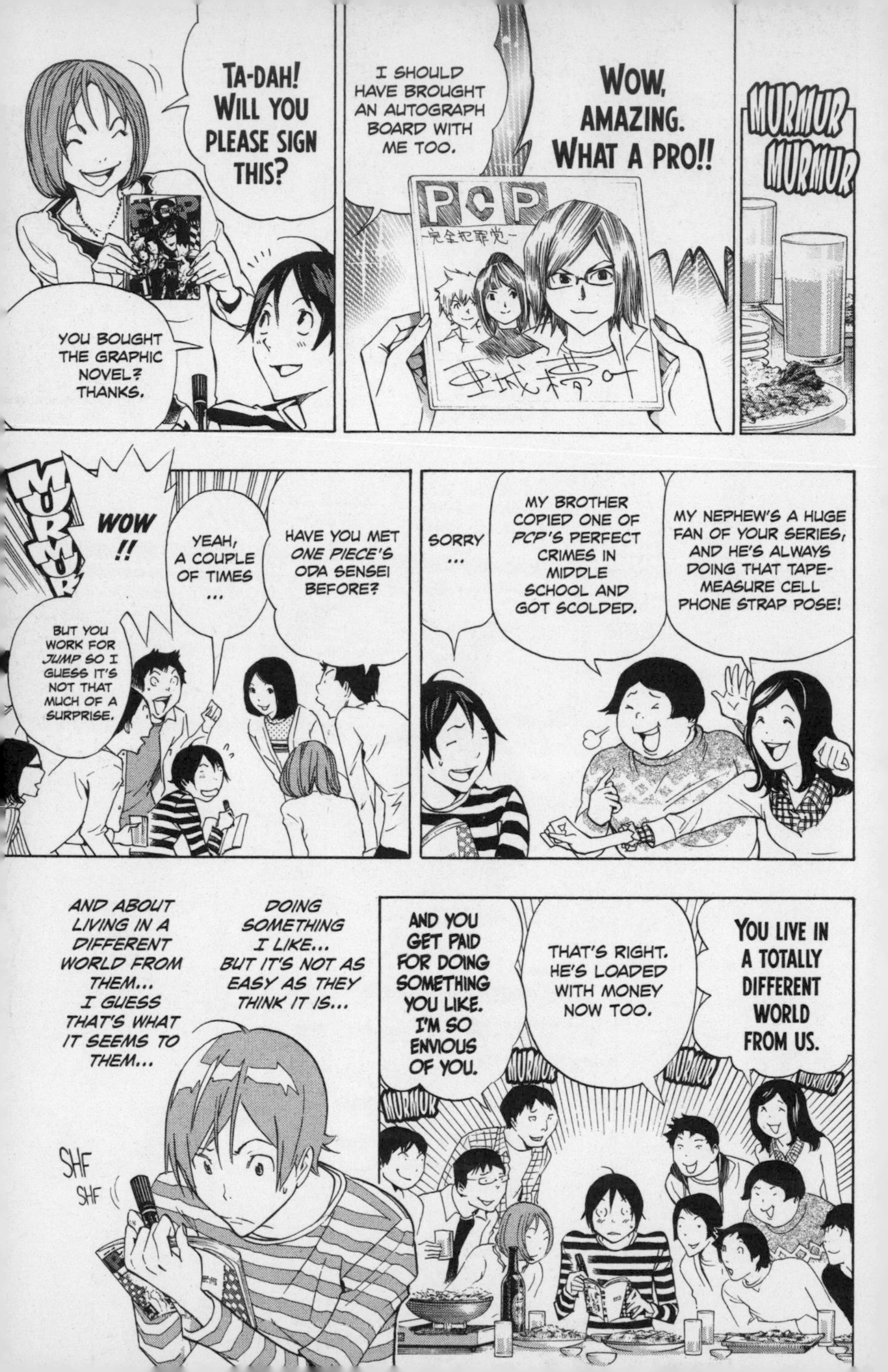

MURMUR MURMUR
WOW, AMAZING. WHAT A PRO!!
I SHOULD HAVE BROUGHT AN AUTOGRAPH BOARD WITH ME TOO.
PCP
完全犯罪党
TA-DAH! WILL YOU PLEASE SIGN THIS?
YOU BOUGHT THE GRAPHIC NOVEL? THANKS.
MY NEPHEW'S A HUGE FAN OF YOUR SERIES, AND HE'S ALWAYS DOING THAT TAPE-MEASURE CELL PHONE STRAP POSE!
MY BROTHER COPIED ONE OF PCP'S PERFECT CRIMES IN MIDDLE SCHOOL AND GOT SCOLDED.
SORRY ...
HAVE YOU MET ONE PIECE'S ODA SENSEI BEFORE?
YEAH, A COUPLE OF TIMES ...
WOW !!
MURMUR
BUT YOU WORK FOR JUMP SO I GUESS IT'S NOT THAT MUCH OF A SURPRISE.
YOU LIVE IN A TOTALLY DIFFERENT WORLD FROM US.
THAT'S RIGHT. HE'S LOADED WITH MONEY NOW TOO.
AND YOU GET PAID FOR DOING SOMETHING YOU LIKE. I'M SO ENVIOUS OF YOU.
MURMUR
MURMUR
MURMUR
MURMUR
DOING SOMETHING I LIKE... BUT IT'S NOT AS EASY AS THEY THINK IT IS...
AND ABOUT LIVING IN A DIFFERENT WORLD FROM THEM... I GUESS THAT'S WHAT IT SEEMS TO THEM...
SHF
SHF

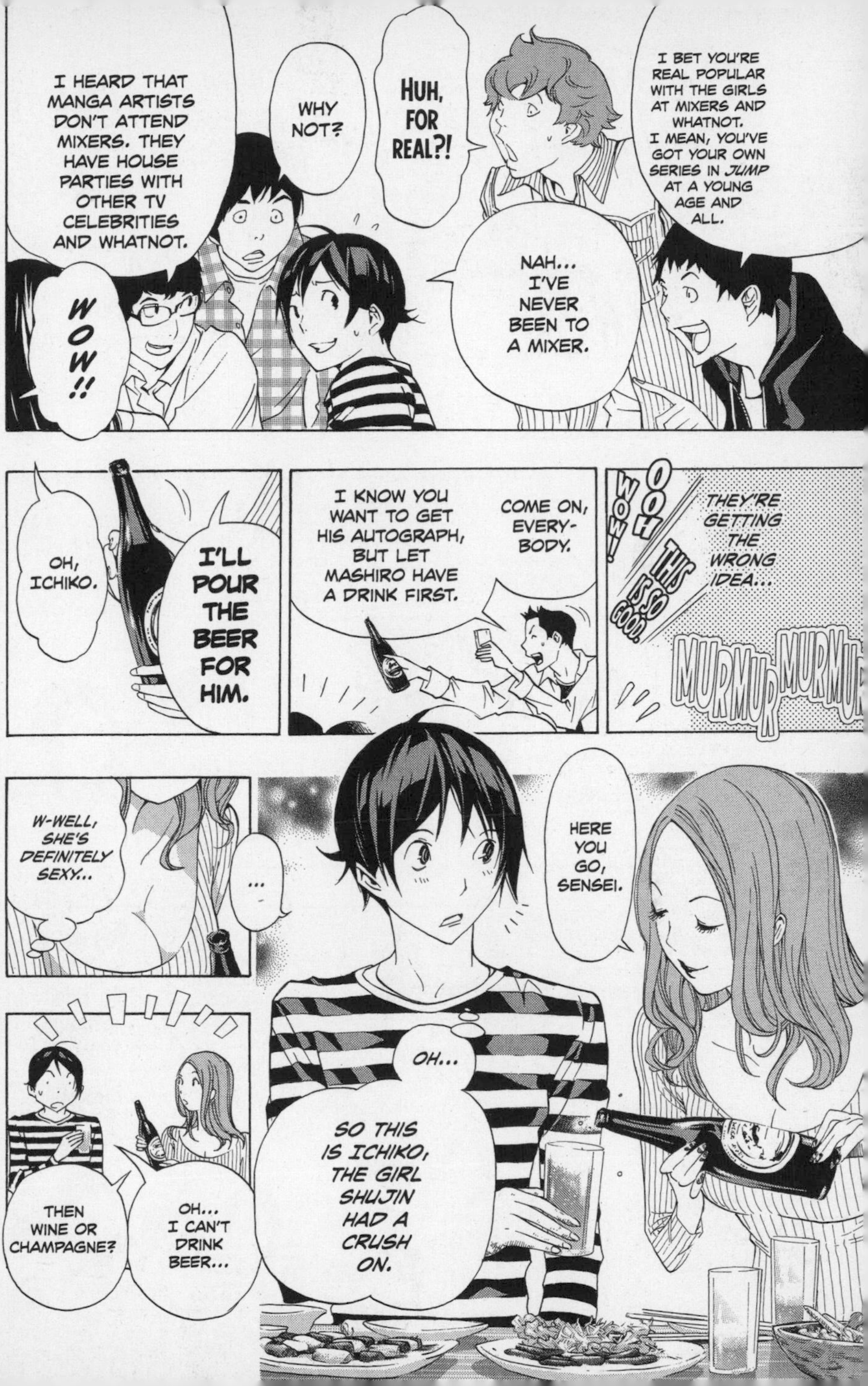
I BET YOU'RE REAL POPULAR WITH THE GIRLS AT MIXERS AND WHATNOT. I MEAN, YOU'VE GOT YOUR OWN SERIES IN *JUMP* AT A YOUNG AGE AND ALL.
NAH... I'VE NEVER BEEN TO A MIXER.
HUH, FOR REAL?!
WHY NOT?
I HEARD THAT MANGA ARTISTS DON'T ATTEND MIXERS. THEY HAVE HOUSE PARTIES WITH OTHER TV CELEBRITIES AND WHATNOT.
WOW!!
OOH
WOW!
THIS IS SO GOOD.
THEY'RE GETTING THE WRONG IDEA...
MURMUR MURMU
COME ON, EVERYBODY.
I KNOW YOU WANT TO GET HIS AUTOGRAPH, BUT LET MASHIRO HAVE A DRINK FIRST.
I'LL POUR THE BEER FOR HIM.
OH, ICHIKO.
HERE YOU GO, SENSEI.
OH...
SO THIS IS ICHIKO, THE GIRL SHUJIN HAD A CRUSH ON.
...
W-WELL, SHE'S DEFINITELY SEXY...
OH... I CAN'T DRINK BEER...
THEN WINE OR CHAMPAGNE?

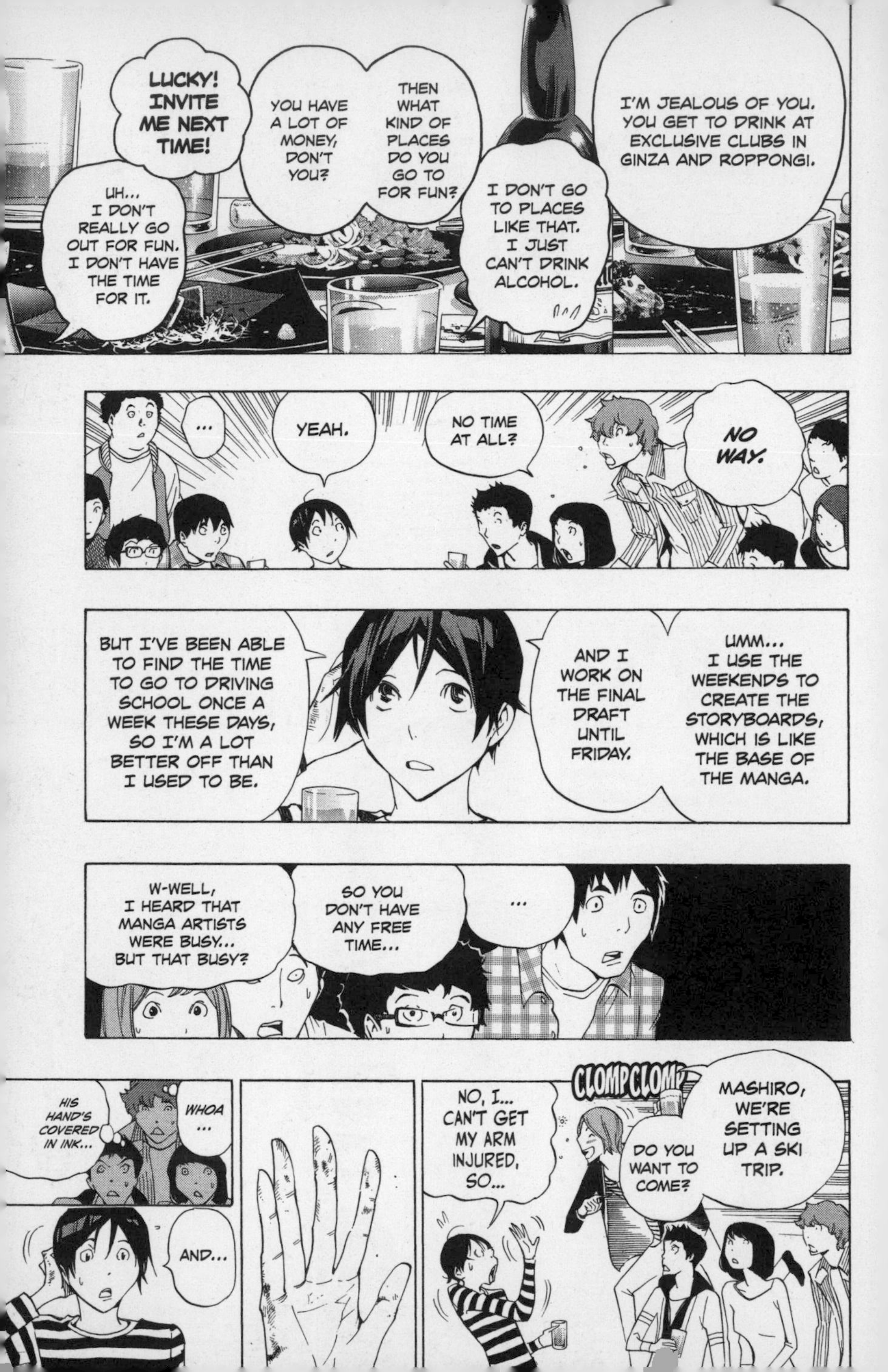
I'M JEALOUS OF YOU. YOU GET TO DRINK AT EXCLUSIVE CLUBS IN GINZA AND ROPPONGI.
I DON'T GO TO PLACES LIKE THAT. I JUST CAN'T DRINK ALCOHOL.
THEN WHAT KIND OF PLACES DO YOU GO TO FOR FUN?
YOU HAVE A LOT OF MONEY, DON'T YOU?
LUCKY! INVITE ME NEXT TIME!
UH... I DON'T REALLY GO OUT FOR FUN. I DON'T HAVE THE TIME FOR IT.
NO WAY.
NO TIME AT ALL?
YEAH.
...
UMM... I USE THE WEEKENDS TO CREATE THE STORYBOARDS, WHICH IS LIKE THE BASE OF THE MANGA.
AND I WORK ON THE FINAL DRAFT UNTIL FRIDAY.
BUT I'VE BEEN ABLE TO FIND THE TIME TO GO TO DRIVING SCHOOL ONCE A WEEK THESE DAYS, SO I'M A LOT BETTER OFF THAN I USED TO BE.
...
SO YOU DON'T HAVE ANY FREE TIME...
W-WELL, I HEARD THAT MANGA ARTISTS WERE BUSY... BUT THAT BUSY?
CLOMPCLOM
MASHIRO, WE'RE SETTING UP A SKI TRIP.
DO YOU WANT TO COME?
NO, I... CAN'T GET MY ARM INJURED, SO...
WHOA ...
HIS HAND'S COVERED IN INK...
AND...

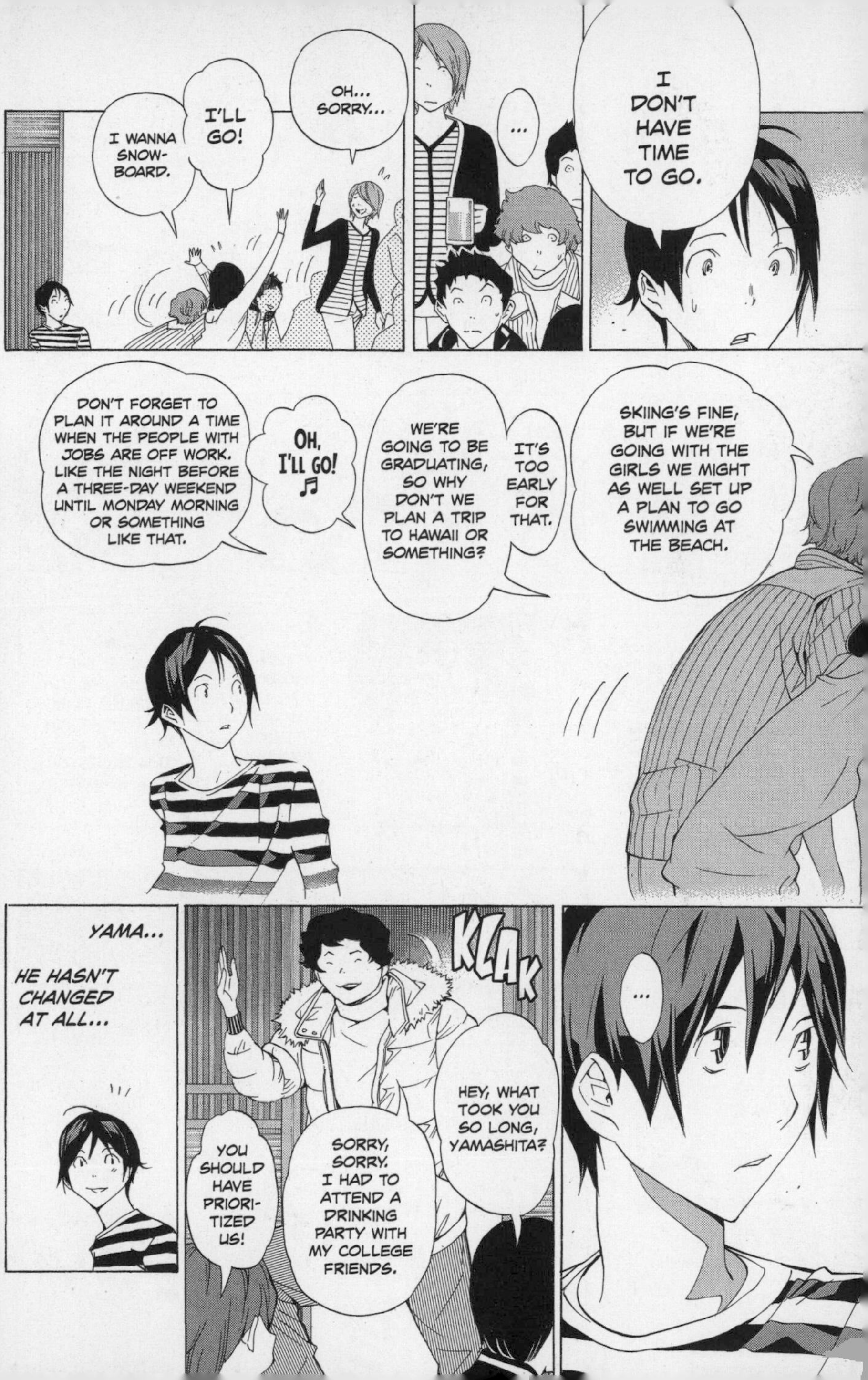
I DON'T HAVE TIME TO GO.
...
OH... SORRY...
I'LL GO!
I WANNA SNOW-BOARD.
SKIING'S FINE, BUT IF WE'RE GOING WITH THE GIRLS WE MIGHT AS WELL SET UP A PLAN TO GO SWIMMING AT THE BEACH.
IT'S TOO EARLY FOR THAT.
WE'RE GOING TO BE GRADUATING, SO WHY DON'T WE PLAN A TRIP TO HAWAII OR SOMETHING?
OH, I'LL GO! ♪
DON'T FORGET TO PLAN IT AROUND A TIME WHEN THE PEOPLE WITH JOBS ARE OFF WORK. LIKE THE NIGHT BEFORE A THREE-DAY WEEKEND UNTIL MONDAY MORNING OR SOMETHING LIKE THAT.
...
KLAK
HEY, WHAT TOOK YOU SO LONG, YAMASHITA?
SORRY, SORRY. I HAD TO ATTEND A DRINKING PARTY WITH MY COLLEGE FRIENDS.
YOU SHOULD HAVE PRIORI-TIZED US!
YAMA...
HE HASN'T CHANGED AT ALL...

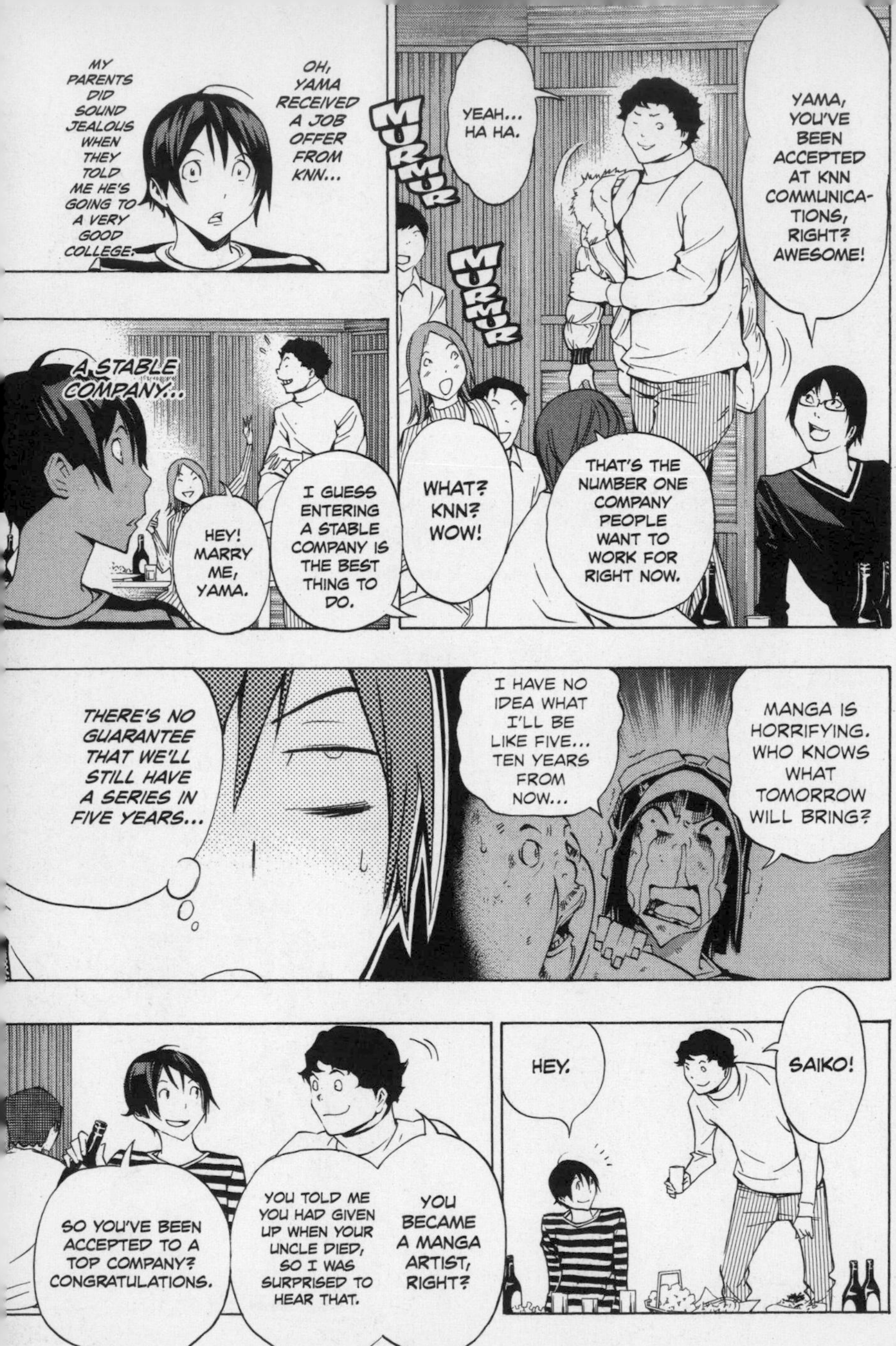

YAMA, YOU'VE BEEN ACCEPTED AT KNN COMMUNICATIONS, RIGHT? AWESOME!
YEAH... HA HA.
MURMUR
MURMUR
THAT'S THE NUMBER ONE COMPANY PEOPLE WANT TO WORK FOR RIGHT NOW.
WHAT? KNN? WOW!
OH, YAMA RECEIVED A JOB OFFER FROM KNN...
MY PARENTS DID SOUND JEALOUS WHEN THEY TOLD ME HE'S GOING TO A VERY GOOD COLLEGE.
A STABLE COMPANY...
I GUESS ENTERING A STABLE COMPANY IS THE BEST THING TO DO.
HEY! MARRY ME, YAMA.
MANGA IS HORRIFYING. WHO KNOWS WHAT TOMORROW WILL BRING?
I HAVE NO IDEA WHAT I'LL BE LIKE FIVE... TEN YEARS FROM NOW...
THERE'S NO GUARANTEE THAT WE'LL STILL HAVE A SERIES IN FIVE YEARS...
SAIKO!
HEY.
YOU BECAME A MANGA ARTIST, RIGHT?
YOU TOLD ME YOU HAD GIVEN UP WHEN YOUR UNCLE DIED, SO I WAS SURPRISED TO HEAR THAT.
SO YOU'VE BEEN ACCEPTED TO A TOP COMPANY? CONGRATULATIONS.

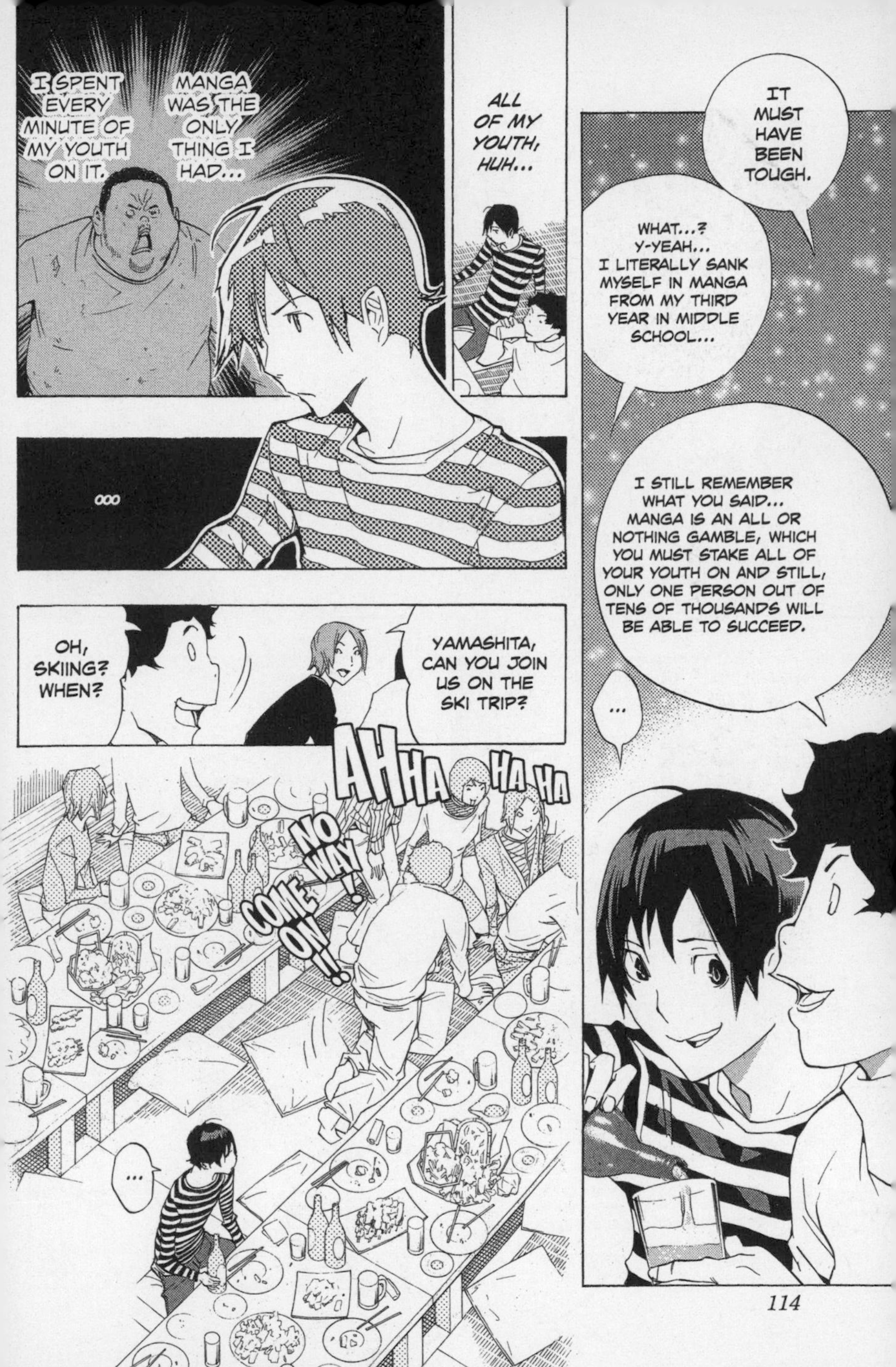
IT MUST HAVE BEEN TOUGH.
WHAT...? Y-YEAH... I LITERALLY SANK MYSELF IN MANGA FROM MY THIRD YEAR IN MIDDLE SCHOOL...
I STILL REMEMBER WHAT YOU SAID... MANGA IS AN ALL OR NOTHING GAMBLE, WHICH YOU MUST STAKE ALL OF YOUR YOUTH ON AND STILL, ONLY ONE PERSON OUT OF TENS OF THOUSANDS WILL BE ABLE TO SUCCEED.
...
ALL OF MY YOUTH, HUH...
MANGA WAS THE ONLY THING I HAD...
I SPENT EVERY MINUTE OF MY YOUTH ON IT.
ooo
YAMASHITA, CAN YOU JOIN US ON THE SKI TRIP?
OH, SKIING? WHEN?
AHHA HA HA HA
NO WAY!
COME ON!!
...

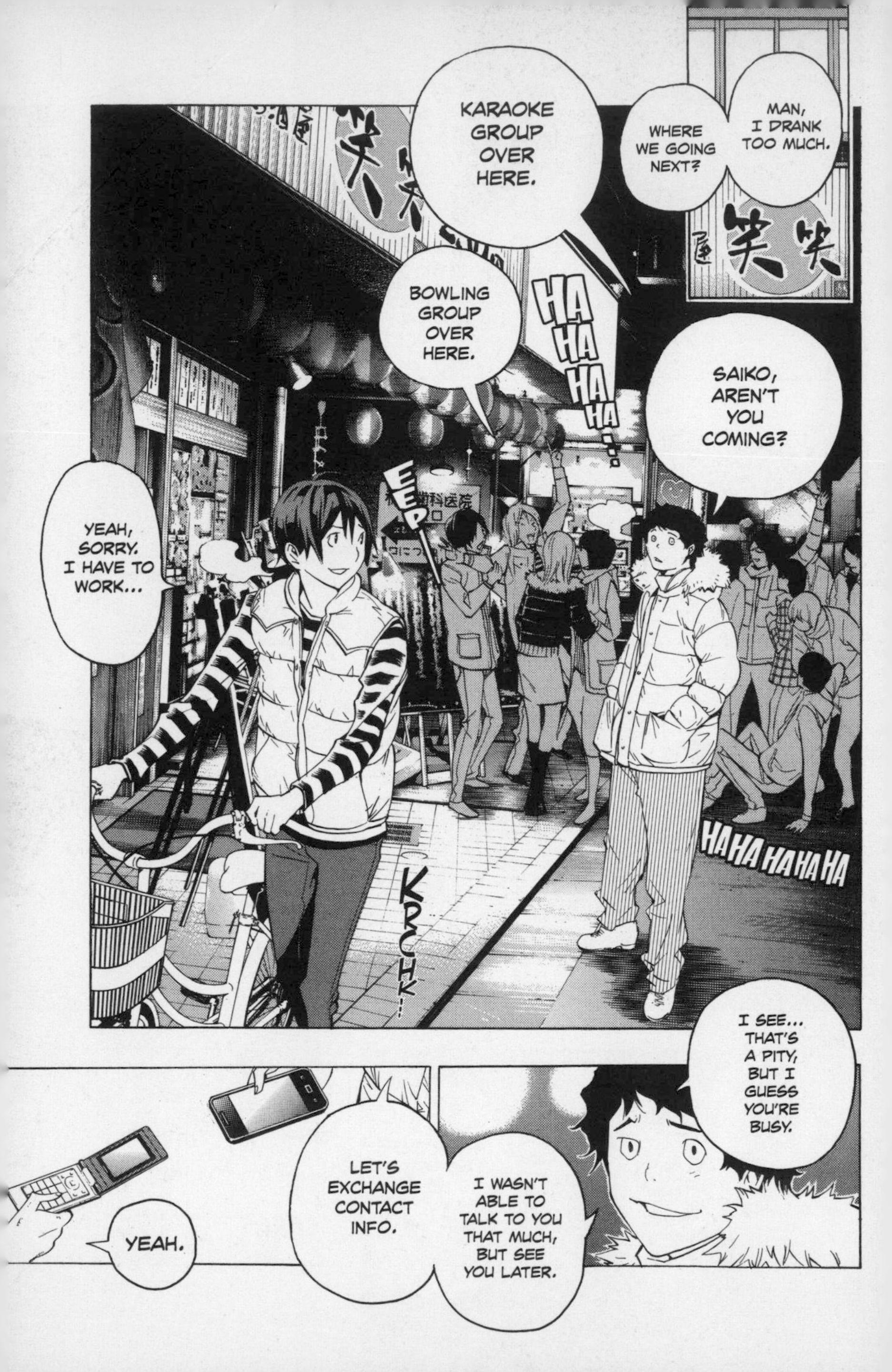
MAN, I DRANK TOO MUCH.
WHERE WE GOING NEXT?
KARAOKE GROUP OVER HERE.
HA HA HA HA..
BOWLING GROUP OVER HERE.
SAIKO, AREN'T YOU COMING?
EEP
YEAH, SORRY. I HAVE TO WORK...
HA HA HA HA HA
KRCHK...
I SEE... THAT'S A PITY, BUT I GUESS YOU'RE BUSY.
I WASN'T ABLE TO TALK TO YOU THAT MUCH, BUT SEE YOU LATER.
LET'S EXCHANGE CONTACT INFO.
YEAH.

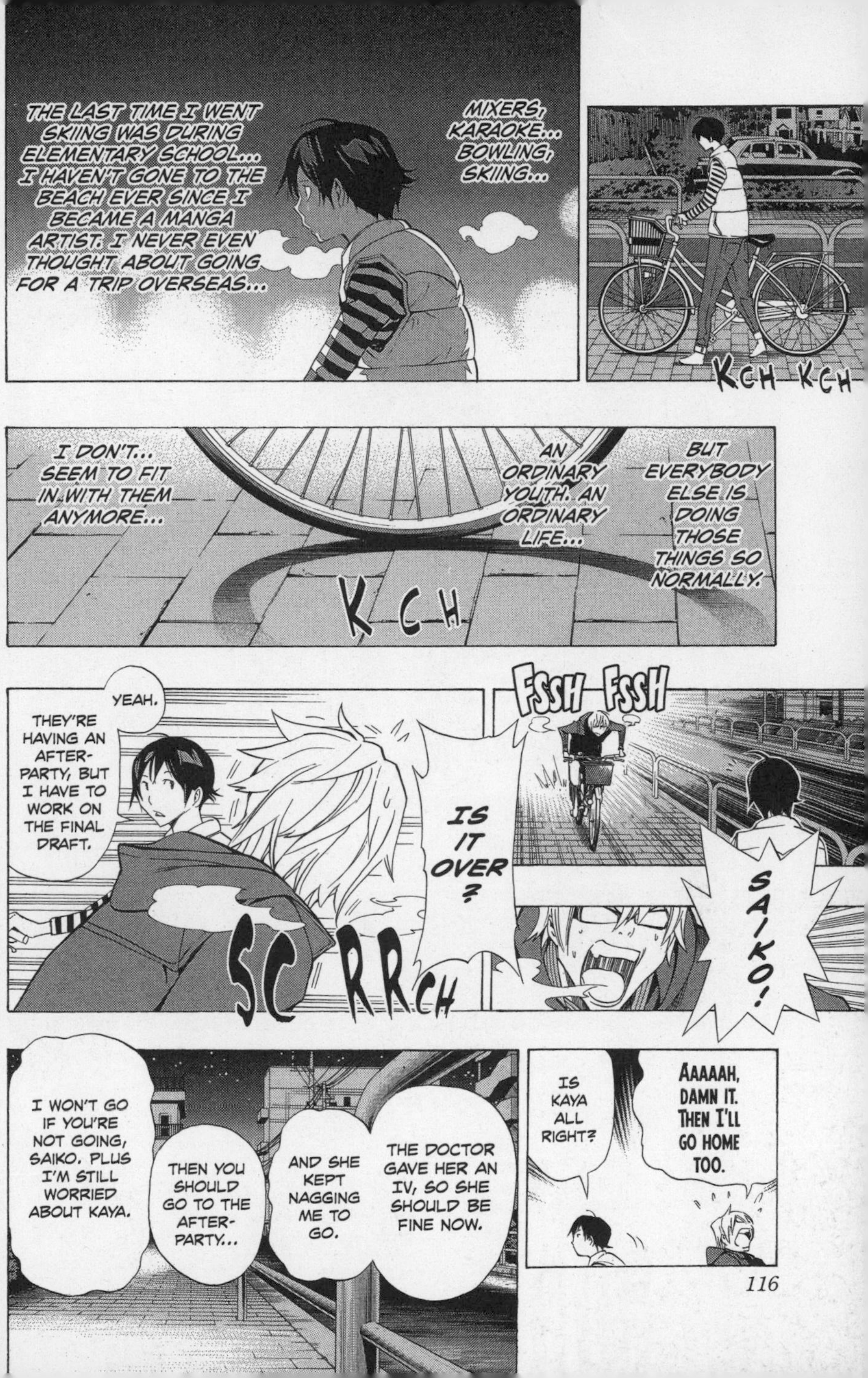
KCH KCH
MIXERS, KARAOKE... BOWLING, SKIING...
THE LAST TIME I WENT SKIING WAS DURING ELEMENTARY SCHOOL... I HAVEN'T GONE TO THE BEACH EVER SINCE I BECAME A MANGA ARTIST. I NEVER EVEN THOUGHT ABOUT GOING FOR A TRIP OVERSEAS...
BUT EVERYBODY ELSE IS DOING THOSE THINGS SO NORMALLY.
AN ORDINARY YOUTH. AN ORDINARY LIFE...
I DON'T... SEEM TO FIT IN WITH THEM ANYMORE...
KCH
FSSH FSSH
SAIKO!
IS IT OVER?
YEAH.
THEY'RE HAVING AN AFTER-PARTY, BUT I HAVE TO WORK ON THE FINAL DRAFT.
SC RRCH
AAAAAH, DAMN IT. THEN I'LL GO HOME TOO.
IS KAYA ALL RIGHT?
THE DOCTOR GAVE HER AN IV, SO SHE SHOULD BE FINE NOW.
AND SHE KEPT NAGGING ME TO GO.
THEN YOU SHOULD GO TO THE AFTER-PARTY...
I WON'T GO IF YOU'RE NOT GOING, SAIKO. PLUS I'M STILL WORRIED ABOUT KAYA.

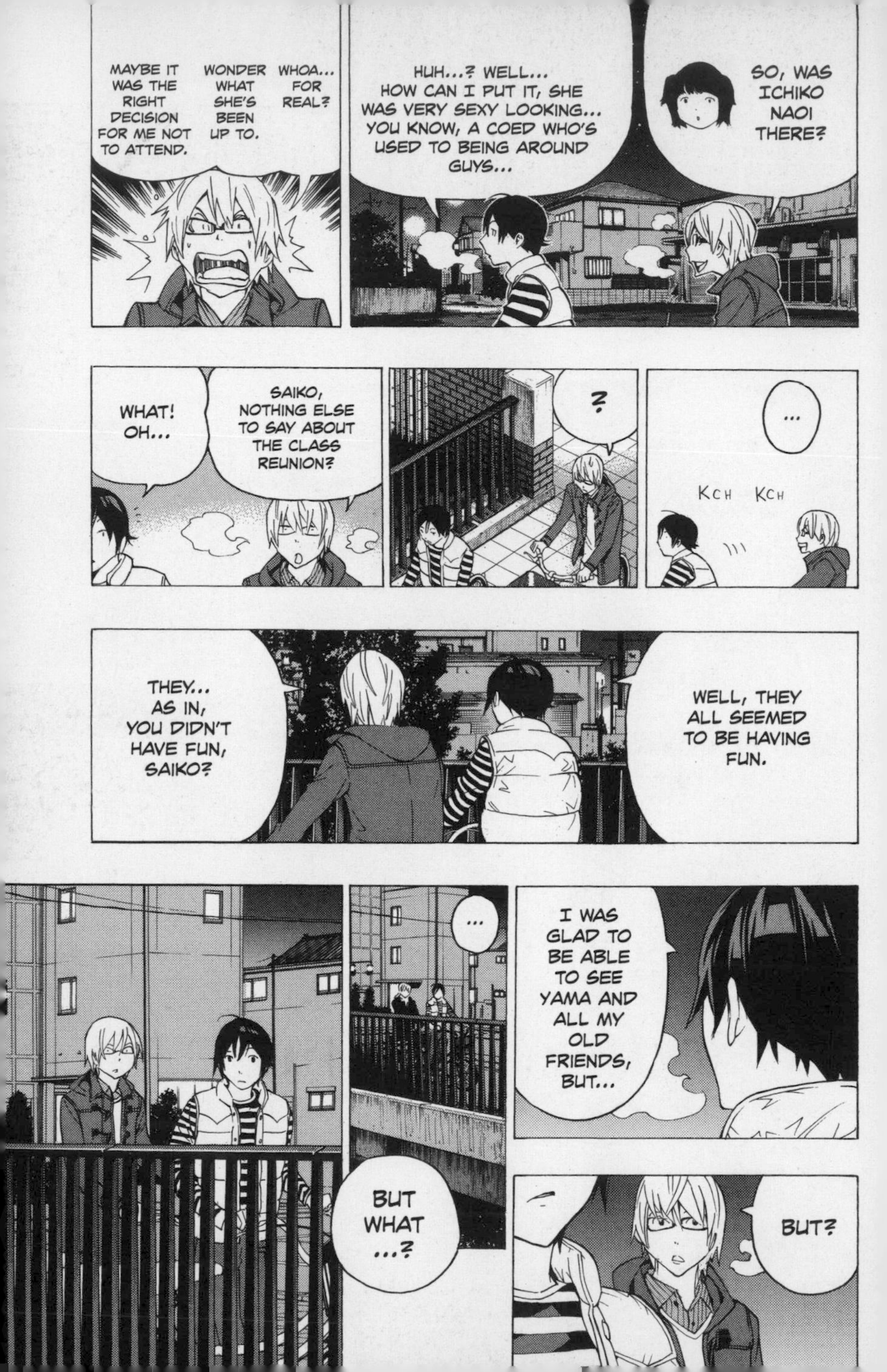
SO, WAS ICHIKO NAOI THERE?
HUH...? WELL... HOW CAN I PUT IT, SHE WAS VERY SEXY LOOKING... YOU KNOW, A COED WHO'S USED TO BEING AROUND GUYS...
WHOA... FOR REAL?
WONDER WHAT SHE'S BEEN UP TO.
MAYBE IT WAS THE RIGHT DECISION FOR ME NOT TO ATTEND.
...
KCH KCH
?
SAIKO, NOTHING ELSE TO SAY ABOUT THE CLASS REUNION?
WHAT! OH...
WELL, THEY ALL SEEMED TO BE HAVING FUN.
THEY... AS IN, YOU DIDN'T HAVE FUN, SAIKO?
I WAS GLAD TO BE ABLE TO SEE YAMA AND ALL MY OLD FRIENDS, BUT...
BUT?
...
BUT WHAT ...?

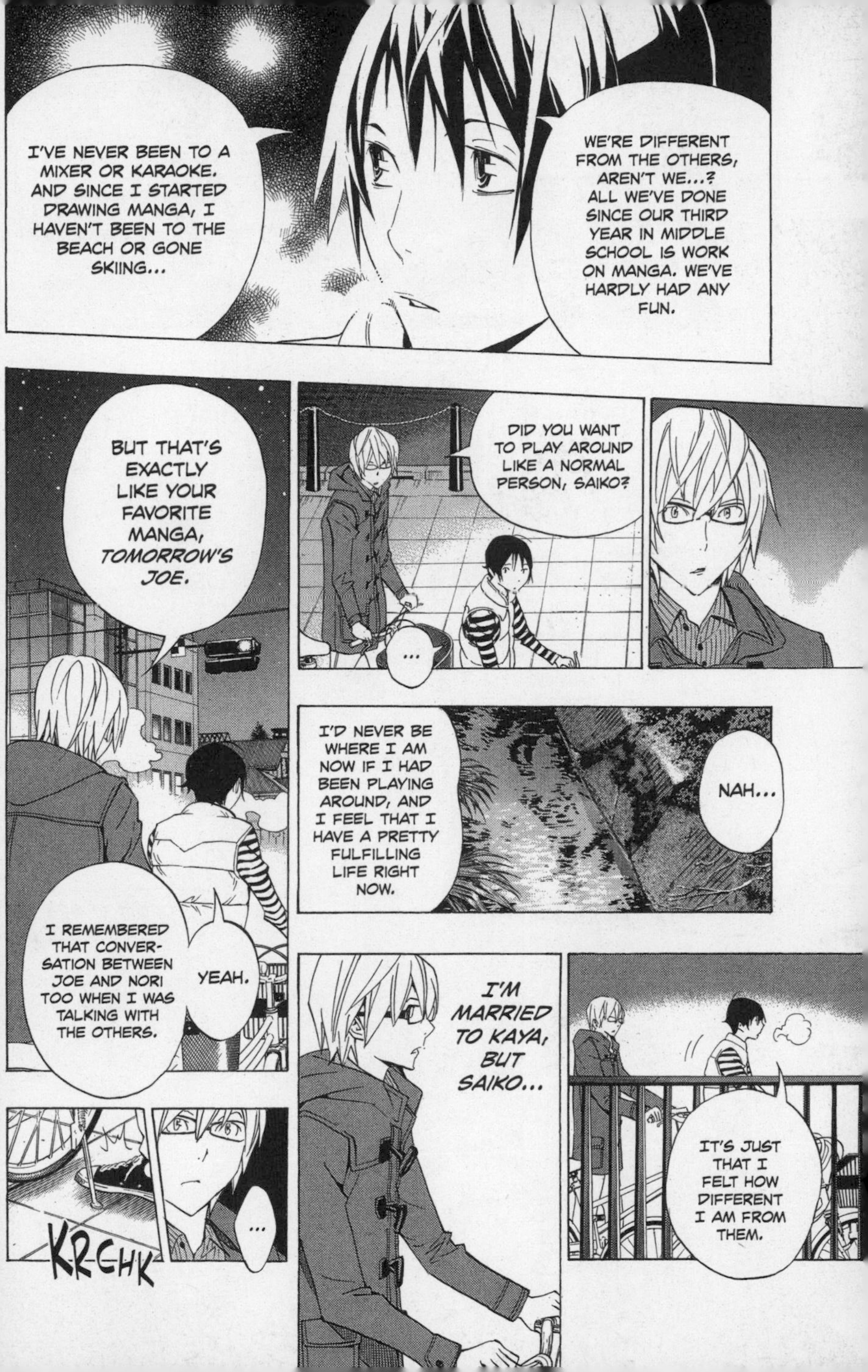
WE'RE DIFFERENT FROM THE OTHERS, AREN'T WE...? ALL WE'VE DONE SINCE OUR THIRD YEAR IN MIDDLE SCHOOL IS WORK ON MANGA. WE'VE HARDLY HAD ANY FUN.
I'VE NEVER BEEN TO A MIXER OR KARAOKE. AND SINCE I STARTED DRAWING MANGA, I HAVEN'T BEEN TO THE BEACH OR GONE SKIING...
DID YOU WANT TO PLAY AROUND LIKE A NORMAL PERSON, SAIKO?
...
NAH...
I'D NEVER BE WHERE I AM NOW IF I HAD BEEN PLAYING AROUND, AND I FEEL THAT I HAVE A PRETTY FULFILLING LIFE RIGHT NOW.
BUT THAT'S EXACTLY LIKE YOUR FAVORITE MANGA, *TOMORROW'S JOE*.
YEAH.
I REMEMBERED THAT CONVER-SATION BETWEEN JOE AND NORI TOO WHEN I WAS TALKING WITH THE OTHERS.
IT'S JUST THAT I FELT HOW DIFFERENT I AM FROM THEM.
I'M MARRIED TO KAYA, BUT SAIKO...
...
KRCHK

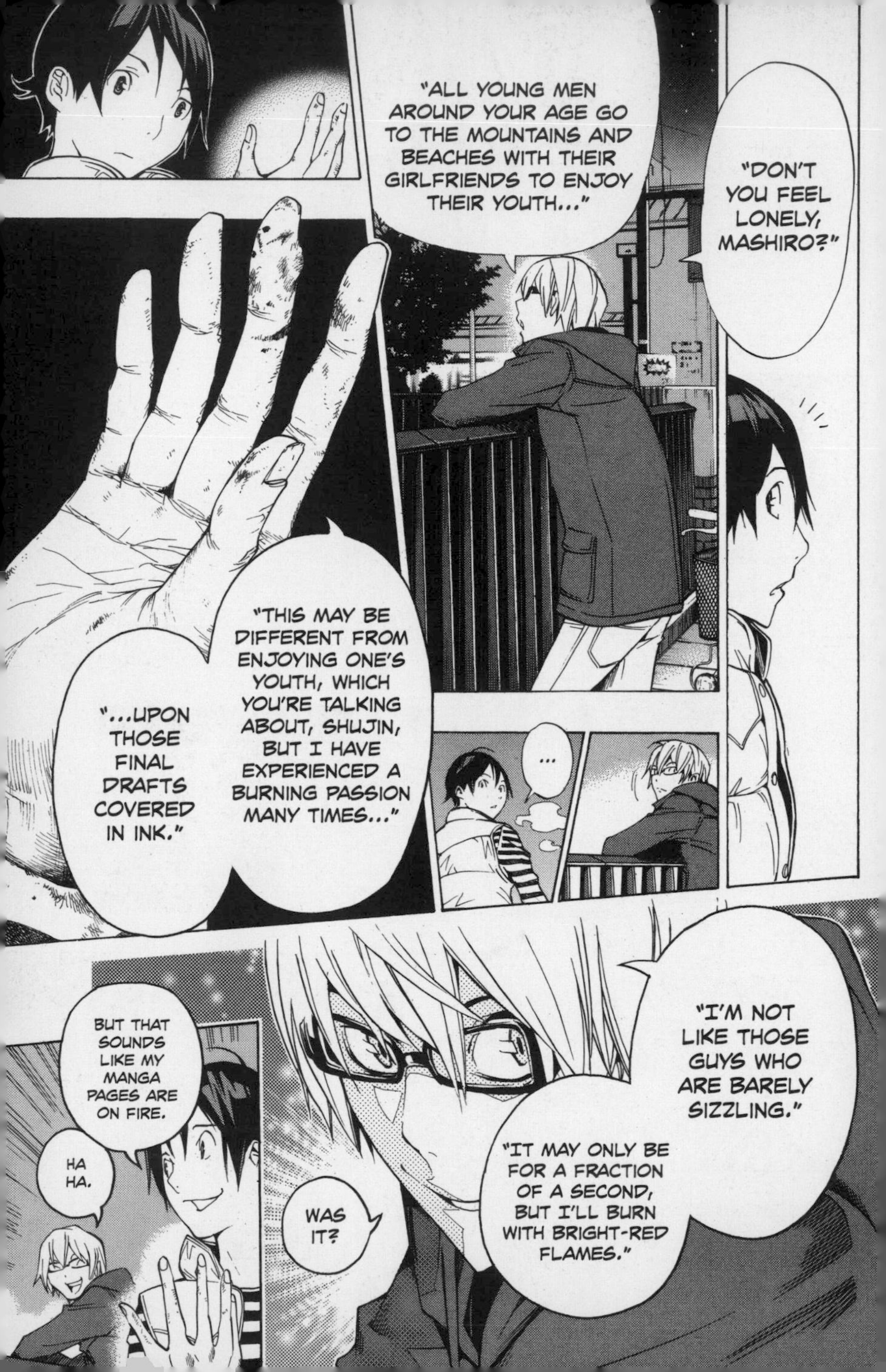
"ALL YOUNG MEN AROUND YOUR AGE GO TO THE MOUNTAINS AND BEACHES WITH THEIR GIRLFRIENDS TO ENJOY THEIR YOUTH..."
"DON'T YOU FEEL LONELY, MASHIRO?"
...
"THIS MAY BE DIFFERENT FROM ENJOYING ONE'S YOUTH, WHICH YOU'RE TALKING ABOUT, SHUJIN, BUT I HAVE EXPERIENCED A BURNING PASSION MANY TIMES..."
"...UPON THOSE FINAL DRAFTS COVERED IN INK."
"I'M NOT LIKE THOSE GUYS WHO ARE BARELY SIZZLING."
"IT MAY ONLY BE FOR A FRACTION OF A SECOND, BUT I'LL BURN WITH BRIGHT-RED FLAMES."
WAS IT?
BUT THAT SOUNDS LIKE MY MANGA PAGES ARE ON FIRE.
HA HA.

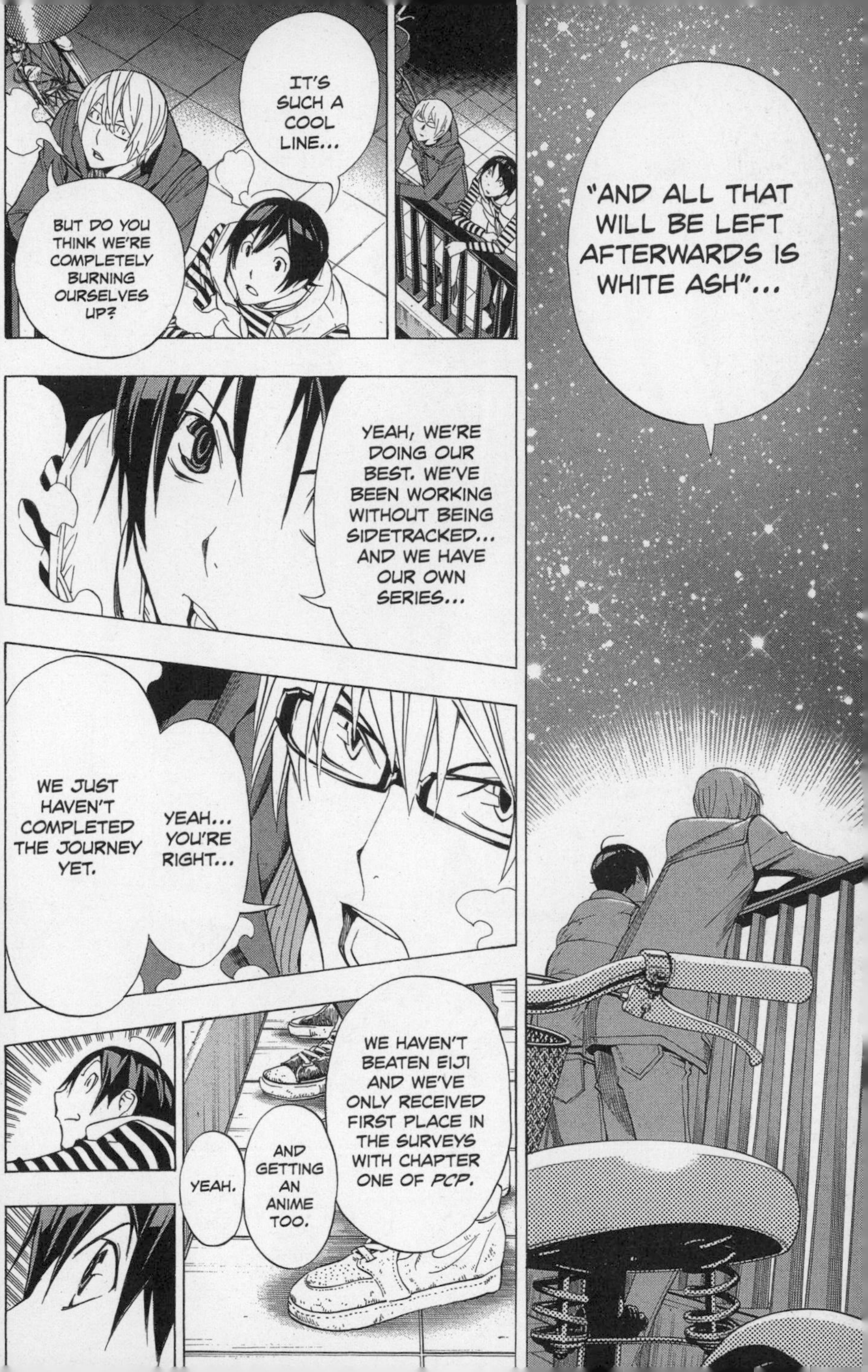
"AND ALL THAT WILL BE LEFT AFTERWARDS IS WHITE ASH"...
IT'S SUCH A COOL LINE...
BUT DO YOU THINK WE'RE COMPLETELY BURNING OURSELVES UP?
YEAH, WE'RE DOING OUR BEST. WE'VE BEEN WORKING WITHOUT BEING SIDETRACKED... AND WE HAVE OUR OWN SERIES...
WE JUST HAVEN'T COMPLETED THE JOURNEY YET.
YEAH... YOU'RE RIGHT...
WE HAVEN'T BEATEN EIJI AND WE'VE ONLY RECEIVED FIRST PLACE IN THE SURVEYS WITH CHAPTER ONE OF *PCP*.
AND GETTING AN ANIME TOO.
YEAH.

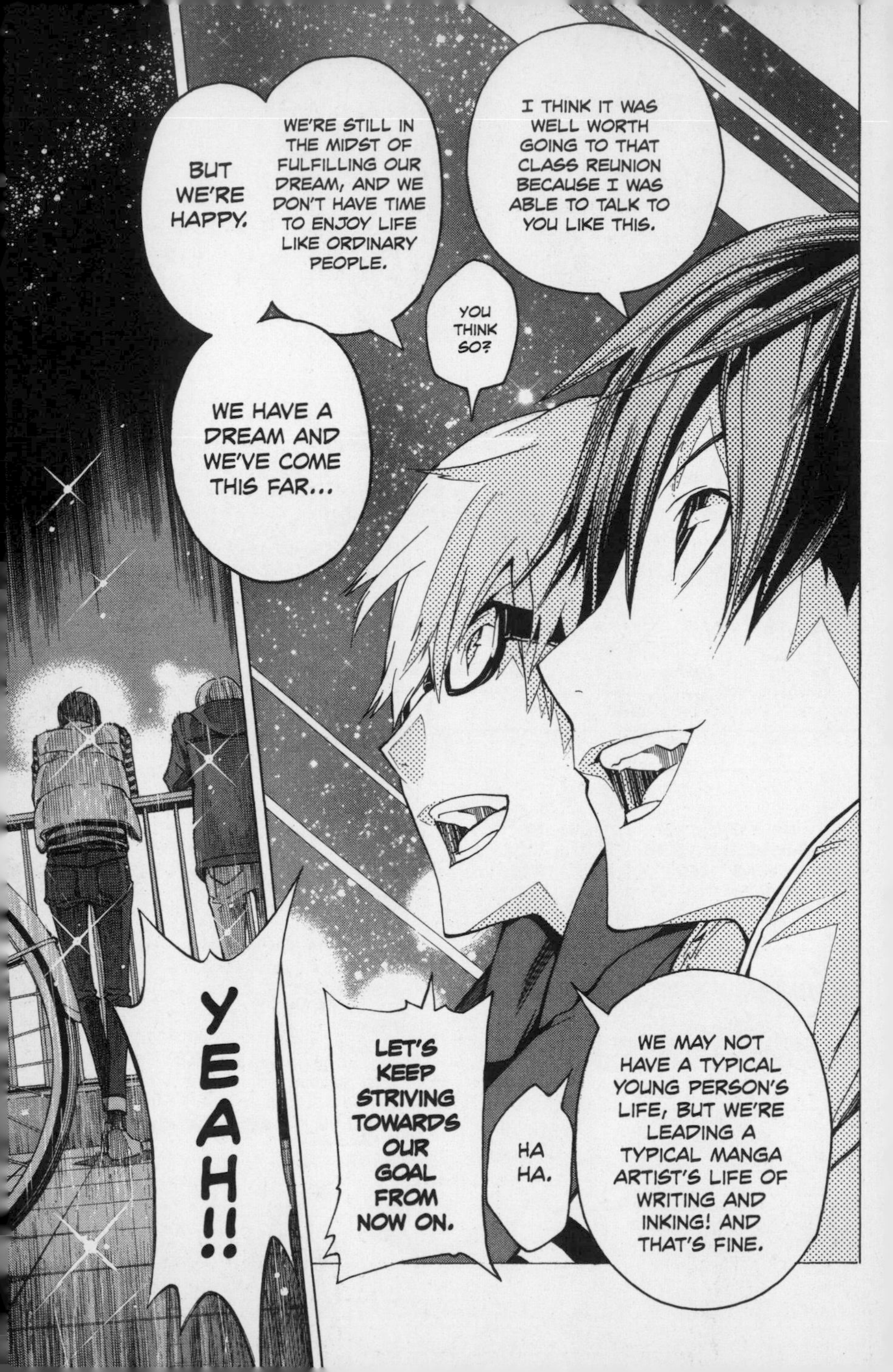

I THINK IT WAS WELL WORTH GOING TO THAT CLASS REUNION BECAUSE I WAS ABLE TO TALK TO YOU LIKE THIS.
YOU THINK SO?
WE'RE STILL IN THE MIDST OF FULFILLING OUR DREAM, AND WE DON'T HAVE TIME TO ENJOY LIFE LIKE ORDINARY PEOPLE.
BUT WE'RE HAPPY.
WE HAVE A DREAM AND WE'VE COME THIS FAR...
WE MAY NOT HAVE A TYPICAL YOUNG PERSON'S LIFE, BUT WE'RE LEADING A TYPICAL MANGA ARTIST'S LIFE OF WRITING AND INKING! AND THAT'S FINE.
HA HA.
LET'S KEEP STRIVING TOWARDS OUR GOAL FROM NOW ON.
YEAH!!

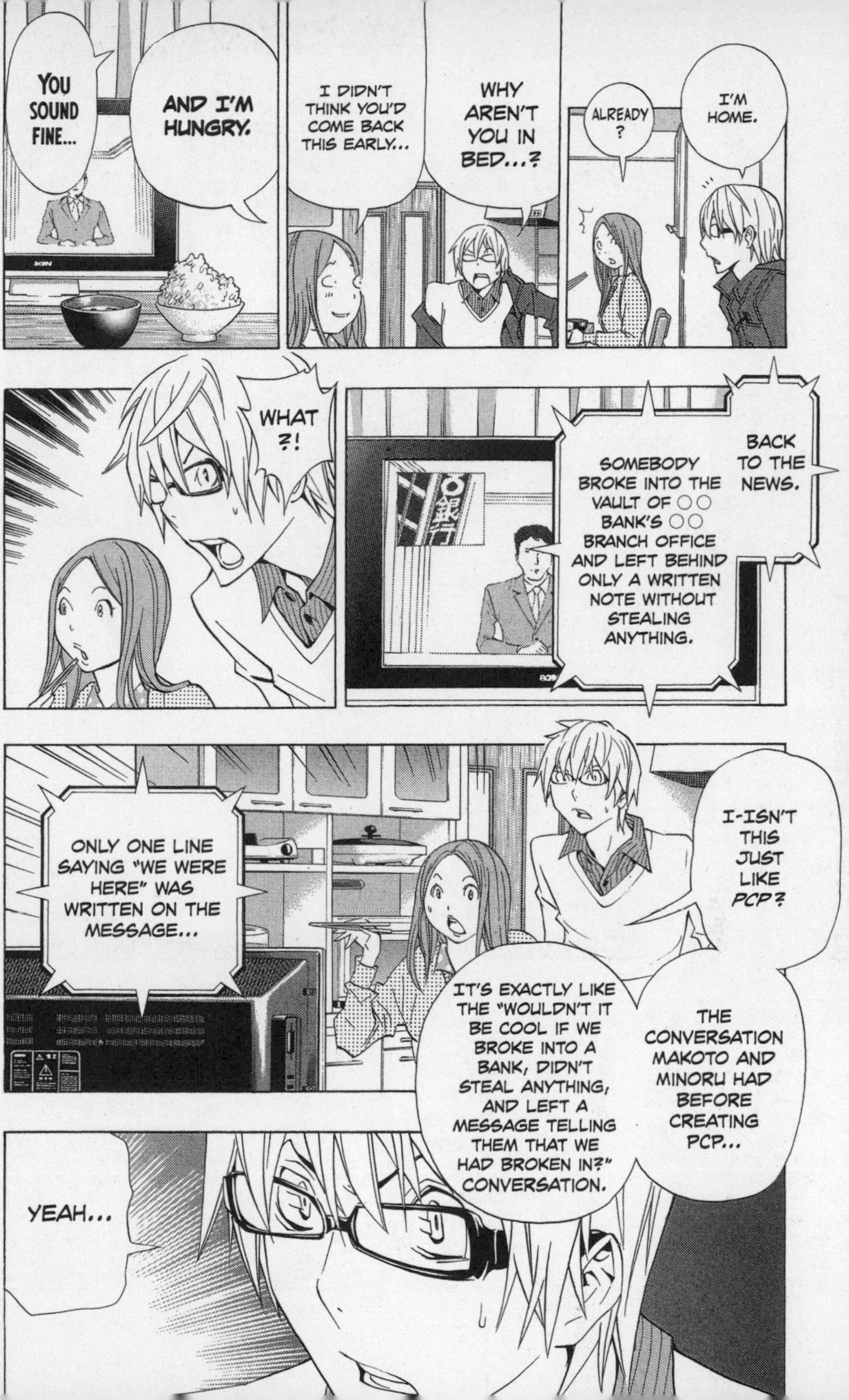
I'M HOME.
ALREADY?
WHY AREN'T YOU IN BED...?
I DIDN'T THINK YOU'D COME BACK THIS EARLY...
AND I'M HUNGRY.
YOU SOUND FINE...
BACK TO THE NEWS.
SOMEBODY BROKE INTO THE VAULT OF ○○ BANK'S ○○ BRANCH OFFICE AND LEFT BEHIND ONLY A WRITTEN NOTE WITHOUT STEALING ANYTHING.
WHAT?!
I-ISN'T THIS JUST LIKE *PCP*?
ONLY ONE LINE SAYING "WE WERE HERE" WAS WRITTEN ON THE MESSAGE...
THE CONVERSATION MAKOTO AND MINORU HAD BEFORE CREATING PCP...
IT'S EXACTLY LIKE THE "WOULDN'T IT BE COOL IF WE BROKE INTO A BANK, DIDN'T STEAL ANYTHING, AND LEFT A MESSAGE TELLING THEM THAT WE HAD BROKEN IN?" CONVERSATION.
YEAH...

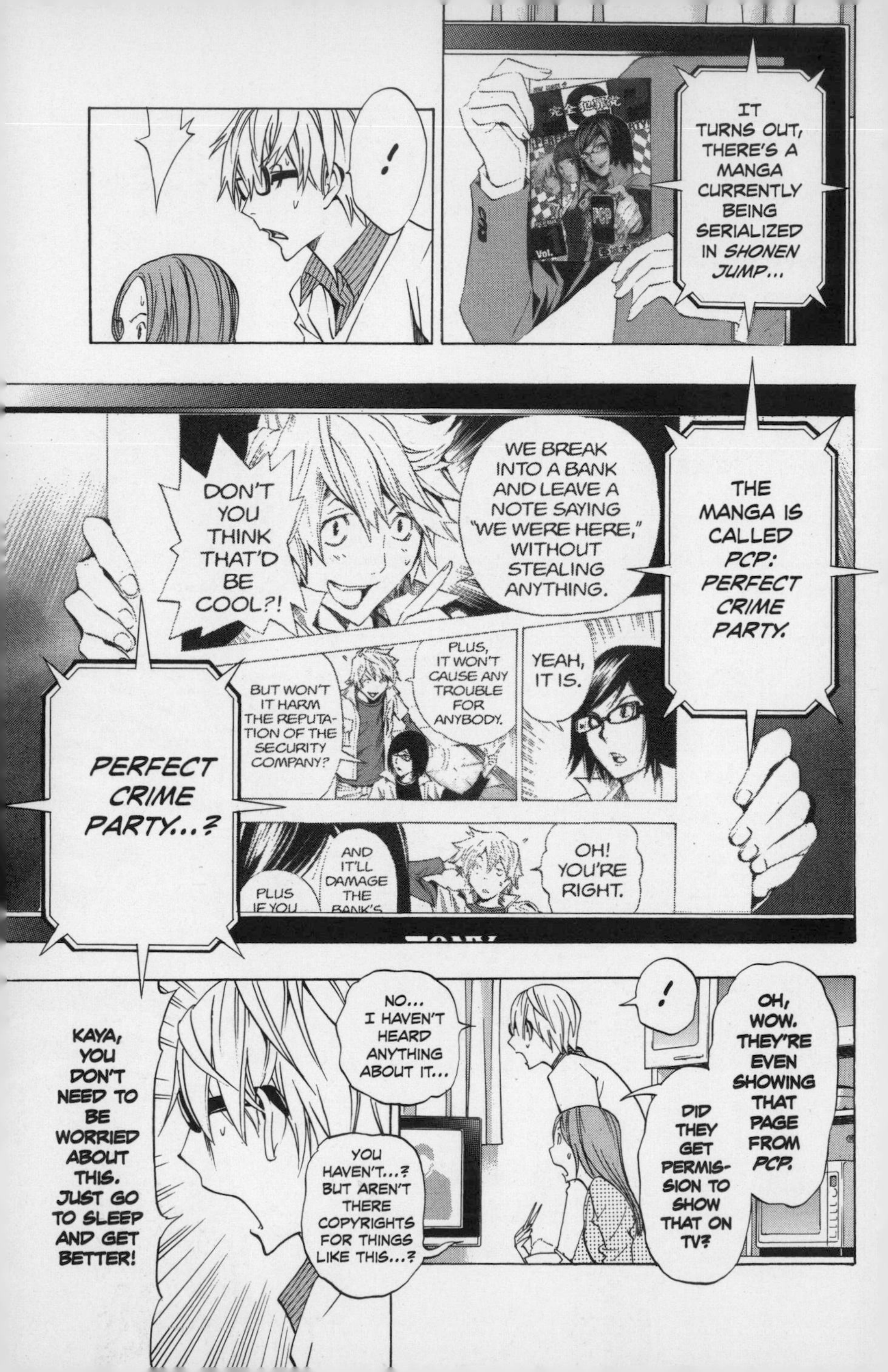
IT TURNS OUT, THERE'S A MANGA CURRENTLY BEING SERIALIZED IN *SHONEN JUMP*...
!
THE MANGA IS CALLED *PCP: PERFECT CRIME PARTY.*
WE BREAK INTO A BANK AND LEAVE A NOTE SAYING "WE WERE HERE," WITHOUT STEALING ANYTHING.
DON'T YOU THINK THAT'D BE COOL?!
YEAH, IT IS.
PLUS, IT WON'T CAUSE ANY TROUBLE FOR ANYBODY.
BUT WON'T IT HARM THE REPUTATION OF THE SECURITY COMPANY?
OH! YOU'RE RIGHT.
AND IT'LL DAMAGE THE
PLUS
PERFECT CRIME PARTY...?
!
OH, WOW. THEY'RE EVEN SHOWING THAT PAGE FROM *PCP.*
DID THEY GET PERMISSION TO SHOW THAT ON TV?
NO... I HAVEN'T HEARD ANYTHING ABOUT IT...
YOU HAVEN'T...? BUT AREN'T THERE COPYRIGHTS FOR THINGS LIKE THIS...?
KAYA, YOU DON'T NEED TO BE WORRIED ABOUT THIS. JUST GO TO SLEEP AND GET BETTER!

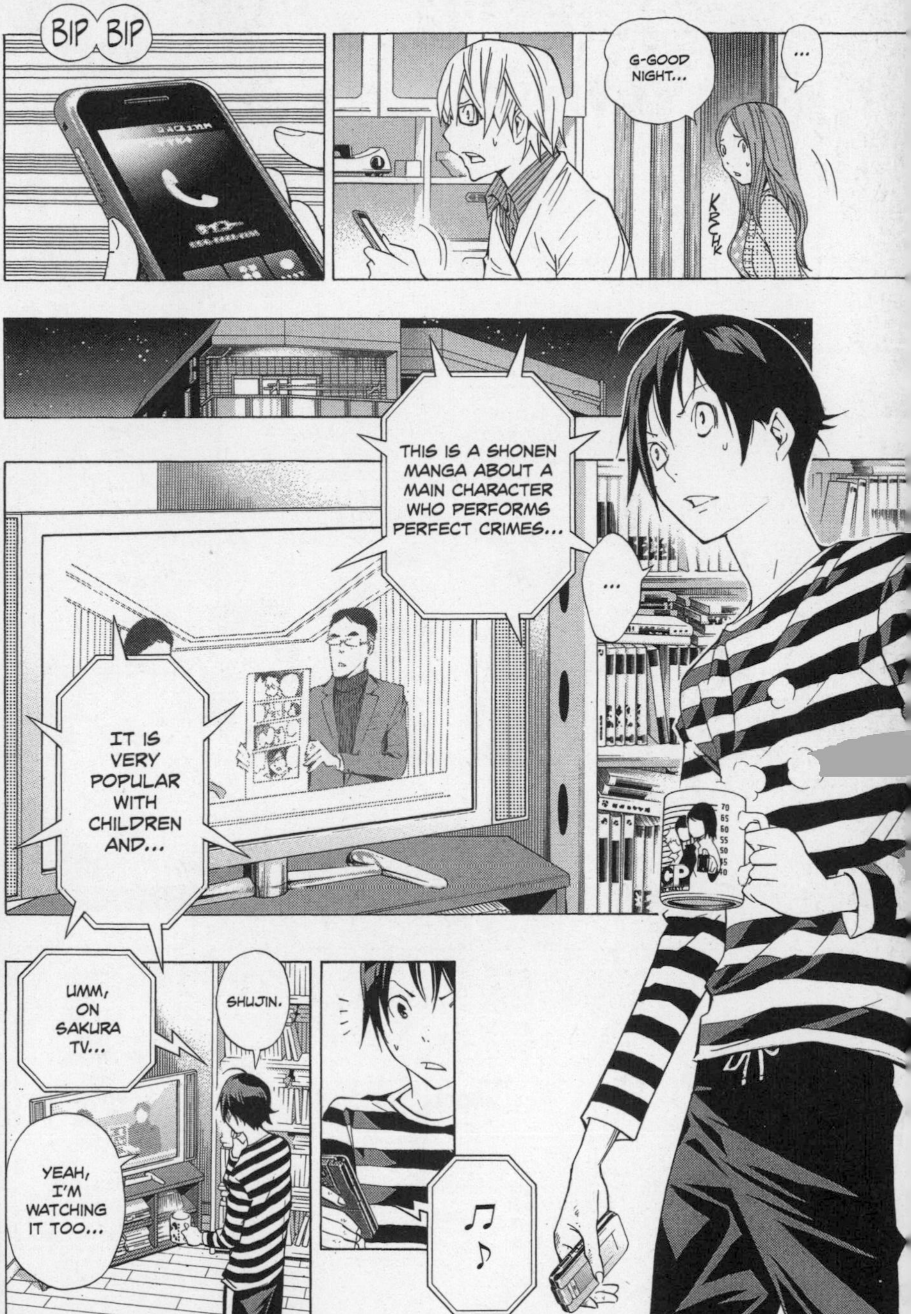
...
G-GOOD NIGHT...
KRCHK
BIP BIP
THIS IS A SHONEN MANGA ABOUT A MAIN CHARACTER WHO PERFORMS PERFECT CRIMES...
...
IT IS VERY POPULAR WITH CHILDREN AND...
♪ ♪
SHUJIN.
UMM, ON SAKURA TV...
YEAH, I'M WATCHING IT TOO...

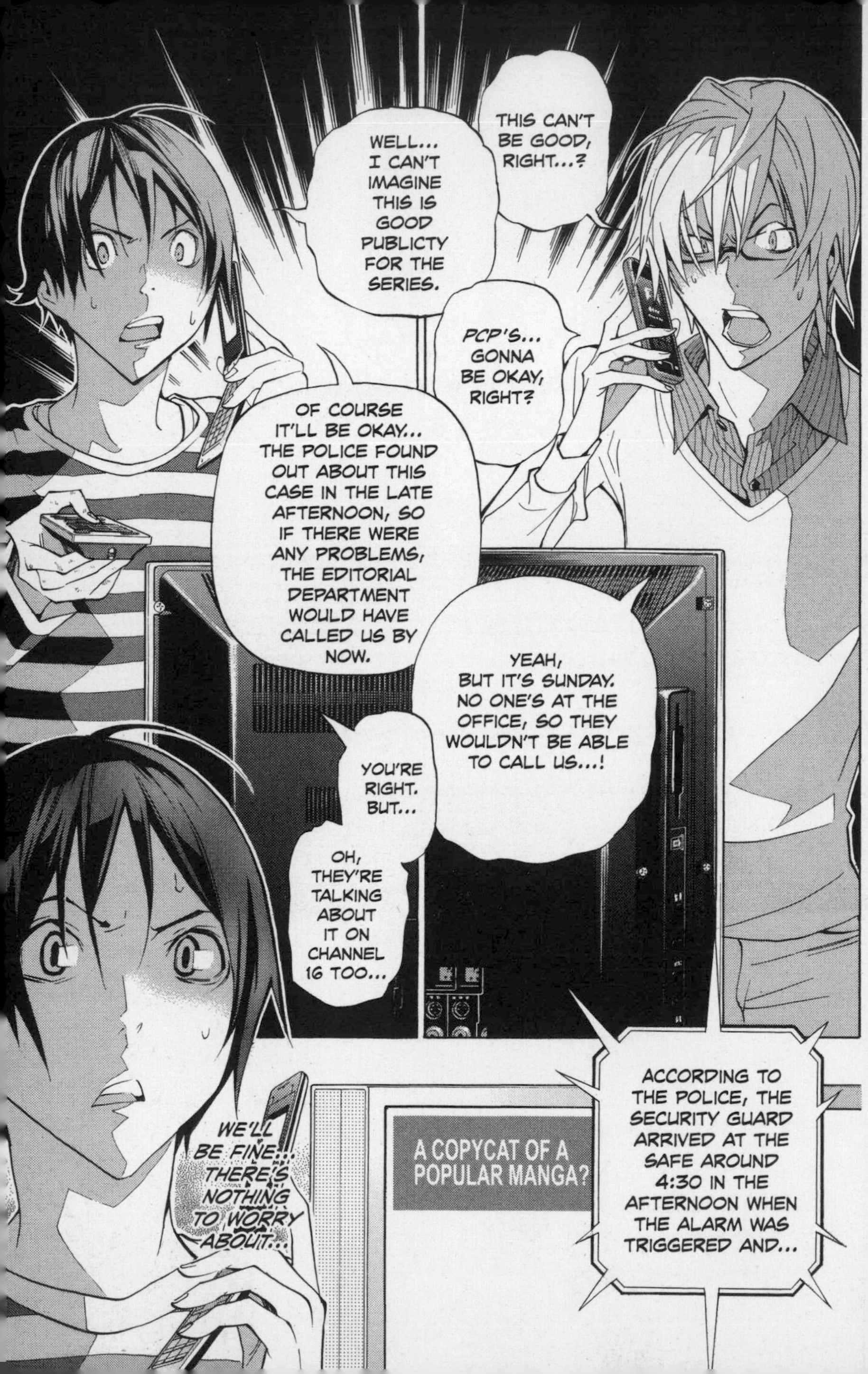
THIS CAN'T BE GOOD, RIGHT...?
WELL... I CAN'T IMAGINE THIS IS GOOD PUBLICTY FOR THE SERIES.
PCP'S... GONNA BE OKAY, RIGHT?
OF COURSE IT'LL BE OKAY... THE POLICE FOUND OUT ABOUT THIS CASE IN THE LATE AFTERNOON, SO IF THERE WERE ANY PROBLEMS, THE EDITORIAL DEPARTMENT WOULD HAVE CALLED US BY NOW.
YEAH, BUT IT'S SUNDAY. NO ONE'S AT THE OFFICE, SO THEY WOULDN'T BE ABLE TO CALL US...!
YOU'RE RIGHT. BUT...
OH, THEY'RE TALKING ABOUT IT ON CHANNEL 16 TOO...
ACCORDING TO THE POLICE, THE SECURITY GUARD ARRIVED AT THE SAFE AROUND 4:30 IN THE AFTERNOON WHEN THE ALARM WAS TRIGGERED AND...
A COPYCAT OF A POPULAR MANGA?
WE'LL BE FINE... THERE'S NOTHING TO WORRY ABOUT...

OHBA'S STORYBOARD

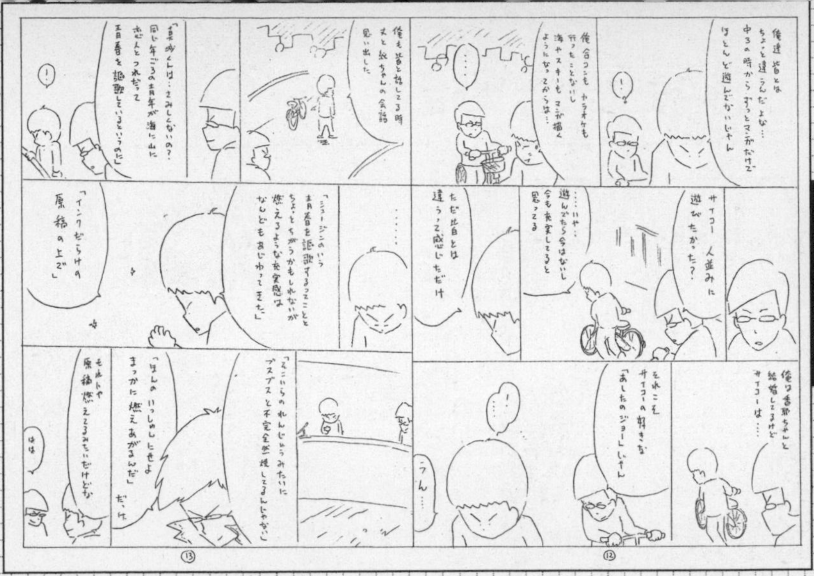
俺達皆とは ちょっと違うんだよな… 中3の時から ずっとマンガだけで ほとんど遊んでないじゃん
!
俺合コンも カラオケも 行ったことないし 海やスキーも マンガ描く ようになってからは…
…
サイコー 人並みに 遊びたかった？
…いや… 遊んでたら今はないし 今も充実してると 思ってる
ただ皆とは 違うって感じただけ
俺は香耶ちゃんと 結婚してるけど サイコーは……
それこそ サイコーの好きな 「あしたのジョー」じゃん
!…
うん……
⑫
俺も皆と話してる時 丈と紀ちゃんの会話 思い出した
「真城くんは…さみしくないの？ 同じ年ごろの青年が海に山に 恋人とつれだって 青春を謳歌しているというのに」
!
……
「ジョージのいう 青春を謳歌するってこととは ちょっとちがうかもしれないが 燃えるような充実感は なんどもあじわってきた」
「インクだらけの 原稿の上で」
「そこいらのれんじゅうみたいに ブスブスと不完全燃焼してるんじゃない」
「ほんの いっしゅんにせよ まっかに燃えあがるんだ」
原稿燃えてるみたいだけどな
はは
⑬

OBATA'S STORYBOARD

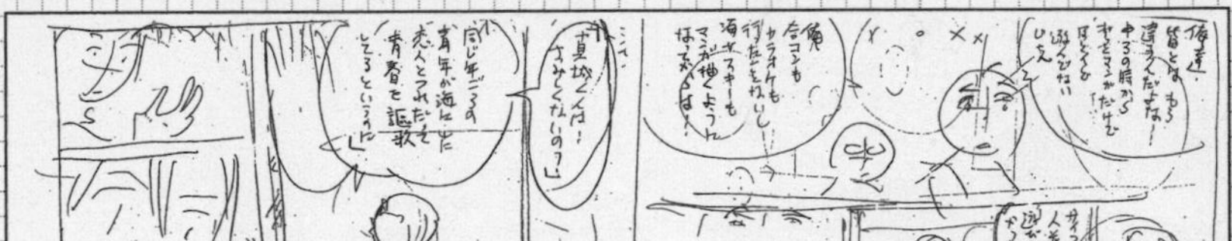

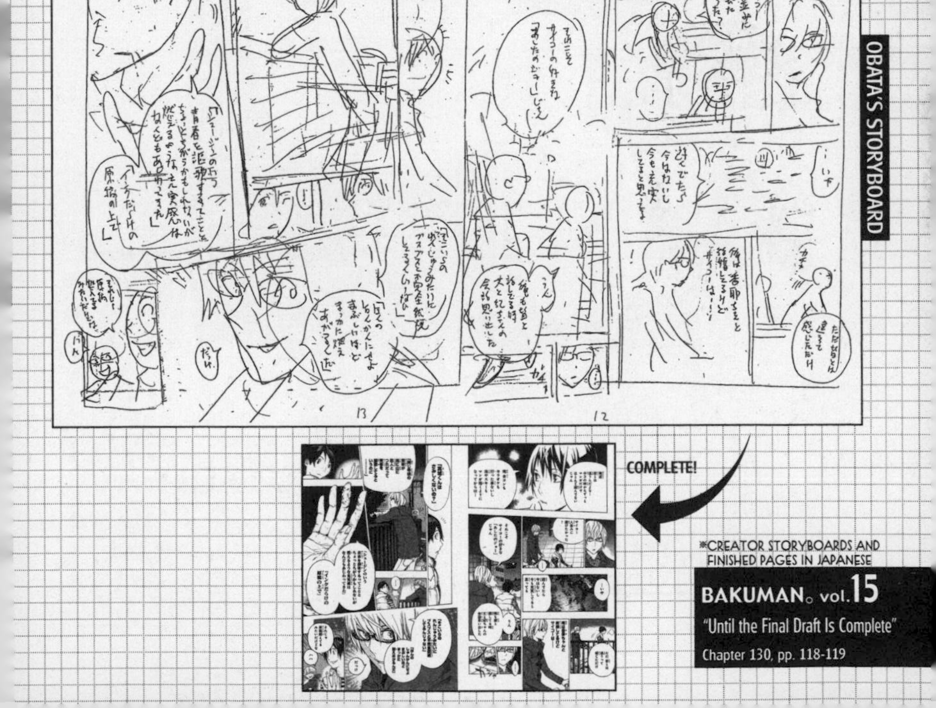

COMPLETE!

※CREATOR STORYBOARDS AND FINISHED PAGES IN JAPANESE

BAKUMAN。 vol.15

"Until the Final Draft Is Complete"

Chapter 130, pp. 118-119

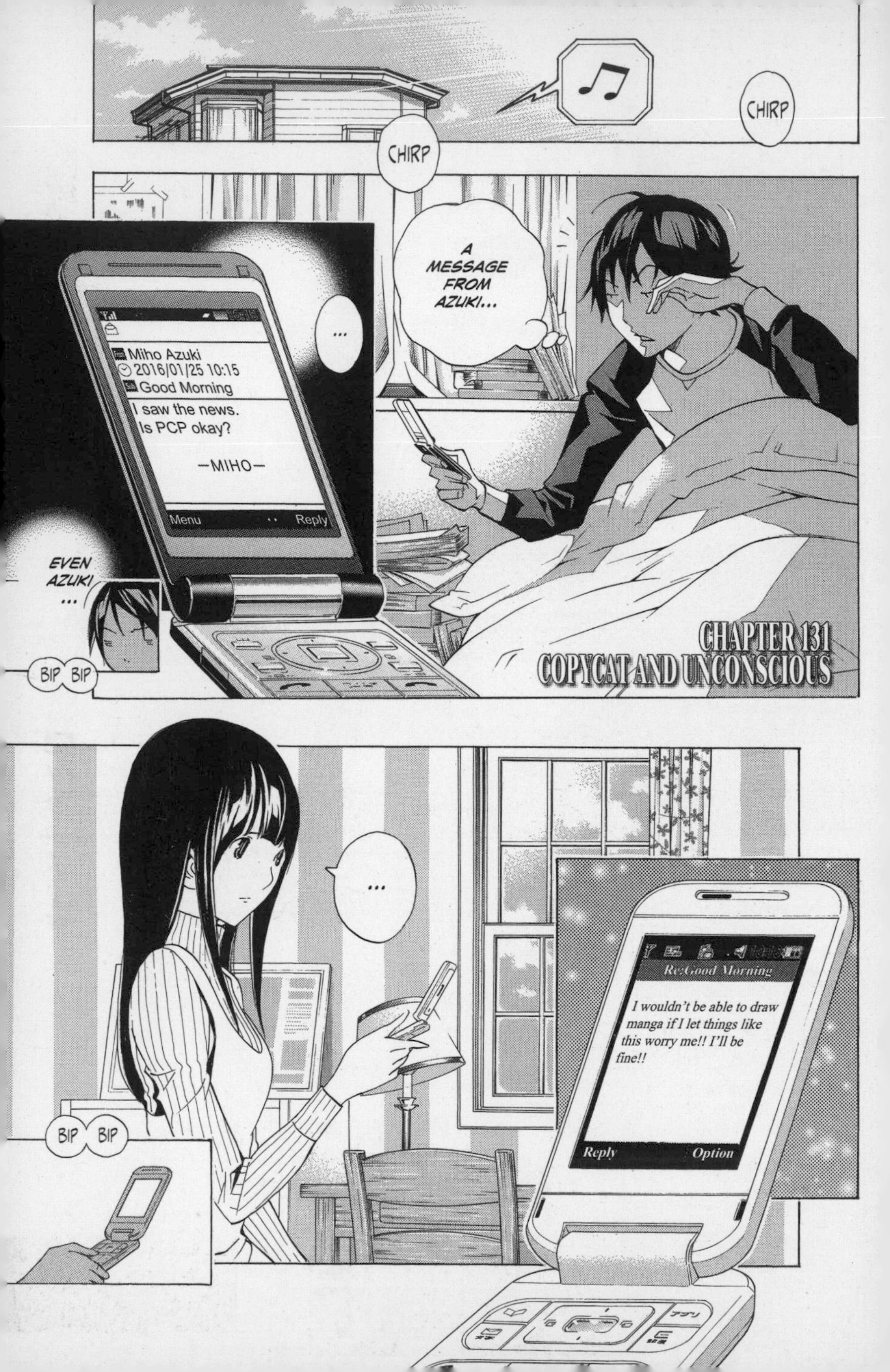
CHIRP
CHIRP
A MESSAGE FROM AZUKI...
CHAPTER 131
COPYCAT AND UNCONSCIOUS
...
Miho Azuki
2016/01/25 10:15
Good Morning
I saw the news. Is PCP okay?
—MIHO—
Menu
Reply
EVEN AZUKI ...
BIP BIP
Re:Good Morning
I wouldn't be able to draw manga if I let things like this worry me!! I'll be fine!!
Reply
Option
...
BIP BIP

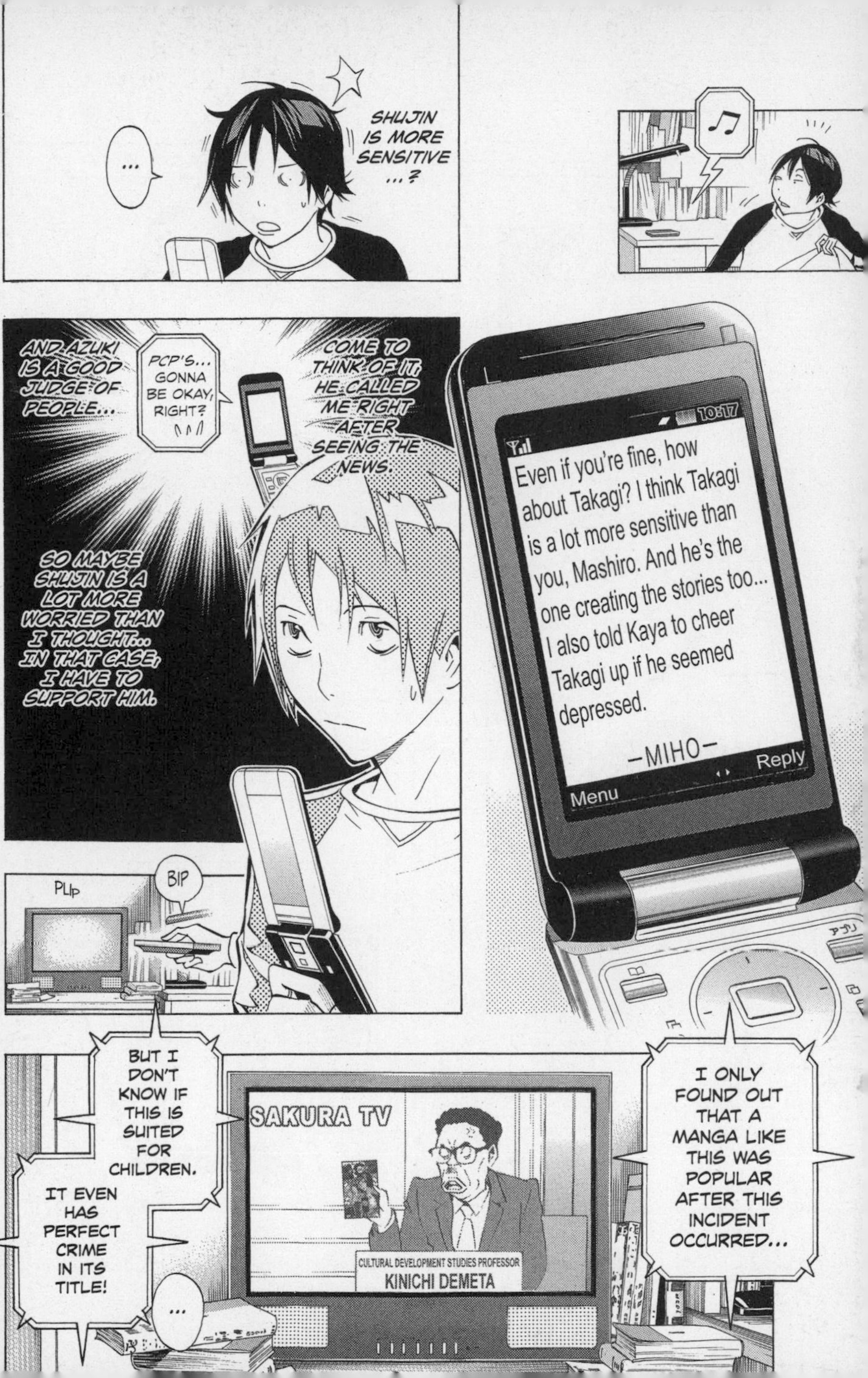
♫
SHUJIN IS MORE SENSITIVE ...?
...
Even if you're fine, how about Takagi? I think Takagi is a lot more sensitive than you, Mashiro. And he's the one creating the stories too... I also told Kaya to cheer Takagi up if he seemed depressed.
—MIHO—
Reply
Menu
10:17
COME TO THINK OF IT, HE CALLED ME RIGHT AFTER SEEING THE NEWS.
PCP'S... GONNA BE OKAY, RIGHT?
AND AZUKI IS A GOOD JUDGE OF PEOPLE...
SO MAYBE SHUJIN IS A LOT MORE WORRIED THAN I THOUGHT... IN THAT CASE, I HAVE TO SUPPORT HIM.
BIP
PLIP
I ONLY FOUND OUT THAT A MANGA LIKE THIS WAS POPULAR AFTER THIS INCIDENT OCCURRED...
SAKURA TV
BUT I DON'T KNOW IF THIS IS SUITED FOR CHILDREN.
IT EVEN HAS PERFECT CRIME IN ITS TITLE!
CULTURAL DEVELOPMENT STUDIES PROFESSOR
KINICHI DEMETA
...

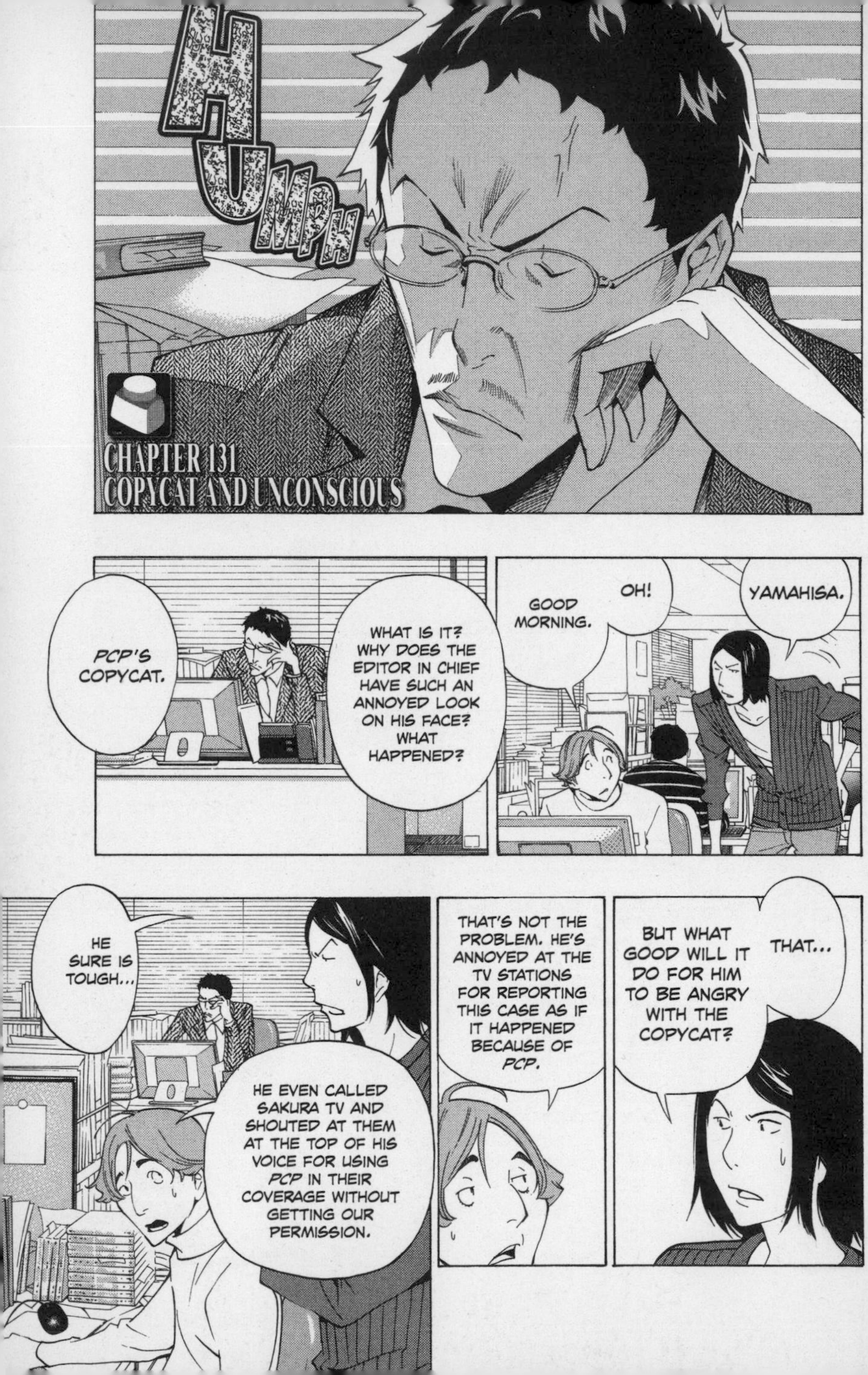
HUMPH
CHAPTER 131
COPYCAT AND UNCONSCIOUS
YAMAHISA.
OH!
GOOD MORNING.
WHAT IS IT? WHY DOES THE EDITOR IN CHIEF HAVE SUCH AN ANNOYED LOOK ON HIS FACE? WHAT HAPPENED?
PCP'S COPYCAT.
THAT...
BUT WHAT GOOD WILL IT DO FOR HIM TO BE ANGRY WITH THE COPYCAT?
THAT'S NOT THE PROBLEM. HE'S ANNOYED AT THE TV STATIONS FOR REPORTING THIS CASE AS IF IT HAPPENED BECAUSE OF *PCP*.
HE SURE IS TOUGH...
HE EVEN CALLED SAKURA TV AND SHOUTED AT THEM AT THE TOP OF HIS VOICE FOR USING *PCP* IN THEIR COVERAGE WITHOUT GETTING OUR PERMISSION.

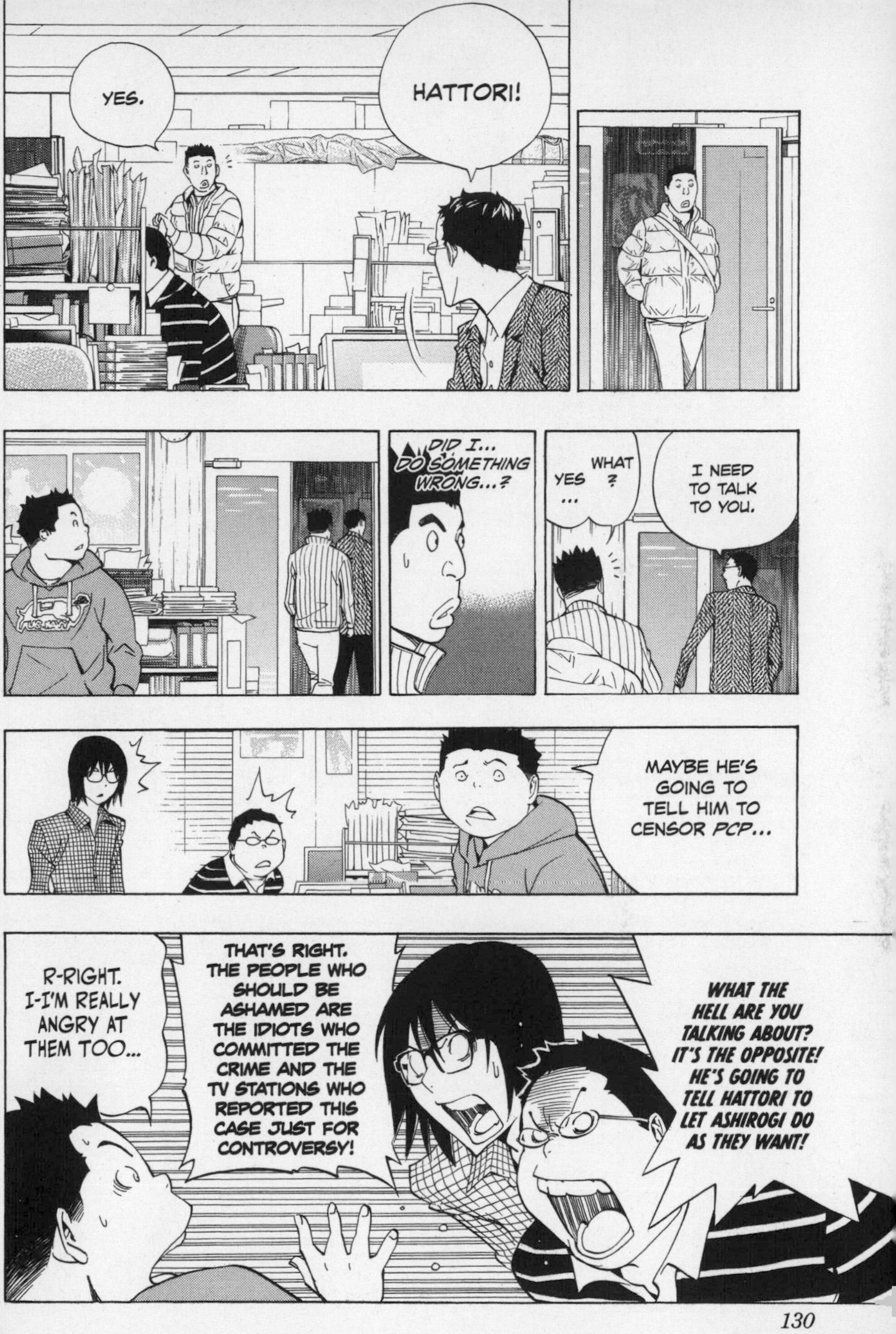
HATTORI!
YES.
I NEED TO TALK TO YOU.
WHAT?
YES...
DID I... DO SOMETHING WRONG...?
MAYBE HE'S GOING TO TELL HIM TO CENSOR *PCP*...
WHAT THE HELL ARE YOU TALKING ABOUT? IT'S THE OPPOSITE! HE'S GOING TO TELL HATTORI TO LET ASHIROGI DO AS THEY WANT!
THAT'S RIGHT. THE PEOPLE WHO SHOULD BE ASHAMED ARE THE IDIOTS WHO COMMITTED THE CRIME AND THE TV STATIONS WHO REPORTED THIS CASE JUST FOR CONTROVERSY!
R-RIGHT. I-I'M REALLY ANGRY AT THEM TOO...

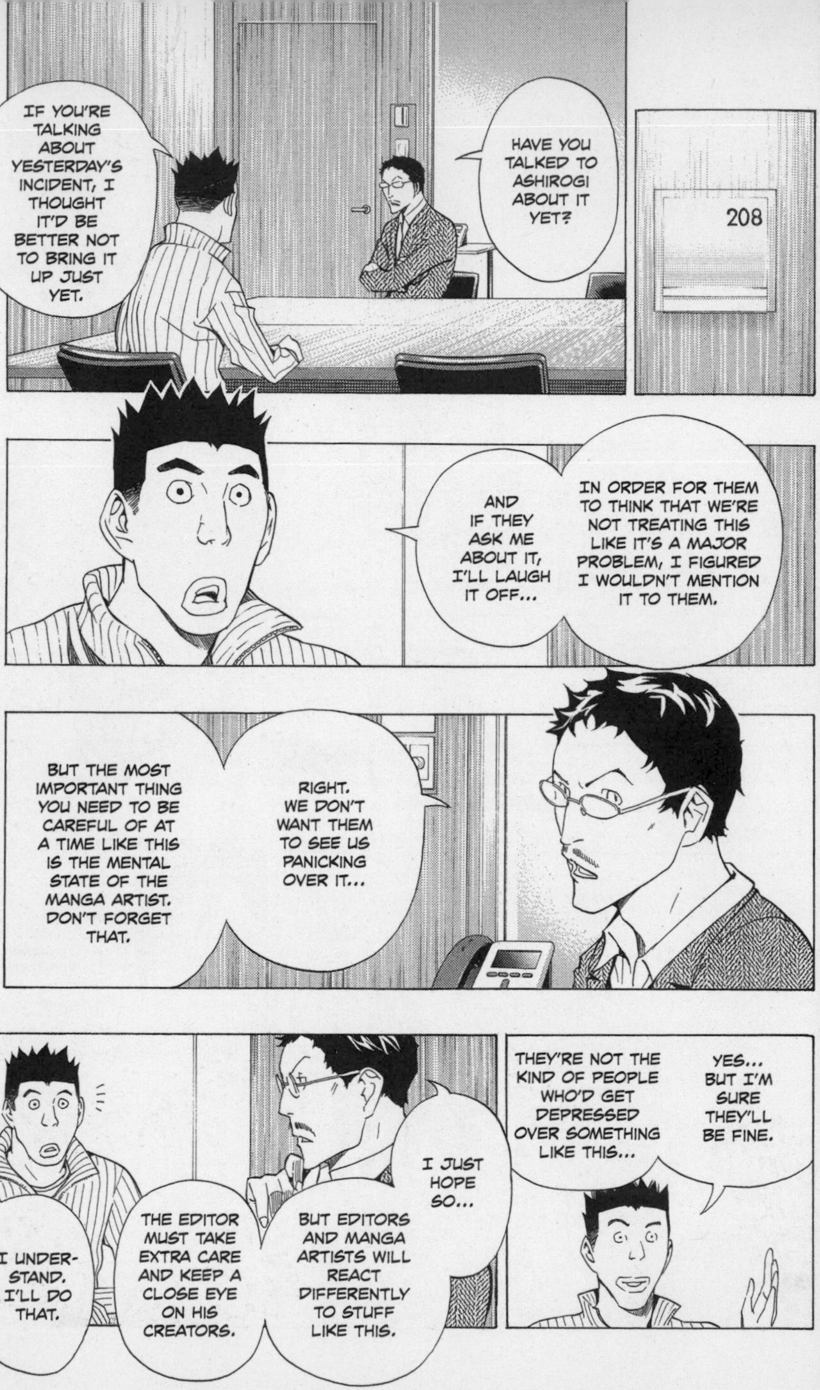
208
HAVE YOU TALKED TO ASHIROGI ABOUT IT YET?
IF YOU'RE TALKING ABOUT YESTERDAY'S INCIDENT, I THOUGHT IT'D BE BETTER NOT TO BRING IT UP JUST YET.
IN ORDER FOR THEM TO THINK THAT WE'RE NOT TREATING THIS LIKE IT'S A MAJOR PROBLEM, I FIGURED I WOULDN'T MENTION IT TO THEM.
AND IF THEY ASK ME ABOUT IT, I'LL LAUGH IT OFF...
RIGHT. WE DON'T WANT THEM TO SEE US PANICKING OVER IT...
BUT THE MOST IMPORTANT THING YOU NEED TO BE CAREFUL OF AT A TIME LIKE THIS IS THE MENTAL STATE OF THE MANGA ARTIST. DON'T FORGET THAT.
YES... BUT I'M SURE THEY'LL BE FINE.
THEY'RE NOT THE KIND OF PEOPLE WHO'D GET DEPRESSED OVER SOMETHING LIKE THIS...
I JUST HOPE SO...
BUT EDITORS AND MANGA ARTISTS WILL REACT DIFFERENTLY TO STUFF LIKE THIS.
THE EDITOR MUST TAKE EXTRA CARE AND KEEP A CLOSE EYE ON HIS CREATORS.
I UNDER-STAND. I'LL DO THAT.

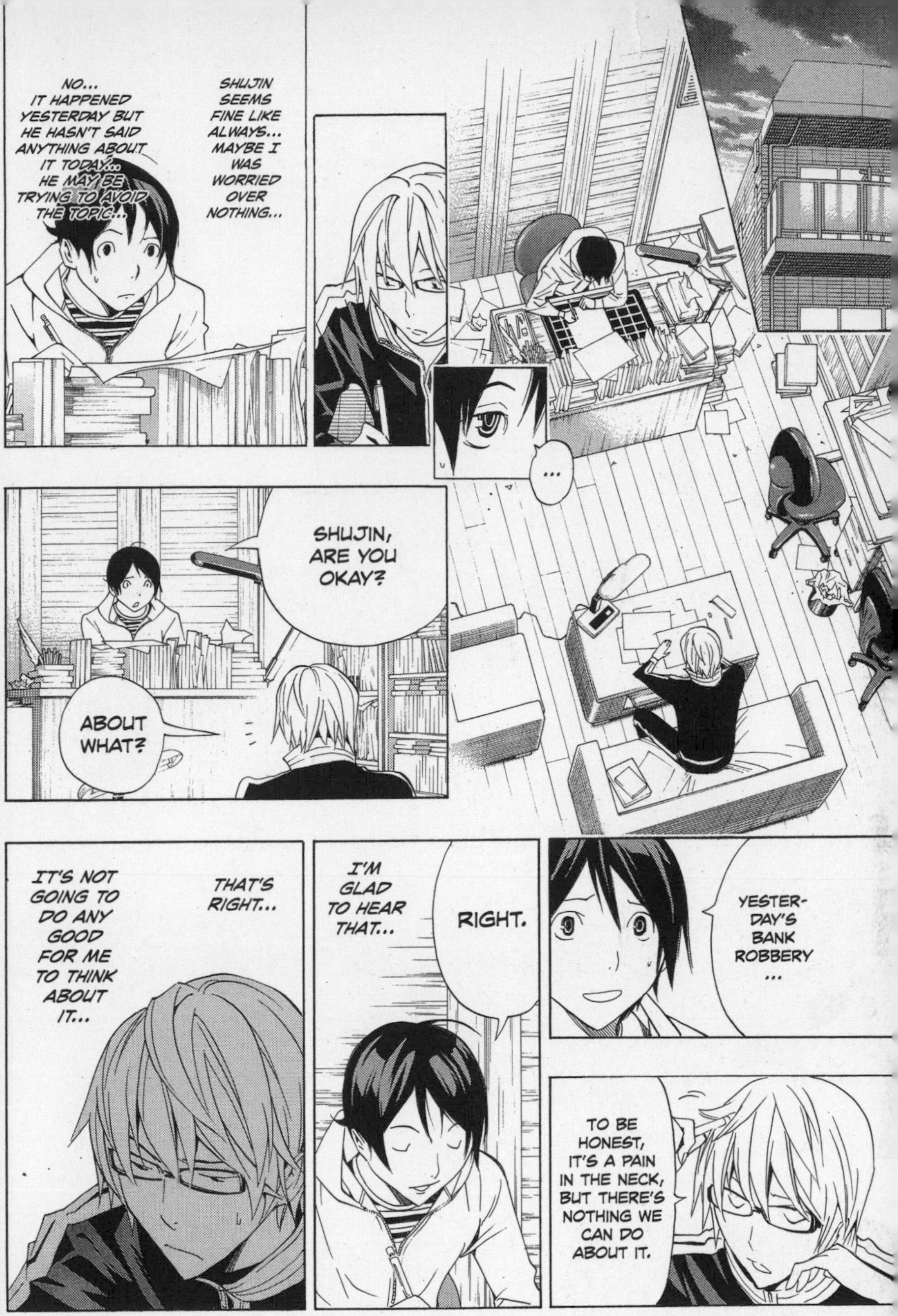
...
SHUJIN SEEMS FINE LIKE ALWAYS... MAYBE I WAS WORRIED OVER NOTHING...
NO... IT HAPPENED YESTERDAY BUT HE HASN'T SAID ANYTHING ABOUT IT TODAY... HE MAY BE TRYING TO AVOID THE TOPIC...
SHUJIN, ARE YOU OKAY?
ABOUT WHAT?
YESTER-DAY'S BANK ROBBERY ...
TO BE HONEST, IT'S A PAIN IN THE NECK, BUT THERE'S NOTHING WE CAN DO ABOUT IT.
RIGHT.
I'M GLAD TO HEAR THAT...
THAT'S RIGHT...
IT'S NOT GOING TO DO ANY GOOD FOR ME TO THINK ABOUT IT...

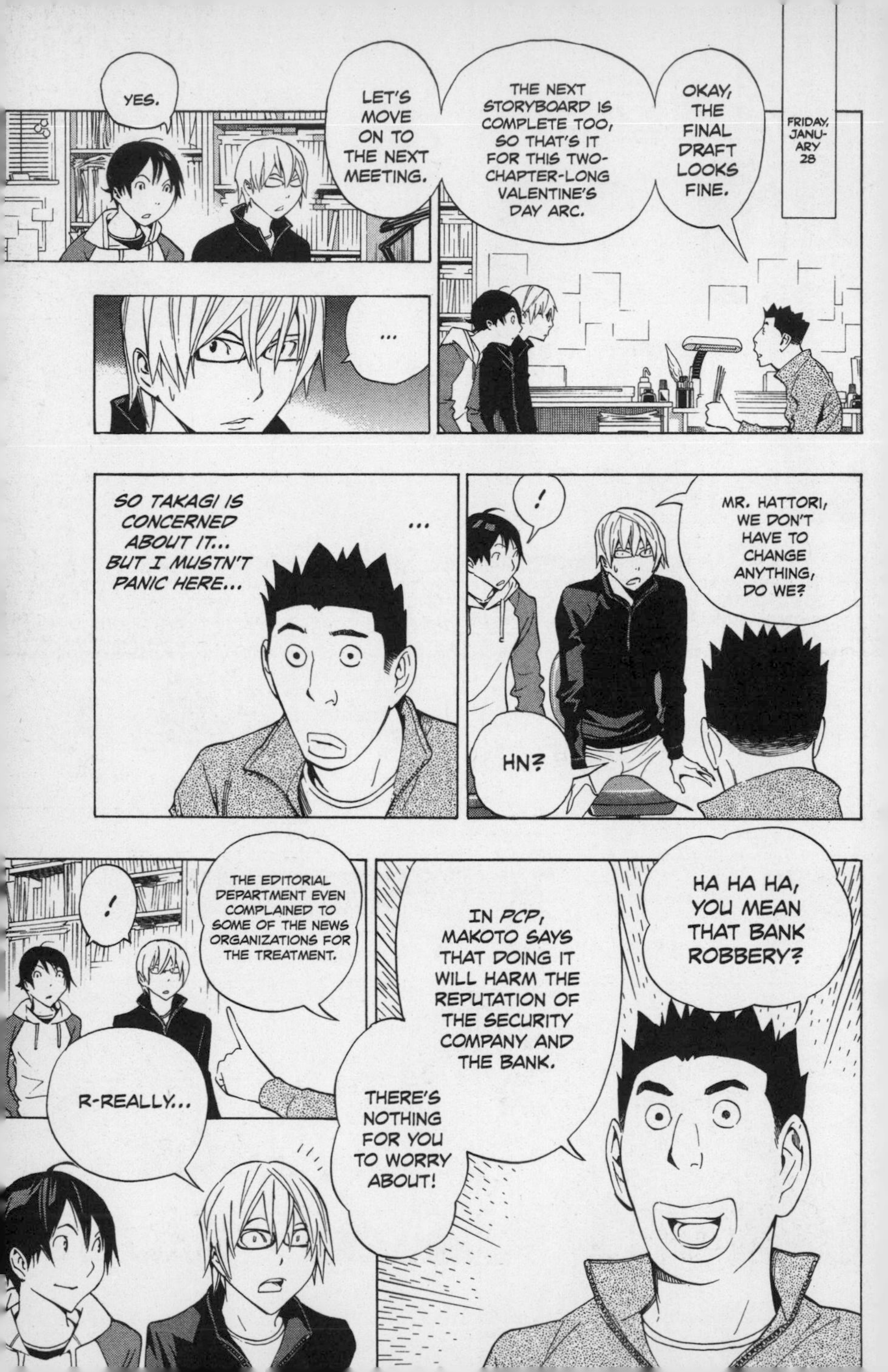
FRIDAY, JANUARY 28
OKAY, THE FINAL DRAFT LOOKS FINE.
THE NEXT STORYBOARD IS COMPLETE TOO, SO THAT'S IT FOR THIS TWO-CHAPTER-LONG VALENTINE'S DAY ARC.
LET'S MOVE ON TO THE NEXT MEETING.
YES.
...
!
MR. HATTORI, WE DON'T HAVE TO CHANGE ANYTHING, DO WE?
HN?
...
SO TAKAGI IS CONCERNED ABOUT IT... BUT I MUSTN'T PANIC HERE...
HA HA HA, YOU MEAN THAT BANK ROBBERY?
IN PCP, MAKOTO SAYS THAT DOING IT WILL HARM THE REPUTATION OF THE SECURITY COMPANY AND THE BANK.
THERE'S NOTHING FOR YOU TO WORRY ABOUT!
THE EDITORIAL DEPARTMENT EVEN COMPLAINED TO SOME OF THE NEWS ORGANIZATIONS FOR THE TREATMENT.
!
R-REALLY...

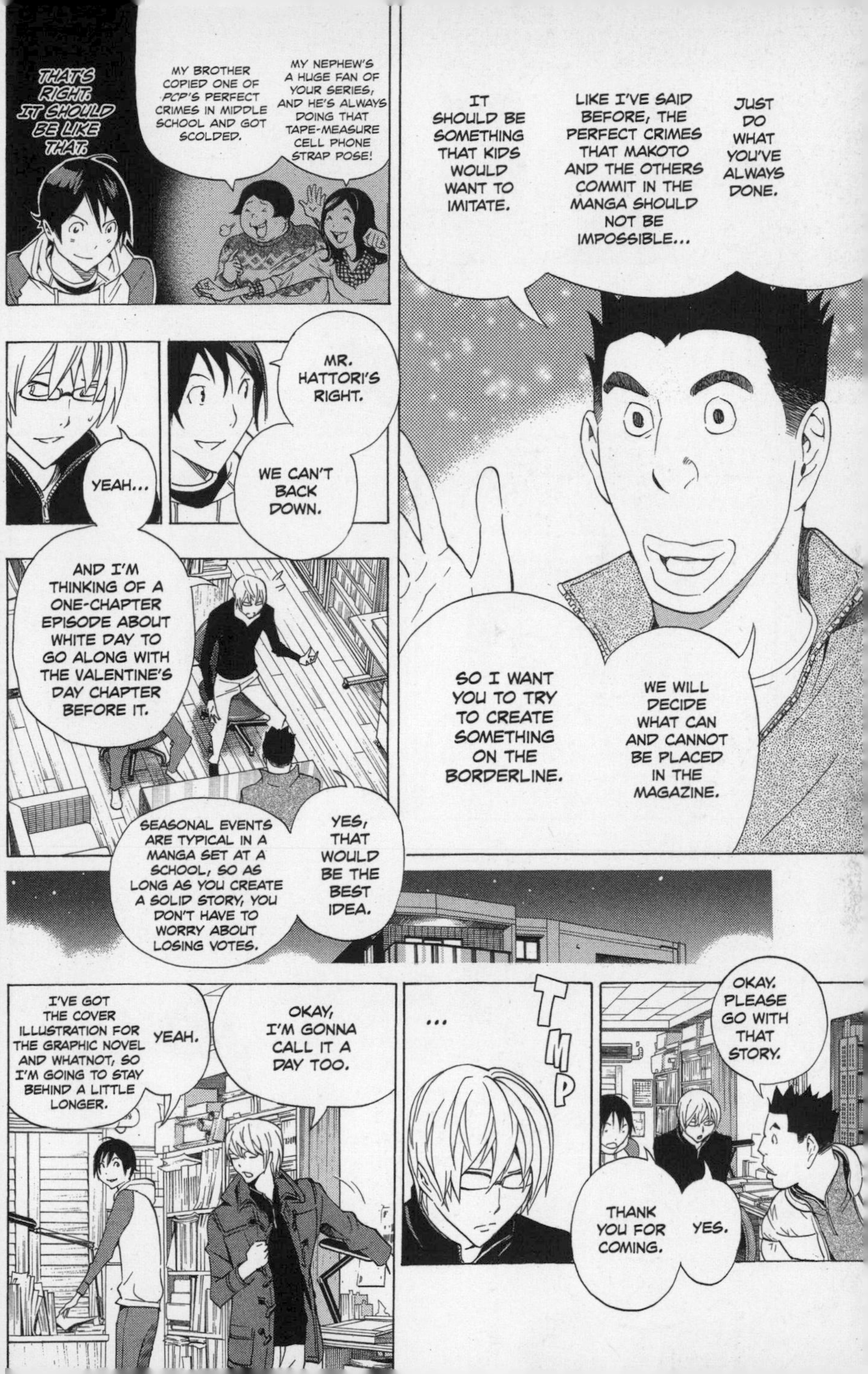
JUST DO WHAT YOU'VE ALWAYS DONE.
LIKE I'VE SAID BEFORE, THE PERFECT CRIMES THAT MAKOTO AND THE OTHERS COMMIT IN THE MANGA SHOULD NOT BE IMPOSSIBLE...
IT SHOULD BE SOMETHING THAT KIDS WOULD WANT TO IMITATE.
WE WILL DECIDE WHAT CAN AND CANNOT BE PLACED IN THE MAGAZINE.
SO I WANT YOU TO TRY TO CREATE SOMETHING ON THE BORDERLINE.
MY NEPHEW'S A HUGE FAN OF YOUR SERIES, AND HE'S ALWAYS DOING THAT TAPE-MEASURE CELL PHONE STRAP POSE!
MY BROTHER COPIED ONE OF PCP'S PERFECT CRIMES IN MIDDLE SCHOOL AND GOT SCOLDED.
THAT'S RIGHT. IT SHOULD BE LIKE THAT.
MR. HATTORI'S RIGHT.
WE CAN'T BACK DOWN.
YEAH...
AND I'M THINKING OF A ONE-CHAPTER EPISODE ABOUT WHITE DAY TO GO ALONG WITH THE VALENTINE'S DAY CHAPTER BEFORE IT.
YES, THAT WOULD BE THE BEST IDEA.
SEASONAL EVENTS ARE TYPICAL IN A MANGA SET AT A SCHOOL, SO AS LONG AS YOU CREATE A SOLID STORY, YOU DON'T HAVE TO WORRY ABOUT LOSING VOTES.
OKAY. PLEASE GO WITH THAT STORY.
YES.
THANK YOU FOR COMING.
TMP
...
OKAY, I'M GONNA CALL IT A DAY TOO.
YEAH.
I'VE GOT THE COVER ILLUSTRATION FOR THE GRAPHIC NOVEL AND WHATNOT, SO I'M GOING TO STAY BEHIND A LITTLE LONGER.

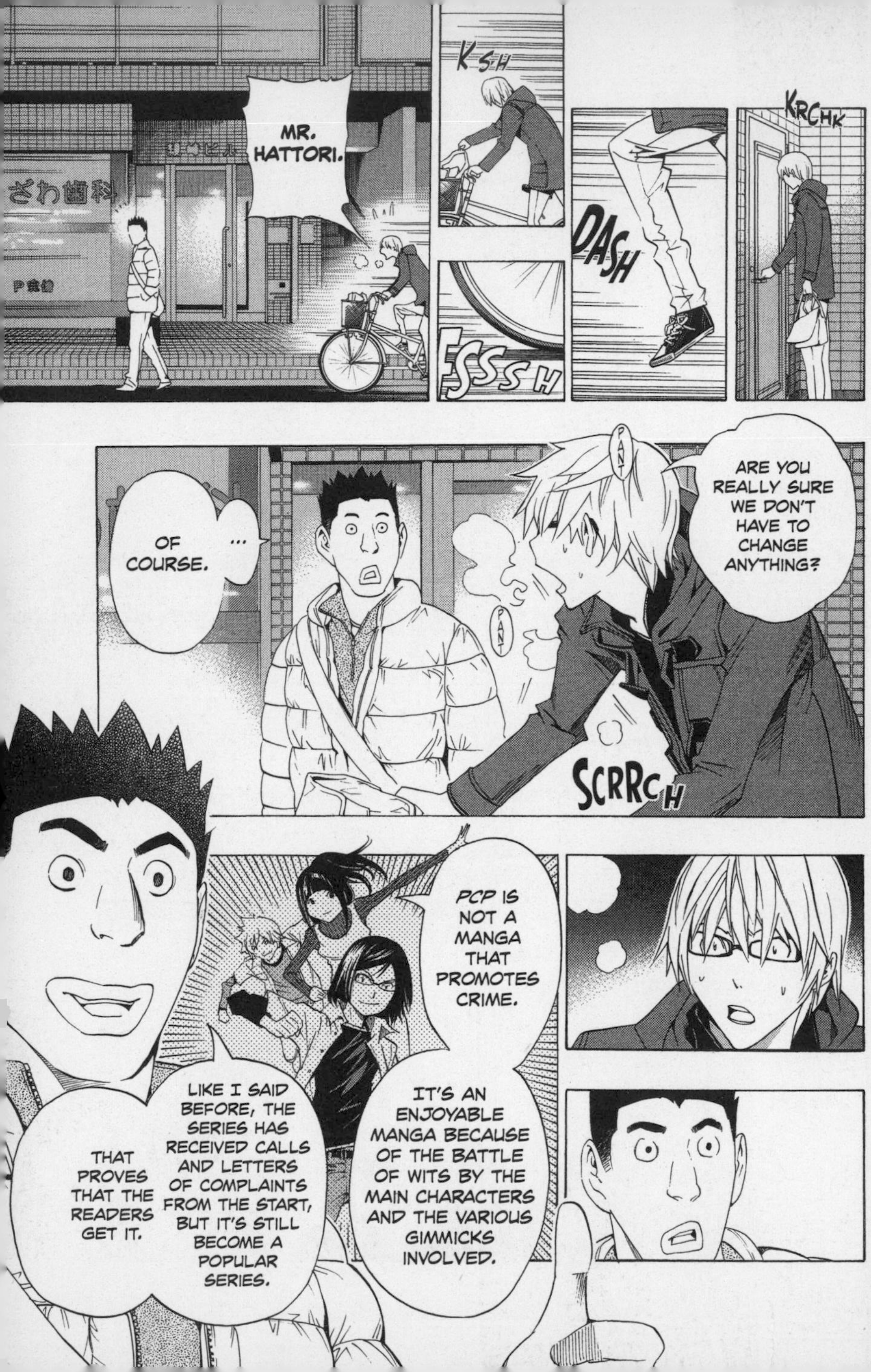
KRCHK
DASH
KSH
ESSSH
MR. HATTORI.
PANT
ARE YOU REALLY SURE WE DON'T HAVE TO CHANGE ANYTHING?
PANT
SCRRCH
...
OF COURSE.
PCP IS NOT A MANGA THAT PROMOTES CRIME.
IT'S AN ENJOYABLE MANGA BECAUSE OF THE BATTLE OF WITS BY THE MAIN CHARACTERS AND THE VARIOUS GIMMICKS INVOLVED.
LIKE I SAID BEFORE, THE SERIES HAS RECEIVED CALLS AND LETTERS OF COMPLAINTS FROM THE START, BUT IT'S STILL BECOME A POPULAR SERIES.
THAT PROVES THAT THE READERS GET IT.

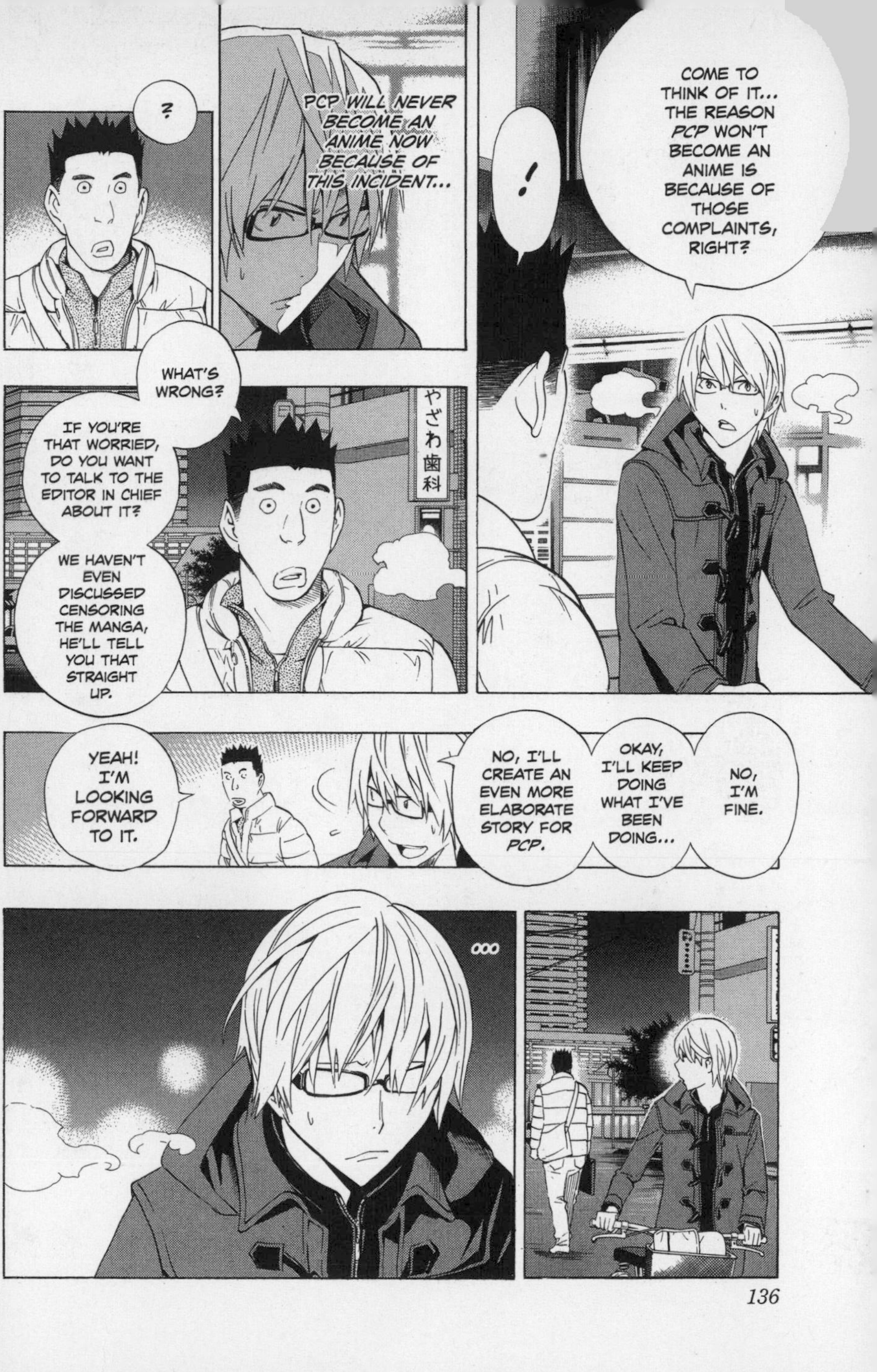
COME TO THINK OF IT... THE REASON *PCP* WON'T BECOME AN ANIME IS BECAUSE OF THOSE COMPLAINTS, RIGHT?
!
PCP WILL NEVER BECOME AN ANIME NOW BECAUSE OF THIS INCIDENT...
?
WHAT'S WRONG?
IF YOU'RE THAT WORRIED, DO YOU WANT TO TALK TO THE EDITOR IN CHIEF ABOUT IT?
WE HAVEN'T EVEN DISCUSSED CENSORING THE MANGA, HE'LL TELL YOU THAT STRAIGHT UP.
やざわ歯科
NO, I'M FINE.
OKAY, I'LL KEEP DOING WHAT I'VE BEEN DOING...
NO, I'LL CREATE AN EVEN MORE ELABORATE STORY FOR *PCP*.
YEAH! I'M LOOKING FORWARD TO IT.
ooo

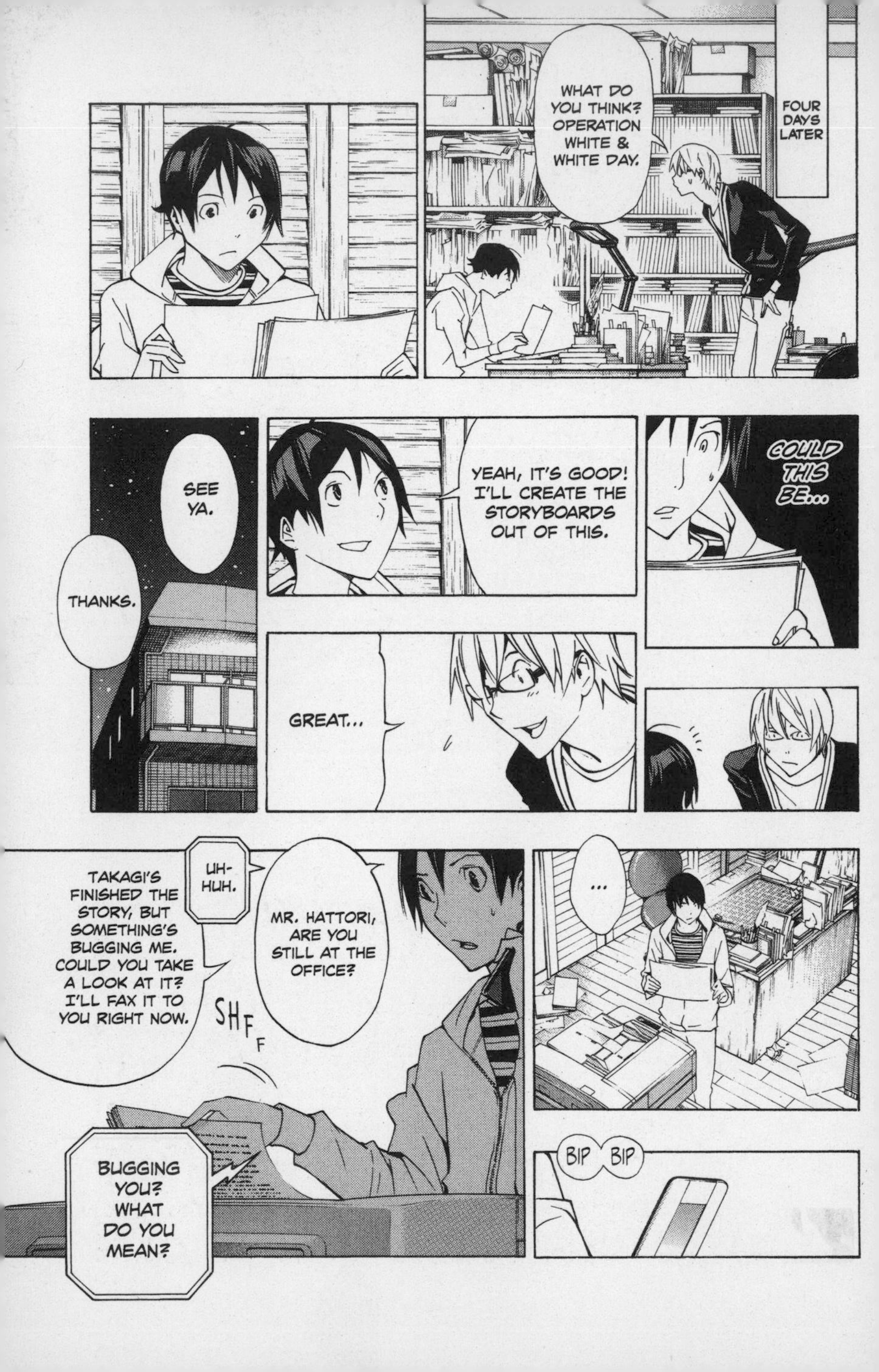
FOUR DAYS LATER
WHAT DO YOU THINK? OPERATION WHITE & WHITE DAY.
COULD THIS BE...
YEAH, IT'S GOOD! I'LL CREATE THE STORYBOARDS OUT OF THIS.
GREAT...
SEE YA.
THANKS.
...
BIP BIP
MR. HATTORI, ARE YOU STILL AT THE OFFICE?
UH-HUH.
TAKAGI'S FINISHED THE STORY, BUT SOMETHING'S BUGGING ME. COULD YOU TAKE A LOOK AT IT? I'LL FAX IT TO YOU RIGHT NOW.
SHFF
BUGGING YOU? WHAT DO YOU MEAN?

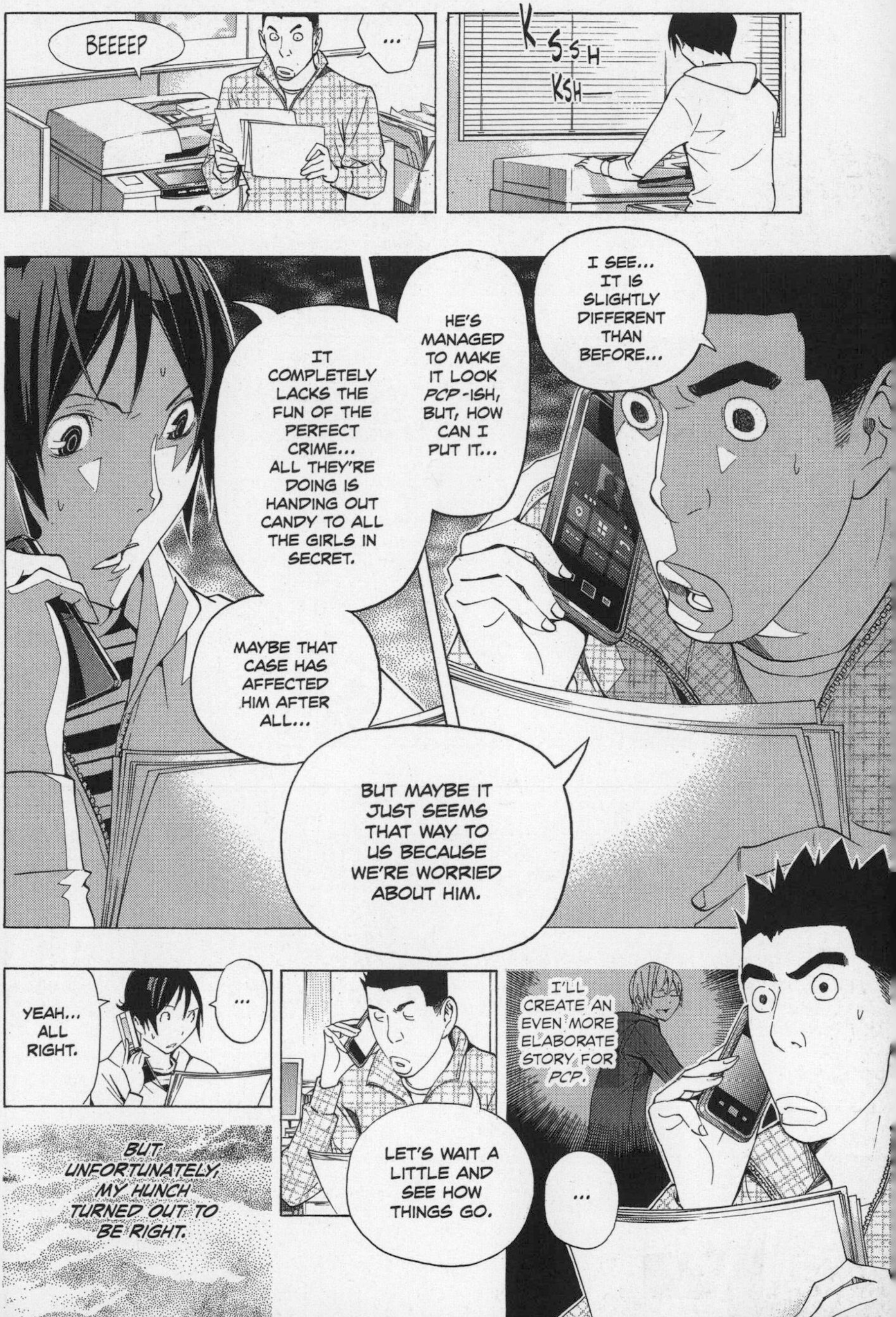
KSSH
KSH
...
BEEEEP
I SEE... IT IS SLIGHTLY DIFFERENT THAN BEFORE...
HE'S MANAGED TO MAKE IT LOOK *PCP*-ISH, BUT, HOW CAN I PUT IT...
IT COMPLETELY LACKS THE FUN OF THE PERFECT CRIME... ALL THEY'RE DOING IS HANDING OUT CANDY TO ALL THE GIRLS IN SECRET.
MAYBE THAT CASE HAS AFFECTED HIM AFTER ALL...
BUT MAYBE IT JUST SEEMS THAT WAY TO US BECAUSE WE'RE WORRIED ABOUT HIM.
I'LL CREATE AN EVEN MORE ELABORATE STORY FOR *PCP*.
...
LET'S WAIT A LITTLE AND SEE HOW THINGS GO.
...
YEAH... ALL RIGHT.
BUT UNFORTUNATELY, MY HUNCH TURNED OUT TO BE RIGHT.

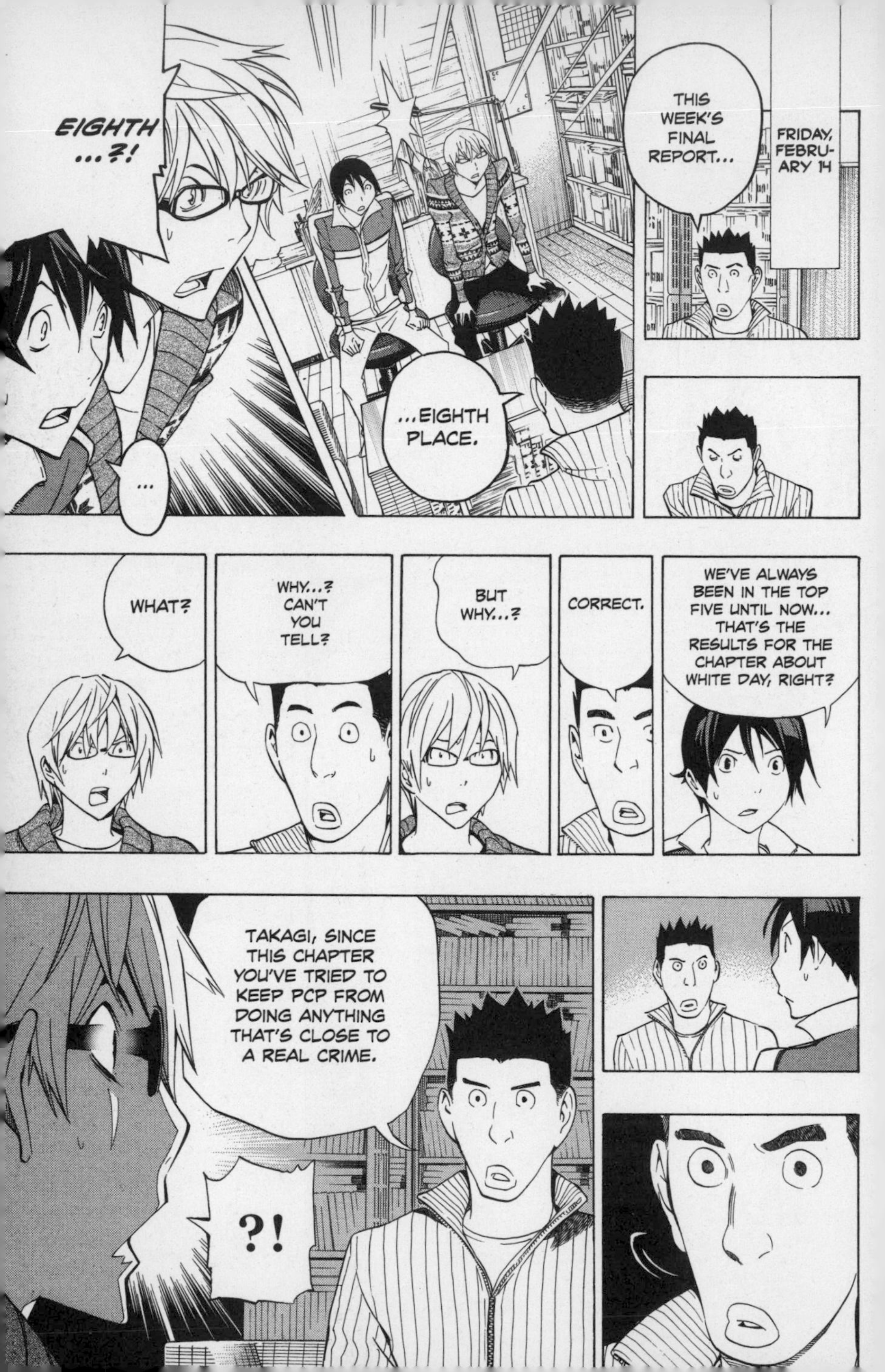
FRIDAY, FEBRUARY 14
THIS WEEK'S FINAL REPORT...
...EIGHTH PLACE.
EIGHTH ...?!
...
WE'VE ALWAYS BEEN IN THE TOP FIVE UNTIL NOW... THAT'S THE RESULTS FOR THE CHAPTER ABOUT WHITE DAY, RIGHT?
CORRECT.
BUT WHY...?
WHY...? CAN'T YOU TELL?
WHAT?
TAKAGI, SINCE THIS CHAPTER YOU'VE TRIED TO KEEP PCP FROM DOING ANYTHING THAT'S CLOSE TO A REAL CRIME.
?!

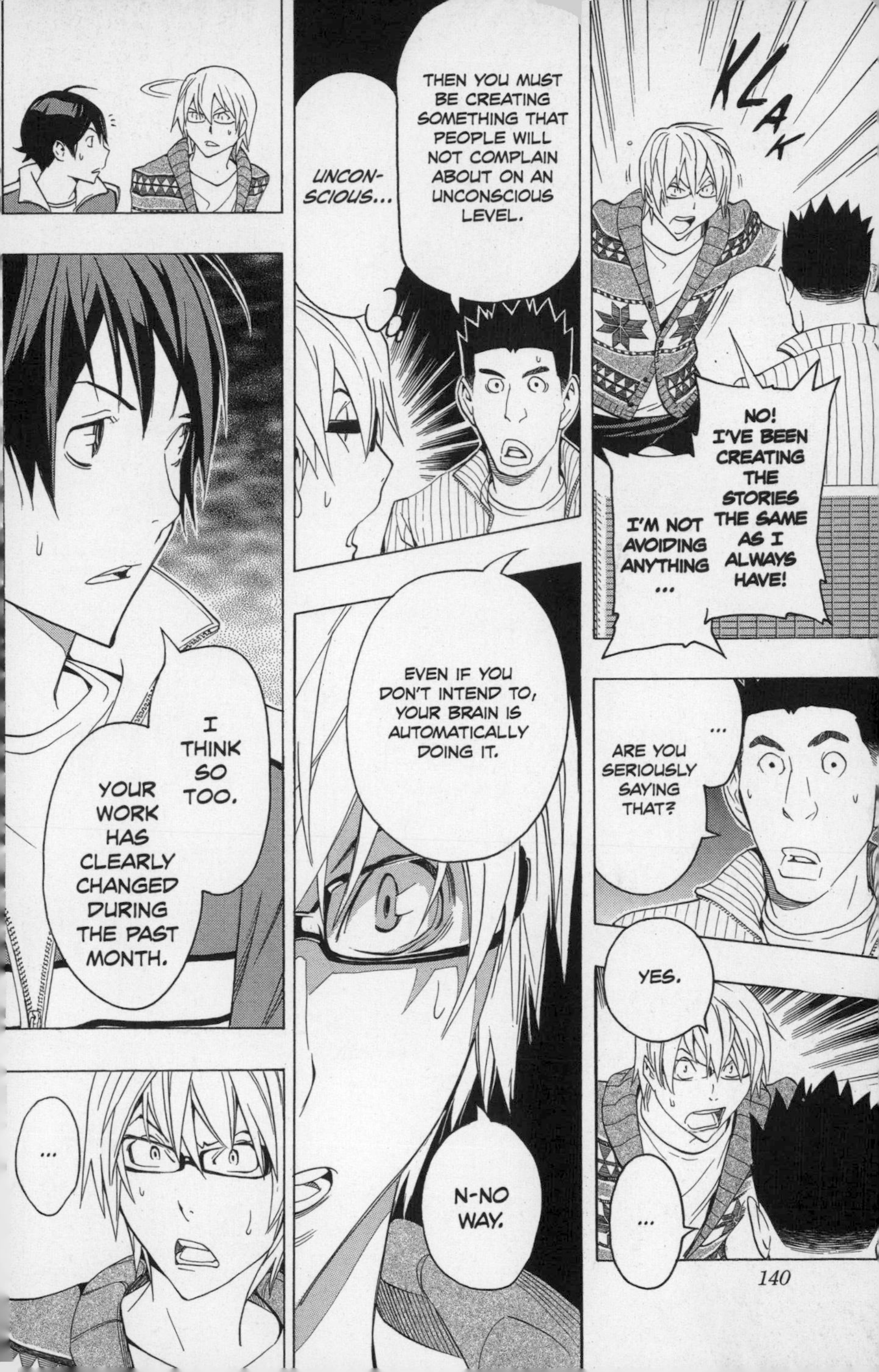
KLAK
NO! I'VE BEEN CREATING THE STORIES THE SAME AS I ALWAYS HAVE!
I'M NOT AVOIDING ANYTHING...
THEN YOU MUST BE CREATING SOMETHING THAT PEOPLE WILL NOT COMPLAIN ABOUT ON AN UNCONSCIOUS LEVEL.
UNCON-SCIOUS...
...
ARE YOU SERIOUSLY SAYING THAT?
EVEN IF YOU DON'T INTEND TO, YOUR BRAIN IS AUTOMATICALLY DOING IT.
I THINK SO TOO.
YOUR WORK HAS CLEARLY CHANGED DURING THE PAST MONTH.
YES.
...
N-NO WAY.
...

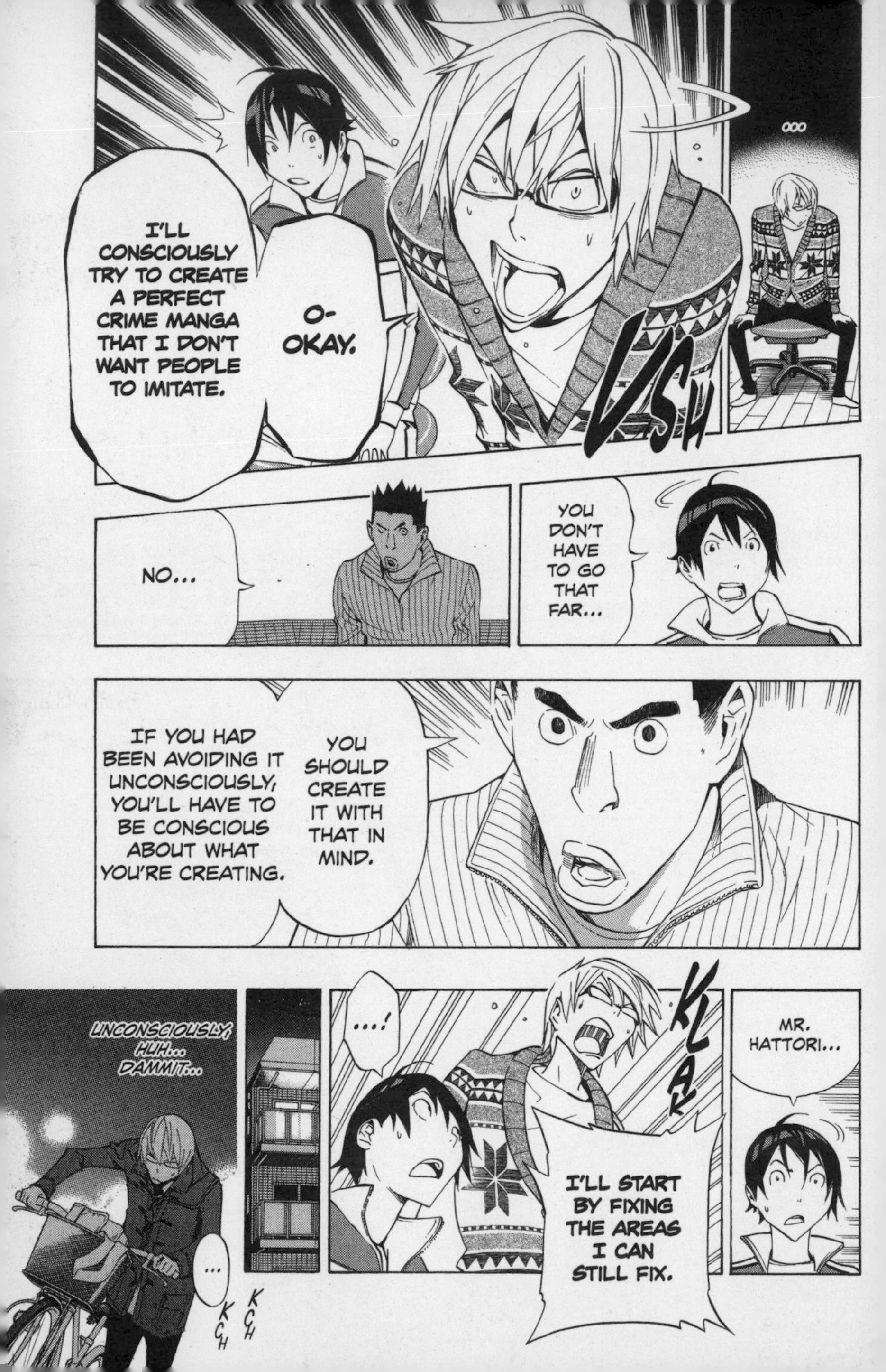
I'LL CONSCIOUSLY TRY TO CREATE A PERFECT CRIME MANGA THAT I DON'T WANT PEOPLE TO IMITATE.
O- OKAY.
VSHH
YOU DON'T HAVE TO GO THAT FAR...
NO...
IF YOU HAD BEEN AVOIDING IT UNCONSCIOUSLY, YOU'LL HAVE TO BE CONSCIOUS ABOUT WHAT YOU'RE CREATING.
YOU SHOULD CREATE IT WITH THAT IN MIND.
MR. HATTORI...
KLAK
...!
I'LL START BY FIXING THE AREAS I CAN STILL FIX.
UNCONSCIOUSLY, HUH... DAMMIT...
...
KCH KCH

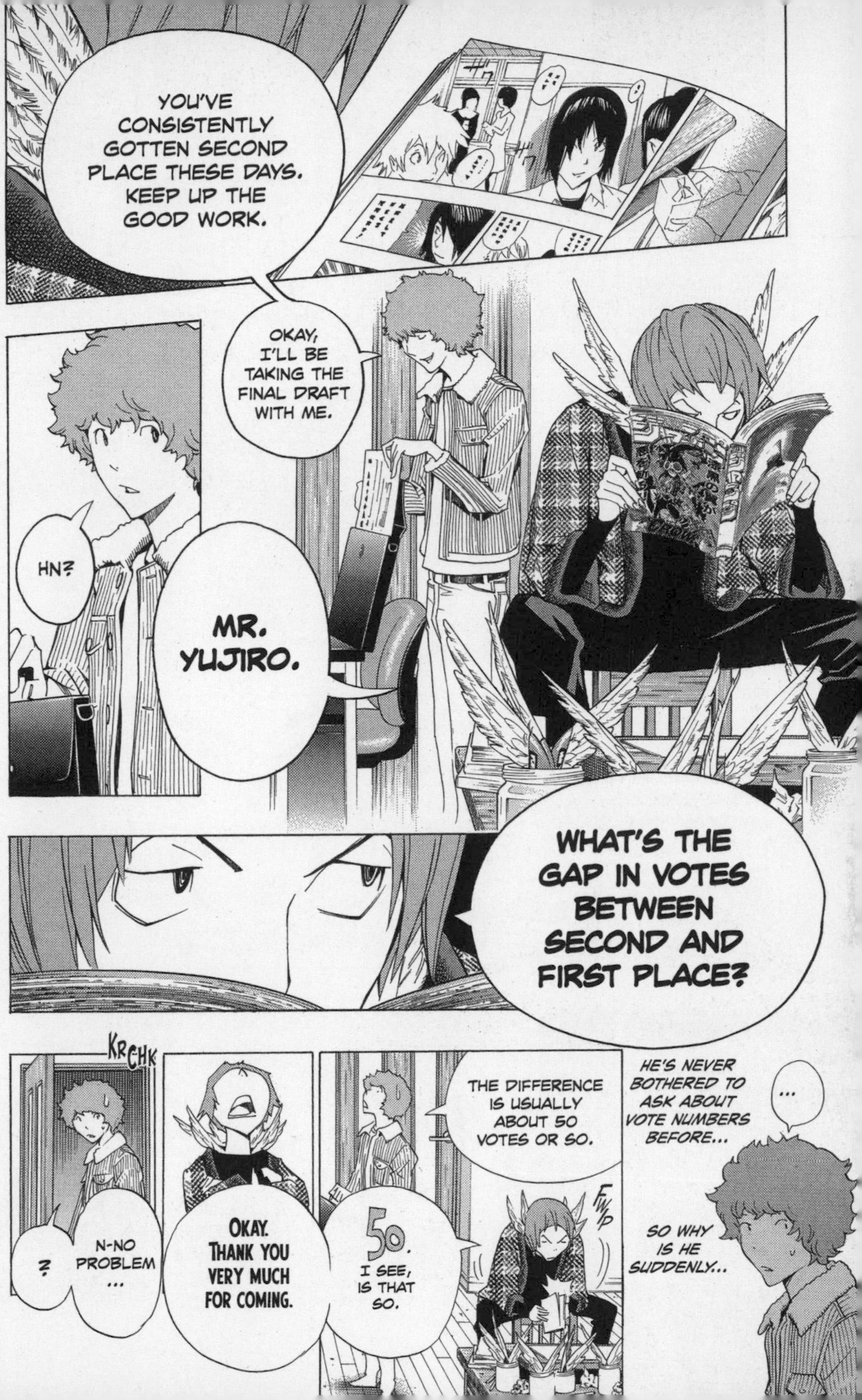
YOU'VE CONSISTENTLY GOTTEN SECOND PLACE THESE DAYS. KEEP UP THE GOOD WORK.
OKAY, I'LL BE TAKING THE FINAL DRAFT WITH ME.
MR. YUJIRO.
HN?
WHAT'S THE GAP IN VOTES BETWEEN SECOND AND FIRST PLACE?
...
HE'S NEVER BOTHERED TO ASK ABOUT VOTE NUMBERS BEFORE...
SO WHY IS HE SUDDENLY...
THE DIFFERENCE IS USUALLY ABOUT 50 VOTES OR SO.
FWIP
50. I SEE, IS THAT SO.
OKAY. THANK YOU VERY MUCH FOR COMING.
KRCHK
N-NO PROBLEM ...
?

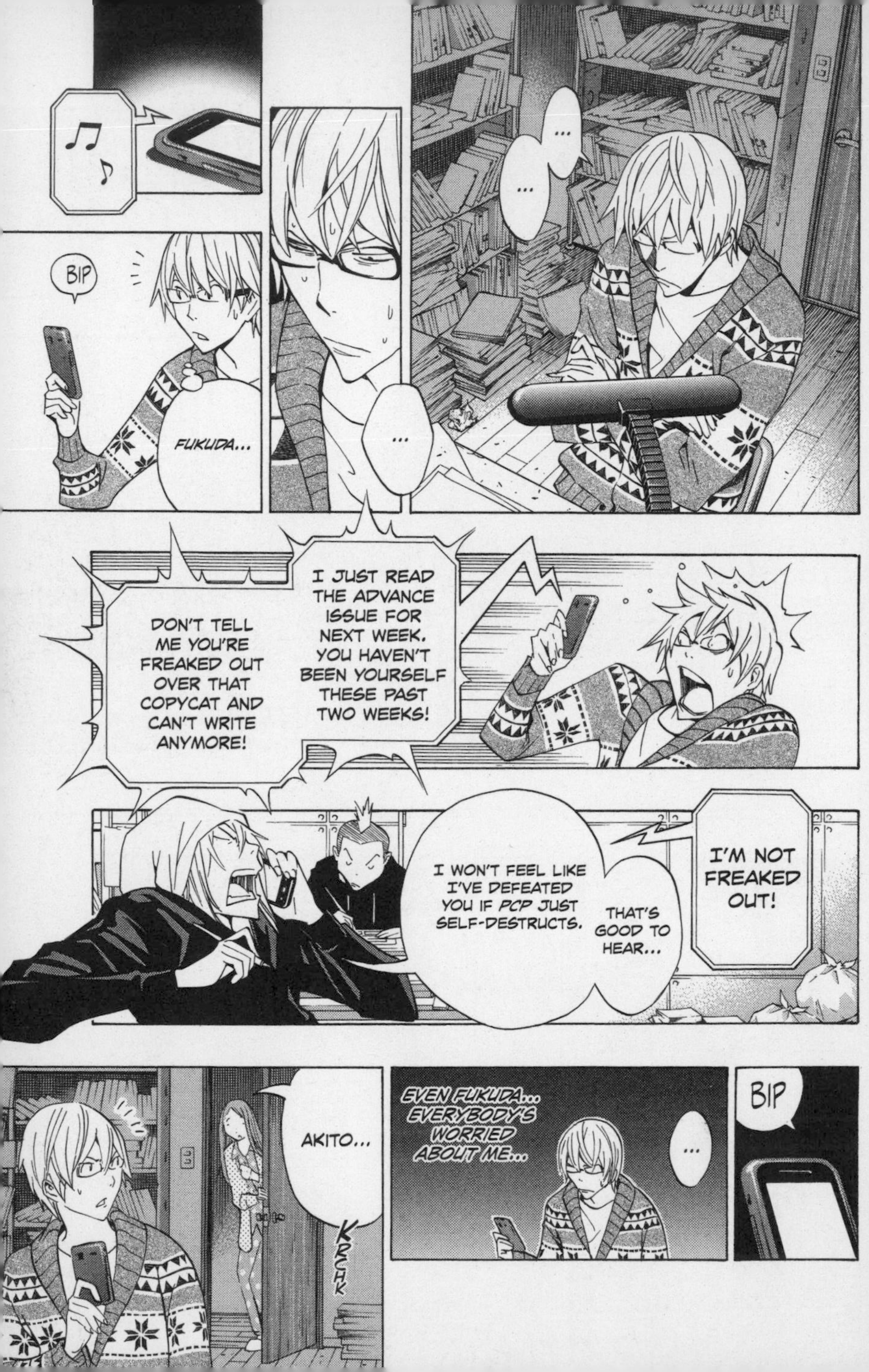
...
...
...
♫ ♪
BIP
FUKUDA...
I JUST READ THE ADVANCE ISSUE FOR NEXT WEEK. YOU HAVEN'T BEEN YOURSELF THESE PAST TWO WEEKS!
DON'T TELL ME YOU'RE FREAKED OUT OVER THAT COPYCAT AND CAN'T WRITE ANYMORE!
I'M NOT FREAKED OUT!
THAT'S GOOD TO HEAR...
I WON'T FEEL LIKE I'VE DEFEATED YOU IF *PCP* JUST SELF-DESTRUCTS.
BIP
EVEN FUKUDA... EVERYBODY'S WORRIED ABOUT ME...
...
AKITO...
KRCHK

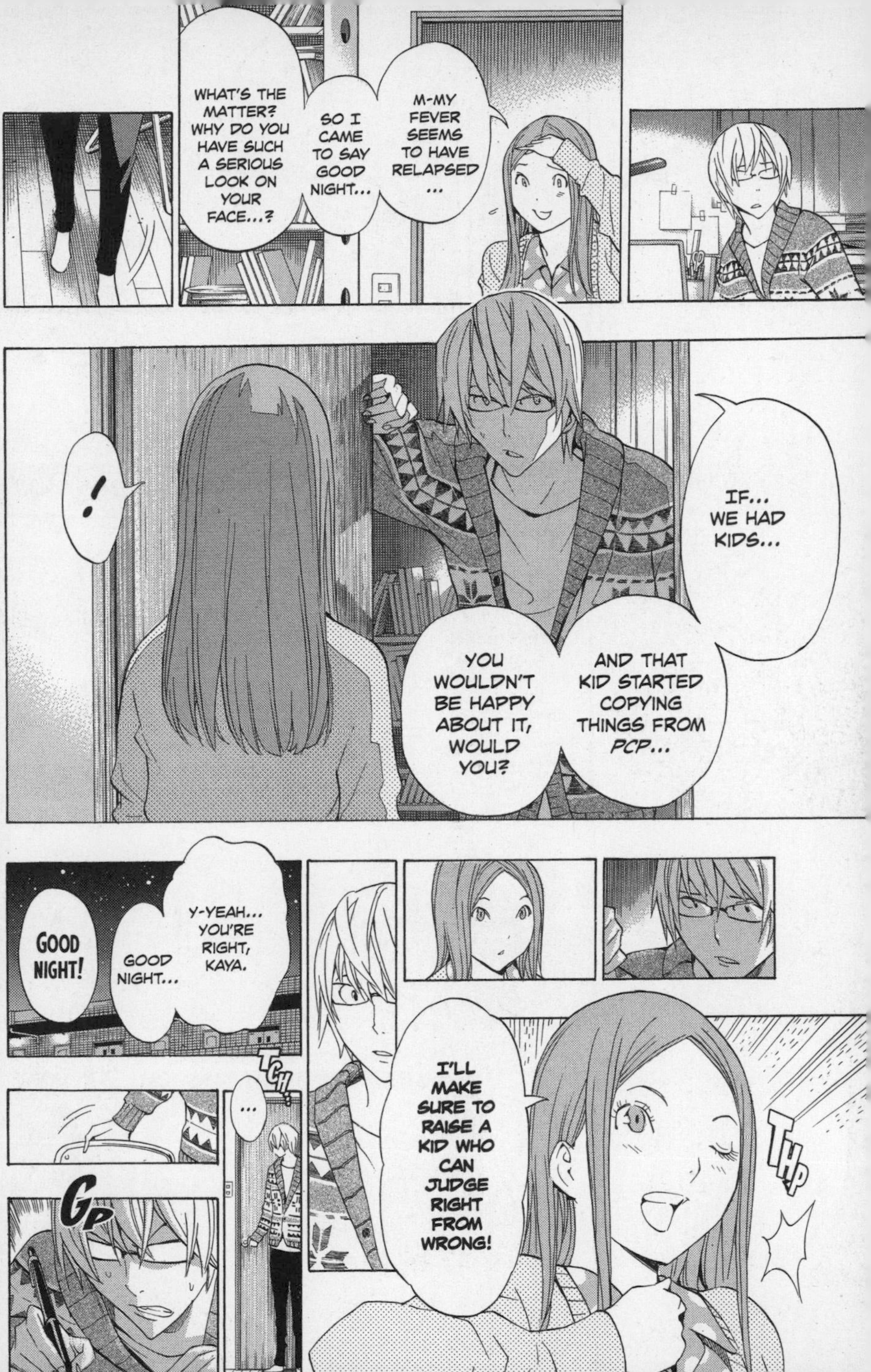
M-MY FEVER SEEMS TO HAVE RELAPSED...
SO I CAME TO SAY GOOD NIGHT...
WHAT'S THE MATTER? WHY DO YOU HAVE SUCH A SERIOUS LOOK ON YOUR FACE...?
IF... WE HAD KIDS...
AND THAT KID STARTED COPYING THINGS FROM *PCP*...
YOU WOULDN'T BE HAPPY ABOUT IT, WOULD YOU?
!
I'LL MAKE SURE TO RAISE A KID WHO CAN JUDGE RIGHT FROM WRONG!
THP
Y-YEAH... YOU'RE RIGHT, KAYA.
GOOD NIGHT...
GOOD NIGHT!
...
TCH
GP

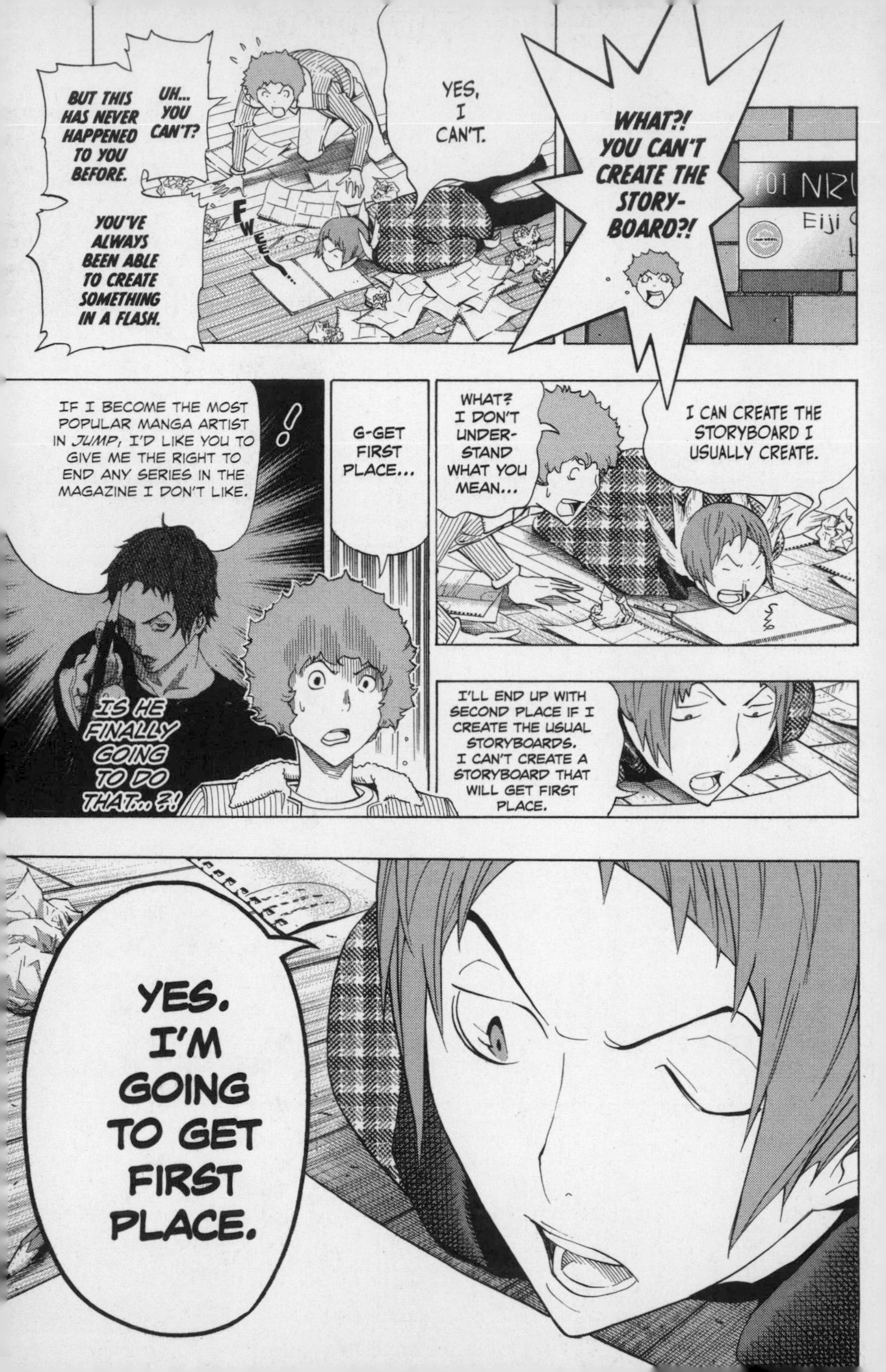
WHAT?! YOU CAN'T CREATE THE STORY-BOARD?!
YES, I CAN'T.
UH... YOU CAN'T?
BUT THIS HAS NEVER HAPPENED TO YOU BEFORE.
YOU'VE ALWAYS BEEN ABLE TO CREATE SOMETHING IN A FLASH.
FWEE...
I CAN CREATE THE STORYBOARD I USUALLY CREATE.
WHAT? I DON'T UNDER-STAND WHAT YOU MEAN...
I'LL END UP WITH SECOND PLACE IF I CREATE THE USUAL STORYBOARDS. I CAN'T CREATE A STORYBOARD THAT WILL GET FIRST PLACE.
G-GET FIRST PLACE...
IF I BECOME THE MOST POPULAR MANGA ARTIST IN JUMP, I'D LIKE YOU TO GIVE ME THE RIGHT TO END ANY SERIES IN THE MAGAZINE I DON'T LIKE.
IS HE FINALLY GOING TO DO THAT...?!
YES. I'M GOING TO GET FIRST PLACE.

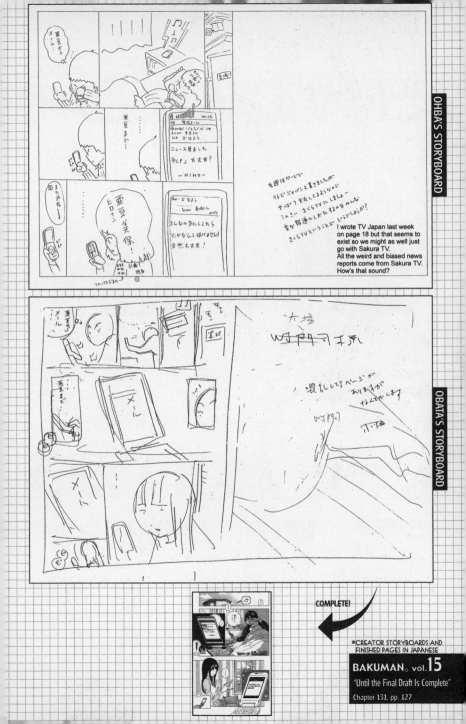

OHBA'S STORYBOARD

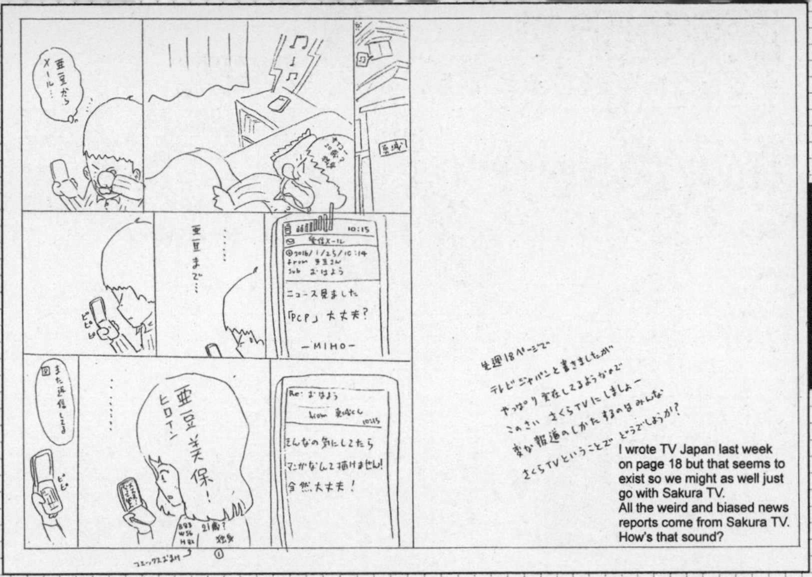
先週18ページで
テレビジャパンと書きましたが
やっぱり実在してるようなので
このさい さくらTVにしましょー
変な報道のしかたするのはみんな
さくらTVということで どうでしょうか?
I wrote TV Japan last week on page 18 but that seems to exist so we might as well just go with Sakura TV.
All the weird and biased news reports come from Sakura TV.
How's that sound?

OBATA'S STORYBOARD

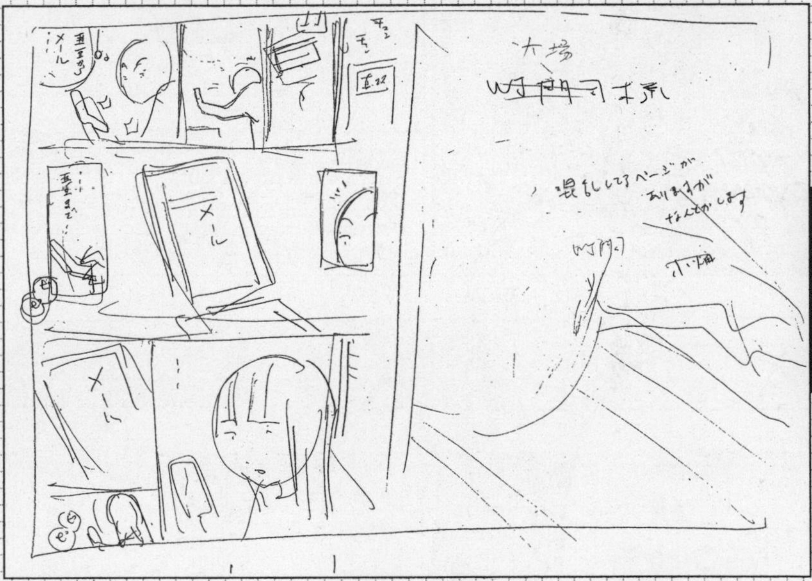

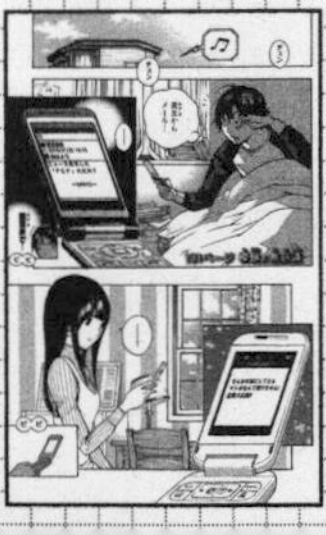

COMPLETE!

*CREATOR STORYBOARDS AND FINISHED PAGES IN JAPANESE

BAKUMAN。 vol.15

"Until the Final Draft Is Complete"

Chapter 131, pp. 127

CHAPTER 132
HANDSTAND AND PULLING TOGETHER

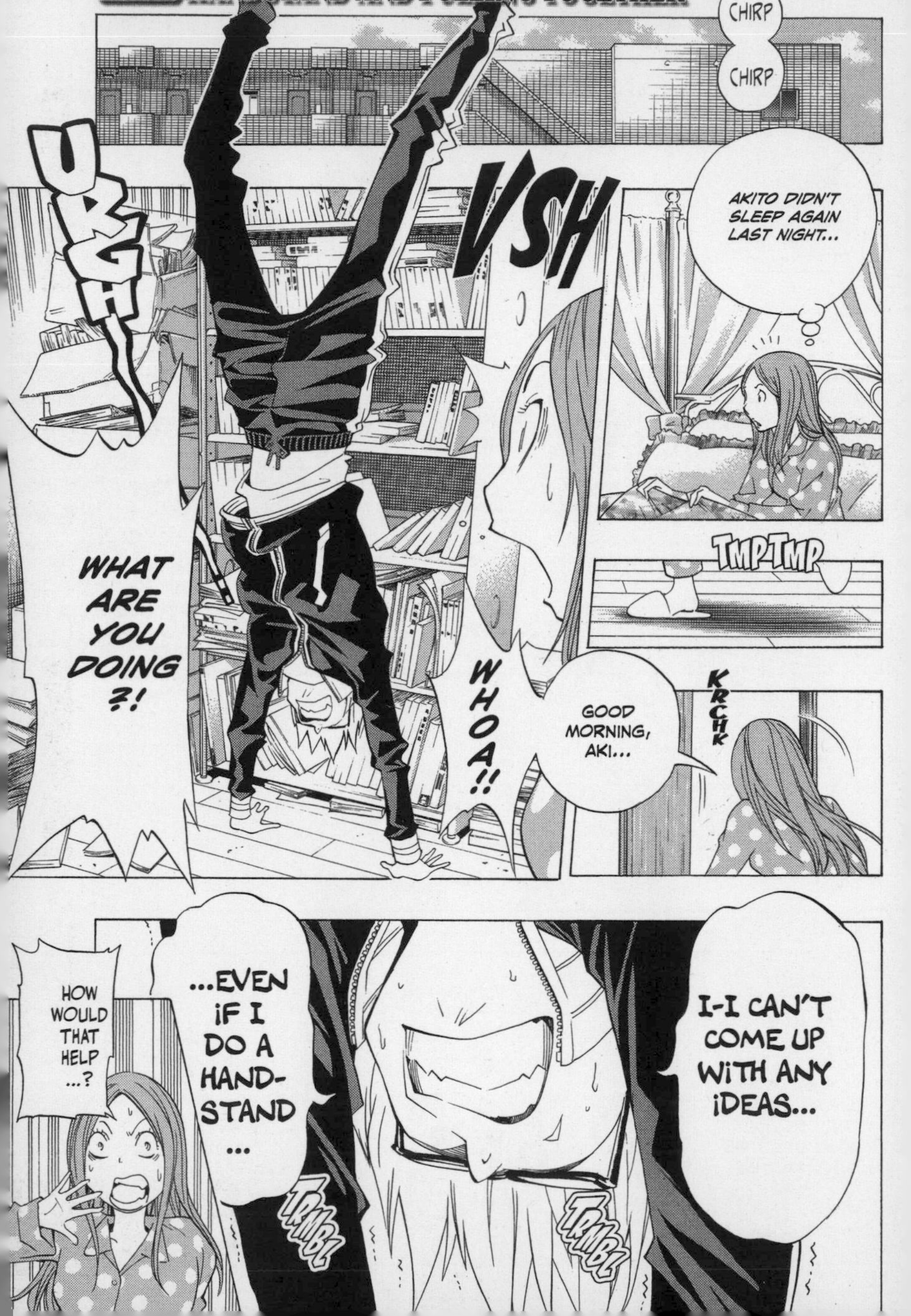

CHIRP
CHIRP
AKITO DIDN'T SLEEP AGAIN LAST NIGHT...
TMPTMP
KRCHK
GOOD MORNING, AKI...
VSH
WHOA!!
URGH
WHAT ARE YOU DOING?!
I-I CAN'T COME UP WITH ANY IDEAS...
...EVEN IF I DO A HAND-STAND...
HOW WOULD THAT HELP...?
TRMBL
TRMBL

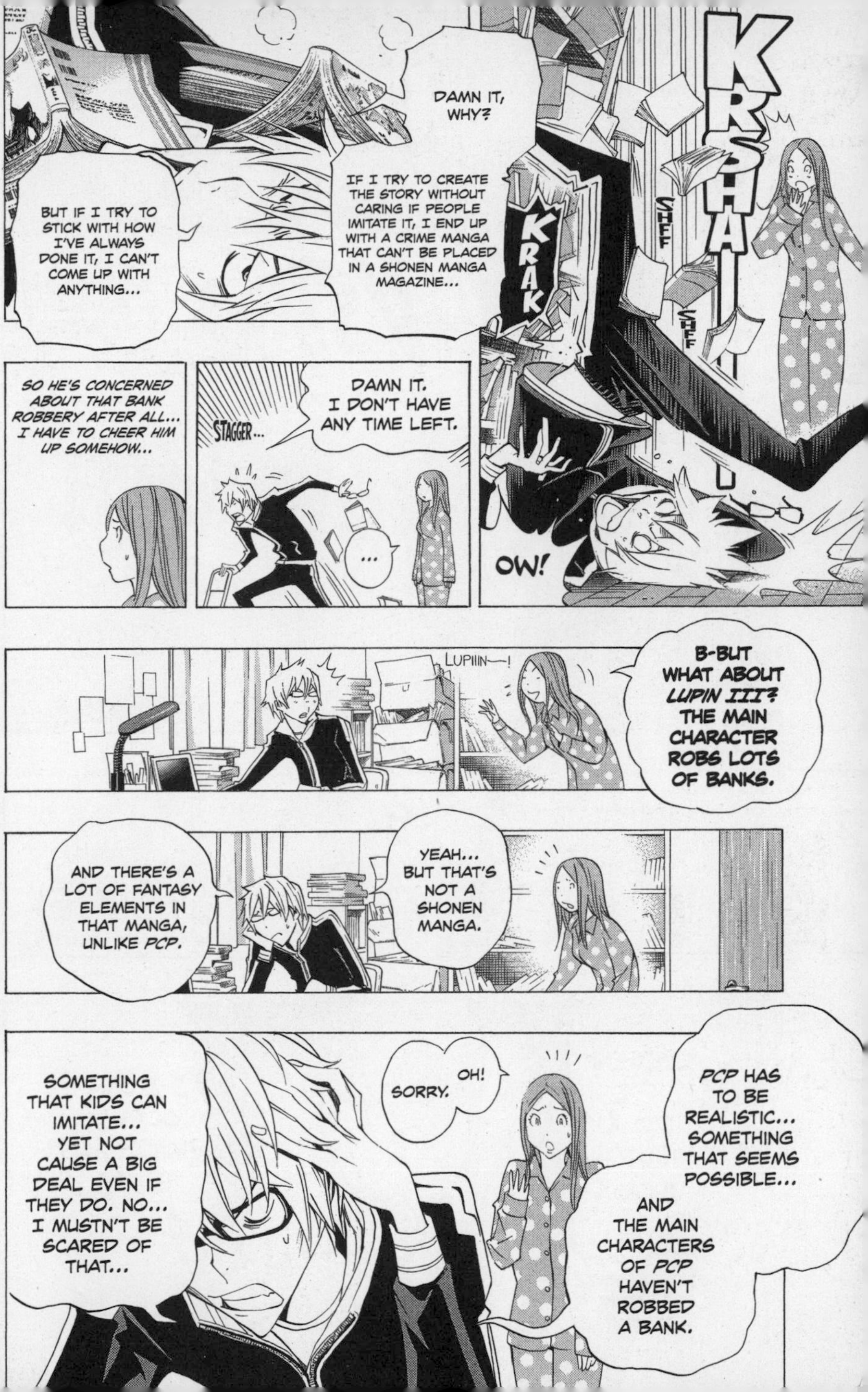
KRSHA
SHFF
SHFF
KRAK
OW!
DAMN IT, WHY?
IF I TRY TO CREATE THE STORY WITHOUT CARING IF PEOPLE IMITATE IT, I END UP WITH A CRIME MANGA THAT CAN'T BE PLACED IN A SHONEN MANGA MAGAZINE...
BUT IF I TRY TO STICK WITH HOW I'VE ALWAYS DONE IT, I CAN'T COME UP WITH ANYTHING...
DAMN IT. I DON'T HAVE ANY TIME LEFT.
STAGGER...
...
SO HE'S CONCERNED ABOUT THAT BANK ROBBERY AFTER ALL... I HAVE TO CHEER HIM UP SOMEHOW...
B-BUT WHAT ABOUT LUPIN III? THE MAIN CHARACTER ROBS LOTS OF BANKS.
LUPIIN—!
YEAH... BUT THAT'S NOT A SHONEN MANGA.
AND THERE'S A LOT OF FANTASY ELEMENTS IN THAT MANGA, UNLIKE PCP.
PCP HAS TO BE REALISTIC... SOMETHING THAT SEEMS POSSIBLE...
AND THE MAIN CHARACTERS OF PCP HAVEN'T ROBBED A BANK.
OH!
SORRY.
SOMETHING THAT KIDS CAN IMITATE... YET NOT CAUSE A BIG DEAL EVEN IF THEY DO. NO... I MUSTN'T BE SCARED OF THAT...

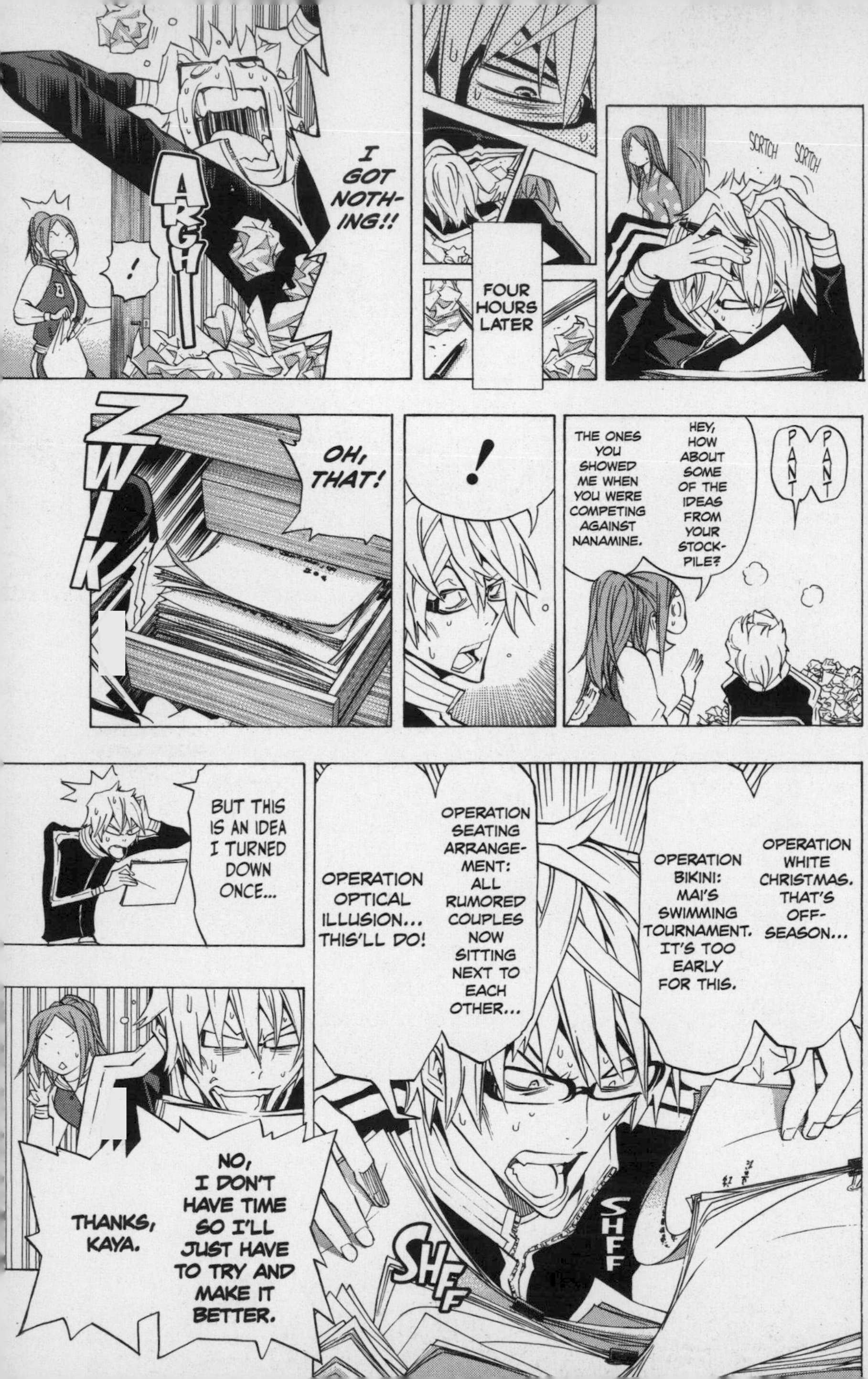
SCRTCH SCRTCH
FOUR HOURS LATER
I GOT NOTHING!!
ARGH
!
HEY, HOW ABOUT SOME OF THE IDEAS FROM YOUR STOCKPILE?
THE ONES YOU SHOWED ME WHEN YOU WERE COMPETING AGAINST NANAMINE.
PANT PANT
!
OH, THAT!
ZWIK
OPERATION WHITE CHRISTMAS. THAT'S OFF-SEASON...
OPERATION BIKINI: MAI'S SWIMMING TOURNAMENT. IT'S TOO EARLY FOR THIS.
OPERATION SEATING ARRANGEMENT: ALL RUMORED COUPLES NOW SITTING NEXT TO EACH OTHER...
OPERATION OPTICAL ILLUSION... THIS'LL DO!
SHFF
SHFF
BUT THIS IS AN IDEA I TURNED DOWN ONCE...
NO, I DON'T HAVE TIME SO I'LL JUST HAVE TO TRY AND MAKE IT BETTER.
THANKS, KAYA.

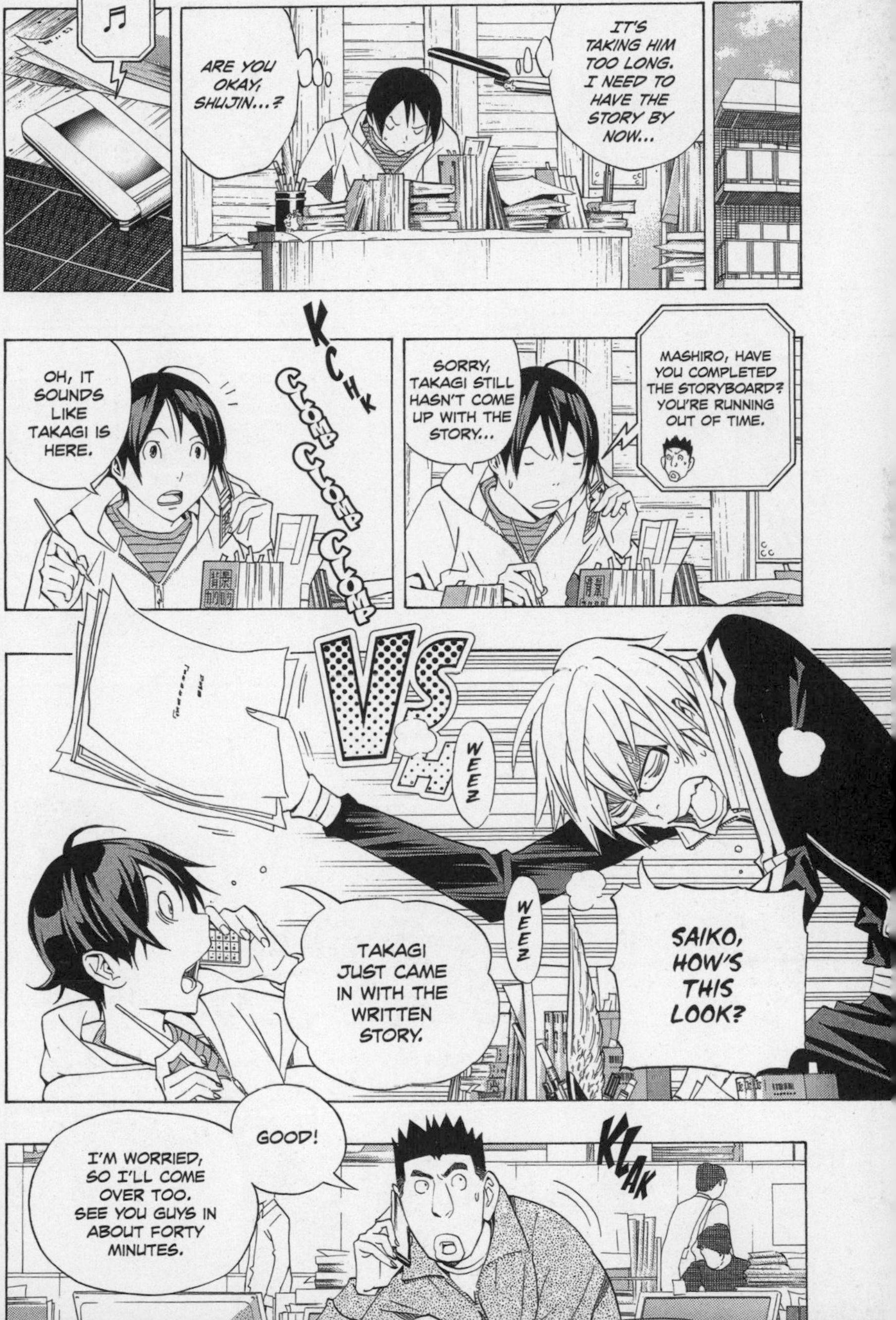
IT'S TAKING HIM TOO LONG. I NEED TO HAVE THE STORY BY NOW...
ARE YOU OKAY, SHUJIN...?
♪
MASHIRO, HAVE YOU COMPLETED THE STORYBOARD? YOU'RE RUNNING OUT OF TIME.
SORRY, TAKAGI STILL HASN'T COME UP WITH THE STORY...
KCHK
CLOMP CLOMP CLOMP CLOMP
OH, IT SOUNDS LIKE TAKAGI IS HERE.
VS
WEEZ
SAIKO, HOW'S THIS LOOK?
WEEZ
TAKAGI JUST CAME IN WITH THE WRITTEN STORY.
KLAK
GOOD!
I'M WORRIED, SO I'LL COME OVER TOO. SEE YOU GUYS IN ABOUT FORTY MINUTES.

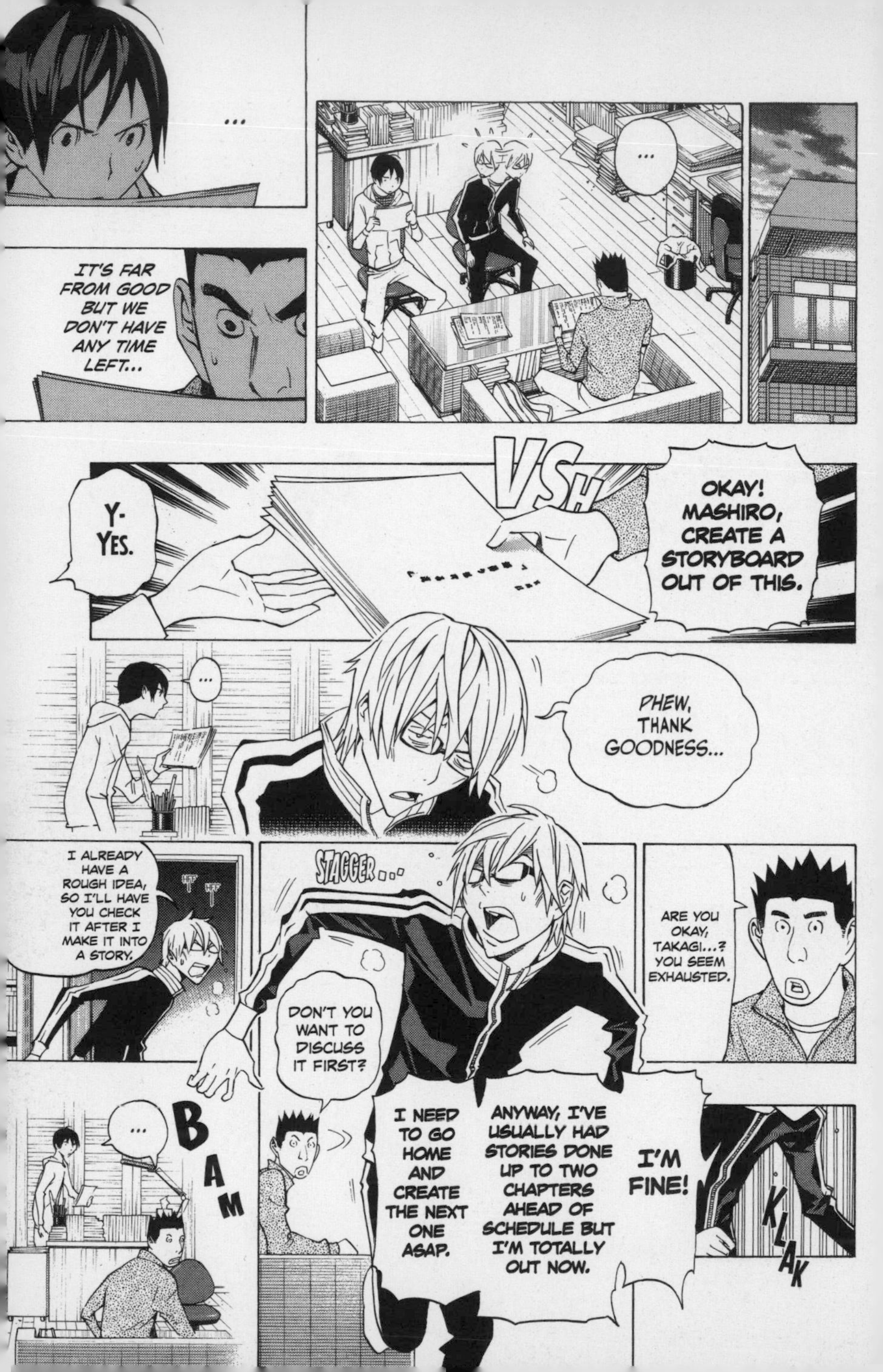
...
...
IT'S FAR FROM GOOD BUT WE DON'T HAVE ANY TIME LEFT...
OKAY! MASHIRO, CREATE A STORYBOARD OUT OF THIS.
VSH
Y-YES.
PHEW, THANK GOODNESS...
...
ARE YOU OKAY, TAKAGI...? YOU SEEM EXHAUSTED.
STAGGER...
I ALREADY HAVE A ROUGH IDEA, SO I'LL HAVE YOU CHECK IT AFTER I MAKE IT INTO A STORY.
DON'T YOU WANT TO DISCUSS IT FIRST?
I'M FINE!
KLAK
ANYWAY, I'VE USUALLY HAD STORIES DONE UP TO TWO CHAPTERS AHEAD OF SCHEDULE BUT I'M TOTALLY OUT NOW.
I NEED TO GO HOME AND CREATE THE NEXT ONE ASAP.
...
BAM

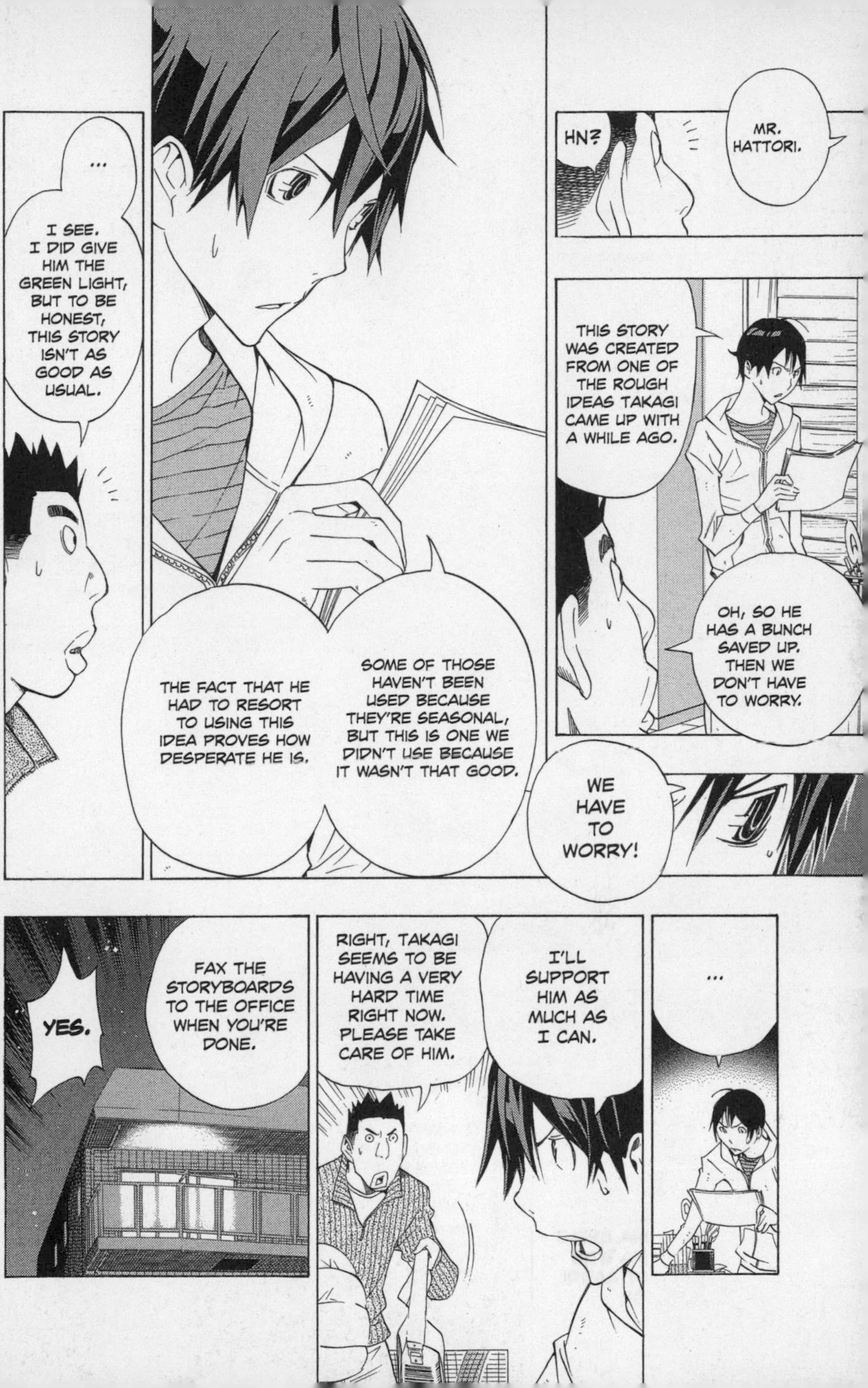
MR. HATTORI.
HN?
THIS STORY WAS CREATED FROM ONE OF THE ROUGH IDEAS TAKAGI CAME UP WITH A WHILE AGO.
OH, SO HE HAS A BUNCH SAVED UP. THEN WE DON'T HAVE TO WORRY.
WE HAVE TO WORRY!
SOME OF THOSE HAVEN'T BEEN USED BECAUSE THEY'RE SEASONAL, BUT THIS IS ONE WE DIDN'T USE BECAUSE IT WASN'T THAT GOOD.
THE FACT THAT HE HAD TO RESORT TO USING THIS IDEA PROVES HOW DESPERATE HE IS.
...
I SEE. I DID GIVE HIM THE GREEN LIGHT, BUT TO BE HONEST, THIS STORY ISN'T AS GOOD AS USUAL.
...
I'LL SUPPORT HIM AS MUCH AS I CAN.
RIGHT, TAKAGI SEEMS TO BE HAVING A VERY HARD TIME RIGHT NOW. PLEASE TAKE CARE OF HIM.
FAX THE STORYBOARDS TO THE OFFICE WHEN YOU'RE DONE.
YES.

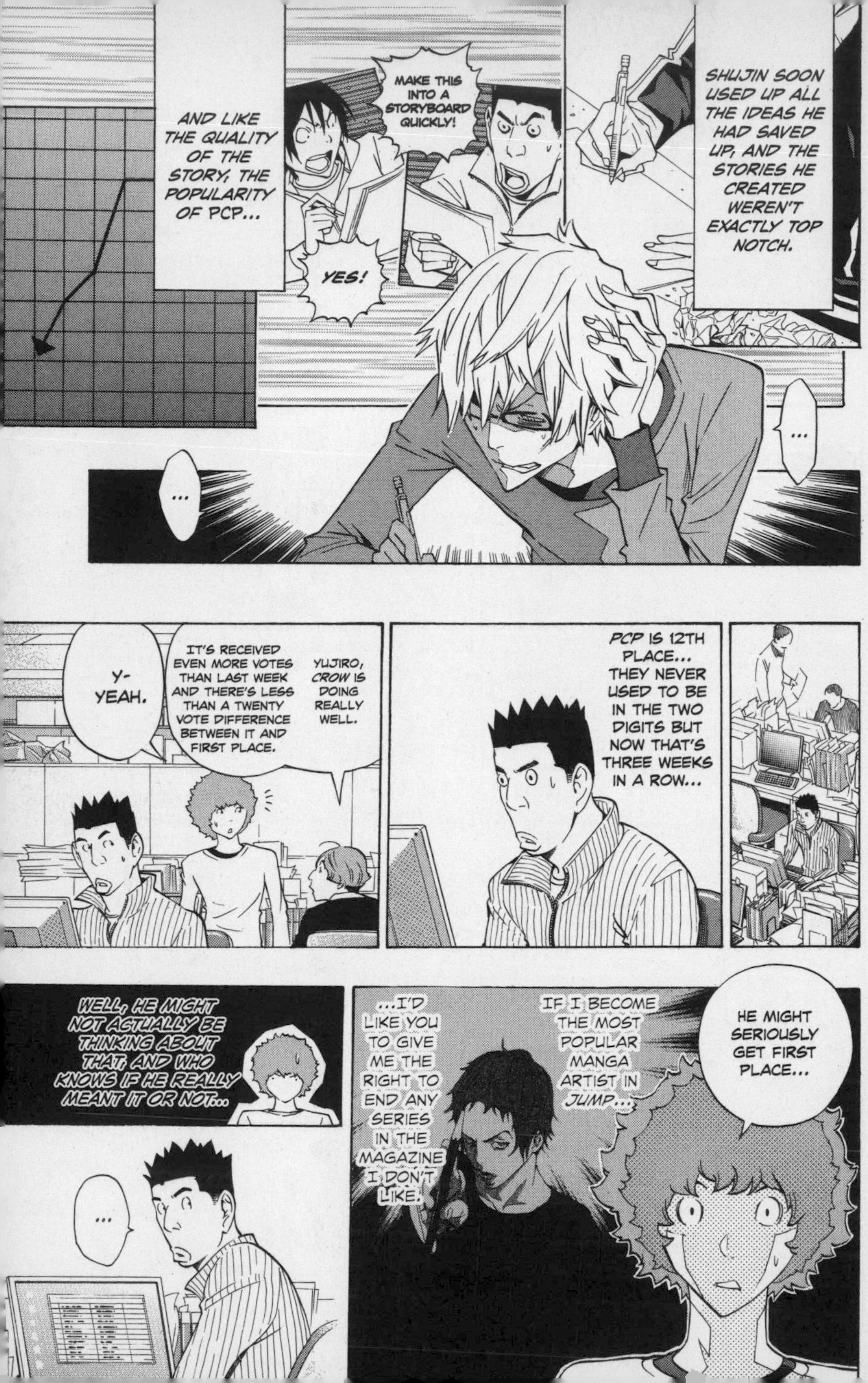
SHUJIN SOON USED UP ALL THE IDEAS HE HAD SAVED UP, AND THE STORIES HE CREATED WEREN'T EXACTLY TOP NOTCH.
MAKE THIS INTO A STORYBOARD QUICKLY!
YES!
AND LIKE THE QUALITY OF THE STORY, THE POPULARITY OF PCP...
...
...
PCP IS 12TH PLACE... THEY NEVER USED TO BE IN THE TWO DIGITS BUT NOW THAT'S THREE WEEKS IN A ROW...
YUJIRO, CROW IS DOING REALLY WELL.
IT'S RECEIVED EVEN MORE VOTES THAN LAST WEEK AND THERE'S LESS THAN A TWENTY VOTE DIFFERENCE BETWEEN IT AND FIRST PLACE.
Y-YEAH.
HE MIGHT SERIOUSLY GET FIRST PLACE...
IF I BECOME THE MOST POPULAR MANGA ARTIST IN JUMP...
...I'D LIKE YOU TO GIVE ME THE RIGHT TO END ANY SERIES IN THE MAGAZINE I DON'T LIKE.
WELL, HE MIGHT NOT ACTUALLY BE THINKING ABOUT THAT, AND WHO KNOWS IF HE REALLY MEANT IT OR NOT...
...

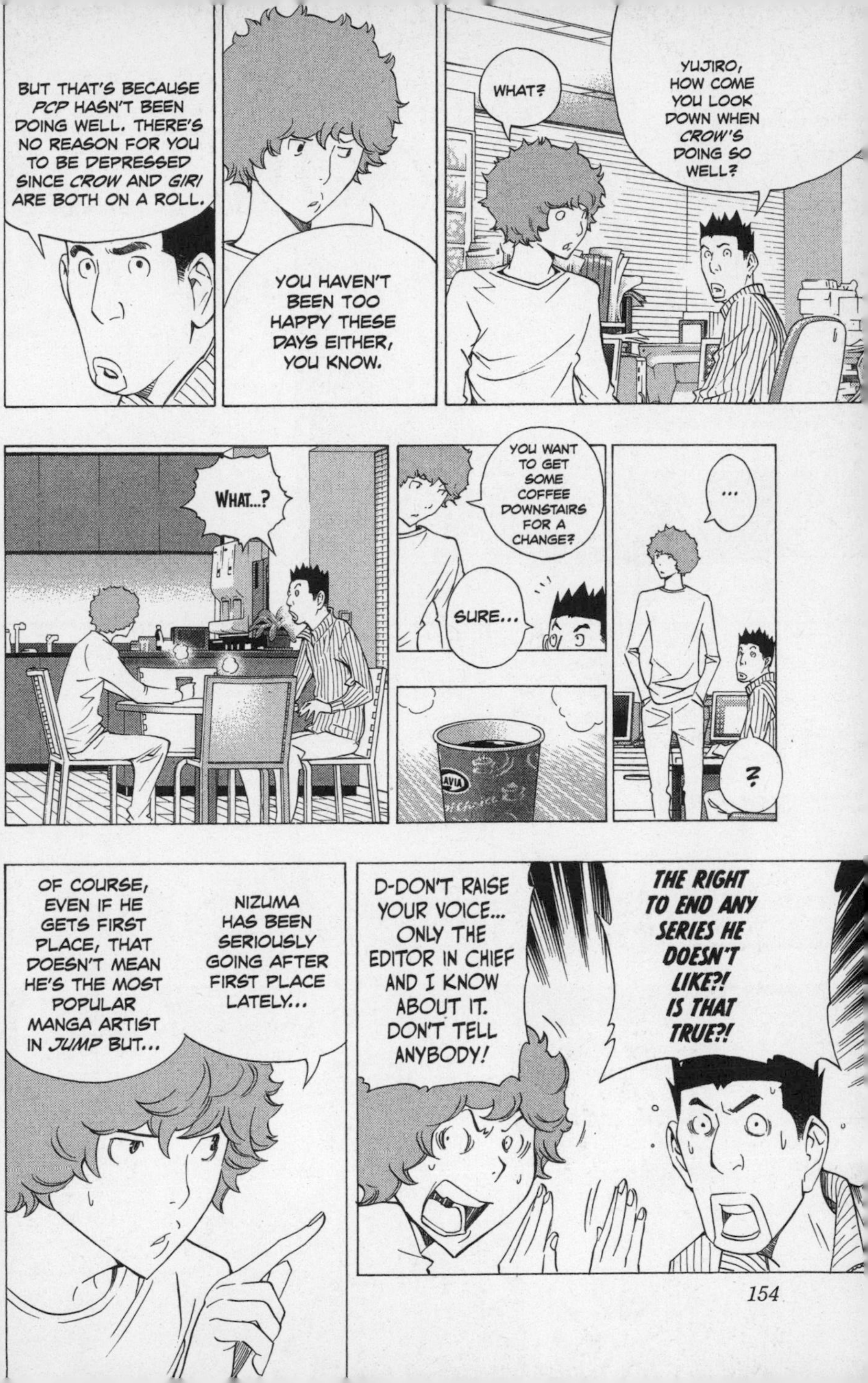
YUJIRO, HOW COME YOU LOOK DOWN WHEN *CROW'S* DOING SO WELL?
WHAT?
YOU HAVEN'T BEEN TOO HAPPY THESE DAYS EITHER, YOU KNOW.
BUT THAT'S BECAUSE *PCP* HASN'T BEEN DOING WELL. THERE'S NO REASON FOR YOU TO BE DEPRESSED SINCE *CROW* AND *GIRI* ARE BOTH ON A ROLL.
...
?
YOU WANT TO GET SOME COFFEE DOWNSTAIRS FOR A CHANGE?
SURE...
WHAT...?
THE RIGHT TO END ANY SERIES HE DOESN'T LIKE?! IS THAT TRUE?!
D-DON'T RAISE YOUR VOICE... ONLY THE EDITOR IN CHIEF AND I KNOW ABOUT IT. DON'T TELL ANYBODY!
NIZUMA HAS BEEN SERIOUSLY GOING AFTER FIRST PLACE LATELY...
OF COURSE, EVEN IF HE GETS FIRST PLACE, THAT DOESN'T MEAN HE'S THE MOST POPULAR MANGA ARTIST IN *JUMP* BUT...

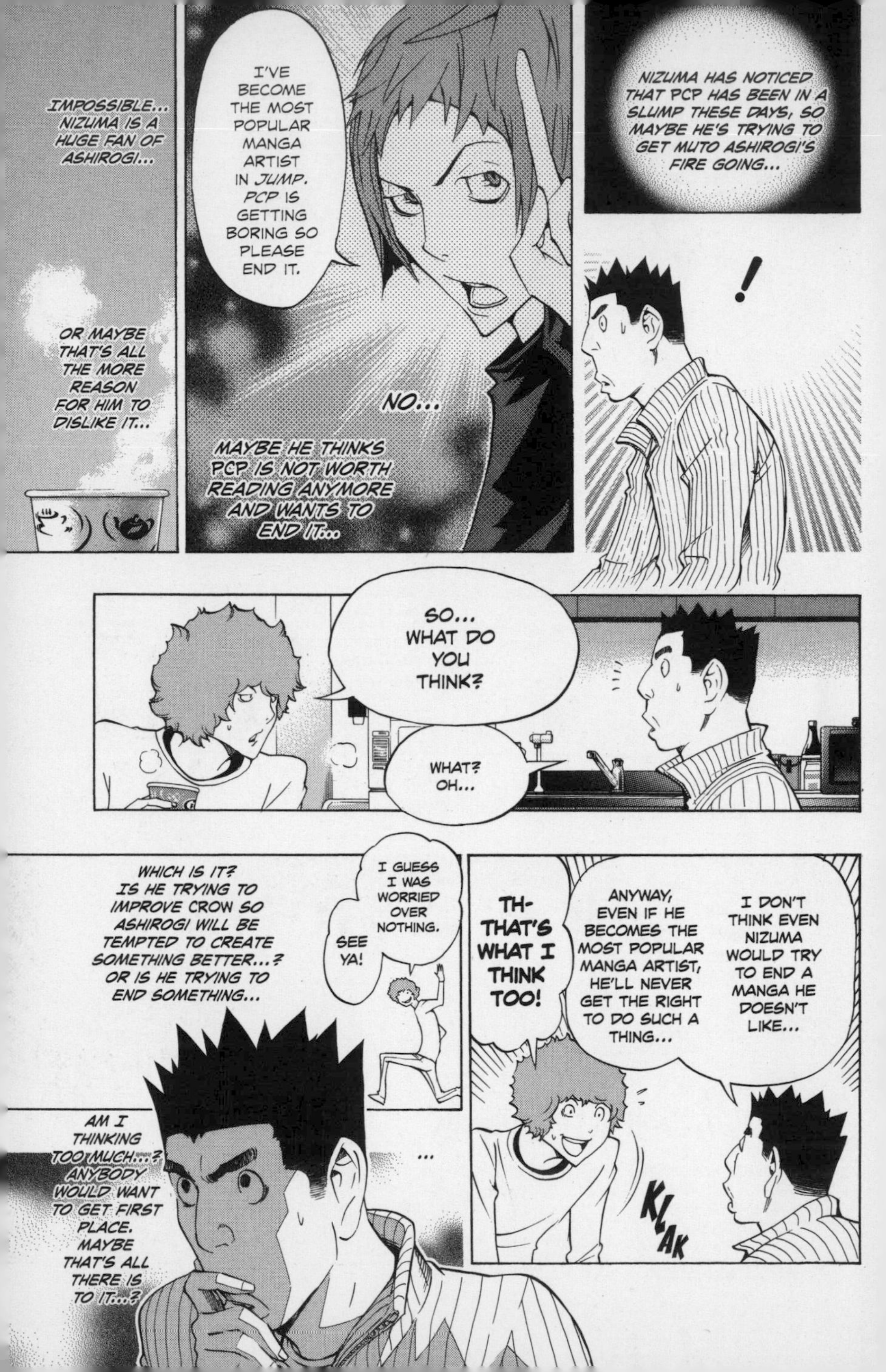
NIZUMA HAS NOTICED THAT PCP HAS BEEN IN A SLUMP THESE DAYS, SO MAYBE HE'S TRYING TO GET MUTO ASHIROGI'S FIRE GOING...
!
I'VE BECOME THE MOST POPULAR MANGA ARTIST IN *JUMP*. *PCP* IS GETTING BORING SO PLEASE END IT.
NO...
MAYBE HE THINKS PCP IS NOT WORTH READING ANYMORE AND WANTS TO END IT...
IMPOSSIBLE... NIZUMA IS A HUGE FAN OF ASHIROGI...
OR MAYBE THAT'S ALL THE MORE REASON FOR HIM TO DISLIKE IT...
SO... WHAT DO YOU THINK?
WHAT? OH...
I DON'T THINK EVEN NIZUMA WOULD TRY TO END A MANGA HE DOESN'T LIKE...
ANYWAY, EVEN IF HE BECOMES THE MOST POPULAR MANGA ARTIST, HE'LL NEVER GET THE RIGHT TO DO SUCH A THING...
TH-THAT'S WHAT I THINK TOO!
KLAK
I GUESS I WAS WORRIED OVER NOTHING.
SEE YA!
WHICH IS IT? IS HE TRYING TO IMPROVE CROW SO ASHIROGI WILL BE TEMPTED TO CREATE SOMETHING BETTER...? OR IS HE TRYING TO END SOMETHING...
...
AM I THINKING TOO MUCH...? ANYBODY WOULD WANT TO GET FIRST PLACE. MAYBE THAT'S ALL THERE IS TO IT...?

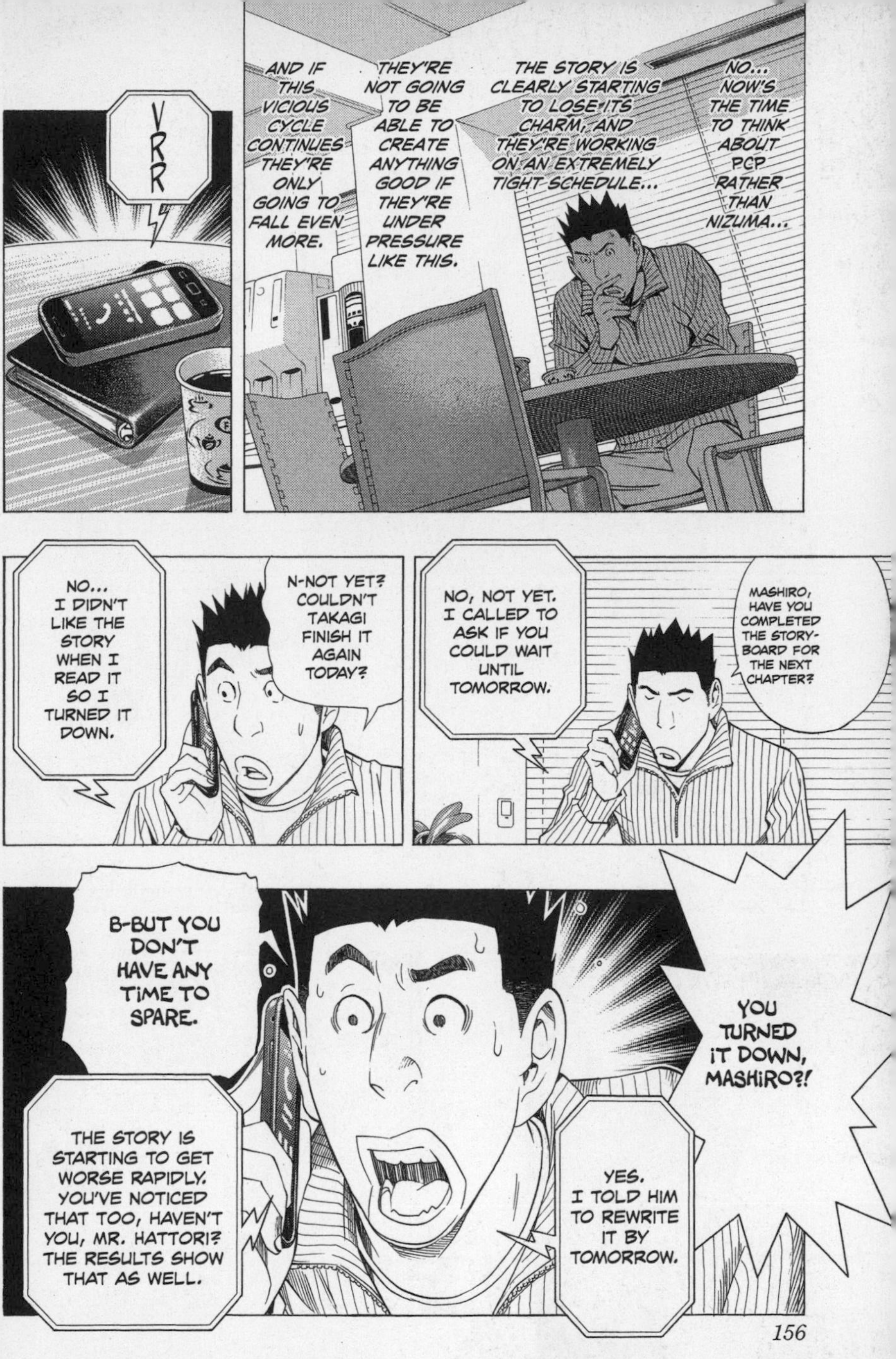
NO... NOW'S THE TIME TO THINK ABOUT PCP RATHER THAN NIZUMA...
THE STORY IS CLEARLY STARTING TO LOSE ITS CHARM, AND THEY'RE WORKING ON AN EXTREMELY TIGHT SCHEDULE...
THEY'RE NOT GOING TO BE ABLE TO CREATE ANYTHING GOOD IF THEY'RE UNDER PRESSURE LIKE THIS.
AND IF THIS VICIOUS CYCLE CONTINUES THEY'RE ONLY GOING TO FALL EVEN MORE.
VRR
MASHIRO, HAVE YOU COMPLETED THE STORY-BOARD FOR THE NEXT CHAPTER?
NO, NOT YET. I CALLED TO ASK IF YOU COULD WAIT UNTIL TOMORROW.
N-NOT YET? COULDN'T TAKAGI FINISH IT AGAIN TODAY?
NO... I DIDN'T LIKE THE STORY WHEN I READ IT SO I TURNED IT DOWN.
YOU TURNED IT DOWN, MASHIRO?!
YES. I TOLD HIM TO REWRITE IT BY TOMORROW.
B-BUT YOU DON'T HAVE ANY TIME TO SPARE.
THE STORY IS STARTING TO GET WORSE RAPIDLY. YOU'VE NOTICED THAT TOO, HAVEN'T YOU, MR. HATTORI? THE RESULTS SHOW THAT AS WELL.

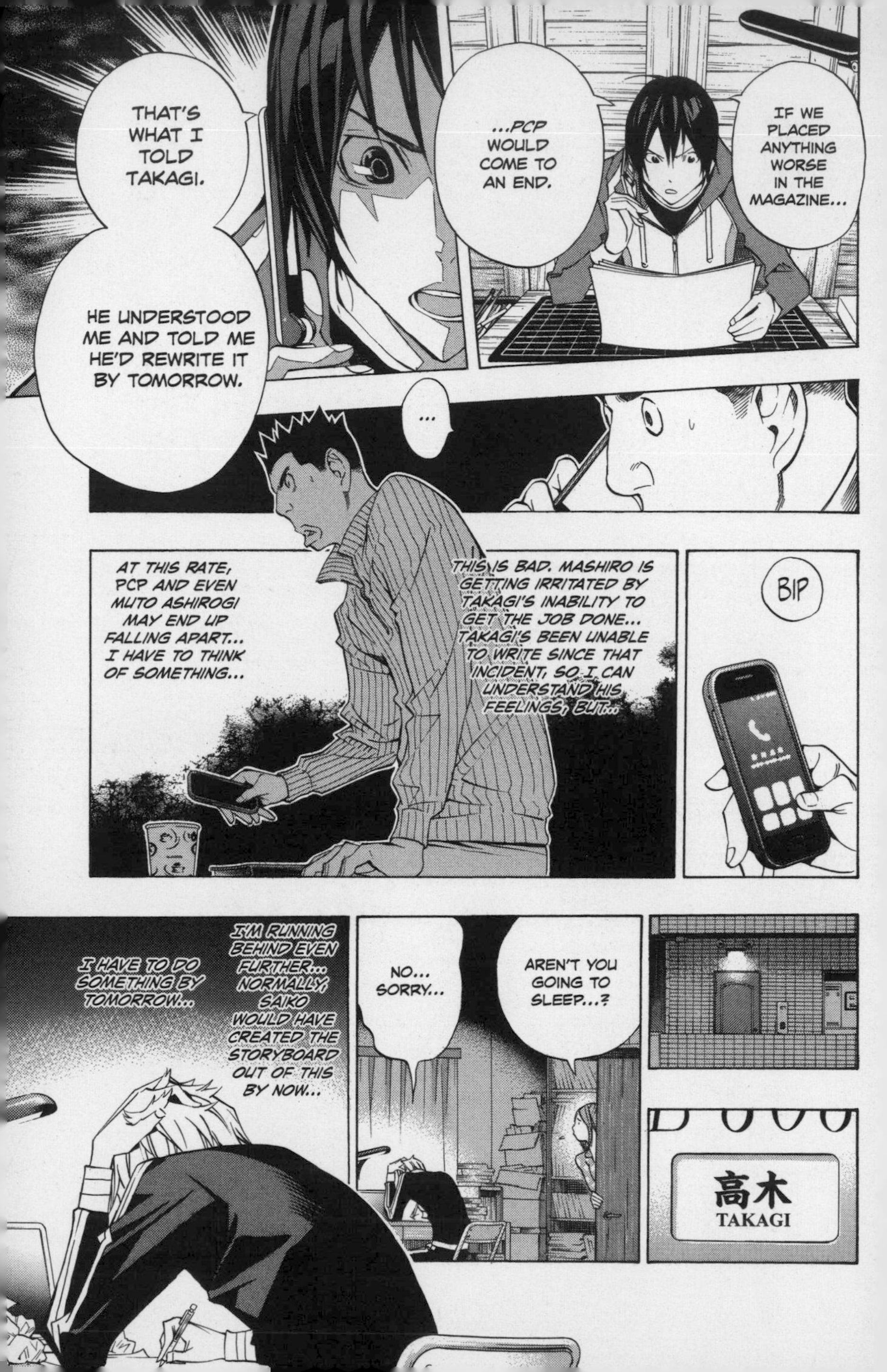
IF WE PLACED ANYTHING WORSE IN THE MAGAZINE...
...PCP WOULD COME TO AN END.
THAT'S WHAT I TOLD TAKAGI.
HE UNDERSTOOD ME AND TOLD ME HE'D REWRITE IT BY TOMORROW.
...
BIP
THIS IS BAD. MASHIRO IS GETTING IRRITATED BY TAKAGI'S INABILITY TO GET THE JOB DONE... TAKAGI'S BEEN UNABLE TO WRITE SINCE THAT INCIDENT, SO I CAN UNDERSTAND HIS FEELINGS, BUT...
AT THIS RATE, PCP AND EVEN MUTO ASHIROGI MAY END UP FALLING APART... I HAVE TO THINK OF SOMETHING...
高木
TAKAGI
AREN'T YOU GOING TO SLEEP...?
NO... SORRY...
I'M RUNNING BEHIND EVEN FURTHER... NORMALLY, SAIKO WOULD HAVE CREATED THE STORYBOARD OUT OF THIS BY NOW...
I HAVE TO DO SOMETHING BY TOMORROW...

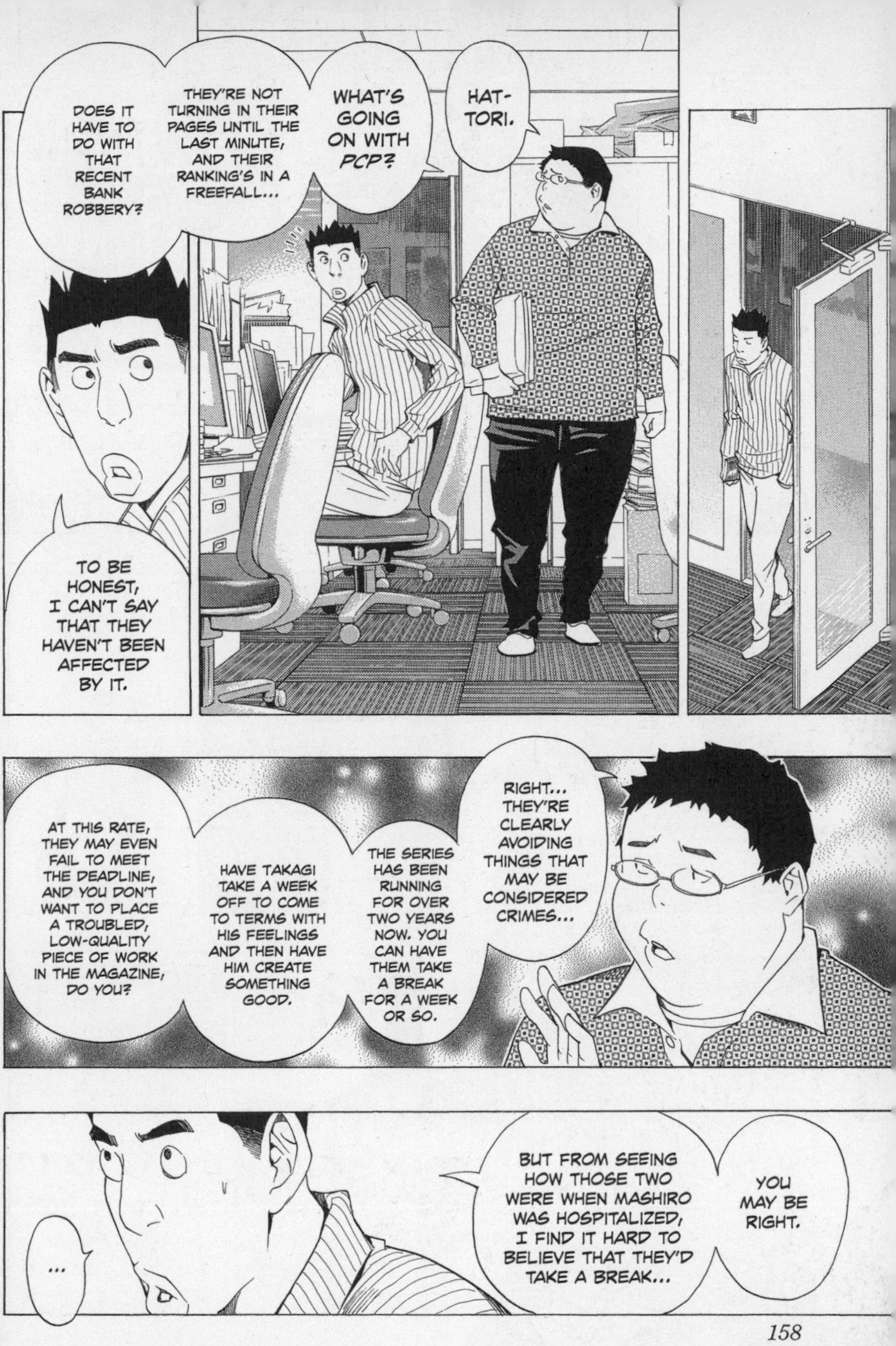
HAT-TORI.
WHAT'S GOING ON WITH PCP?
THEY'RE NOT TURNING IN THEIR PAGES UNTIL THE LAST MINUTE, AND THEIR RANKING'S IN A FREEFALL...
DOES IT HAVE TO DO WITH THAT RECENT BANK ROBBERY?
TO BE HONEST, I CAN'T SAY THAT THEY HAVEN'T BEEN AFFECTED BY IT.
RIGHT... THEY'RE CLEARLY AVOIDING THINGS THAT MAY BE CONSIDERED CRIMES...
THE SERIES HAS BEEN RUNNING FOR OVER TWO YEARS NOW. YOU CAN HAVE THEM TAKE A BREAK FOR A WEEK OR SO.
HAVE TAKAGI TAKE A WEEK OFF TO COME TO TERMS WITH HIS FEELINGS AND THEN HAVE HIM CREATE SOMETHING GOOD.
AT THIS RATE, THEY MAY EVEN FAIL TO MEET THE DEADLINE, AND YOU DON'T WANT TO PLACE A TROUBLED, LOW-QUALITY PIECE OF WORK IN THE MAGAZINE, DO YOU?
YOU MAY BE RIGHT.
BUT FROM SEEING HOW THOSE TWO WERE WHEN MASHIRO WAS HOSPITALIZED, I FIND IT HARD TO BELIEVE THAT THEY'D TAKE A BREAK...
...

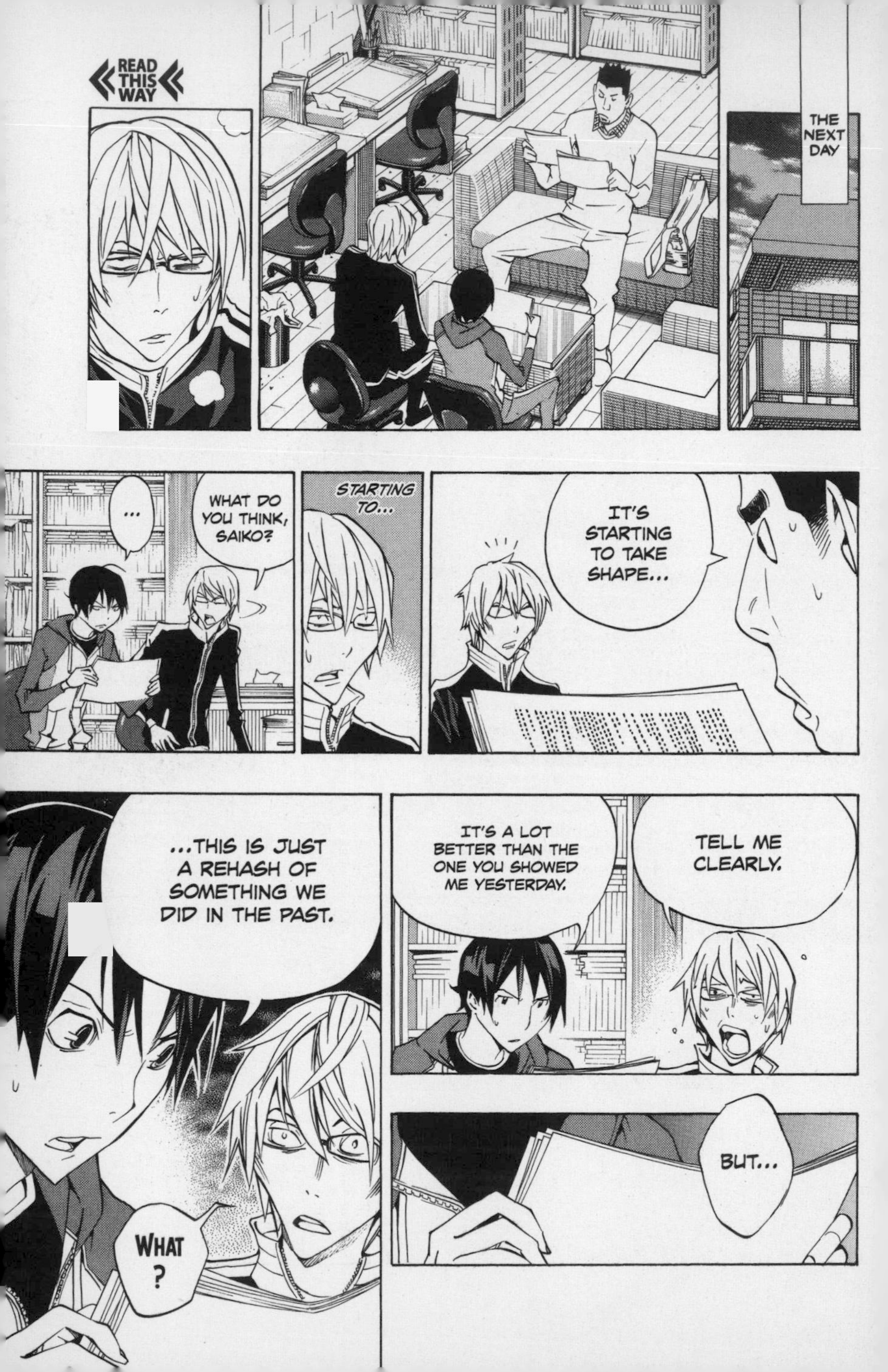
READ THIS WAY
THE NEXT DAY
IT'S STARTING TO TAKE SHAPE...
STARTING TO...
WHAT DO YOU THINK, SAIKO?
...
TELL ME CLEARLY.
IT'S A LOT BETTER THAN THE ONE YOU SHOWED ME YESTERDAY.
BUT...
...THIS IS JUST A REHASH OF SOMETHING WE DID IN THE PAST.
WHAT?

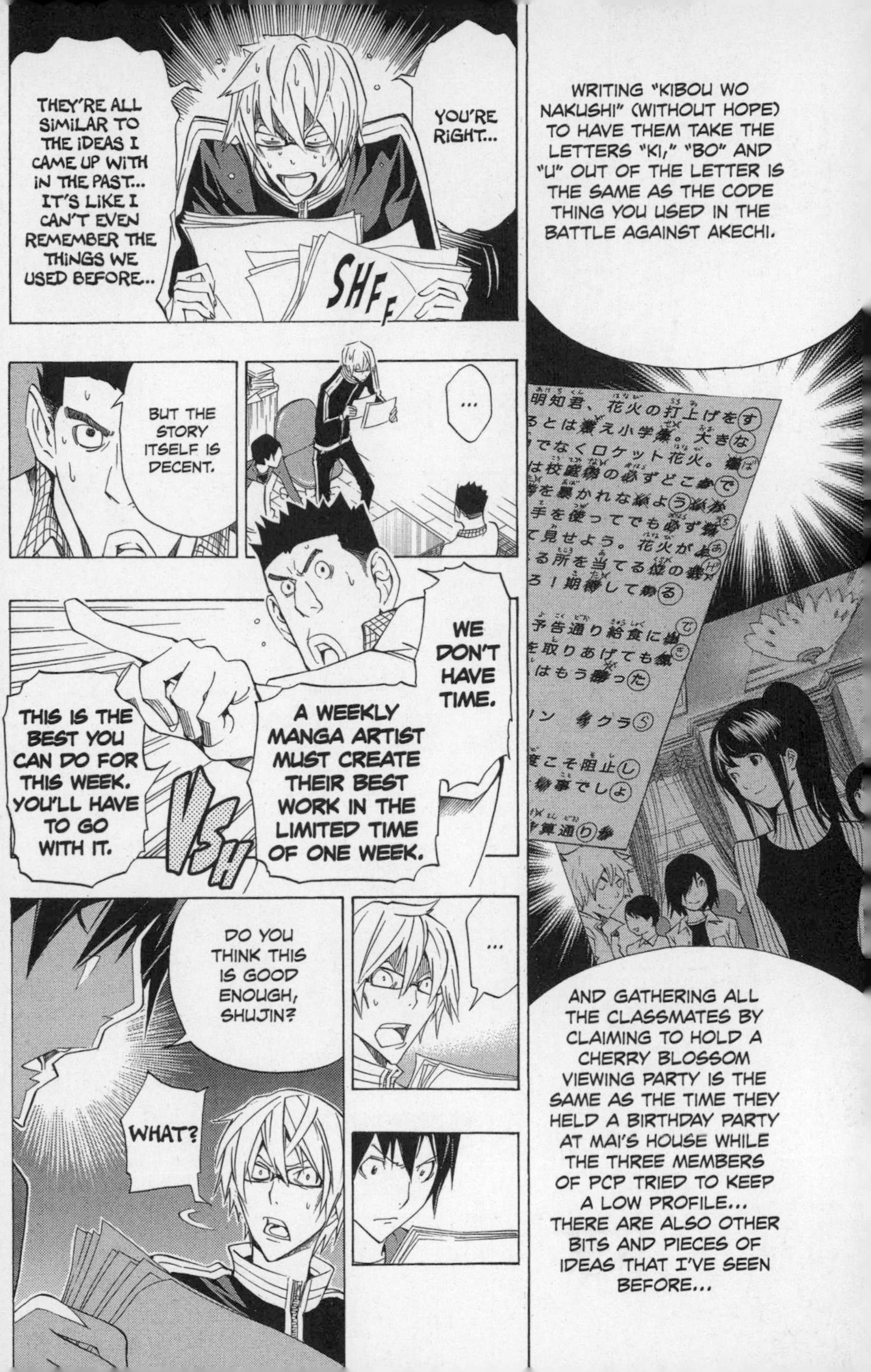
WRITING "KIBOU WO NAKUSHI" (WITHOUT HOPE) TO HAVE THEM TAKE THE LETTERS "KI," "BO" AND "U" OUT OF THE LETTER IS THE SAME AS THE CODE THING YOU USED IN THE BATTLE AGAINST AKECHI.
AND GATHERING ALL THE CLASSMATES BY CLAIMING TO HOLD A CHERRY BLOSSOM VIEWING PARTY IS THE SAME AS THE TIME THEY HELD A BIRTHDAY PARTY AT MAI'S HOUSE WHILE THE THREE MEMBERS OF PCP TRIED TO KEEP A LOW PROFILE... THERE ARE ALSO OTHER BITS AND PIECES OF IDEAS THAT I'VE SEEN BEFORE...
YOU'RE RIGHT...
THEY'RE ALL SIMILAR TO THE IDEAS I CAME UP WITH IN THE PAST... IT'S LIKE I CAN'T EVEN REMEMBER THE THINGS WE USED BEFORE...
SHFF
...
BUT THE STORY ITSELF IS DECENT.
WE DON'T HAVE TIME.
A WEEKLY MANGA ARTIST MUST CREATE THEIR BEST WORK IN THE LIMITED TIME OF ONE WEEK.
THIS IS THE BEST YOU CAN DO FOR THIS WEEK. YOU'LL HAVE TO GO WITH IT.
VSH
...
DO YOU THINK THIS IS GOOD ENOUGH, SHUJIN?
WHAT?

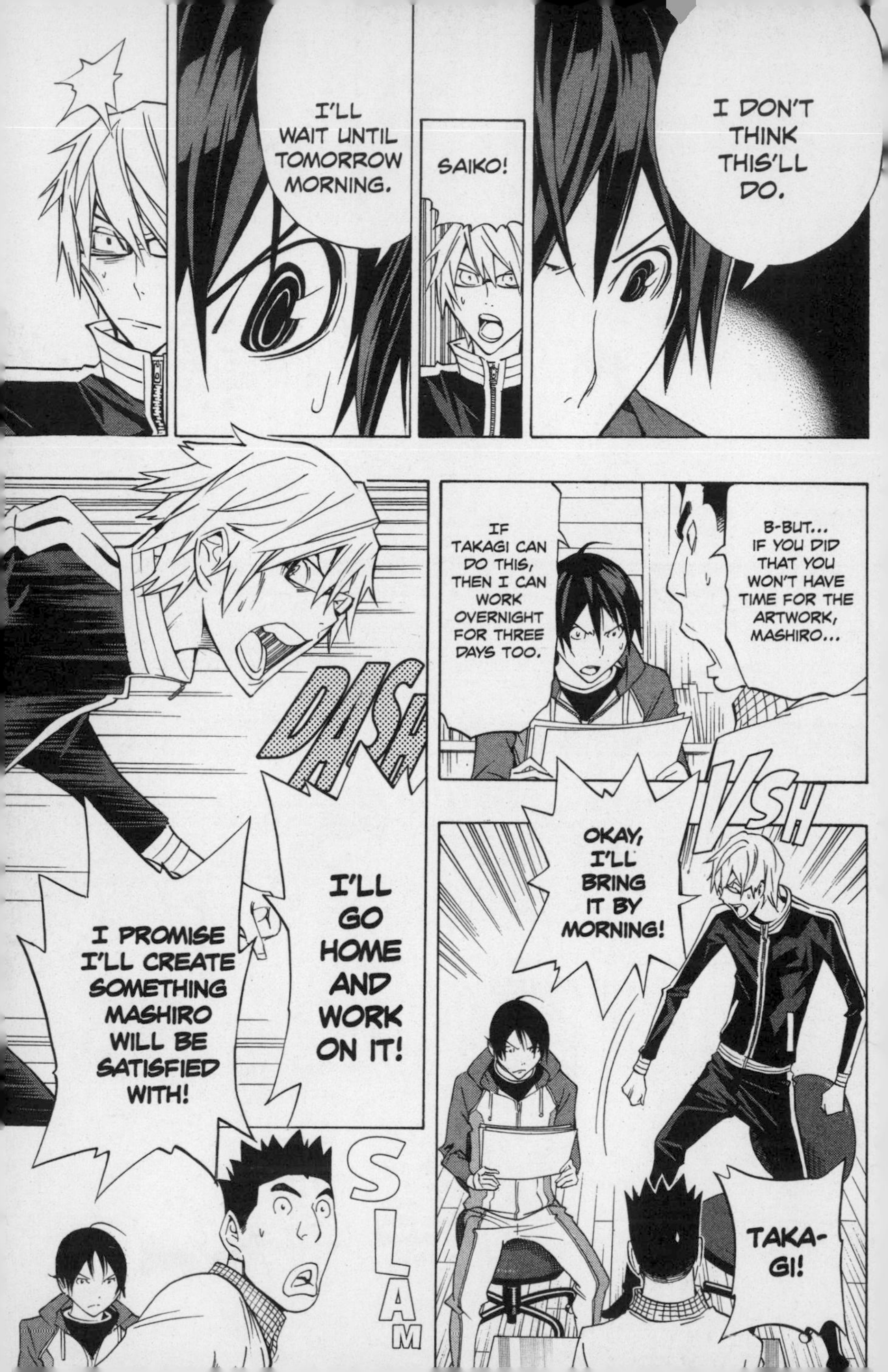
I DON'T THINK THIS'LL DO.
SAIKO!
I'LL WAIT UNTIL TOMORROW MORNING.
B-BUT... IF YOU DID THAT YOU WON'T HAVE TIME FOR THE ARTWORK, MASHIRO...
IF TAKAGI CAN DO THIS, THEN I CAN WORK OVERNIGHT FOR THREE DAYS TOO.
VSH
OKAY, I'LL BRING IT BY MORNING!
TAKA-GI!
DASH
I'LL GO HOME AND WORK ON IT!
I PROMISE I'LL CREATE SOMETHING MASHIRO WILL BE SATISFIED WITH!
SLAM

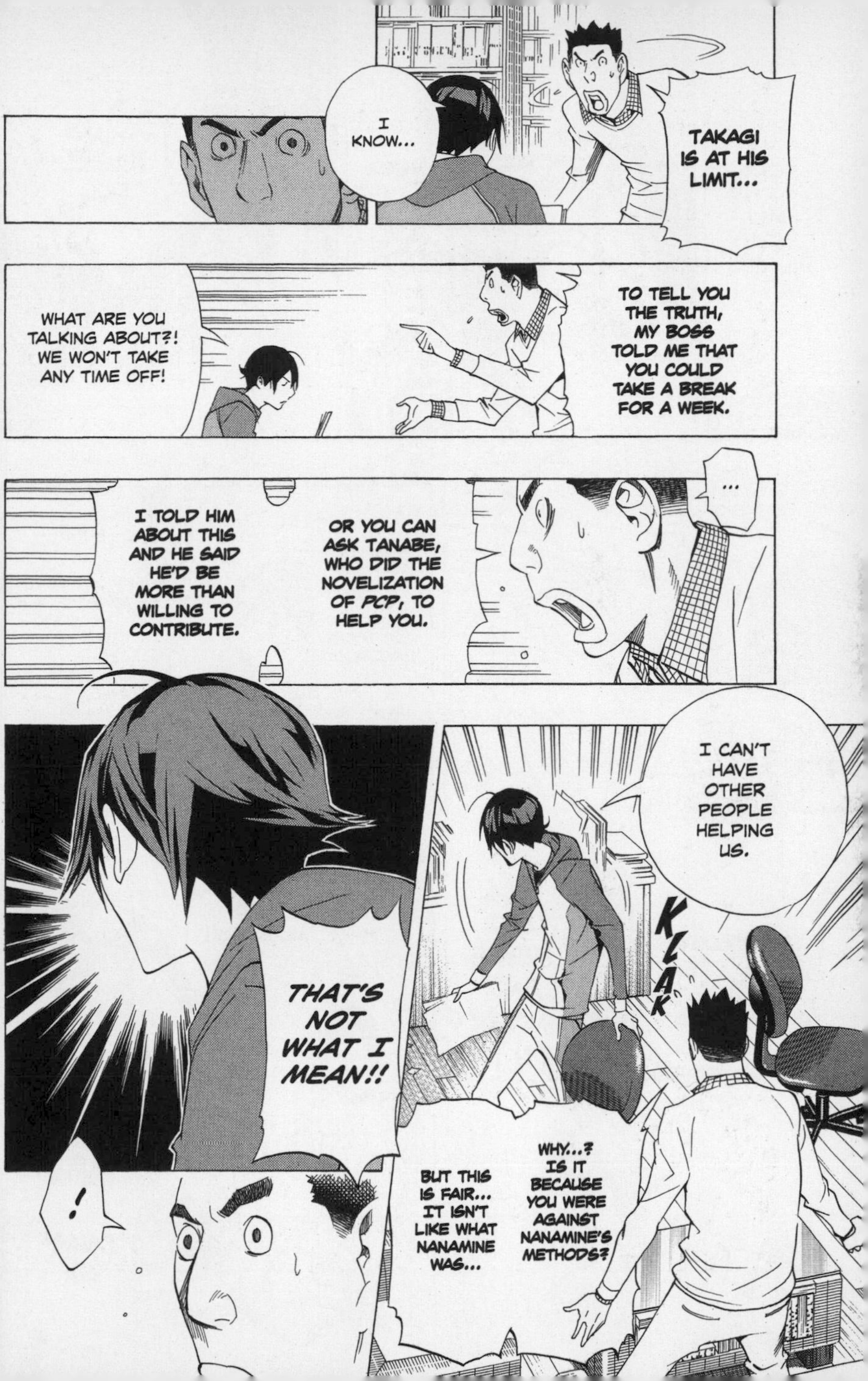

TAKAGI IS AT HIS LIMIT...
I KNOW...
TO TELL YOU THE TRUTH, MY BOSS TOLD ME THAT YOU COULD TAKE A BREAK FOR A WEEK.
WHAT ARE YOU TALKING ABOUT?! WE WON'T TAKE ANY TIME OFF!
...
OR YOU CAN ASK TANABE, WHO DID THE NOVELIZATION OF *PCP*, TO HELP YOU.
I TOLD HIM ABOUT THIS AND HE SAID HE'D BE MORE THAN WILLING TO CONTRIBUTE.
I CAN'T HAVE OTHER PEOPLE HELPING US.
KLAK
THAT'S NOT WHAT I MEAN!!
WHY...? IS IT BECAUSE YOU WERE AGAINST NANAMINE'S METHODS?
BUT THIS IS FAIR... IT ISN'T LIKE WHAT NANAMINE WAS...
!

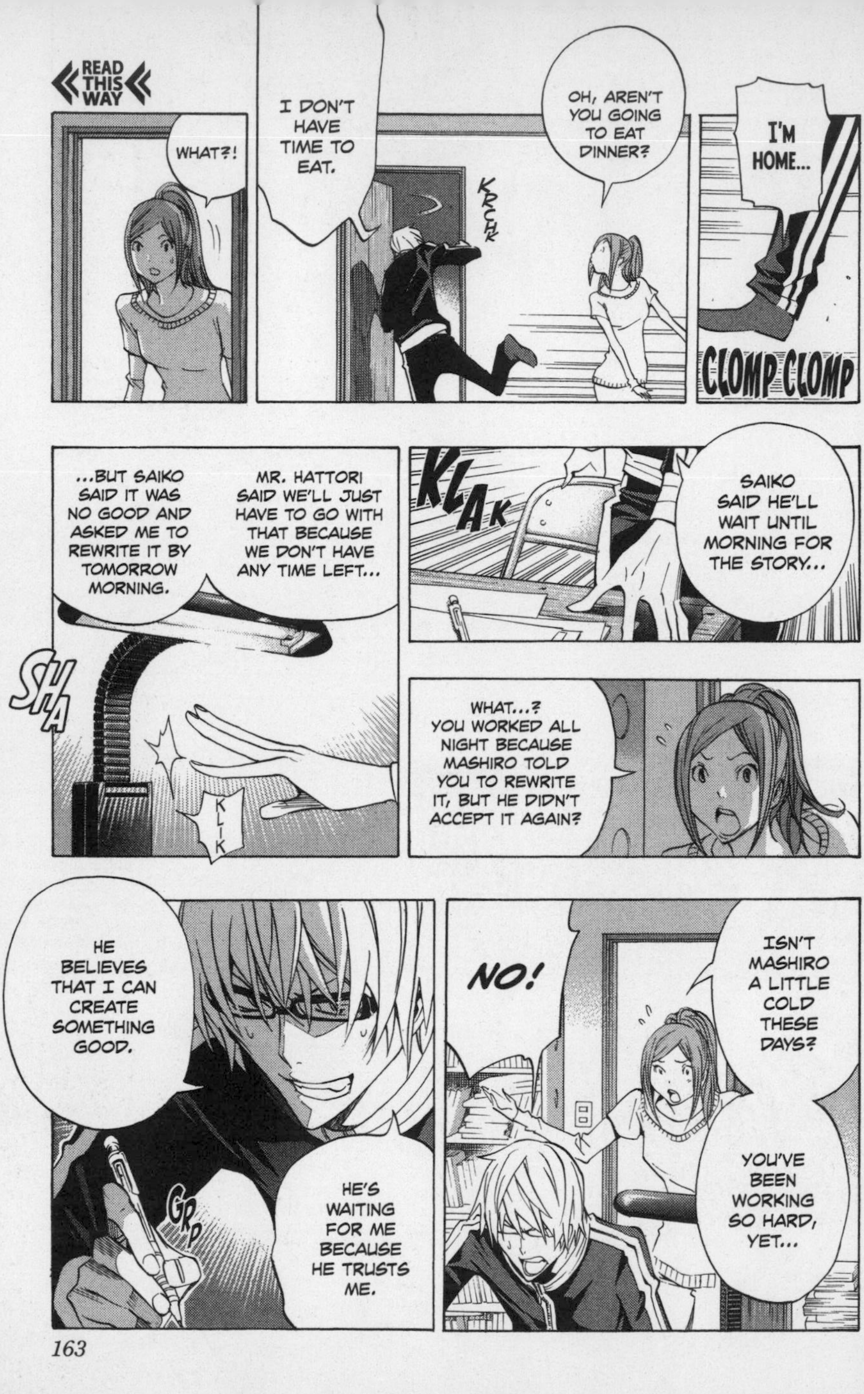
READ THIS WAY
I'M HOME...
CLOMP CLOMP
OH, AREN'T YOU GOING TO EAT DINNER?
KRCHK
I DON'T HAVE TIME TO EAT.
WHAT?!
SAIKO SAID HE'LL WAIT UNTIL MORNING FOR THE STORY...
KLAK
WHAT...? YOU WORKED ALL NIGHT BECAUSE MASHIRO TOLD YOU TO REWRITE IT, BUT HE DIDN'T ACCEPT IT AGAIN?
MR. HATTORI SAID WE'LL JUST HAVE TO GO WITH THAT BECAUSE WE DON'T HAVE ANY TIME LEFT...
...BUT SAIKO SAID IT WAS NO GOOD AND ASKED ME TO REWRITE IT BY TOMORROW MORNING.
SHA
KLIK
ISN'T MASHIRO A LITTLE COLD THESE DAYS?
YOU'VE BEEN WORKING SO HARD, YET...
NO!
HE BELIEVES THAT I CAN CREATE SOMETHING GOOD.
HE'S WAITING FOR ME BECAUSE HE TRUSTS ME.
GRP

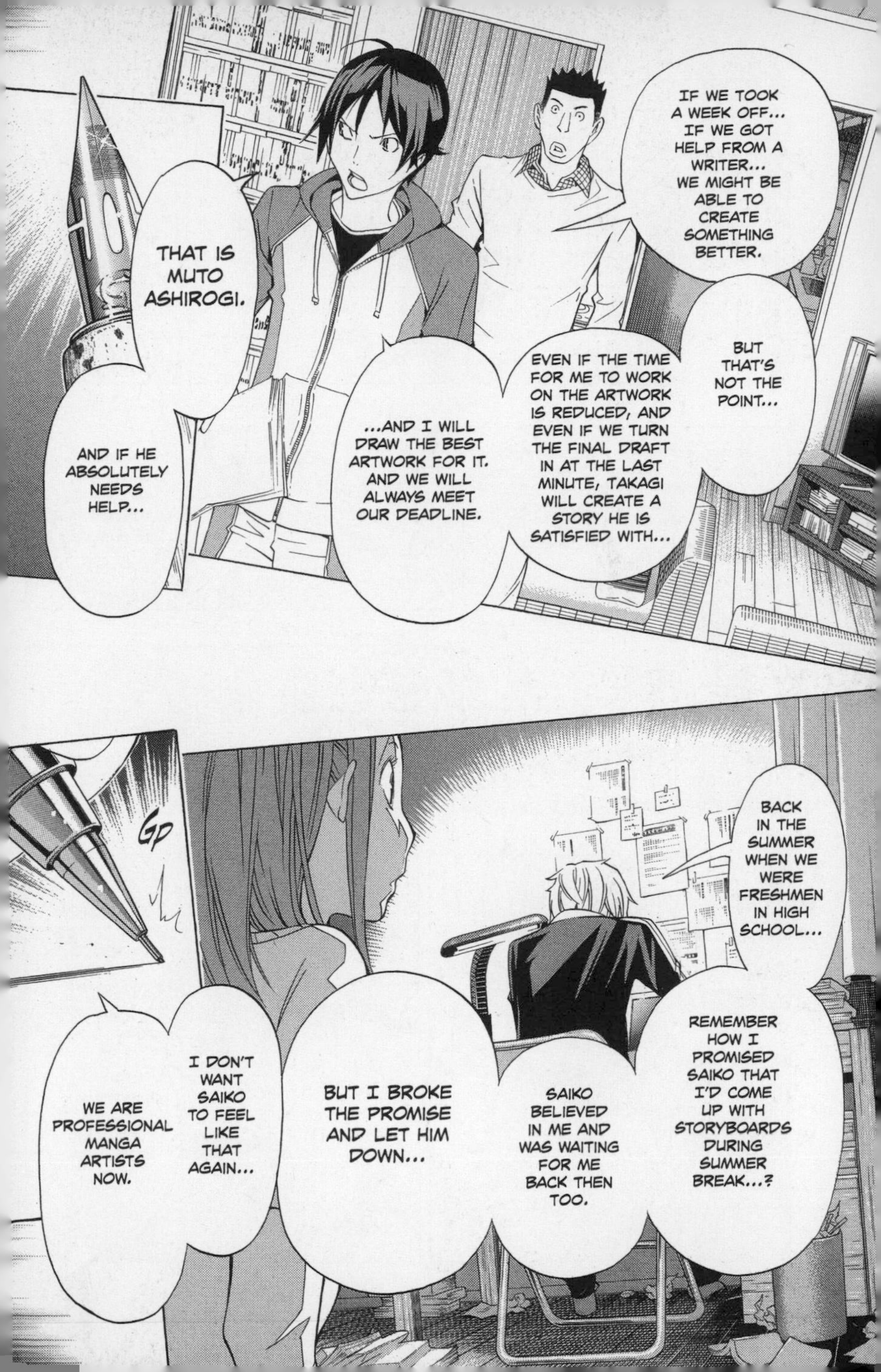
IF WE TOOK A WEEK OFF... IF WE GOT HELP FROM A WRITER... WE MIGHT BE ABLE TO CREATE SOMETHING BETTER.
BUT THAT'S NOT THE POINT...
EVEN IF THE TIME FOR ME TO WORK ON THE ARTWORK IS REDUCED, AND EVEN IF WE TURN THE FINAL DRAFT IN AT THE LAST MINUTE, TAKAGI WILL CREATE A STORY HE IS SATISFIED WITH...
...AND I WILL DRAW THE BEST ARTWORK FOR IT. AND WE WILL ALWAYS MEET OUR DEADLINE.
THAT IS MUTO ASHIROGI.
AND IF HE ABSOLUTELY NEEDS HELP...
BACK IN THE SUMMER WHEN WE WERE FRESHMEN IN HIGH SCHOOL...
Gp
REMEMBER HOW I PROMISED SAIKO THAT I'D COME UP WITH STORYBOARDS DURING SUMMER BREAK...?
SAIKO BELIEVED IN ME AND WAS WAITING FOR ME BACK THEN TOO.
BUT I BROKE THE PROMISE AND LET HIM DOWN...
I DON'T WANT SAIKO TO FEEL LIKE THAT AGAIN...
WE ARE PROFESSIONAL MANGA ARTISTS NOW.

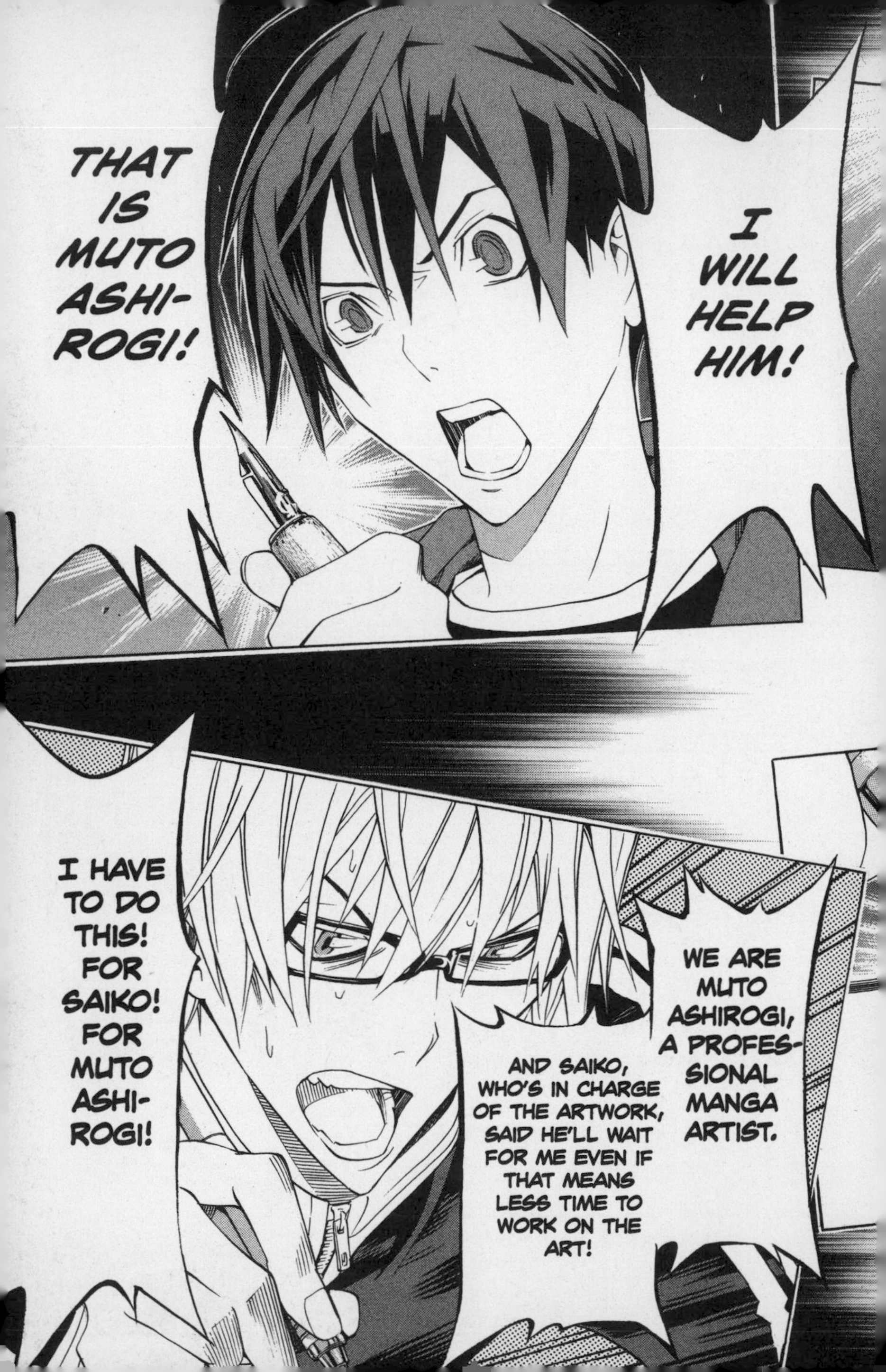
I WILL HELP HIM!
THAT IS MUTO ASHI-ROGI!
WE ARE MUTO ASHIROGI, A PROFES-SIONAL MANGA ARTIST.
AND SAIKO, WHO'S IN CHARGE OF THE ARTWORK, SAID HE'LL WAIT FOR ME EVEN IF THAT MEANS LESS TIME TO WORK ON THE ART!
I HAVE TO DO THIS! FOR SAIKO! FOR MUTO ASHI-ROGI!

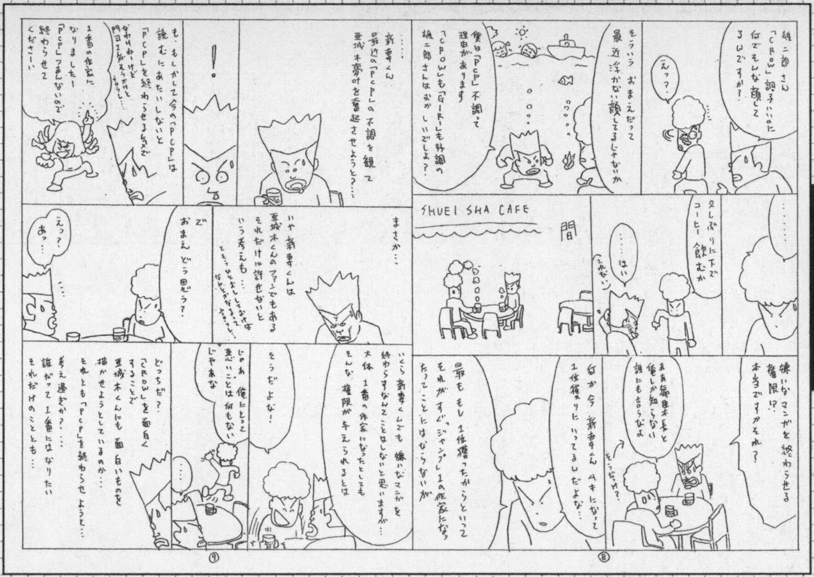
雄二郎さん「CROW」調子いいのに何でそんな顔してるんですか!
えっ?
そういうおまえだって最近浮かない顔してるじゃないか
ウウ…
僕は「PCP」不調って理由があります
「CROW」も「GIRL」も好調の雄二郎さんはおかしいでしょ?
……
久しぶりに下でコーヒー飲むか
……はい
SHUEI SHA CAFE
間
嫌いなマンガを終わらせる権限!? 本当ですかそれ?
ああ 編集長と俺しか知らない 誰にも言うなよ
何か今 新妻くん ムキになって1位獲りにいってるんだよな…
最ももし1位獲ったからといってそれがすぐ「ジャンプ」1の作家になったってことにはならないが
⑧
……新妻くん最近の「PCP」の不調を観て亜城木夢叶を奮起させようと?……
!
も・もしかして今の「PCP」は読むにあたいしないと「PCP」を終わらせる気で
1番の作家になりました「PCP」つまんないので終わらせてください
まさか…
いや新妻くんは亜城木くんのファンでもある それだけは許せないという考えも…
で おまえどう思う?
えっ? あっ…
いくら新妻くんでも嫌いなマンガを終わらせるなんてことはしないと思いますが… 大体1番の作家になったとしてもそんな権限が与えられるとは
そうだよな!
……
どっちだ? 「CROW」を面白くすることで亜城木くんにも面白いものを描かせようとしているのか… それとも「PCP」を終わらせようと…
考え過ぎか?… 誰だって1番にはなりたい それだけのことかも…
⑨

OHBA'S STORYBOARD

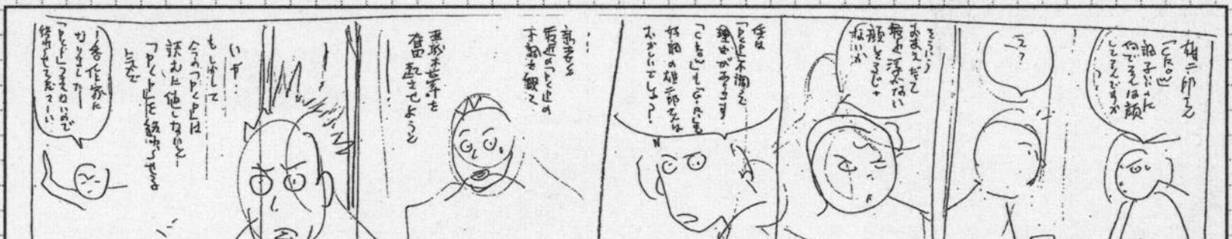

OBATA'S STORYBOARD

COMPLETE!

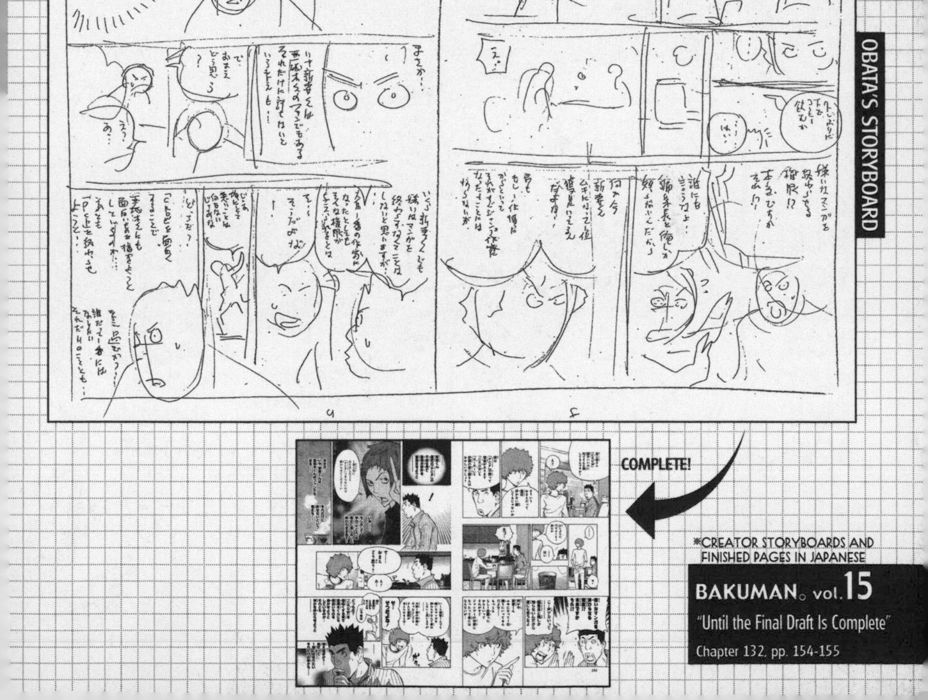

*CREATOR STORYBOARDS AND FINISHED PAGES IN JAPANESE

BAKUMAN。 vol.15

"Until the Final Draft Is Complete"

Chapter 132, pp. 154-155

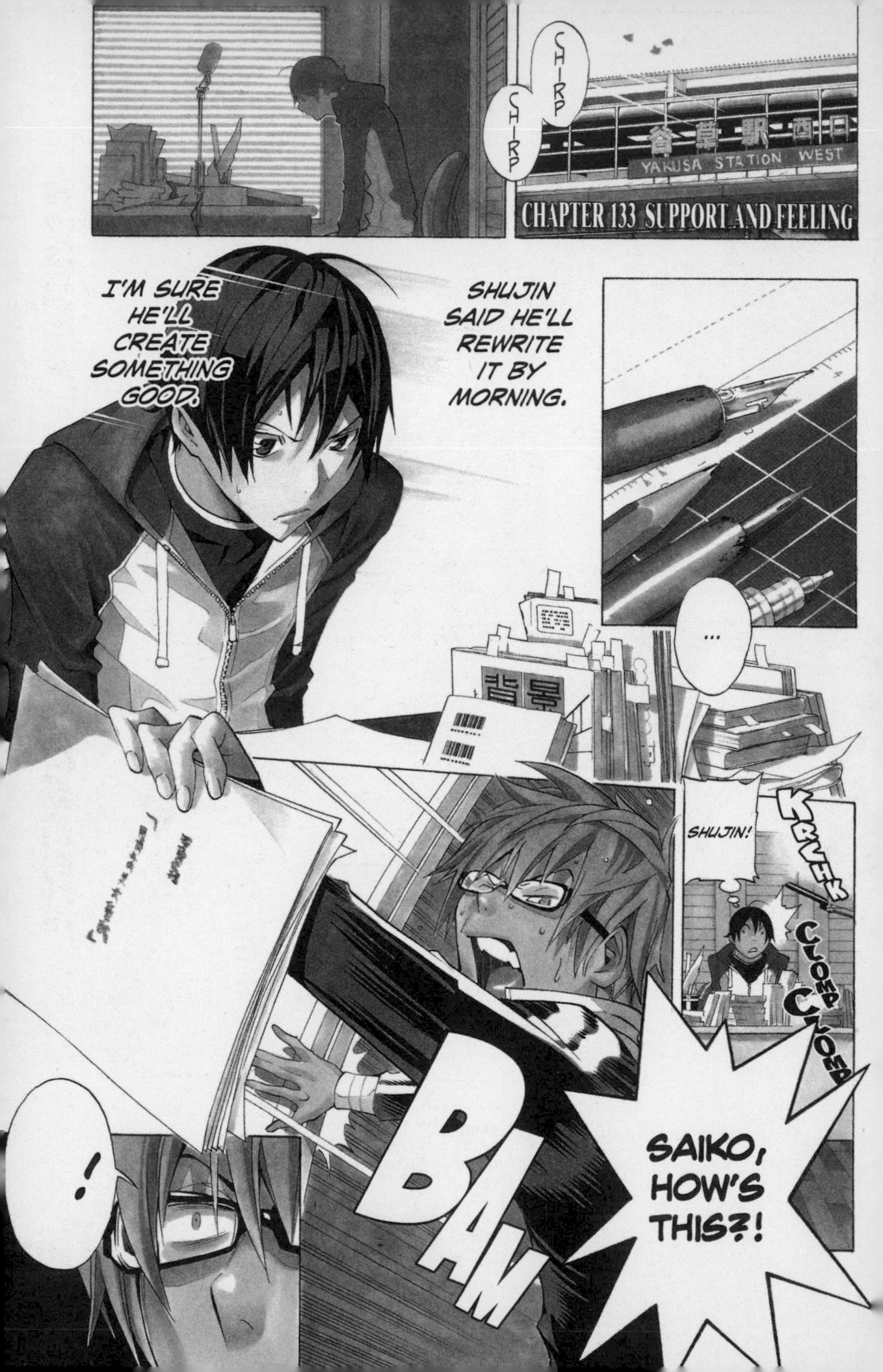
CHAPTER 133 SUPPORT AND FEELING
谷草駅西口
YAKUSA STATION WEST
CHIRP
CHIRP
SHUJIN SAID HE'LL REWRITE IT BY MORNING.
I'M SURE HE'LL CREATE SOMETHING GOOD.
...
SHUJIN!
KRUHK
CLOMP
CLOMP
SAIKO, HOW'S THIS?!
BAM
!

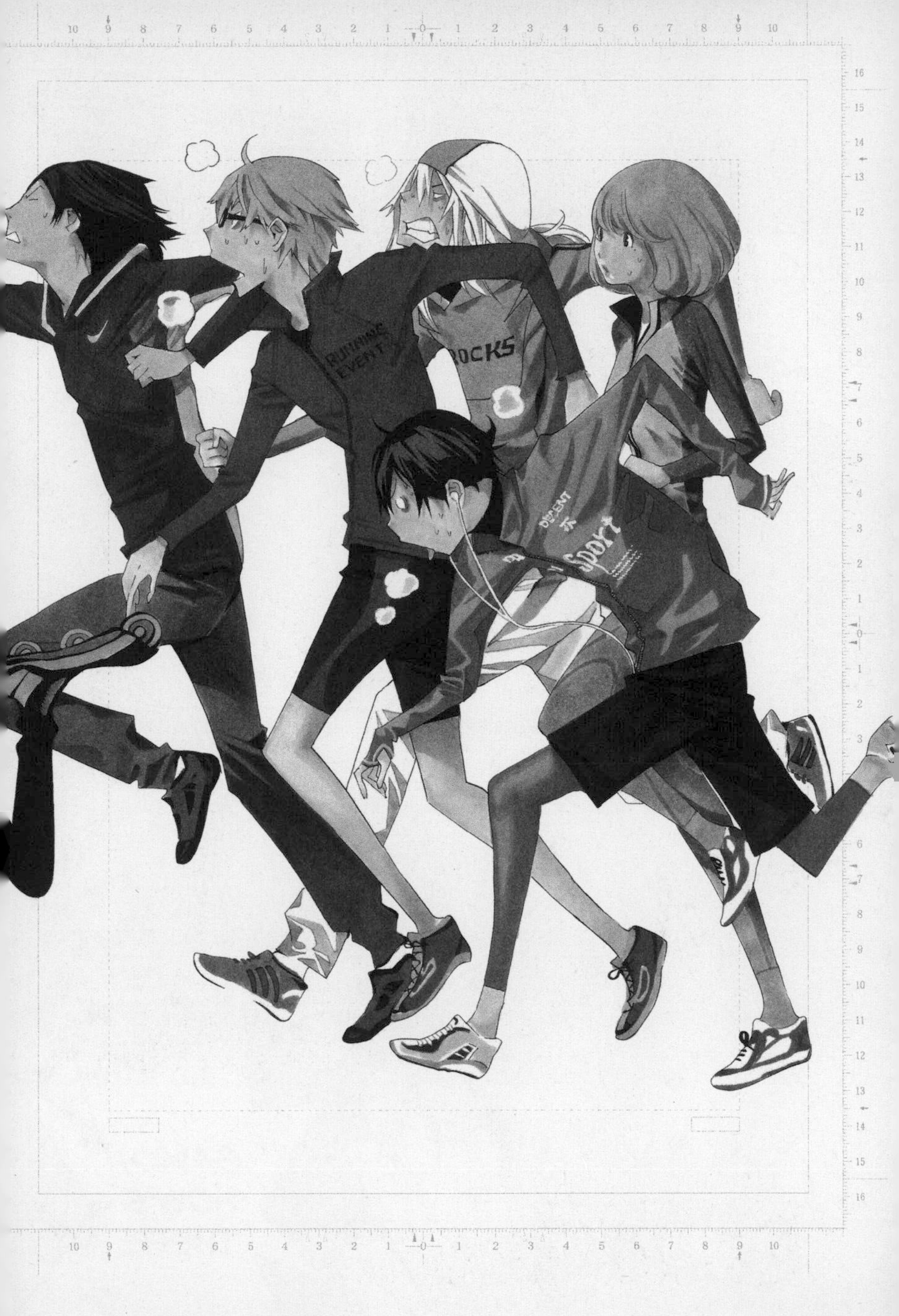
RUNNING EVENT
sport

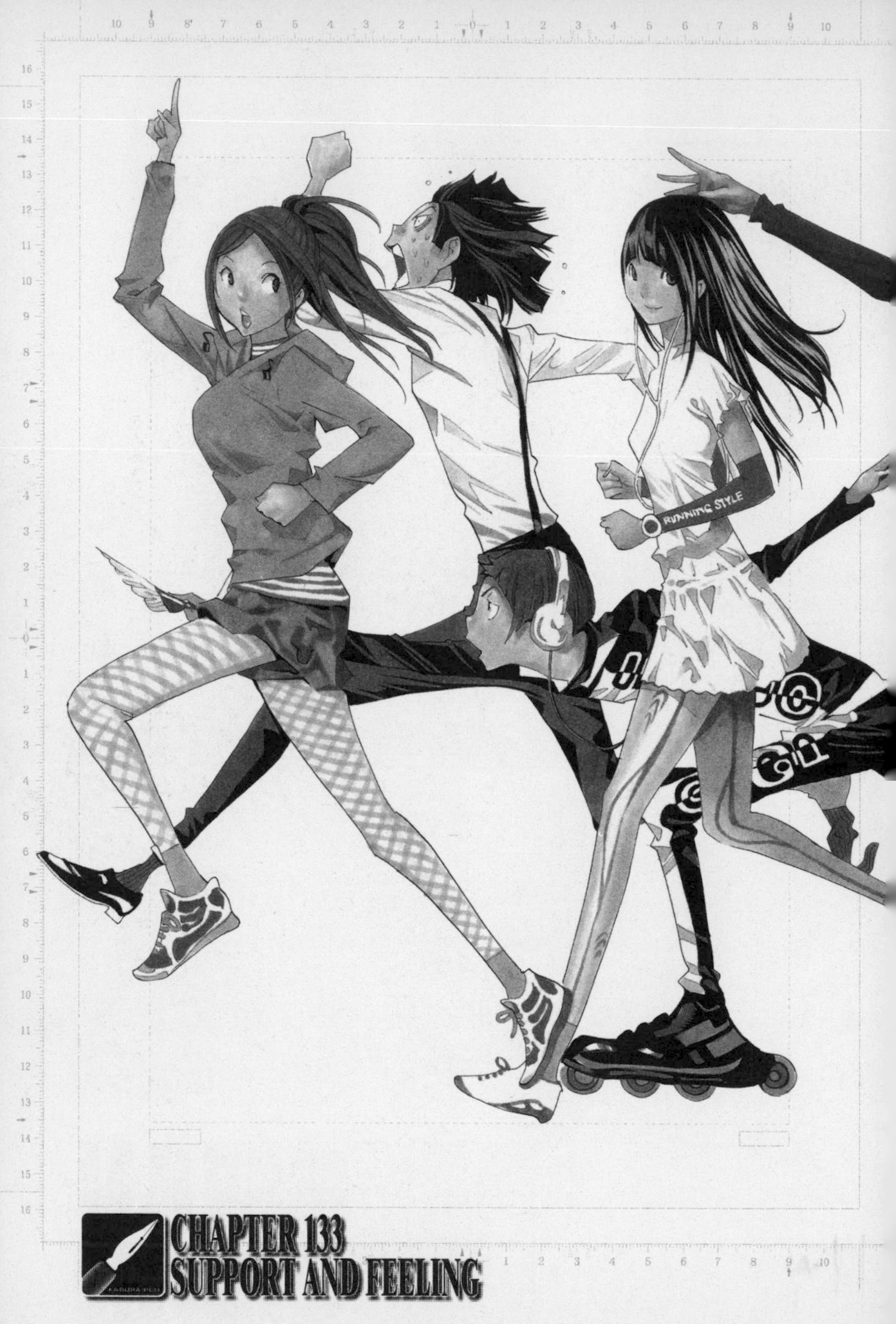
RUNNING STYLE

CHAPTER 133
SUPPORT AND FEELING

BAKUMAN。

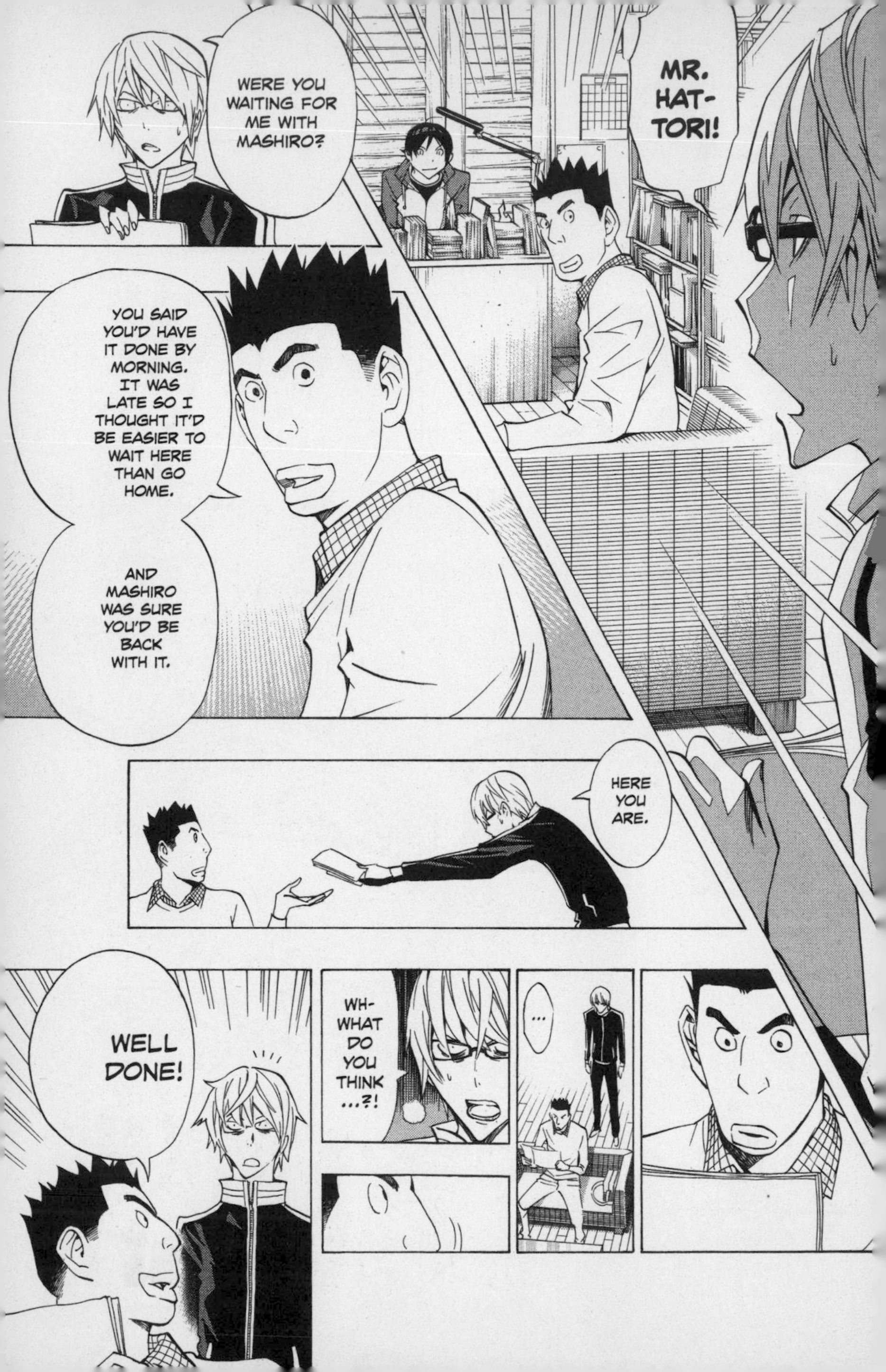
MR. HAT-TORI!
WERE YOU WAITING FOR ME WITH MASHIRO?
YOU SAID YOU'D HAVE IT DONE BY MORNING. IT WAS LATE SO I THOUGHT IT'D BE EASIER TO WAIT HERE THAN GO HOME.
AND MASHIRO WAS SURE YOU'D BE BACK WITH IT.
HERE YOU ARE.
...
WH-WHAT DO YOU THINK ...?!
WELL DONE!

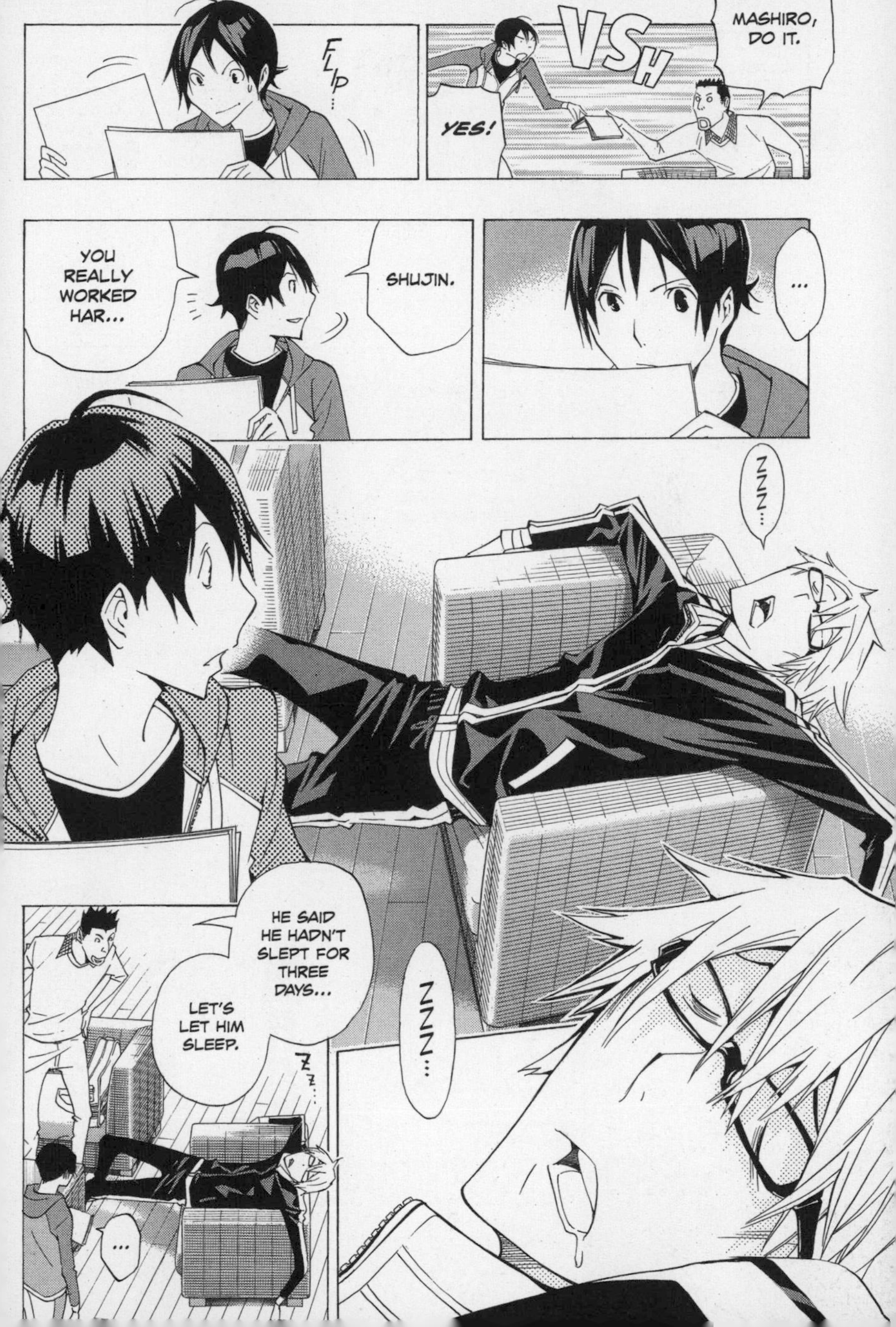
MASHIRO, DO IT.
VSH
YES!
FLIP...
...
SHUJIN.
YOU REALLY WORKED HAR...
ZZZ...
ZZZ...
HE SAID HE HADN'T SLEPT FOR THREE DAYS...
LET'S LET HIM SLEEP.
Z z z...
...

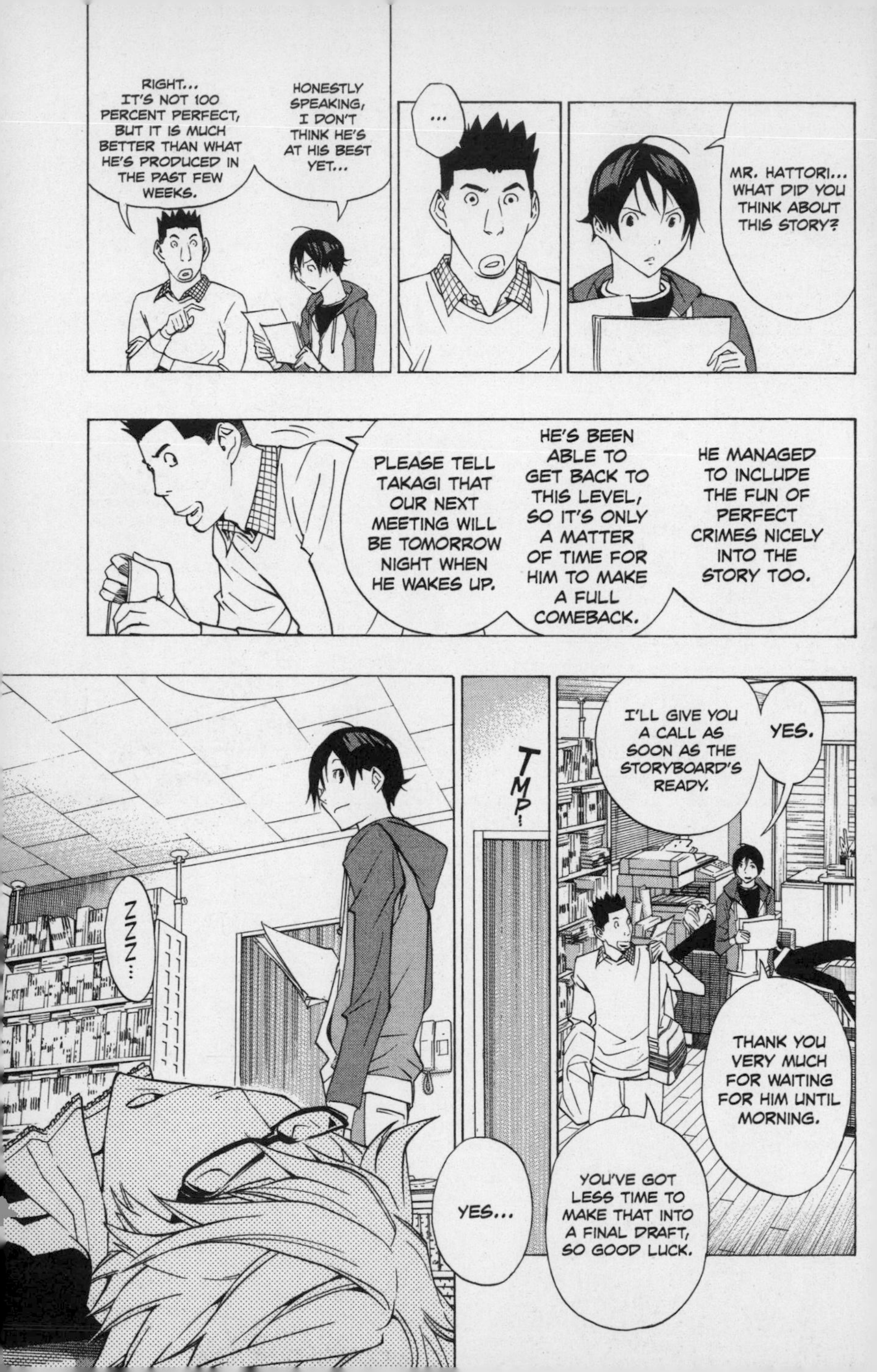
MR. HATTORI... WHAT DID YOU THINK ABOUT THIS STORY?
...
HONESTLY SPEAKING, I DON'T THINK HE'S AT HIS BEST YET...
RIGHT... IT'S NOT 100 PERCENT PERFECT, BUT IT IS MUCH BETTER THAN WHAT HE'S PRODUCED IN THE PAST FEW WEEKS.
HE MANAGED TO INCLUDE THE FUN OF PERFECT CRIMES NICELY INTO THE STORY TOO.
HE'S BEEN ABLE TO GET BACK TO THIS LEVEL, SO IT'S ONLY A MATTER OF TIME FOR HIM TO MAKE A FULL COMEBACK.
PLEASE TELL TAKAGI THAT OUR NEXT MEETING WILL BE TOMORROW NIGHT WHEN HE WAKES UP.
YES.
I'LL GIVE YOU A CALL AS SOON AS THE STORYBOARD'S READY.
THANK YOU VERY MUCH FOR WAITING FOR HIM UNTIL MORNING.
YOU'VE GOT LESS TIME TO MAKE THAT INTO A FINAL DRAFT, SO GOOD LUCK.
YES...
TMP...
ZZZ...

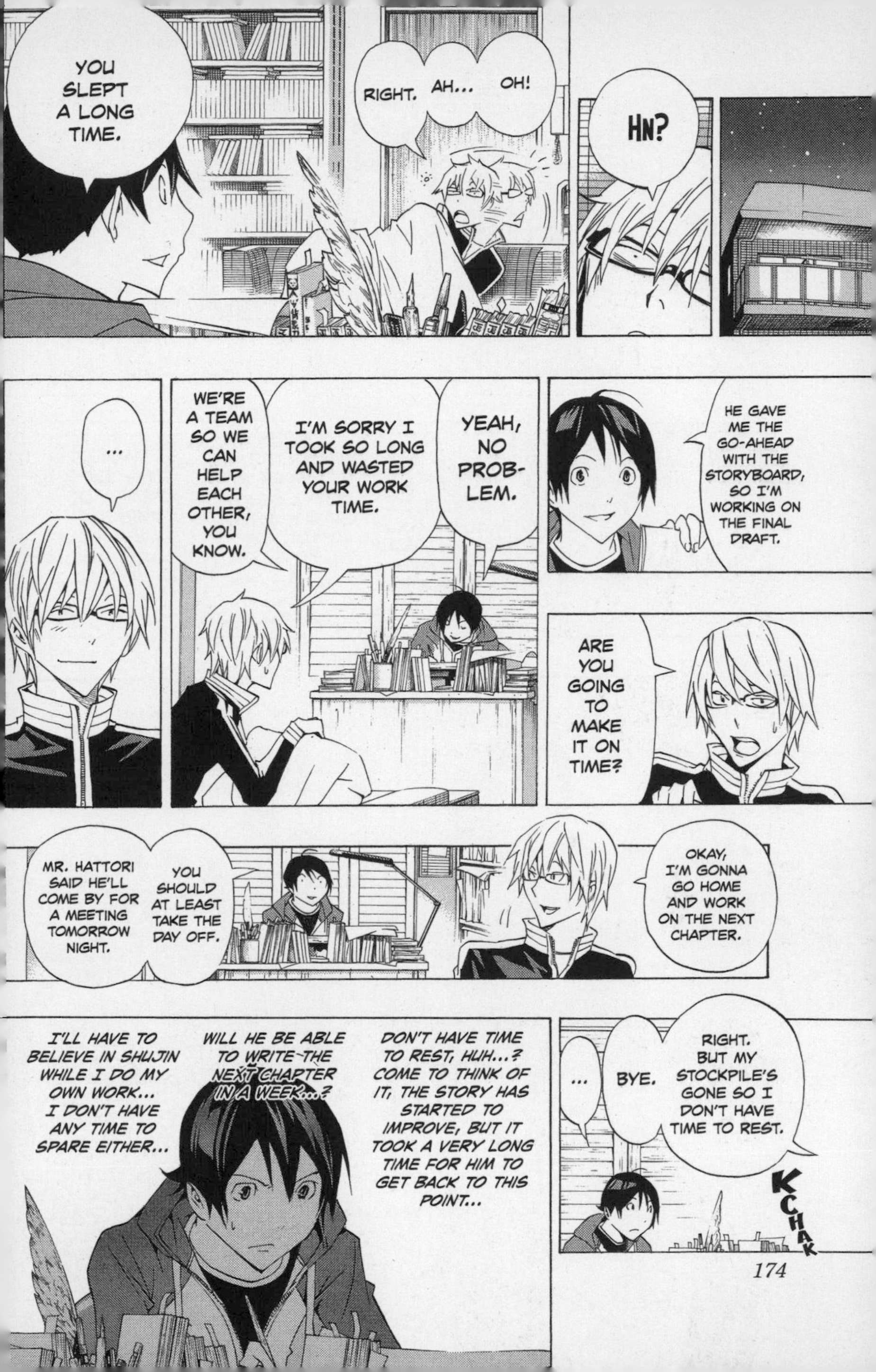
HN?
OH!
AH...
RIGHT.
YOU SLEPT A LONG TIME.
HE GAVE ME THE GO-AHEAD WITH THE STORYBOARD, SO I'M WORKING ON THE FINAL DRAFT.
ARE YOU GOING TO MAKE IT ON TIME?
YEAH, NO PROB-LEM.
I'M SORRY I TOOK SO LONG AND WASTED YOUR WORK TIME.
WE'RE A TEAM SO WE CAN HELP EACH OTHER, YOU KNOW.
...
OKAY, I'M GONNA GO HOME AND WORK ON THE NEXT CHAPTER.
YOU SHOULD AT LEAST TAKE THE DAY OFF.
MR. HATTORI SAID HE'LL COME BY FOR A MEETING TOMORROW NIGHT.
RIGHT. BUT MY STOCKPILE'S GONE SO I DON'T HAVE TIME TO REST.
BYE.
...
KCHAK
DON'T HAVE TIME TO REST, HUH...? COME TO THINK OF IT, THE STORY HAS STARTED TO IMPROVE, BUT IT TOOK A VERY LONG TIME FOR HIM TO GET BACK TO THIS POINT...
WILL HE BE ABLE TO WRITE THE NEXT CHAPTER IN A WEEK...?
I'LL HAVE TO BELIEVE IN SHUJIN WHILE I DO MY OWN WORK... I DON'T HAVE ANY TIME TO SPARE EITHER...

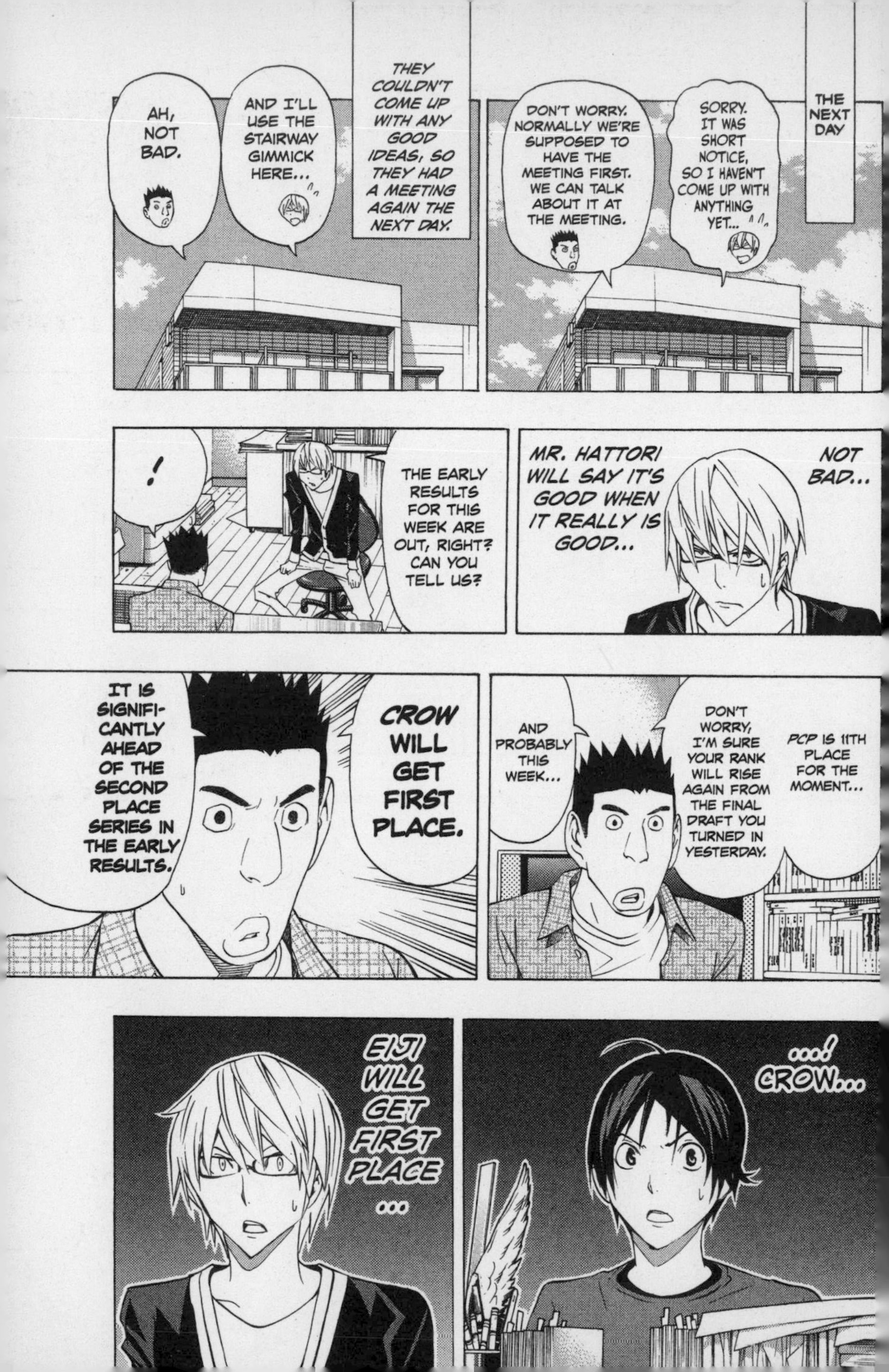
THE NEXT DAY
SORRY. IT WAS SHORT NOTICE, SO I HAVEN'T COME UP WITH ANYTHING YET...
DON'T WORRY. NORMALLY WE'RE SUPPOSED TO HAVE THE MEETING FIRST. WE CAN TALK ABOUT IT AT THE MEETING.
THEY COULDN'T COME UP WITH ANY GOOD IDEAS, SO THEY HAD A MEETING AGAIN THE NEXT DAY.
AND I'LL USE THE STAIRWAY GIMMICK HERE...
AH, NOT BAD.
NOT BAD...
MR. HATTORI WILL SAY IT'S GOOD WHEN IT REALLY IS GOOD...
THE EARLY RESULTS FOR THIS WEEK ARE OUT, RIGHT? CAN YOU TELL US?
!
PCP IS 11TH PLACE FOR THE MOMENT...
DON'T WORRY, I'M SURE YOUR RANK WILL RISE AGAIN FROM THE FINAL DRAFT YOU TURNED IN YESTERDAY.
AND PROBABLY THIS WEEK...
CROW WILL GET FIRST PLACE.
IT IS SIGNIFICANTLY AHEAD OF THE SECOND PLACE SERIES IN THE EARLY RESULTS.
...! CROW...
EIJI WILL GET FIRST PLACE...

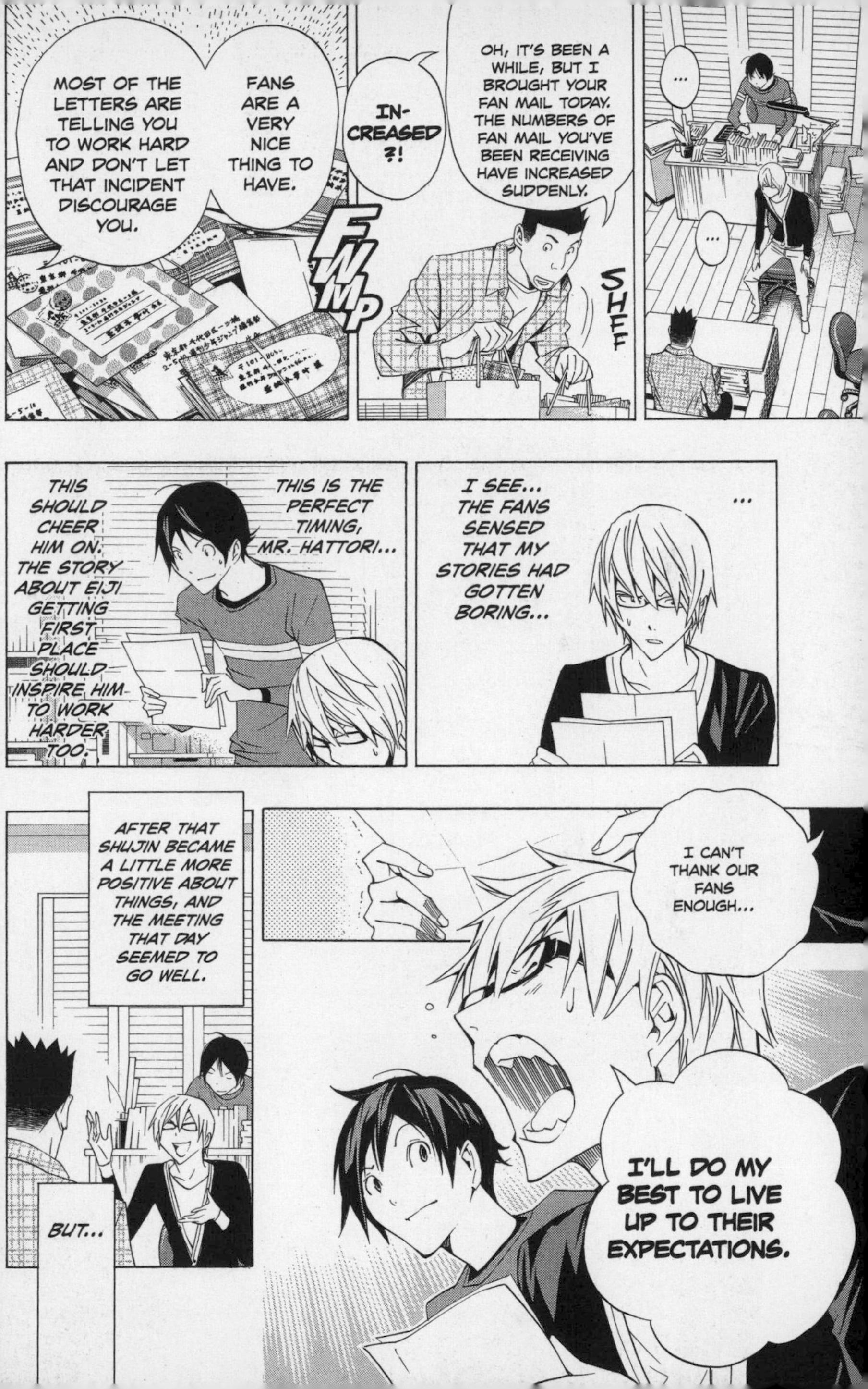
...
...
OH, IT'S BEEN A WHILE, BUT I BROUGHT YOUR FAN MAIL TODAY. THE NUMBERS OF FAN MAIL YOU'VE BEEN RECEIVING HAVE INCREASED SUDDENLY.
IN-CREASED ?!
SHEFF
FWMP
FANS ARE A VERY NICE THING TO HAVE.
MOST OF THE LETTERS ARE TELLING YOU TO WORK HARD AND DON'T LET THAT INCIDENT DISCOURAGE YOU.
...
I SEE... THE FANS SENSED THAT MY STORIES HAD GOTTEN BORING...
THIS IS THE PERFECT TIMING, MR. HATTORI...
THIS SHOULD CHEER HIM ON. THE STORY ABOUT EIJI GETTING FIRST PLACE SHOULD INSPIRE HIM TO WORK HARDER TOO.
I CAN'T THANK OUR FANS ENOUGH...
I'LL DO MY BEST TO LIVE UP TO THEIR EXPECTATIONS.
AFTER THAT SHUJIN BECAME A LITTLE MORE POSITIVE ABOUT THINGS, AND THE MEETING THAT DAY SEEMED TO GO WELL.
BUT...

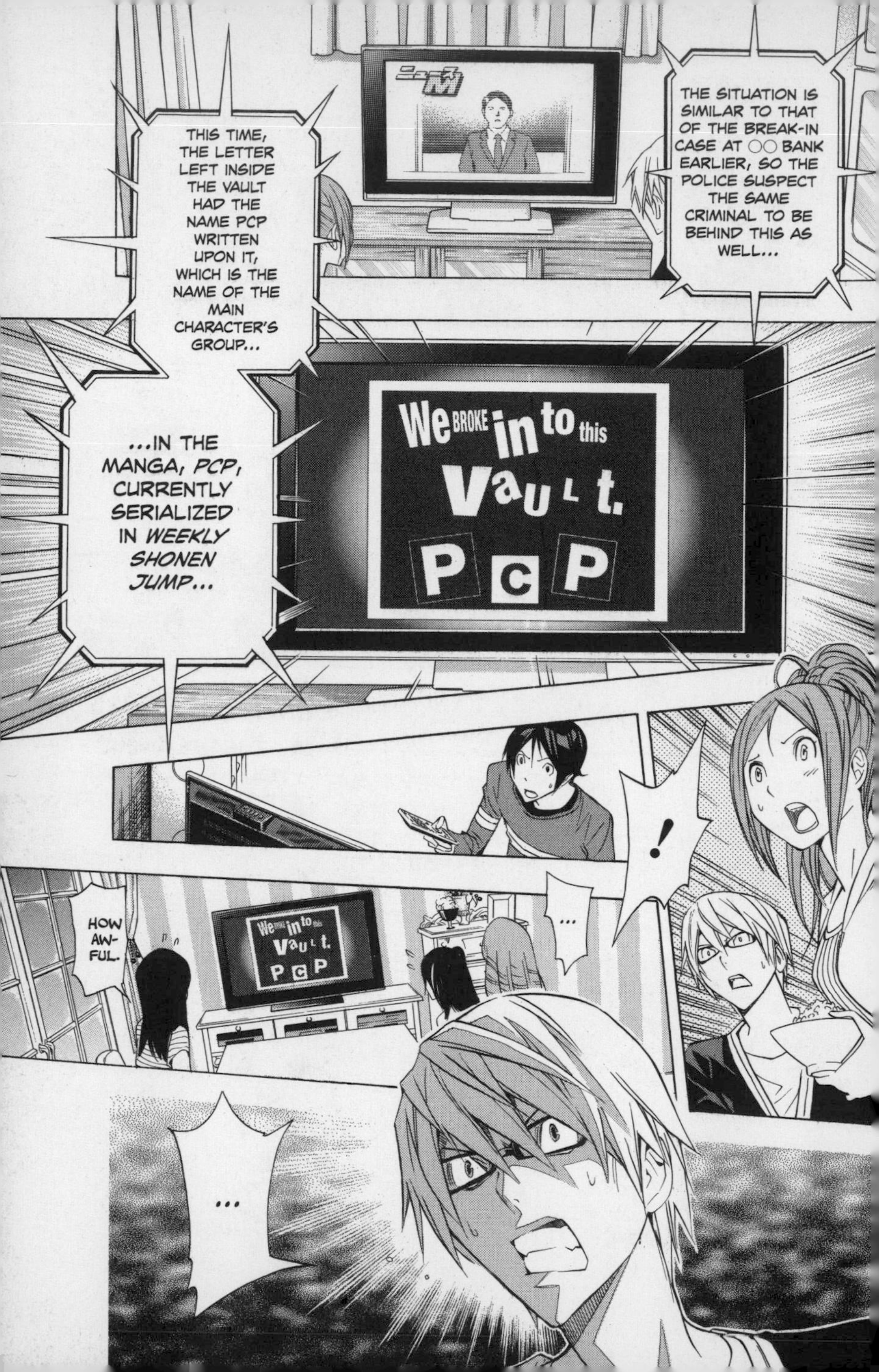
THE SITUATION IS SIMILAR TO THAT OF THE BREAK-IN CASE AT ○○ BANK EARLIER, SO THE POLICE SUSPECT THE SAME CRIMINAL TO BE BEHIND THIS AS WELL...
THIS TIME, THE LETTER LEFT INSIDE THE VAULT HAD THE NAME PCP WRITTEN UPON IT, WHICH IS THE NAME OF THE MAIN CHARACTER'S GROUP...
We BROKE in to this VauLt.
PCP
...IN THE MANGA, *PCP*, CURRENTLY SERIALIZED IN *WEEKLY SHONEN JUMP*...
!
...
HOW AW-FUL.
...

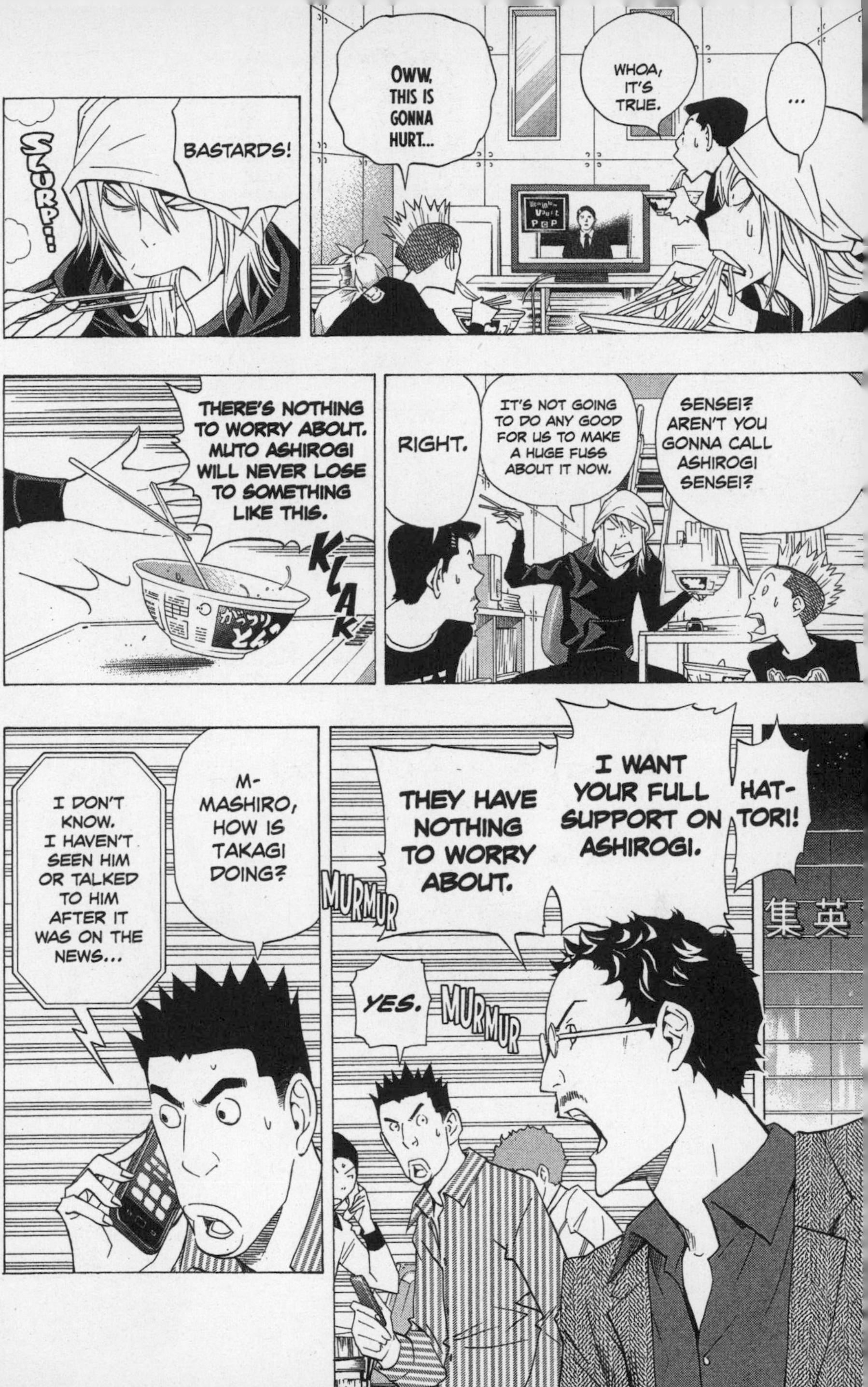
...
WHOA, IT'S TRUE.
OWW, THIS IS GONNA HURT...
BASTARDS!
SLURP...
SENSEI? AREN'T YOU GONNA CALL ASHIROGI SENSEI?
IT'S NOT GOING TO DO ANY GOOD FOR US TO MAKE A HUGE FUSS ABOUT IT NOW.
RIGHT.
THERE'S NOTHING TO WORRY ABOUT. MUTO ASHIROGI WILL NEVER LOSE TO SOMETHING LIKE THIS.
KLAK
HAT-TORI!
I WANT YOUR FULL SUPPORT ON ASHIROGI.
THEY HAVE NOTHING TO WORRY ABOUT.
MURMUR
YES.
MURMUR
集英
M-MASHIRO, HOW IS TAKAGI DOING?
I DON'T KNOW. I HAVEN'T SEEN HIM OR TALKED TO HIM AFTER IT WAS ON THE NEWS...

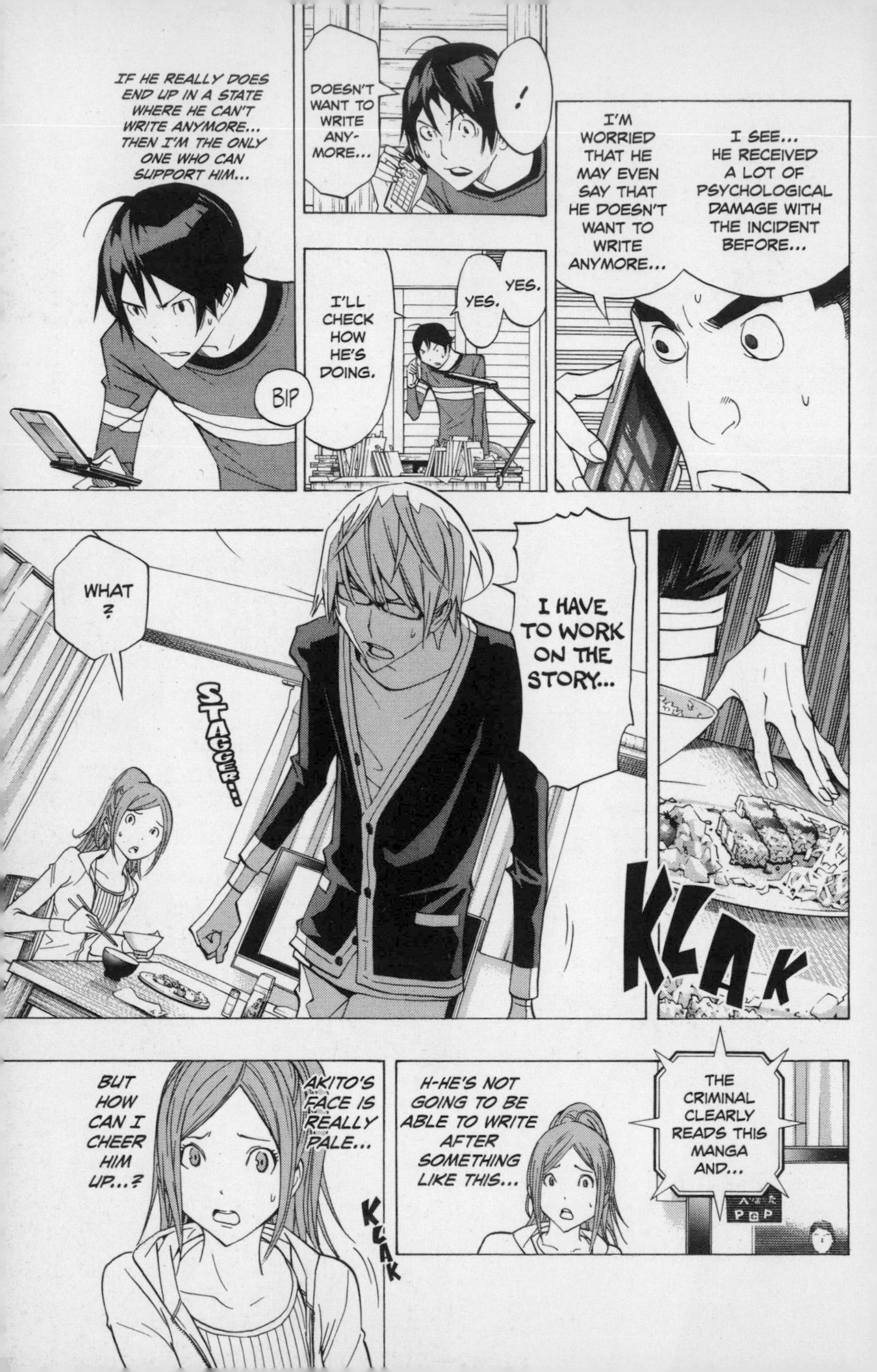
I SEE... HE RECEIVED A LOT OF PSYCHOLOGICAL DAMAGE WITH THE INCIDENT BEFORE...
I'M WORRIED THAT HE MAY EVEN SAY THAT HE DOESN'T WANT TO WRITE ANYMORE...
!
DOESN'T WANT TO WRITE ANY-MORE...
YES.
YES.
I'LL CHECK HOW HE'S DOING.
IF HE REALLY DOES END UP IN A STATE WHERE HE CAN'T WRITE ANYMORE... THEN I'M THE ONLY ONE WHO CAN SUPPORT HIM...
BIP
KLAK
I HAVE TO WORK ON THE STORY...
WHAT?
STAGGER...
THE CRIMINAL CLEARLY READS THIS MANGA AND...
H-HE'S NOT GOING TO BE ABLE TO WRITE AFTER SOMETHING LIKE THIS...
AKITO'S FACE IS REALLY PALE...
BUT HOW CAN I CHEER HIM UP...?
KLAK

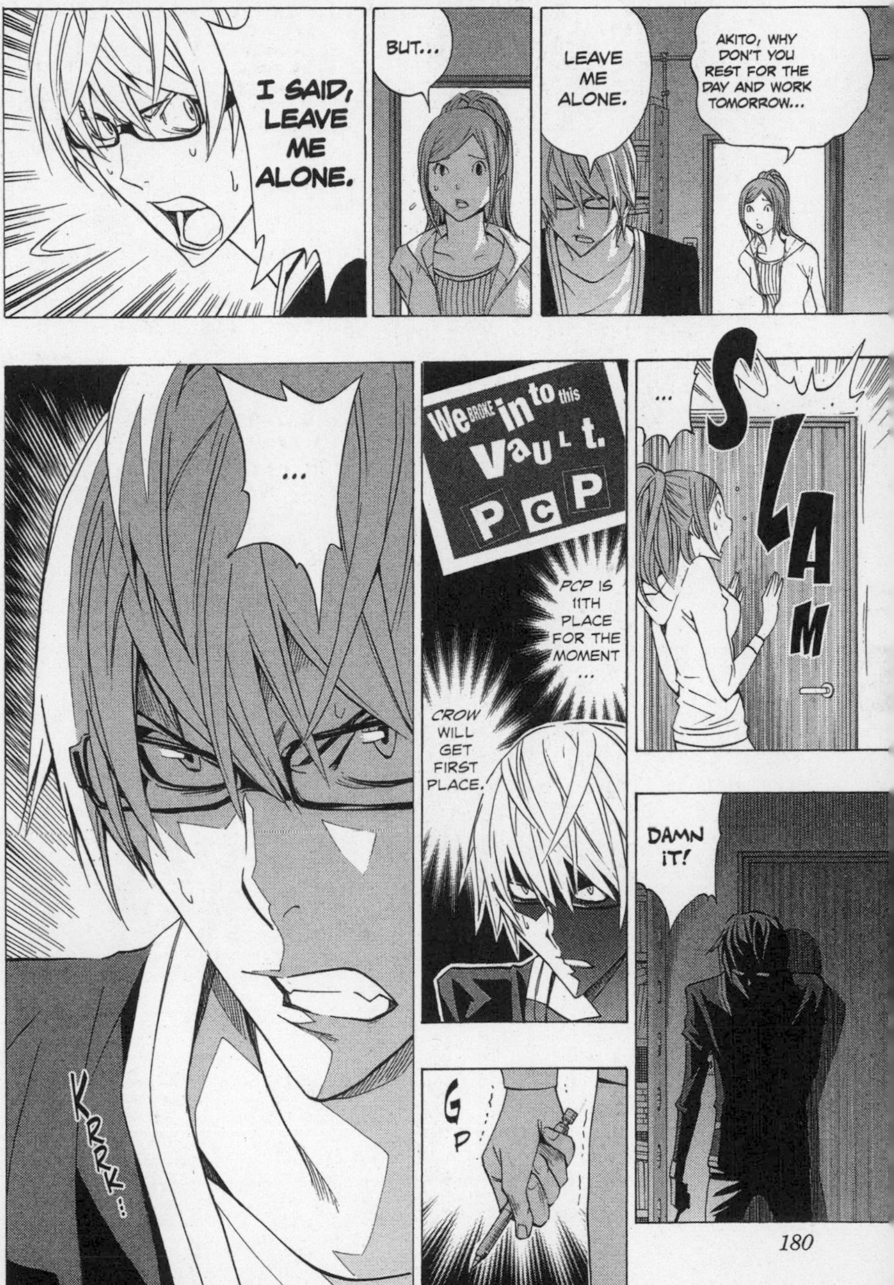
AKITO, WHY DON'T YOU REST FOR THE DAY AND WORK TOMORROW...
LEAVE ME ALONE.
BUT...
I SAID, LEAVE ME ALONE.
...
SLAM
DAMN IT!
We BROKE in to this VauLt.
PCP
PCP IS 11TH PLACE FOR THE MOMENT...
CROW WILL GET FIRST PLACE.
GP
...
KRRK..

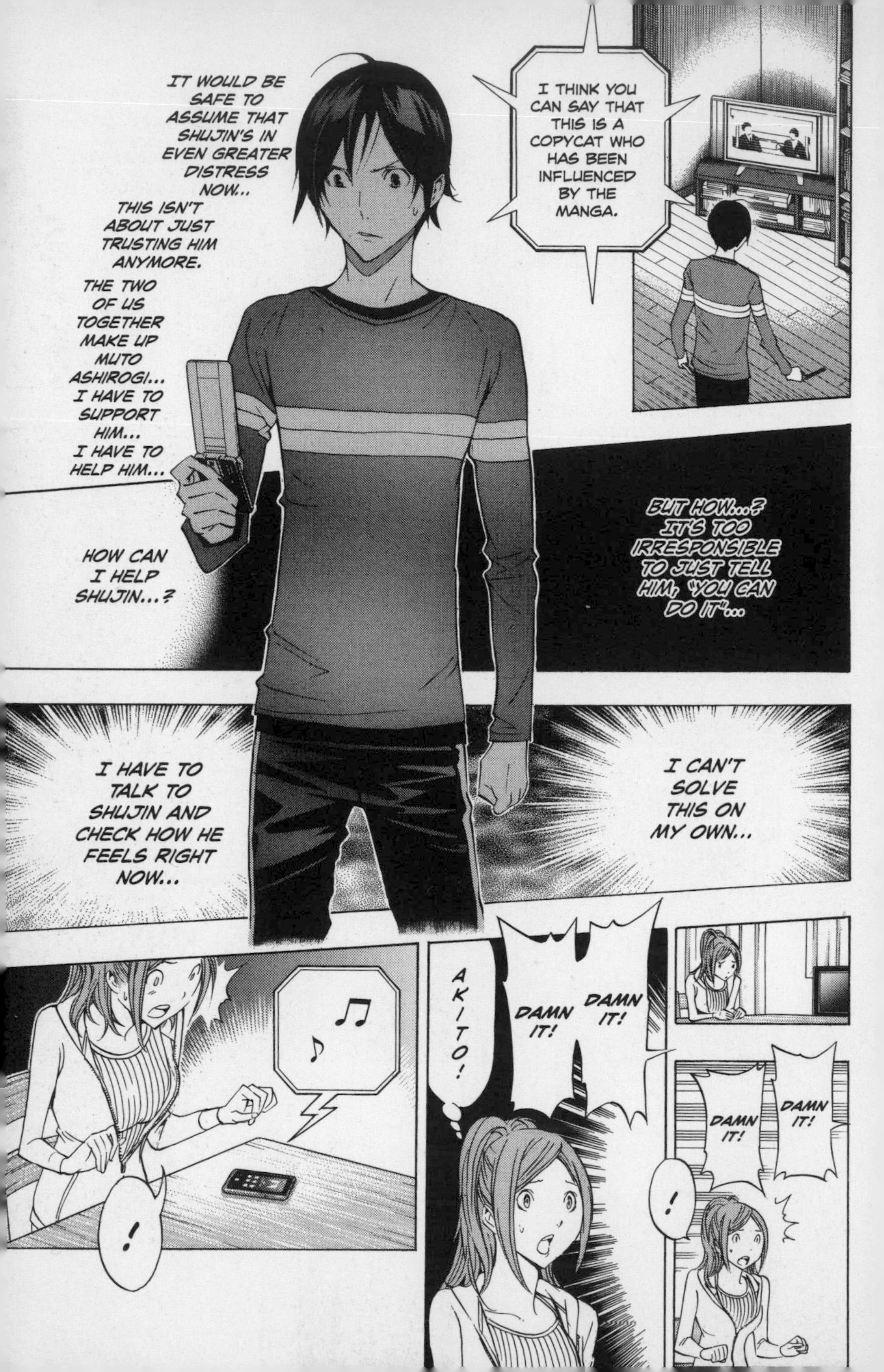
I THINK YOU CAN SAY THAT THIS IS A COPYCAT WHO HAS BEEN INFLUENCED BY THE MANGA.
IT WOULD BE SAFE TO ASSUME THAT SHUJIN'S IN EVEN GREATER DISTRESS NOW...
THIS ISN'T ABOUT JUST TRUSTING HIM ANYMORE.
THE TWO OF US TOGETHER MAKE UP MUTO ASHIROGI... I HAVE TO SUPPORT HIM... I HAVE TO HELP HIM...
BUT HOW...? IT'S TOO IRRESPONSIBLE TO JUST TELL HIM, "YOU CAN DO IT"...
HOW CAN I HELP SHUJIN...?
I CAN'T SOLVE THIS ON MY OWN...
I HAVE TO TALK TO SHUJIN AND CHECK HOW HE FEELS RIGHT NOW...
DAMN IT!
DAMN IT!
!
DAMN IT!
DAMN IT!
AKITO!
♫ ♪
!

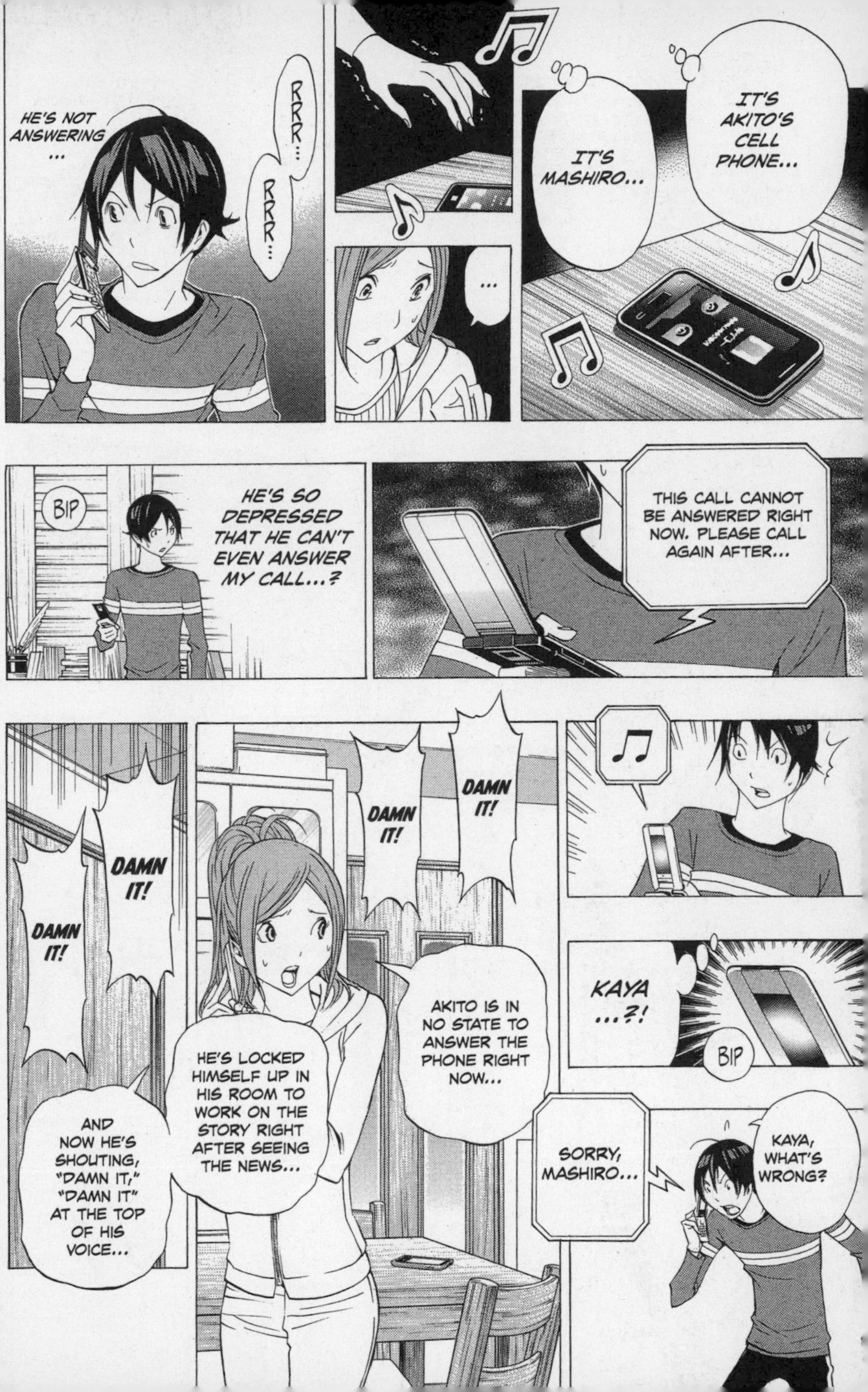
IT'S AKITO'S CELL PHONE...
IT'S MASHIRO...
...
RRR... RRR...
HE'S NOT ANSWERING ...
THIS CALL CANNOT BE ANSWERED RIGHT NOW. PLEASE CALL AGAIN AFTER...
HE'S SO DEPRESSED THAT HE CAN'T EVEN ANSWER MY CALL...?
BIP
KAYA ...?!
BIP
KAYA, WHAT'S WRONG?
SORRY, MASHIRO...
DAMN IT!
DAMN IT!
DAMN IT!
DAMN IT!
AKITO IS IN NO STATE TO ANSWER THE PHONE RIGHT NOW...
HE'S LOCKED HIMSELF UP IN HIS ROOM TO WORK ON THE STORY RIGHT AFTER SEEING THE NEWS...
AND NOW HE'S SHOUTING, "DAMN IT," "DAMN IT" AT THE TOP OF HIS VOICE...

READ THIS WAY

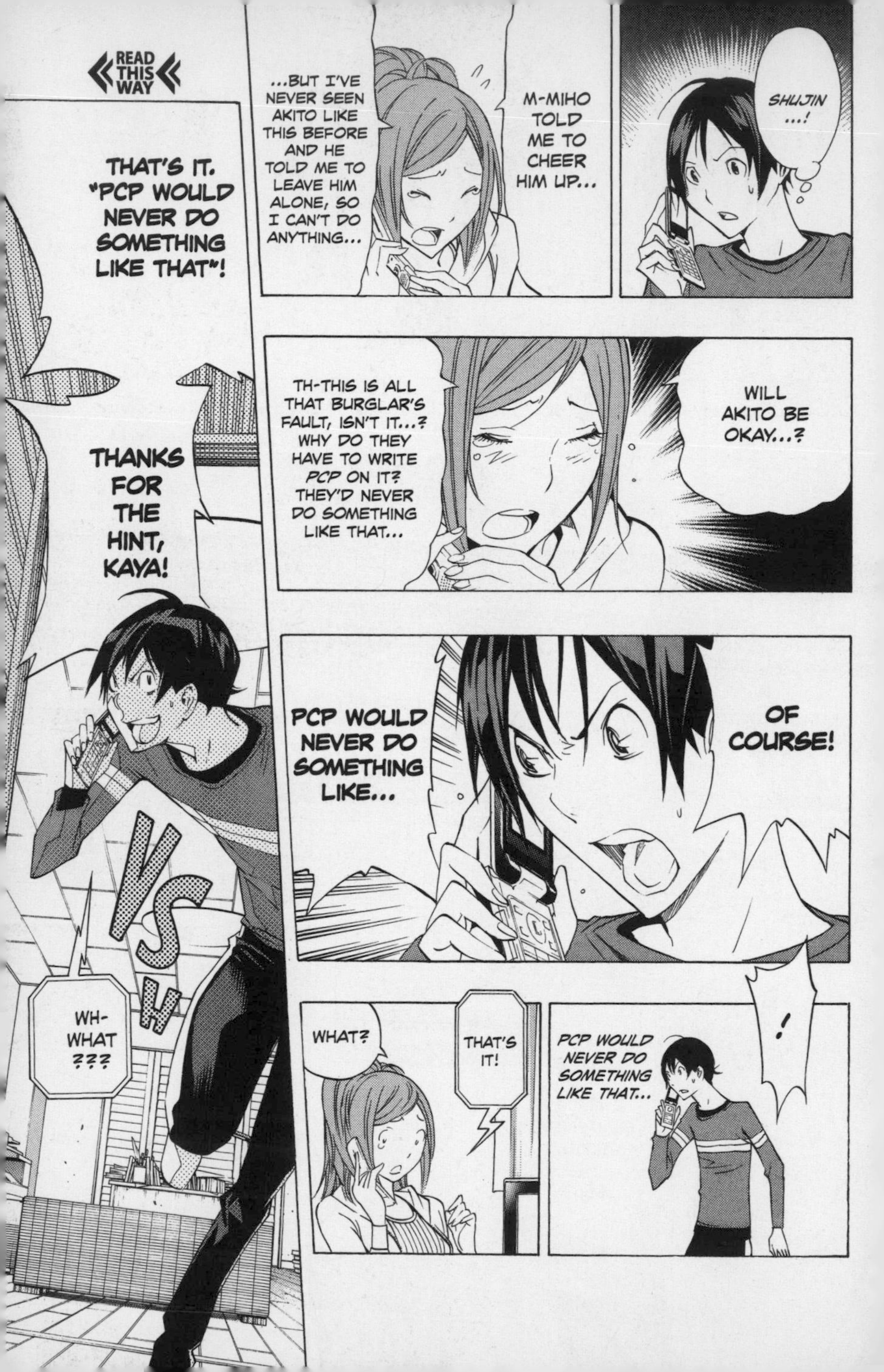
SHUJIN ...!
M-MIHO TOLD ME TO CHEER HIM UP...
...BUT I'VE NEVER SEEN AKITO LIKE THIS BEFORE AND HE TOLD ME TO LEAVE HIM ALONE, SO I CAN'T DO ANYTHING...
WILL AKITO BE OKAY...?
TH-THIS IS ALL THAT BURGLAR'S FAULT, ISN'T IT...? WHY DO THEY HAVE TO WRITE PCP ON IT? THEY'D NEVER DO SOMETHING LIKE THAT...
OF COURSE!
PCP WOULD NEVER DO SOMETHING LIKE...
!
PCP WOULD NEVER DO SOMETHING LIKE THAT...
THAT'S IT!
WHAT?
THAT'S IT. "PCP WOULD NEVER DO SOMETHING LIKE THAT"!
THANKS FOR THE HINT, KAYA!
VSH
WH-WHAT ???

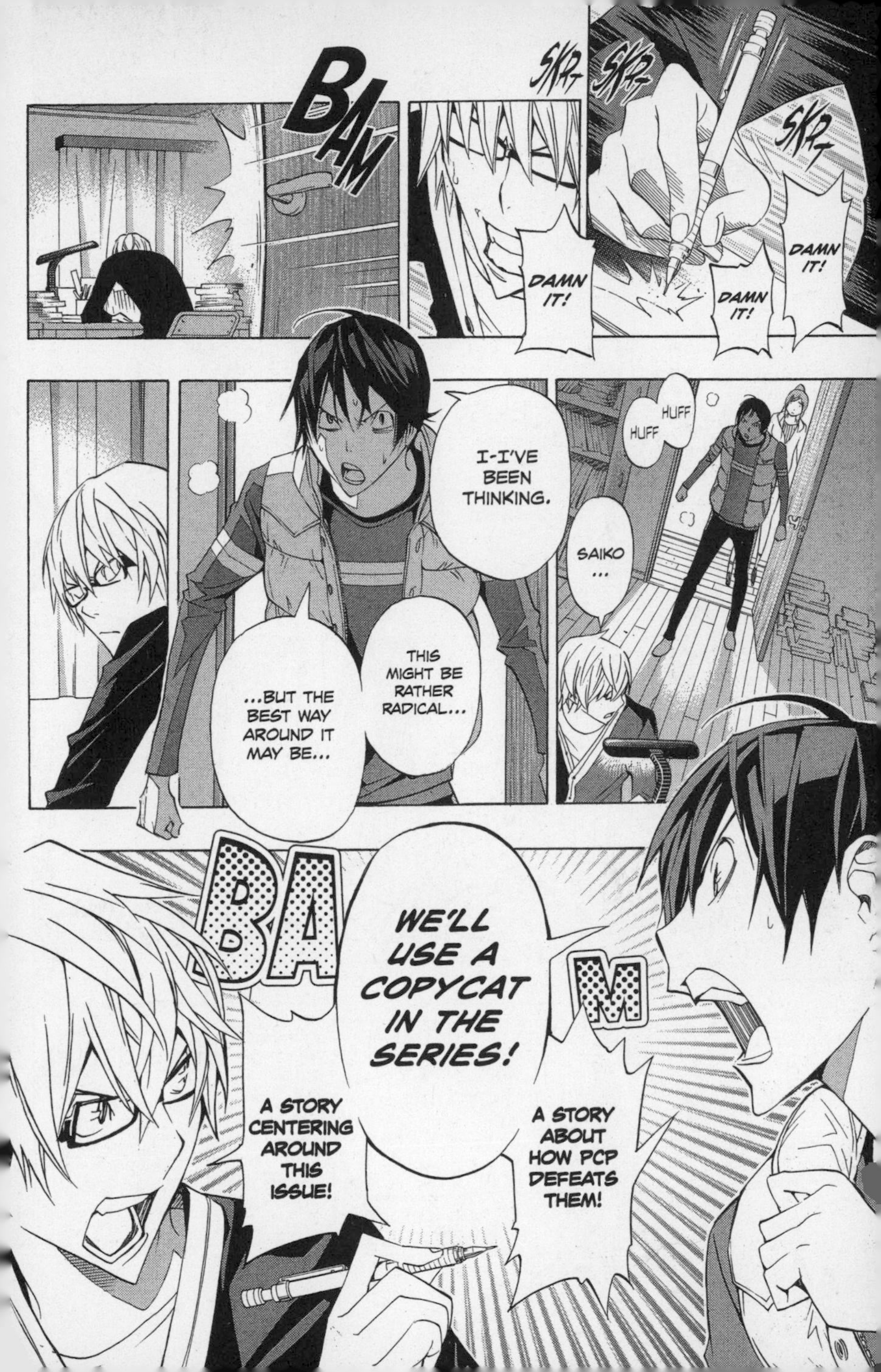
SKRT
SKRT
SKRT
DAMN IT!
DAMN IT!
DAMN IT!
BAM
HUFF
HUFF
SAIKO...
I-I'VE BEEN THINKING.
THIS MIGHT BE RATHER RADICAL...
...BUT THE BEST WAY AROUND IT MAY BE...
BAM
WE'LL USE A COPYCAT IN THE SERIES!
A STORY ABOUT HOW PCP DEFEATS THEM!
A STORY CENTERING AROUND THIS ISSUE!

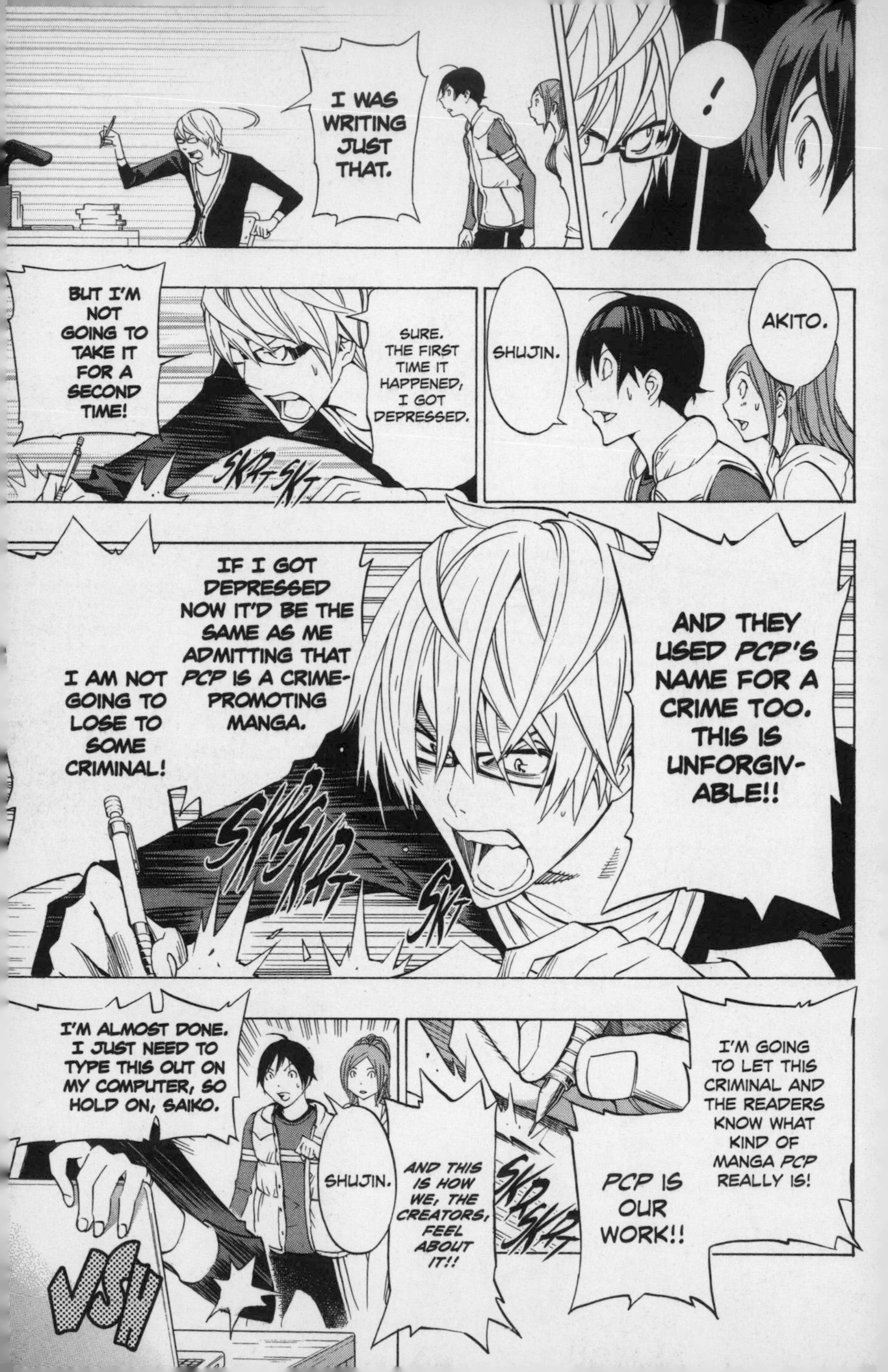
!
I WAS WRITING JUST THAT.
AKITO.
SHUJIN.
SURE. THE FIRST TIME IT HAPPENED, I GOT DEPRESSED.
BUT I'M NOT GOING TO TAKE IT FOR A SECOND TIME!
AND THEY USED *PCP'S* NAME FOR A CRIME TOO. THIS IS UNFORGIV-ABLE!!
IF I GOT DEPRESSED NOW IT'D BE THE SAME AS ME ADMITTING THAT *PCP* IS A CRIME-PROMOTING MANGA.
I AM NOT GOING TO LOSE TO SOME CRIMINAL!
I'M GOING TO LET THIS CRIMINAL AND THE READERS KNOW WHAT KIND OF MANGA *PCP* REALLY IS!
PCP IS OUR WORK!!
AND THIS IS HOW WE, THE CREATORS, FEEL ABOUT IT!!
SHUJIN.
I'M ALMOST DONE. I JUST NEED TO TYPE THIS OUT ON MY COMPUTER, SO HOLD ON, SAIKO.
VSH

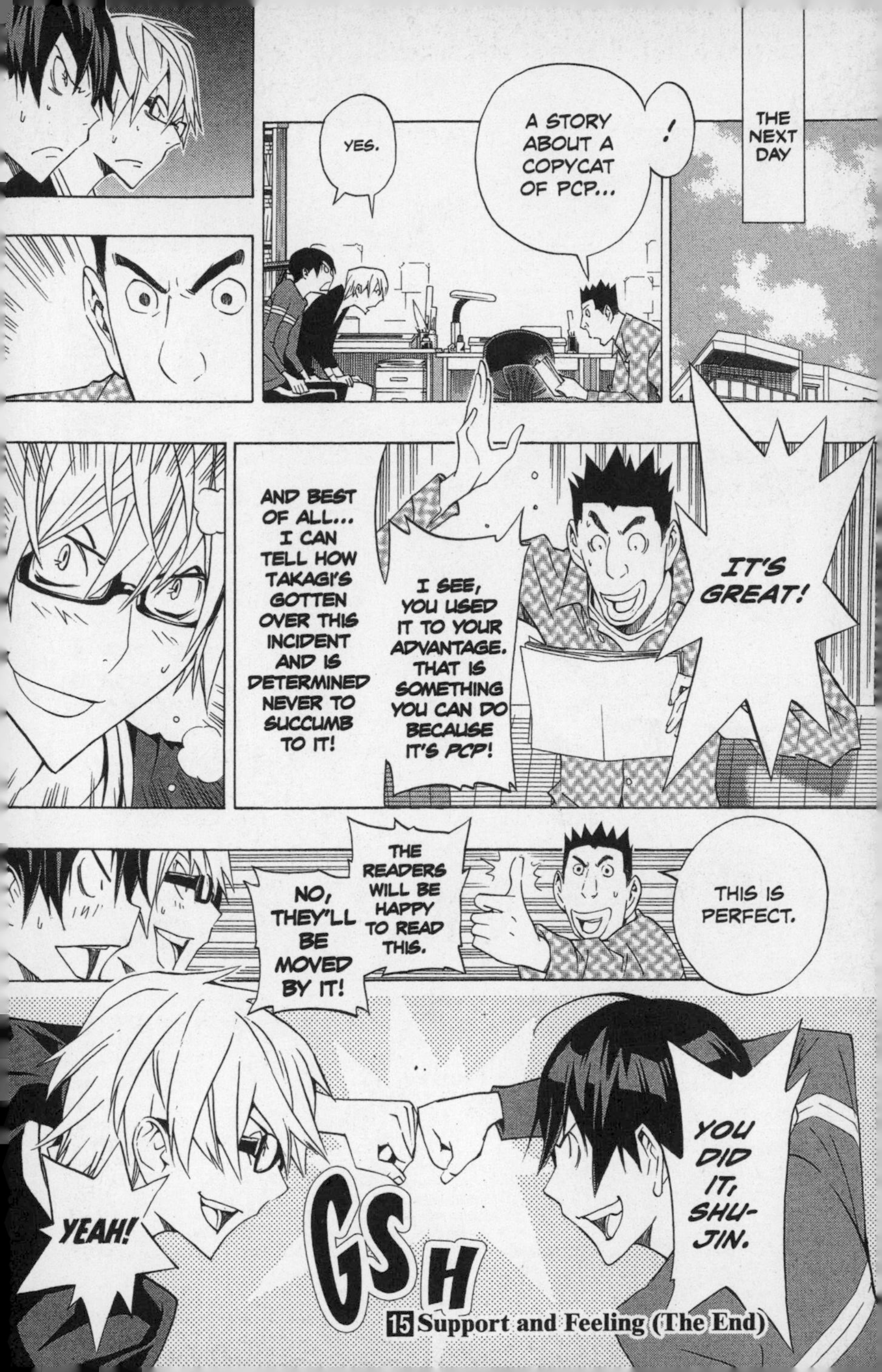
THE NEXT DAY
A STORY ABOUT A COPYCAT OF PCP...
!
YES.
IT'S GREAT!
I SEE, YOU USED IT TO YOUR ADVANTAGE. THAT IS SOMETHING YOU CAN DO BECAUSE IT'S *PCP*!
AND BEST OF ALL... I CAN TELL HOW TAKAGI'S GOTTEN OVER THIS INCIDENT AND IS DETERMINED NEVER TO SUCCUMB TO IT!
THIS IS PERFECT.
THE READERS WILL BE HAPPY TO READ THIS.
NO, THEY'LL BE MOVED BY IT!
YOU DID IT, SHUJIN.
GSH
YEAH!

15 Support and Feeling (The End)

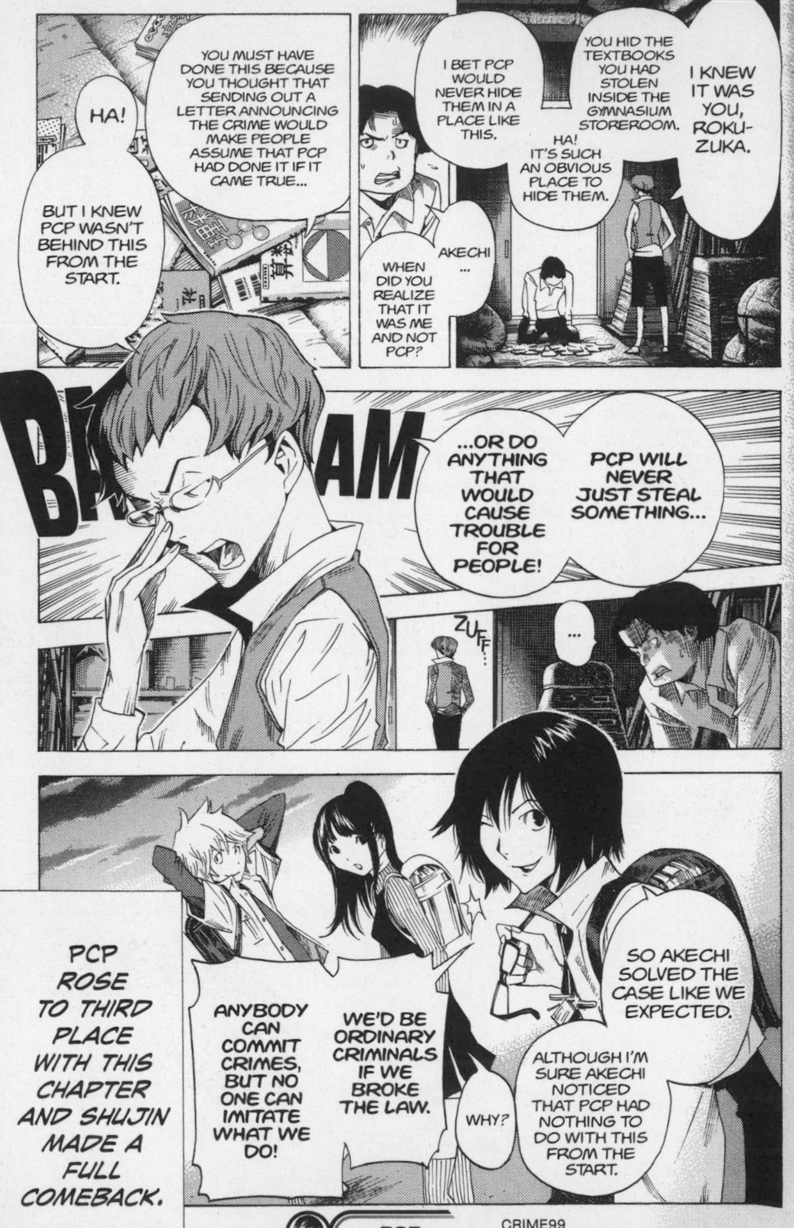
I KNEW IT WAS YOU, ROKU-ZUKA.
YOU HID THE TEXTBOOKS YOU HAD STOLEN INSIDE THE GYMNASIUM STOREROOM.
I BET PCP WOULD NEVER HIDE THEM IN A PLACE LIKE THIS.
HA! IT'S SUCH AN OBVIOUS PLACE TO HIDE THEM.
AKECHI ...
WHEN DID YOU REALIZE THAT IT WAS ME AND NOT PCP?
YOU MUST HAVE DONE THIS BECAUSE YOU THOUGHT THAT SENDING OUT A LETTER ANNOUNCING THE CRIME WOULD MAKE PEOPLE ASSUME THAT PCP HAD DONE IT IF IT CAME TRUE...
HA!
BUT I KNEW PCP WASN'T BEHIND THIS FROM THE START.
PCP WILL NEVER JUST STEAL SOMETHING...
...OR DO ANYTHING THAT WOULD CAUSE TROUBLE FOR PEOPLE!
ZUFF...
...
SO AKECHI SOLVED THE CASE LIKE WE EXPECTED.
ALTHOUGH I'M SURE AKECHI NOTICED THAT PCP HAD NOTHING TO DO WITH THIS FROM THE START.
WHY?
WE'D BE ORDINARY CRIMINALS IF WE BROKE THE LAW.
ANYBODY CAN COMMIT CRIMES, BUT NO ONE CAN IMITATE WHAT WE DO!
PCP ROSE TO THIRD PLACE WITH THIS CHAPTER AND SHUJIN MADE A FULL COMEBACK.
PCP
CRIME99
/The End

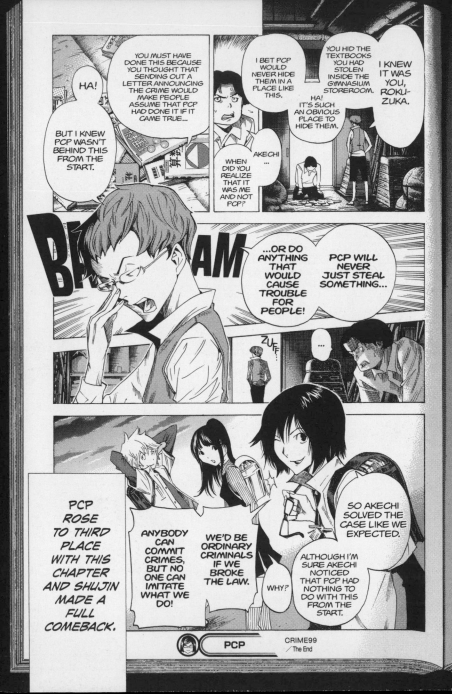

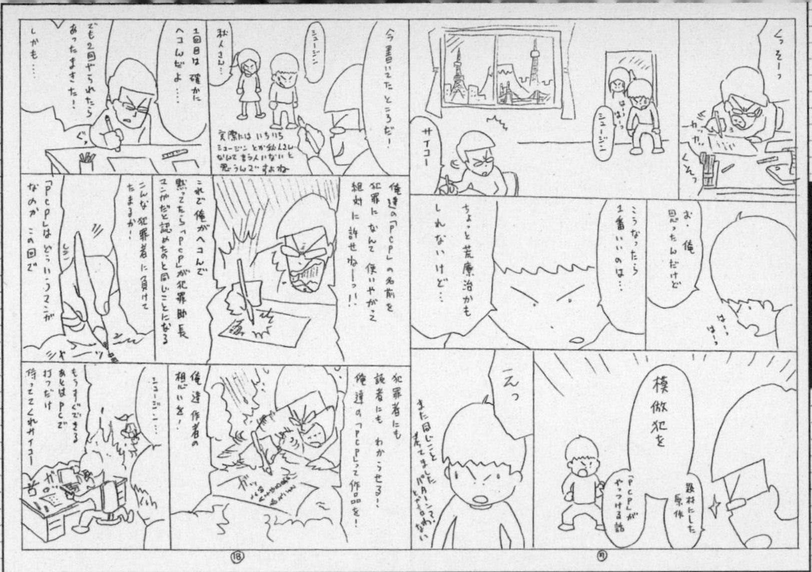
くっそーっ
ガッ ガッ
くそっ
はーっ はーっ
シュージン
サイコー
お・俺 思ったんだけど
こうなったら 1番いいのは…
ちょっと荒原治かも しれないけど…
模倣犯を
題材にした原作
「PCP」がやっつける話
えっ
今書いてたところだ!
シュージン
秋人さん…
実際には いちいち シュージン とか 秋人さん なんて言う人いないと思うんですよね
1回目は確かにヘコんだよ…
でも2回やられたら あったまきた!
しかも…
俺達の「PCP」の名前を 犯罪になんて使いやがって 絶対に許せねーっ!!
これで俺がヘコんで 黙ってたら「PCP」が犯罪助長 マンガだと認めたのと同じことになる
こんな犯罪者に負けて たまるか!
「PCP」はどういうマンガ なのか この回で
犯罪者にも 読者にも わからせる! 俺達の「PCP」って作品を!
俺達作者の 想いを!
シュージン…
もうすぐできる あとはPCで 打つだけ 待っててくれサイコー

OHBA'S STORYBOARD

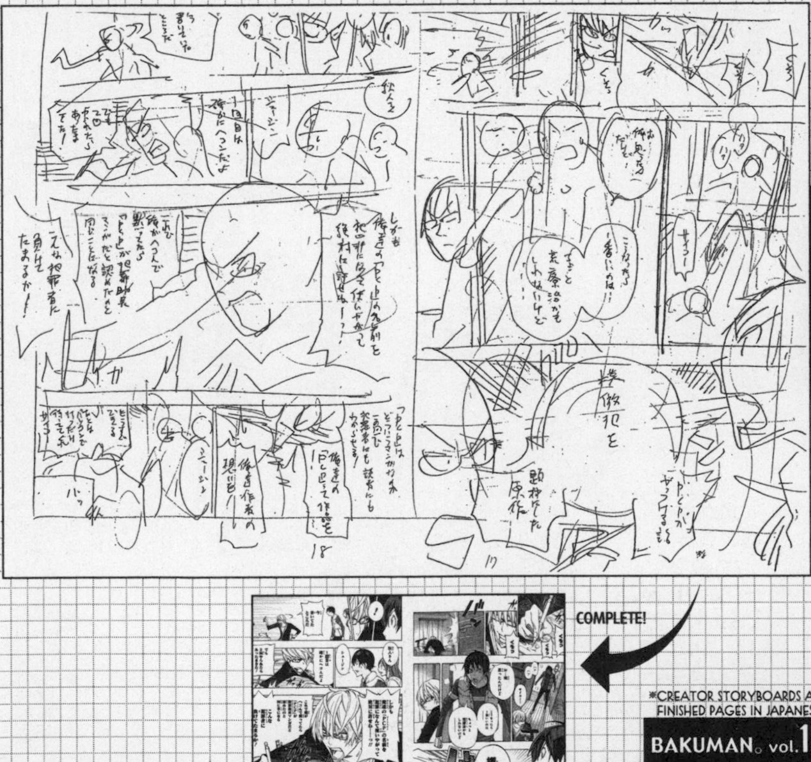

OBATA'S STORYBOARD

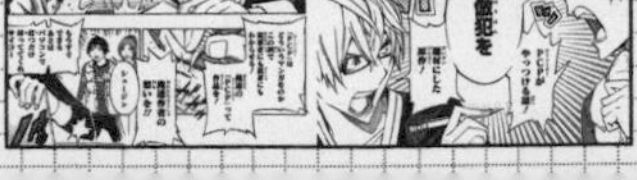

COMPLETE!

*CREATOR STORYBOARDS AND FINISHED PAGES IN JAPANESE

BAKUMAN。 vol.15

"Until the Final Draft Is Complete"

Chapter 133, pp. 184-185

BAKUMAN。

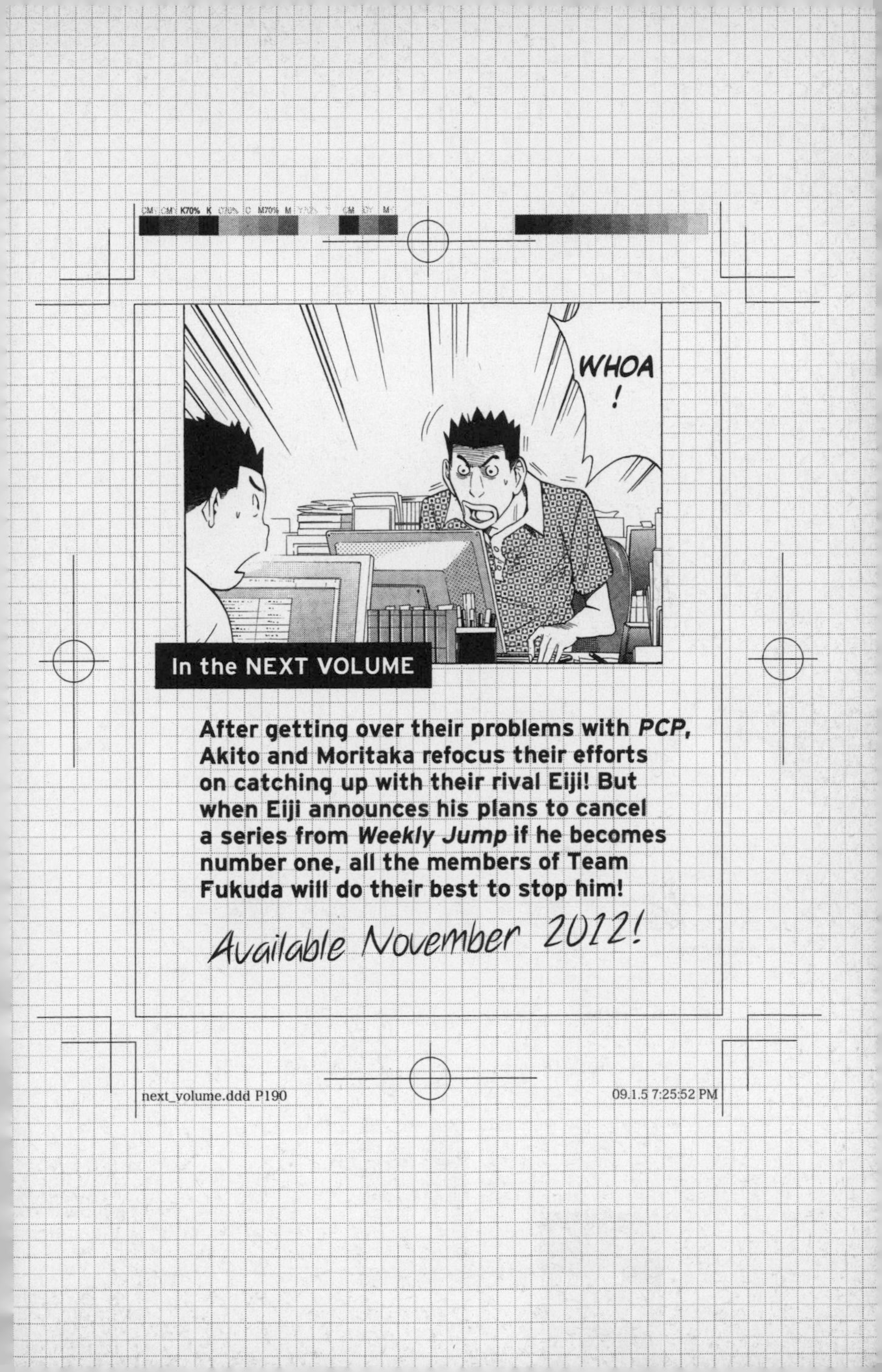
WHOA
!

In the NEXT VOLUME

After getting over their problems with *PCP*, Akito and Moritaka refocus their efforts on catching up with their rival Eiji! But when Eiji announces his plans to cancel a series from *Weekly Jump* if he becomes number one, all the members of Team Fukuda will do their best to stop him!

Available November 2012!

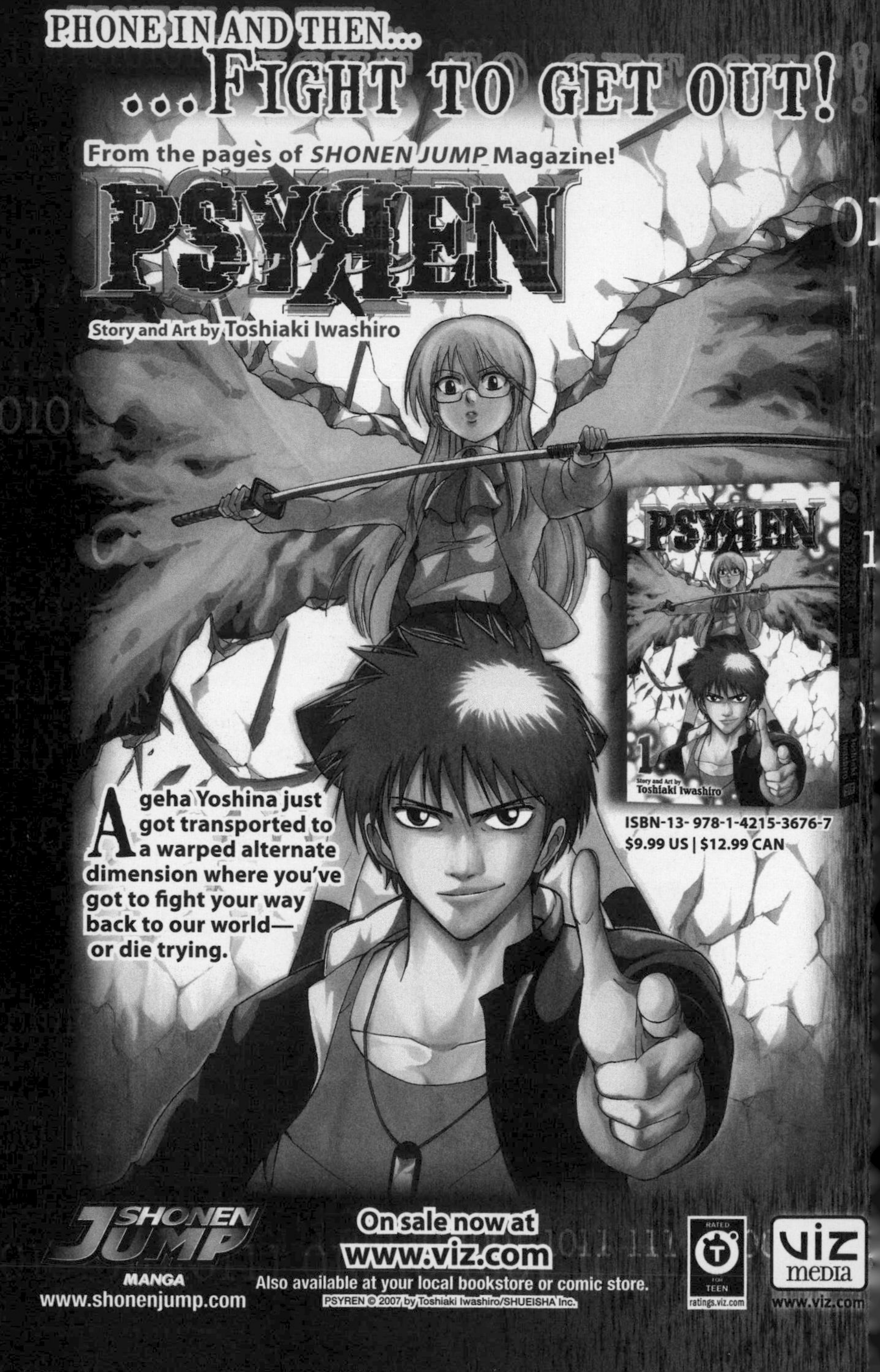
PHONE IN AND THEN...
...FIGHT TO GET OUT!
From the pages of SHONEN JUMP Magazine!
PSYREN
Story and Art by Toshiaki Iwashiro
Ageha Yoshina just got transported to a warped alternate dimension where you've got to fight your way back to our world—or die trying.
PSYREN
1
Story and Art by Toshiaki Iwashiro
ISBN-13- 978-1-4215-3676-7
$9.99 US | $12.99 CAN
SHONEN JUMP MANGA
www.shonenjump.com
On sale now at www.viz.com
Also available at your local bookstore or comic store.
PSYREN © 2007 by Toshiaki Iwashiro/SHUEISHA Inc.
RATED T FOR TEEN
ratings.viz.com
VIZ media
www.viz.com

This is the LAST PAGE.

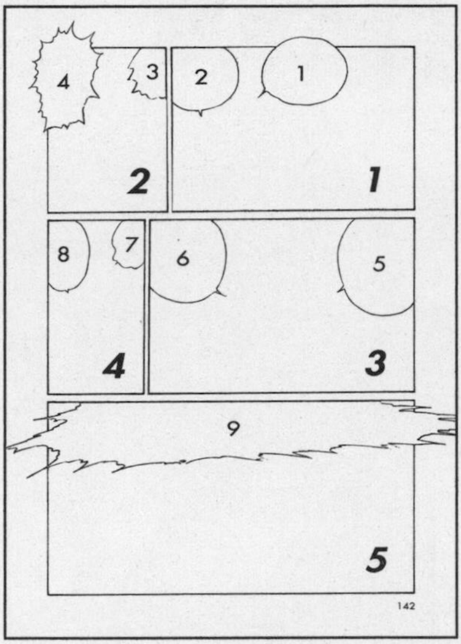
1
2
1
3
4
2
5
6
3
7
8
4
9
5
142

← Follow the action this way.

BAKUMAN。 has been printed in the original Japanese format in order to preserve the orientation of the original artwork.

Please turn it around and begin reading from right to left. Unlike English, Japanese is read right to left, so Japanese comics are read in reverse order from the way English comics are typically read. Have fun with it!

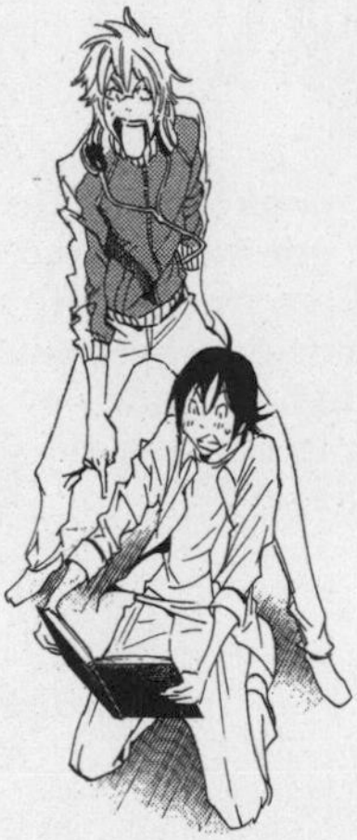